PRENTICE HALL MATHEMATICS

ALGEBRA 1

ALL-IN-ONE
Student Workbook
VERSION A

PEARSON
Prentice
Hall

Boston, Massachusetts
Upper Saddle River, New Jersey

ISBN 0-13-165718-6

14 15 16 17 18 19 V001 12 11

Daily Notetaking Guide

Practice, Guided Problem Solving, Vocabulary

Chapter 1 Variables, Function Patterns, and Graphs

Chapter 2 Rational Numbers

Chapter 3 Solving Equations

Chapter 4 Solving Inequalities

Chapter 5 Graphs and Functions

Chapter 6 Linear Equations and Their Graphs

Chapter 7 Systems of Equations and Inequalities

Chapter 8 Exponents and Exponential Functions

Chapter 9 Polynomials and Factoring

Chapter 10 Quadratic Equations and Functions

Chapter 11 Radical Expressions and Equations

© Pearson Education, Inc., publishing as Pearson Prentice Hall.

Chapter 12 Rational Expressions and Functions

A Note to the Student:

This section of your workbook contains notetaking pages for each lesson in your student edition. They are structured to help you take effective notes in class. They will also serve as a study guide as you prepare for tests and quizzes.

Lesson 1-1

Using Variables

Lesson Objectives	NAEP 2005 Strand: Algebra
▼ Model relationships with variables	**Topic:** Variables, Expressions, and Operations
▼ Model relationships with equations	**Local Standards:** _____

Vocabulary

A variable is _____

_____

An algebraic expression is _____

_____

An equation is _____

_____

An open sentence is _____

Examples

❶ **Writing an Algebraic Expression** Write an algebraic expression for "the sum of n and 8."

"Sum" indicates addition. Add the first number, ☐, and the second number, ☐.

n ☐ 8

❷ **Writing an Algebraic Expression** Define a variable and write an algebraic expression for "ten more than twice a number."

Relate | ten more than | twice | a number |

Define Let | y | = the number.

Write | ☐ | ☐ | ☐ |

☐ + ☐

❸ **Writing an Equation** Write an equation to show the total income from selling tickets to a school play for $5 each.

Relate The | total income | is | 5 | times | the number of tickets sold |.

Define Let | t | = the number of tickets sold.

Let | i | = the total income.

Write ☐ = ☐ · ☐

☐ = ☐

❹ Writing an Equation from a Table Write an equation for the data in the table.

Gallons	4	6	8	10
Miles	80	120	160	200

Relate | Miles traveled | equals | 20 | times | the number of gallons |

Define Let m = the number of miles traveled.

Let g = the number of gallons.

Write ☐ = ☐ · ☐

☐ = ☐

Quick Check

1. Write an algebraic expression for each phrase.

   a. the quotient of 4.2 and c **b.** t minus 15

2. Define a variable and write an algebraic expression for each phrase.

   a. 9 less than a number

   b. the sum of twice a number and 31

3. Suppose the price of a CD is $15. Write an equation to find the cost of n CDs.

4. Write an equation for the data in the table.

amount earned	$15	$20	$25	$30
amount saved	$7.50	$10	$12.50	$15

Lesson 1-2

Lesson Objectives

▼ Simplify and evaluate expressions and formulas

▼ Simplify and evaluate expressions containing grouping symbols

NAEP 2005 Strand: Algebra

Topic: Variables, Expressions, and Operations

Local Standards: _____

Vocabulary and Key Concepts

Order of Operations

1. Perform any operation(s) [   ].

2. Simplify [   ].

3. [   ] in order from left to right.

4. [   ] in order from left to right.

Simplify means _____

_____

An exponent is _____

_____

A base is _____

A power is _____

_____

$$2^4 = 2 \cdot 2 \cdot 2 \cdot 2$$

Evaluate means _____

_____

Examples

❶ Simplifying a Numerical Expression Simplify $32 + 6^2 - 14 \cdot 3$.

$32 + 6^2 - 14 \cdot 3 = 32 + \boxed{} - 14 \cdot 3$ **Simplify the power:** $6^2 = 6 \cdot \boxed{} = \boxed{}$.

$= 32 + \boxed{} - \boxed{}$ **Multiply 14 and 3.**

$= \boxed{} - 42$ **Add and subtract in order from left to right.**

$= \boxed{}$ **Subtract.**

❷ Evaluating an Algebraic Expression Find the total cost of a pair of jeans that costs $32 and has an 8% sales tax.

total cost		original price		sales tax
↓		↓		↓
C	$=$	p	$+$	$r \cdot p$
				↑
				sales tax rate

$C = \boxed{} + \boxed{} \cdot \boxed{}$

$= \boxed{} + \boxed{} \cdot \boxed{}$ Substitute $\boxed{}$ for p. Change 8% to 0.08 and substitute $\boxed{}$ for r.

$= 32 + \boxed{}$ **Multiply first.**

$= \boxed{}$ **Then add.**

The total cost of the jeans is $\boxed{}$.

❸ Evaluating Expressions with Exponents Evaluate each expression for $x = 11$ and $z = 16$.

a. $(xz)^2$

$(xz)^2 = \left(\boxed{} \cdot \boxed{}\right)^2$ **Substitute** $\boxed{}$ **for** x **and** $\boxed{}$ **for** z.

$= \left(\boxed{}\right)^2$ **Simplify within parentheses.**

$= \boxed{}$ **Simplify the power.**

b. xz^2

$xz^2 = \boxed{} \cdot \boxed{}^2$ **Substitute** $\boxed{}$ **for** x **and** $\boxed{}$ **for** z.

$= 11 \cdot \boxed{}$ **Simplify the power.**

$= \boxed{}$ **Multiply.**

Quick Check

1. Simplify each expression.

a. $6 - 10 \div 5$ **b.** $3 \cdot 6 - 4^2 \div 2$ **c.** $4 \cdot 7 + 4 \div 2^2$ **d.** $5^3 + 90 \div 10$

2. Evaluate each expression for $c = 2$ and $d = 5$.

a. $4c - 2d \div c$ **b.** $d + 6c \div 4$ **c.** $c^4 - d \cdot 2$ **d.** $40 - d^2 + cd \cdot 3$

Examples

❹ Simplifying an Expression Simplify $4[(2 \cdot 9) + (15 \div 3)^2]$.

$4[(2 \cdot 9) + (15 \div 3)^2] = 4\left[\boxed{} + \left(\boxed{}\right)^2\right]$ **First simplify (2 · 9) and (15 ÷ 3).**

$\qquad\qquad\qquad = 4\left[18 + \boxed{}\right]$ **Simplify the power.**

$\qquad\qquad\qquad = 4\left[\boxed{}\right]$ **Add within brackets.**

$\qquad\qquad\qquad = \boxed{}$ **Multiply.**

❺ Carpentry A carpenter wants to build three decks in the shape of regular hexagons. The perimeter p of each deck will be 60 ft. The perpendicular distance a from the center of each deck to one of the sides will be 8.7 ft. Use the formula $A = 3\left(\dfrac{pa}{2}\right)$ to find the total area of all three decks.

$A = 3\left(\dfrac{pa}{2}\right)$

$= 3\left(\dfrac{\boxed{} \cdot \boxed{}}{2}\right)$ **Substitute** $\boxed{}$ **for p and** $\boxed{}$ **for a.**

$= 3\left(\dfrac{\boxed{}}{2}\right)$ **Simplify the numerator.**

$= 3\left(\boxed{}\right)$ **Simplify the fraction.**

$= \boxed{}$ **Multiply.**

The total area of all three decks is $\boxed{}$ ft^2.

Quick Check

3. Evaluate each expression for $r = 9$ and $t = 14$.

  a. rt^2 **b.** r^2t **c.** $(rt)^2$

4. Simplify each expression.

  a. $5[4 + 3(2^2 + 1)]$ **b.** $12 + 3[18 - 5(16 - 13)]$

5. The area of a trapezoid can be found using the formula $\frac{1}{2}h(b_1 + b_2)$. Find the area of a trapezoid with height $h = 300$ ft and bases $b_1 = 250$ ft and $b_2 = 170$ ft.

Lesson 1-3

Exploring Real Numbers

Lesson Objectives	NAEP 2005 Strand: Number Properties and Operations
▼ 1 Classify numbers ▼ 2 Compare numbers	**Topic:** Number Sense **Local Standards:** _____

Vocabulary and Key Concepts

Real Numbers

Natural numbers are _____ $1, 2, 3, \ldots$

_____

Whole numbers are _____ $0, 1, 2, 3, \ldots$

_____

Integers are _____ $\ldots -2, -1, 0, 1, 2, \ldots$

_____

Rational numbers are _____

_____

_____

Irrational numbers are _____

_____

_____

$$0.101001000\ldots \qquad \pi \qquad \sqrt{10}$$

**Decimal representations of each of these
are nonrepeating and nonterminating.**

Real numbers are _____

_____

A counterexample is _____

_____

An inequality is _____

_____

Opposites are _____

_____

Absolute value is _____

_____

Examples

❶ Classifying Numbers Name the set(s) of numbers to which each number belongs.

a. -13 [ ]

b. 3.28 [ ]

❷ Using Counterexamples Determine whether the statement is true or false. If it is false, give a counterexample.

All negative numbers are integers.

A negative number can be a [ ], such as $-\frac{2}{3}$. This is not an integer. The statement is [ ].

❸ Ordering Fractions Write $-\frac{3}{4}$, $-\frac{7}{12}$, and $-\frac{5}{8}$ in order from least to greatest.

$-\frac{3}{4} =$ [ ]

$-\frac{7}{12} =$ [ ] **Write each fraction as a decimal.**

$-\frac{5}{8} =$ [ ]

[ ] < [ ] < [ ] **Order the decimals from least to greatest.**

From least to greatest, the fractions are [ ], [ ], and [ ].

❹ Finding Absolute Value Find each absolute value.

a. $|-2.5|$ -2.5 is [ ] units from 0 on a number line. $|-2.5| =$ [ ]

b. $|7|$ 7 is [ ] units from 0 on a number line. $|7| =$ [ ]

Name_____ Class_____ Date _____

Quick Check

1. Name the set(s) of numbers to which each number belongs.

   a. -12

   b. $\frac{5}{12}$

   c. -4.67

   d. 6

2. Is each statement true or false? If it is false, give a counterexample.

   a. All whole numbers are integers.

   b. No fractions are whole numbers.

3. Write $\frac{1}{12}$, $-\frac{2}{3}$, and $-\frac{5}{8}$ in order from least to greatest.

4. Find each absolute value.

   a. $|5|$ **b.** $|-4|$ **c.** $|-3.7|$ **d.** $\left|\frac{5}{7}\right|$

Lesson 1-4

Patterns and Functions

Lesson Objectives	NAEP 2005 Strand: Algebra
▼ Write a function rule	**Topic:** Patterns, Relations, and Functions
▼ Understand relationships of quantities in a function	**Local Standards:** _____

Vocabulary

A function _____

A function rule _____

The value of the dependent variable [   ] the value of the independent variable.

The possible values for the input, or independent variable, of a function are the

[   ] of the function. The possible values of the output, or the dependent

variable, are the [   ] of the function.

Example

❶ **Writing a Function Rule** Suppose you are making batches of muffins for a bake sale. The relationship between the number of batches (input) and the number of muffins (output) is a function. Use the table to write a function rule.

Number of Batches	1	2	3	4
Number of Muffins	12	24	36	48

Relate   Total number of muffins is [   ]

Define   Let $n =$ [   ]   The number of batches is the input.

           Let $m =$ [   ]   The total number of muffins is the output.

Write $m = \boxed{} n$

The function rule is [   ] .

Quick Check

1. Write a function rule for the relationship between the number of hours (input) and the number of miles (output).

Hours	1	2	3	4
Total Miles	60	120	180	240

[   ]

Example

② Identifying Independent and Dependent Quantities
The table and graph model a function relating time of
day and temperature. Identify the independent and
dependent quantities.

Time of Day	Temperature (°F)
10:00 AM	66
2:00 PM	71
6:00 PM	63
10:00 PM	54

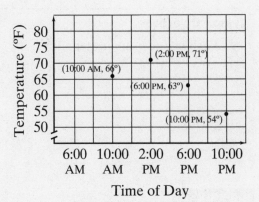

The [   ] is the dependent quantity because it depends on the [   ].

[   ] is the independent quantity.

Quick Check

2. The cooking time for an unstuffed turkey is about 20 minutes per pound.
   What are the independent quantity and dependent quantity for this situation?

Example

③ Reasonable Domain and Range Mateen has 3 hours a night for homework
and fun. He never has more than 2 hours of homework each night.

a. Identify the independent and dependent quantities for this situation. The
amount of time for [   ] depends on the amount of time for [   ].

So the amount of time for fun is the [   ] variable. The amount of
time for homework is the [   ] variable.

b. Find reasonable domain and range values for this situation. A reasonable
domain is from [ ] to [ ] hours. If Mateen has no homework, he has [   ]
for fun. If he has [   ] of homework, he has [   ] for fun.

Quick Check

3. Charlie downloads songs for $.75 each. He has between $3.00 and $6.00 to spend
   on songs. Identify the independent and dependent quantities for this situation
   and find reasonable domain and range values.

Lesson 1-5

Scatter Plots

Lesson Objectives	NAEP 2005 Strand: Algebra; Data Analysis and Probability
▼ Analyze data using scatter plots	**Topics:** Algebraic Representations; Data Representation (Histograms, Line Graphs, Scatter Plots, Box Plots, Circle Graphs, Stem and Leaf Plots, Frequency Distributions, and Tables); Characteristics of Data Sets
	Local Standards: _____

Vocabulary

A scatter plot is _____

_____

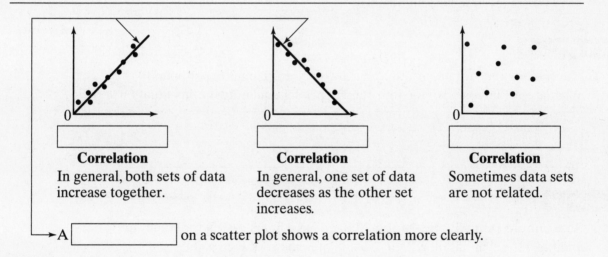

Correlation
In general, both sets of data increase together.

Correlation
In general, one set of data decreases as the other set increases.

Correlation
Sometimes data sets are not related.

➤ A [   ] on a scatter plot shows a correlation more clearly.

Examples

1 **Making a Scatter Plot** The table shows the number of hours worked and the amount of money each person earned. Make a scatter plot of the data.

Name	Hours Worked	Amount Earned
Janel	6	$25.50
Roscoe	12	$51.00
Victoria	11	$46.75
Alex	9	$38.25
Jordan	15	$63.75
Jennifer	10	$42.50

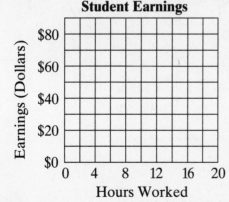

The greatest amount earned is [   ] . A reasonable scale on the vertical axis is from 0 to 70 with every $10 labeled.

For 6 hours worked and earnings of $25.50, plot
([   ] , [   ]).

❷ Identifying a Correlation from a Scatter Plot Use the scatter plot in Example 1 to answer the following question: Is there a positive correlation, negative correlation, or no correlation between the number of hours worked and the amount earned? Explain.

As the number of hours worked increases, the earnings [   ].

There is a [   ] correlation between hours worked and earnings.

Quick Check

1. Use the data in the table. Make a scatter plot of the data.

Year	Daily Newspaper Circulation (millions)	Households With Television (millions)
1950	54	4
1960	59	46
1970	62	59
1980	62	76
1990	62	92
2000	55	101

2. Use the scatter plot from Example 1.

a. Critical Thinking What does the data point at (11, 46.75) represent?

b. Use the graph to predict how much Conrad would earn if he worked 2 hours.

Lesson 1-6

Mean, Median, Mode, and Range

Lesson Objectives	**NAEP 2005 Strand:** Data Analysis and Probability
1 Find mean, median, and mode **2** Make and use stem-and-leaf plots	**Topics:** Data Representation; Characteristics of Data Sets **Local Standards:** _____

Vocabulary and Key Concepts

Mean, Median, Mode

Mean = $\dfrac{\boxed{}}{\boxed{}}$

The mean is often referred to as the $\boxed{}$.

Use the mean to describe the middle of a set of data that $\boxed{}$ have an outlier.

An outlier is a _____

_____

The median is _____

_____

For a set containing an $\boxed{}$ of data items, the median is the

$\boxed{}$ of the two middle data values.

Use the median to describe the middle of a set of data that $\boxed{}$ have an outlier.

The mode is _____

It is possible for a set of data to have $\boxed{}$ mode, $\boxed{}$ mode, or

$\boxed{}$ mode.

Use the mode when the data are $\boxed{}$ or when choosing

the $\boxed{}$ item.

Measures of central tendency are used to _____

The range of a set of data is _____

_____

A stem-and-leaf plot is _____

_____

Name_____ Class_____ Date _____

Examples

❶ Applying Measures of Central Tendency Find the mean, median, and mode of the data below. Which measure of central tendency best describes the data?

$$14 \quad 10 \quad 2 \quad 13 \quad 16 \quad 3 \quad 12 \quad 11$$

Mean: $\dfrac{14 + 10 + 2 + 13 + 16 + 3 + 12 + 11}{\boxed{}} = \boxed{}$

↳ total number of data items

Median: $2 \quad 3 \quad 10 \quad \underline{11} \quad \underline{12} \quad 13 \quad 14 \quad 16$ List the data in order.

$\dfrac{11 + 12}{2} = \boxed{}$ For an even number of data items, find the mean of the two middle terms.

Mode: none   the data item that occurs most often

The mean is $\boxed{}$, the median is $\boxed{}$, and there is $\boxed{}$ mode. The mean is less than $\boxed{}$ of the 8 data items because of the outliers 2 and $\boxed{}$. The $\boxed{}$ best describes the data.

❷ Solving an Equation Suppose your grades on three science exams are 82, 94, and 89. What grade do you need on your next exam to have an average of 90?

Let $x =$ the grade of the fourth exam.

Mean (average): $\dfrac{82 + 94 + 89 + x}{\boxed{}} = 90$

$\dfrac{\boxed{} + x}{4} = 90$ Simplify the numerator.

$\boxed{}\left(\dfrac{265 + x}{4}\right) = \boxed{}(90)$ Multiply each side by $\boxed{}$.

$265 + x = \boxed{}$ Simplify.

$265 + x - \boxed{} = 360 - \boxed{}$ Subtract $\boxed{}$ from each side.

$x = \boxed{}$ Simplify.

Your grade on the next exam must be a $\boxed{}$ for you to have an average of 90.

❸ Making a Stem-and-Leaf Plot Make a stem-and-leaf plot for the data.

$$56 \quad 44 \quad 63 \quad 58 \quad 51 \quad 59 \quad 47$$
$$51 \quad 67 \quad 50 \quad 65 \quad 49 \quad 66 \quad 63$$

4	4 7 □
5	0 1 □ □ □ 9
6	3 3 □ □ □

5|1 means $\boxed{}$.

Quick Check

1. a. The hourly wages of employees at a local restaurant are listed in the line plot below. Find the mean, median, and mode of the data.

Wages of Employees per Hour

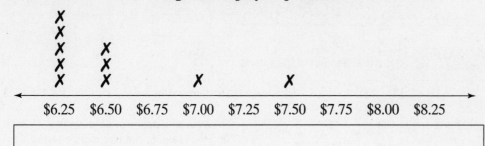

$6.25 $6.50 $6.75 $7.00 $7.25 $7.50 $7.75 $8.00 $8.25

b. Critical Thinking Which measure best describes the data? Explain why.

2. Critical Thinking Suppose your grades on three history exams are 80, 93, and 91. If 100 is the highest possible score on the fourth exam, is it possible to raise your average to 92? Explain.

3. Make a stem-and-leaf plot for the data below.

4.5	4.3	0.8	3.5	2.6
1.4	0.2	0.8	4.3	6.0

Name_____ Class_____ Date_____

Lesson 2-1

Adding Rational Numbers

Lesson Objectives	NAEP 2005 Strand: Number Properties and Operations
▼1 Add real numbers using models and rules ▼2 Apply addition	**Topic:** Number Operations **Local Standards:** _____

Vocabulary and Key Concepts

Identity Property of Addition

For every rational number n, [_____].

Examples $-5 + 0 = $ [____] $0 + 5 = $ [____]

Inverse Property of Addition

For every rational number n, there is an additive inverse $-n$ such that [_____].

Examples $17 + (-17) = $ [____] $-17 + 17 = $ [____]

Adding Numbers With the Same Sign

To add two numbers with the same sign, [_____] their absolute values.

The sum has the [_____] sign as the addends.

Examples $2 + 6 = $ [____] $-2 + (-6) = $ [____]

Adding Numbers With Different Signs

To add two numbers with different signs, find the [_____] of

their absolute values. The sum has the same sign as the addend with the

[_____] absolute value.

Examples $-2 + 6 = $ [____] $2 + (-6) = $ [____]

An additive inverse is _____

The sum of additive inverses is _____

A matrix is _____

An element is _____

Name_____ Class_____ Date _____

Examples

❶ Using a Number Line Model Use a number line to simplify the expression.

a. $3 + (-5)$

$3 + (-5) = $ ☐

−3 −2 −1 0 1 2 3 4

Start at ☐ .

Move left ☐ units.

b. $-3 + 5$

$-3 + 5 = $ ☐

−4 −3 −2 −1 0 1 2 3

Start at ☐ .

Move right ☐ units.

❷ Adding Numbers Simplify each expression.

a. $12 + (-23) = $ ☐   The difference of the absolute values is ☐ . The ☐

addend has the greater absolute value, so the sum is ☐ .

b. $-6.4 + (-8.6) = $ ☐   Since both addends are ☐ , add their absolute values.

The sum is ☐ .

❸ Evaluating Expressions A scuba diver who is 88 ft below sea level begins to ascend to the surface.

a. Write an expression to represent the diver's depth below sea level after rising any number of feet.

Relate | 88 ft below sea level | plus | feet diver rises |

Define   Let | r | = the number of feet diver rises.

Write   ☐   +   ☐

☐ + ☐

b. Find the new depth of the scuba diver after rising 37 ft.

$-88 + r = -88 + $ ☐   Substitute ☐ for r.

$= $ ☐   Simplify.

The scuba diver is ☐ ft below sea level.

❹ Adding Matrices Add $\begin{bmatrix} -6 & 8.6 & 11 \\ 2.3 & 5 & -3 \end{bmatrix} + \begin{bmatrix} 7 & -5.4 & -2 \\ 11.1 & 3 & -1 \end{bmatrix}$.

$\begin{bmatrix} -6 & 8.6 & 11 \\ 2.3 & 5 & -3 \end{bmatrix} + \begin{bmatrix} 7 & -5.4 & -2 \\ 11.1 & 3 & -1 \end{bmatrix}$

$= \begin{bmatrix} ☐ + ☐ & ☐ + (☐) & ☐ + (☐) \\ ☐ + ☐ & ☐ + ☐ & ☐ + (☐) \end{bmatrix}$ Add corresponding elements.

$= \begin{bmatrix} ☐ & ☐ & ☐ \\ ☐ & ☐ & ☐ \end{bmatrix}$ Simplify.

Quick Check

1. Use the number line to find each sum.

$$-11\ -10\ -9\ -8\ -7\ -6\ -5\ -4\ -3\ -2\ -1\ \ 0\ \ 1\ \ 2\ \ 3\ \ 4\ \ 5\ \ 6\ \ 7\ \ 8\ \ 9\ \ 10\ \ 11$$

a. $-6 + 4$ **b.** $4 + (-6)$ **c.** $-3 + (-8)$ **d.** $9 + (-3)$

2. Find each sum.

a. $-7 + (-4)$ **b.** $-26.3 + 8.9$ **c.** $-\frac{3}{4} + \left(-\frac{1}{2}\right)$ **d.** $\frac{8}{9} + \left(-\frac{5}{6}\right)$

3. The temperature one winter morning is $-14°F$. Define a variable and write an expression to find the temperature after it changes. Then evaluate your expression for a decrease of 11 degrees Fahrenheit.

4. Find each sum.

a. $\begin{bmatrix} 5 \\ 3.2 \\ -4.9 \end{bmatrix} + \begin{bmatrix} -9 \\ -1.7 \\ -11.1 \end{bmatrix} = \begin{bmatrix} \boxed{} + \boxed{} \\ \boxed{} + \boxed{} \\ \boxed{} + \boxed{} \end{bmatrix} = \begin{bmatrix} \boxed{} \\ \boxed{} \\ \boxed{} \end{bmatrix}$

b. $\begin{bmatrix} -4 & \frac{7}{8} \\ \frac{3}{4} & 0 \end{bmatrix} + \begin{bmatrix} -5 & -\frac{3}{4} \\ \frac{1}{2} & -1 \end{bmatrix} = \begin{bmatrix} \boxed{} + \boxed{} & \boxed{} + \boxed{} \\ \boxed{} + \boxed{} & \boxed{} + \boxed{} \end{bmatrix} = \begin{bmatrix} \boxed{} & \boxed{} \\ \boxed{} & \boxed{} \end{bmatrix}$

Lesson 2-2

Subtracting Rational Numbers

Lesson Objectives	NAEP 2005 Strand: Number Properties and Operations
▼ Subtract rational numbers	**Topic:** Number Operations
▼ Apply subtraction	**Local Standards:** _____

Key Concepts

Subtracting Numbers

To subtract a number, add $\boxed{}$.

Examples $3 - 5 = 3 + \boxed{} = -2$ $3 - (-5) = 3 + \boxed{} = 8$

Examples

❶ Absolute Values Simplify $|-13 - (-21)|$.

$|-13 - (-21)| = \left|-13 + \boxed{}\right|$ **The opposite of −21 is** $\boxed{}$ **.**

$= \left|\boxed{}\right|$ **Add within absolute value symbols.**

$= \boxed{}$ **Find the absolute value.**

❷ Evaluating Expressions Evaluate $x - (-y)$ for $x = -3$ and $y = -6$.

$x - (-y) = \boxed{} - \left[-\left(\boxed{}\right)\right]$ **Substitute** $\boxed{}$ **for x and** $\boxed{}$ **for y.**

$= \boxed{} - \boxed{}$ **The opposite of −6 is** $\boxed{}$ **.**

$= \boxed{}$ **Subtract.**

❸ Temperature The temperature in Montreal, Canada, at 6:00 P.M. was −8°C. Find the temperature at 10:00 P.M. if it fell 7°C.

Find the temperature at 10:00 P.M. by subtracting $\boxed{}$ from the temperature at 6:00 P.M.

$-8 - 7 = \boxed{} + \left(\boxed{}\right)$ **Add the opposite.**

$= \boxed{}$ **Simplify.**

The temperature at 10:00 P.M. was $\boxed{}$ °C.

Quick Check

1. Simplify each expression.

   a. $|8 - 7|$

   b. $|7 - 8|$

   c. $|-10 - (-4)|$

   d. $|-4 - (-10)|$

2. Evaluate each expression for $t = -2$ and $r = -7$.

   a. $r - t$

   b. $t - r$

   c. $-t - r$

   d. $-r - (-t)$

3. The closing price of stock PQR on Thursday was $14.23. It had fallen $1.23 since the close on Wednesday. Find its closing price on Wednesday.

Lesson 2-3

Multiplying and Dividing Rational Numbers

Lesson Objectives	NAEP 2005 Strand: Number Properties and Operations
▼ Multiply real numbers	Topic: Number Operations
▼ Divide real numbers	Local Standards: _____

Vocabulary and Key Concepts

Identity Property of Multiplication

For every real number n, [ ].

Examples $1 \cdot 5 =$ [ ] $1 \cdot (-5) =$ [ ]

Multiplication Property of Zero

For every real number n, [ ].

Examples $35 \cdot 0 =$ [ ] $-35 \cdot 0 =$ [ ]

Multiplication Property of -1

For every real number n, [ ].

Examples $-1 \cdot 5 =$ [ ] $-1 \cdot (-5) =$ [ ]

Multiplying Numbers With the Same Sign

The product of two positive numbers or two negative numbers is [ ].

Examples $5 \cdot 2 =$ [ ] $-5(-2) =$ [ ]

Multiplying Numbers With Different Signs

The product of a positive number and a negative number, or a negative

number and a positive number, is [ ].

Examples $3(-6) =$ [ ] $-3 \cdot 6 =$ [ ]

Dividing Numbers With the Same Sign

The quotient of two positive numbers or two negative numbers is [ ].

Examples $6 \div 3 =$ [ ] $-6 \div (-3) =$ [ ]

Dividing Numbers With Different Signs

The quotient of a positive number and a negative number, or a negative

number and a positive number, is [ ].

Examples $-6 \div 3 =$ [ ] $6 \div (-3) =$ [ ]

Inverse Property of Multiplication

For every nonzero real number a, there is a multiplicative inverse $\frac{1}{a}$ such

that [ ].

Examples $5\left(\frac{1}{5}\right) =$ [ ] $-5\left(-\frac{1}{5}\right) =$ [ ]

The multiplicative inverse of a nonzero rational number $\frac{a}{b}$ is _____

A reciprocal is _____

Examples

❶ Multiplying Numbers Simplify the expression $-6\left(\frac{3}{4}\right)$.

$-6\left(\frac{3}{4}\right) = -\dfrac{\boxed{}}{\boxed{}}$ **The product of a positive number and a negative number is** $\boxed{}$.

$= -\boxed{}$ **Write** $-\dfrac{\boxed{}}{\boxed{}}$ **as a mixed number.**

❷ Evaluating Expressions Use the function $t = -5.5\left(\frac{a}{1,000}\right)°F$ to calculate the change in temperature t for an increase in altitude a of 7,200 ft.

$t = -5.5\left(\dfrac{\boxed{}}{1,000}\right)$ **Substitute** $\boxed{}$ **for** a.

$= -5.5\left(\boxed{}\right)$ **Divide within parentheses.**

$= \boxed{}°F$ **Multiply.**

❸ Simplifying Exponential Expressions Use the order of operations to simplify each expression.

a. $-0.2^4 = -\left(\boxed{} \cdot \boxed{} \cdot \boxed{} \cdot \boxed{}\right)$ **Write as repeated multiplication.**

$= -\boxed{}$ **Simplify.**

b. $(-0.2)^4 = \left(\boxed{}\right) \cdot \left(\boxed{}\right) \cdot \left(\boxed{}\right) \cdot \left(\boxed{}\right)$ **Write as repeated multiplication.**

$= \boxed{}$ **Simplify.**

Quick Check

1. Simplify each expression.

a. $4(-6)$

b. $-10(-5)$

c. $-4.9(-8)$

d. $-\frac{2}{3}\left(\frac{3}{4}\right)$

2. Use the expression in Example 2 to find the change in temperature if a balloon rises 4,500 ft from the ground.

Examples

④ Dividing Numbers Simplify the expression $-54 \div (-9)$.

$-54 \div (-9) = \boxed{}$ **The quotient of a negative number and a negative number is** $\boxed{}$.

⑤ Evaluating Expressions Evaluate $-\frac{x}{y} - 4z^2$ for $x = 4$, $y = -2$, and $z = -4$.

$-\dfrac{x}{y} - 4z^2 = -\left(\dfrac{\boxed{}}{\boxed{}}\right) - 4\left(\boxed{}\right)^2$ **Substitute** $\boxed{}$ **for x,** $\boxed{}$ **for y, and** $\boxed{}$ **for z.**

$= -\left(\dfrac{\boxed{}}{\boxed{}}\right) - 4\left(\boxed{}\right)$ **Simplify the power.**

$= \left(\boxed{}\right) - \boxed{}$ **Divide and multiply.**

$= \boxed{}$ **Subtract.**

⑥ Division Using the Reciprocal Evaluate $\frac{p}{r}$ for $p = \frac{3}{2}$ and $r = -\frac{3}{4}$.

$\dfrac{p}{r} = \boxed{} \div \boxed{}$ **Rewrite the equation.**

$= \dfrac{\boxed{}}{\boxed{}} \div \left(\boxed{}\dfrac{\boxed{}}{\boxed{}}\right)$ **Substitute** $\dfrac{\boxed{}}{\boxed{}}$ **for p and** $\boxed{}\dfrac{\boxed{}}{\boxed{}}$ **for r.**

$= \dfrac{3}{2}\left(\boxed{}\dfrac{\boxed{}}{\boxed{}}\right)$ **Multiply by** $\boxed{}\dfrac{\boxed{}}{\boxed{}}$**, the reciprocal of** $-\dfrac{3}{4}$**.**

$= \boxed{}$ **Simplify.**

Quick Check

Simplify each expression.

3. a. -4^3

b. $(-2)^4$

4. a. $-42 \div 7$

b. $-8 \div (-2)$

5. Evaluate each expression for $x = 8$, $y = -5$, and $z = -3$.

a. $3x \div (2z) + y \div 10$

b. $\dfrac{2z + x}{2y}$

6. Evaluate $\dfrac{x}{y}$ for $x = 8$ and $y = -\dfrac{4}{5}$

Lesson 2-4

The Distributive Property

Lesson Objectives	NAEP 2005 Strand: Algebra
▼ 1 Use the Distributive Property ▼ 2 Simplify algebraic expressions	**Topic:** Variables, Expressions, and Operations **Local Standards:** _____

Vocabulary and Key Concepts

Distributive Property

For every real number a, b, and c,

$a(b + c) =$ [_____] $(b + c)a =$ [_____]

$a(b - c) =$ [_____] $(b - c)a =$ [_____]

Examples

$5(20 + 6) =$ [_____] $+$ [_____]

$(20 + 6)5 =$ [_____] $+$ [_____]

$9(30 - 2) =$ [_____] $-$ [_____]

$(30 - 2)9 =$ [_____] $-$ [_____]

A term is _____

_____

A constant is _____

A coefficient is _____

_____

Like terms are _____

_____

Examples

❶ Simplifying a Numerical Expression Find the total cost of 4 CDs that cost $12.99 each.

$4(12.99) = 4\left(\,[\underline{\qquad}]\,\right)$ Rewrite 12.99 as 13 − [_____].

$= [\_](\,[\underline{\quad}]\,) - [\_](\,[\underline{\quad}]\,)$ Use the Distributive Property.

$= [\underline{\quad}] - [\underline{\quad}]$ Multiply.

$= [\underline{\quad}]$ Simplify.

The total cost of 4 CDs is [_____].

❷ Simplifying an Expression Simplify $3(4m - 7)$.

$3(4m - 7) = $ ☐$($☐$) - $☐$($☐$)$ **Use the Distributive Property.**

$\quad\quad\quad = $ ☐$m - $☐ **Simplify.**

❸ Using the Multiplication Property of −1 Simplify $-(5q - 6)$.

$-(5q - 6) = $ ☐$(5q - 6)$ **Rewrite the expression using −1.**

$\quad\quad\quad = $ ☐☐$($☐$) - $☐☐$($☐$)$ **Use the Distributive Property.**

$\quad\quad\quad = $ ☐$q + $☐ **Simplify.**

Quick Check

1. Find the total cost of 6 pairs of socks that cost $2.95 per pair.

2. Simplify each expression.

a. $2(3 - 7t)$

b. $(0.4 + 1.1c)(3)$

3. Simplify each expression.

a. $-(2x + 1)$

b. $(3 - 8a)(-1)$

Examples

❹ Combining Like Terms Simplify $-2w^2 + w^2$.

$-2w^2 + w^2 = \left(\boxed{} + \boxed{}\right)w^2$ **Use the Distributive Property.**

$= \boxed{}$ **Simplify.**

❺ Writing an Expression Write an expression for the product of -6 and the quantity 7 minus m.

Relate $\boxed{-6}$ times $\boxed{\text{the quantity 7 minus } m}$

Write $\boxed{}$ $\cdot$ $\boxed{}$

$-6(7 - \boxed{})$

Quick Check

4. Simplify each expression.

  a. $7y + 6y$

  b. $3t - t$

  c. $-9w^3 - 3w^3$

  d. $8d + d$

5. Write an expression for each phrase.

  a. -2 times the quantity t plus 7

  b. the product of 14 and the quantity 8 plus w

Lesson 2-5

Properties of Numbers

Lesson Objectives	NAEP 2005 Strand: Geometry
▼ Identify properties	Topic: Mathematical Reasoning
▼ Use deductive reasoning	Local Standards: _____

Vocabulary and Key Concepts

Properties of Real Numbers

For every real number $a, b,$ and $c,$

Commutative Property of Addition

[ ]

Example $3 + 7 = \boxed{} + \boxed{}$

Commutative Property of Multiplication

[ ]

Example $3 \cdot 7 = \boxed{} \cdot \boxed{}$

Associative Property of Addition

[ ]

Example $(6 + 4) + 5 = \boxed{} + \left(\boxed{} + \boxed{}\right)$

Associative Property of Multiplication

[ ]

Example $(6 \cdot 4) \cdot 5 = \boxed{} \cdot \left(\boxed{} \cdot \boxed{}\right)$

Identity Property of Addition

[ ]

Example $9 + 0 = \boxed{}$

Identity Property of Multiplication

[ ]

Example $6 \cdot 1 = \boxed{}$

Inverse Property of Addition

For every a, there is an additive inverse $\boxed{}$ such that $\boxed{}$.

Example $5 + (-5) = \boxed{}$

Inverse Property of Multiplication

For every a $(a \neq 0)$, there is a multiplicative inverse $\frac{1}{a}$ such that $\boxed{}$.

Example $5 \cdot \boxed{} = 1$

Distributive Property

$a(b + c) = \boxed{}$ **Example** $5(4 + 2) = \boxed{} + \boxed{}$

$a(b - c) = \boxed{}$ **Example** $5(4 - 2) = \boxed{} - \boxed{}$

Multiplication Property of Zero

For every real number $n,$ $\boxed{}$.

Example $-35 \cdot 0 = \boxed{}$

Multiplication Property of –1

For every real number $n,$ $\boxed{}$.

Example $-1 \cdot (-5) = \boxed{}$

Deductive reasoning is _____

_____

Examples

❶ Identifying Properties Name the property each equation illustrates. Explain.

a. $3 \cdot a = a \cdot 3$

[_____] , because

_____

b. $p \cdot 0 = 0$

[_____] , because

_____

c. $6 + (-6) = 0$

[_____] , because

_____

d. $z\left(\frac{1}{z}\right) = 1$ for $z \neq 0$

[_____] , because

_____

❷ Shopping Suppose you buy a shirt for $14.85, a pair of pants for $21.95, and a pair of shoes for $25.15. Find the total amount you spent.

$14.85 + 21.95 + 25.15 = 14.85 +$ [_____] $+$ [_____]   [_____] **Property of Addition**

$= ($ [_____] $+$ [_____] $) +$ [_____]   [_____] **Property of Addition**

$=$ [_____] $+$ [_____]   **Add within parentheses first.**

$=$ [_____]   **Simplify.**

The total amount you spent was $ [_____] .

❸ Justifying Steps Simplify $3x - 4(x - 8)$. Justify each step.

$3x - 4(x - 8) = 3x -$ [_____] $+$ [_____]   [_____] **Property**

$= ($ [_____] $)x + 32$ [_____] **Property**

$=$ [_____] $x + 32$ **Subtract.**

$=$ [_____] $+ 32$ [_____] **of Multiplication**

Quick Check

1. Name the property that each equation illustrates. Explain.

   a. $1m = m$

   b. $(-3 + 4) + 5 = -3 + (4 + 5)$

   c. $3(8 \cdot 0) = (3 \cdot 8)0$

   d. $2 + 0 = 2$

   e. $np = pn$

   f. $p + q = q + p$

2. At the supermarket, you buy a package of cheese for \$2.50, a loaf of bread for \$2.15, a cucumber for \$.65, and some tomatoes for \$3.50. Find the total cost of the groceries.

3. Simplify each expression. Justify each step.

   a. $5a + 6 + a$

   b. $2(3t - 1) + 2$

Lesson 2-6

Theoretical and Experimental Probability

Lesson Objectives	NAEP 2005 Strand: Data Analysis and Probability
▼1 Find theoretical probability ▼2 Find experimental probability	**Topic:** Probability **Local Standards:** _____

Vocabulary

The probability of an event, or P(event), is _____

An outcome is _____

An event is _____

A sample space is _____

event	sample space	favorable outcome
↓	↓	↓
rolling an even number on a number cube		

Theoretical probability is _____

_____

Probability

← less likely	more likely →

impossible event	equally likely and unlikely	**certain event**
rolling a 7 on a number cube	getting a head when flipping a coin	rolling a number less than 7 on a number cube

The complement of an event is _____

possible outcomes for rolling a number cube	outcomes for rolling an even number	complement of rolling an even number
↓	↓	↓

Experimental probability is _____

_____

Odds describes _____

Name_____ Class_____ Date _____

Examples

❶ Finding Theoretical Probability A bowl contains 12 slips of paper, each with a different name of a month on it. Find the theoretical probability that a slip selected at random from the bowl has the name of a month that ends with "ber."

$$P(\text{event}) = \frac{\text{number of favorable outcomes}}{\text{number of possible outcomes}}$$

$$= \frac{\boxed{}}{12} \quad \textbf{There are } \boxed{} \textbf{ months out of 12 that end with "ber":}$$
$$\textbf{September, October, November, and December.}$$

$$= \frac{\boxed{}}{\boxed{}} \quad \textbf{Simplify.}$$

The probability of picking a month that ends with "ber" is $\boxed{}$.

❷ Finding the Complement of an Event For a number cube, find the probability of *not* rolling a number divisible by 3.

$$P(\div 3) = \frac{\text{number of favorable outcomes}}{\text{number of possible outcomes}} = \frac{\boxed{}}{6} \text{ or } \frac{\boxed{}}{\boxed{}}$$

$$P(not \div 3) = \boxed{} - P(\div 3) \quad \textbf{Use the complement formula.}$$

$$= 1 - \frac{\boxed{}}{\boxed{}} = \frac{\boxed{}}{\boxed{}} \quad \textbf{Simplify.}$$

The probability of *not* rolling a number divisible by 3 is $\boxed{}$.

Quick Check

1. Suppose you write the names of days of the week on identical pieces of paper. Find the theoretical probability of picking a piece of paper at random that has the name of a day that starts with the letter T.

2. Critical Thinking A solid with *n* sides is numbered 1 to *n*. What happens to *P*(*not* rolling a 3) as *n* increases?

Examples

❸ Finding Odds Find the odds in favor of tossing a number cube and getting a number greater than 4.

Favorable outcomes: ▢ .

Unfavorable outcomes: ▢ .

The odds are ▢ in favor of the event.

❹ Finding Experimental Probability Quality control inspected 500 belts at random. They found no defects in 485 belts. What is the probability that a belt selected at random will pass quality control? Express your answer as a percent.

$$P(\text{no defects}) = \frac{\text{number of times an event occurs}}{\text{number of time the experiment is done}}$$

$$= \frac{\boxed{}}{500} \qquad \textbf{Substitute.}$$

$$= \boxed{} = \boxed{}\% \qquad \textbf{Simplify. Write as a percent.}$$

The probability that a belt has no defects is ▢ %.

❺ Using Experimental Probability If the belt manufacturer from Example 3 has 6,258 belts, predict how many belts are likely to have no defects.

number with no defects = $P(\text{no defects}) \cdot$ number of belts

$$= \boxed{} \cdot 6{,}258 \qquad \textbf{Substitute. Use } \boxed{} \textbf{ for 97\%.}$$

$$= \boxed{} \qquad \textbf{Simplify.}$$

Approximately ▢ belts are likely to have no defects.

Quick Check

3. In Example 3, find the odds against getting a number less than or equal to 5.

4. A manufacturer decides to inspect 2,500 skateboards. There are 2,450 skateboards that have no defects. Find the probability that a skateboard selected at random has no defects.

5. A manufacturer inspects 700 light bulbs. She finds that the probability that a light bulb works is 99.6%. There are 35,400 light bulbs in the warehouse. Predict how many light bulbs are likely to work.

Lesson 2-7

Probability of Compound Events

Lesson Objectives	NAEP 2005 Strand: Data Analysis and Probability
▼ 1 Find the probability of independent events ▼ 2 Find the probability of dependent events	Topic: Probability Local Standards: _____

Vocabulary and Key Concepts

Probability of Two Independent Events

If A and B are independent events,

$P(A \text{ and } B) = P(A) \cdot P(B)$

Probability of Two Dependent Events

If A and B are dependent events,

$P(A \text{ then } B) = P(A) \cdot P(B \text{ after } A)$

Independent events are _____

_____

Dependent events are _____

_____

Examples

❶ Independent Events Suppose you roll two number cubes. What is the probability that you will roll an odd number on the first cube and a multiple of 3 on the second cube?

$P(\text{odd}) = \dfrac{\boxed{}}{6} = \dfrac{\boxed{}}{\boxed{}}$ **There are $\boxed{}$ odd numbers out of six numbers.**

$P(\text{multiple of 3}) = \dfrac{\boxed{}}{6} = \dfrac{\boxed{}}{\boxed{}}$ **There are $\boxed{}$ multiples of 3 out of six numbers.**

$P(\text{odd and multiple of 3}) = P(\text{odd}) \cdot P(\text{multiple of 3})$

$= \dfrac{\boxed{}}{\boxed{}} \cdot \dfrac{\boxed{}}{\boxed{}}$ **Substitute.**

$= \dfrac{\boxed{}}{\boxed{}}$ **Simplify.**

The probability that you will roll an odd number on the first cube and a multiple of 3 on the second cube is $\boxed{}$.

❷ Selecting Without Replacement Suppose you have 3 quarters and
5 dimes in your pocket. You take out one coin, but you do not put it back.
Then you take out another coin. What is the probability of first taking out
a dime and then a quarter?

Since you do not replace the first coin, the events are [   ].

$$P(\text{dime}) = \frac{\boxed{}}{\boxed{}}$$ **There are** $\boxed{}$ **out of** $\boxed{}$ **coins that are dimes.**

$$P(\text{quarter after dime}) = \frac{\boxed{}}{\boxed{}}$$ **There are** $\boxed{}$ **out of the** $\boxed{}$ **remaining coins that are quarters.**

$$P(\text{dime then quarter}) = P(\text{dime}) \cdot P(\text{quarter after dime})$$

$$= \frac{\boxed{}}{\boxed{}} \cdot \frac{\boxed{}}{\boxed{}} \quad \textbf{Multiply.}$$

$$= \frac{\boxed{}}{\boxed{}}$$

The probability that you will take out a dime and then a quarter is $\boxed{}$.

Quick Check

1. Suppose you roll a red number cube and a blue number cube. What is the
   probability that you will roll a 5 on the red cube and a 1 or 2 on the blue cube?

2. Looking at the letter tiles, find the probability of picking a *U* and then an *O* without replacing the first tile.

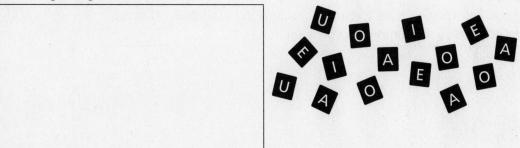

Example

❸ **Applying Probabilities of Compound Events** A teacher must select 2 students for a conference. The teacher randomly picks names from among 3 freshmen, 2 sophomores, 4 juniors, and 4 seniors. What is the probability that a junior and then a senior are chosen?

$P(\text{junior}) = \dfrac{\boxed{}}{\boxed{}}$ **There are** $\boxed{}$ **juniors among** $\boxed{}$ **students.**

$P(\text{senior after junior}) = \dfrac{\boxed{}}{\boxed{}}$ **There are** $\boxed{}$ **seniors among the** $\boxed{}$ **remaining students.**

$P(\text{junior then senior}) = P(\text{junior}) \cdot P(\text{senior after junior})$

$= \dfrac{\boxed{}}{\boxed{}} \cdot \dfrac{\boxed{}}{\boxed{}}$ **Substitute.**

$= \dfrac{\boxed{}}{\boxed{}}$ **Simplify.**

Quick Check

3. a. Using the information from Example 3, what is the probability that the teacher chooses a sophomore and then a junior?

b. What is the probability that the teacher chooses a junior and then a sophomore?

c. Critical Thinking Does the probability of choosing without replacement change if the order of the events is reversed? Explain.

Lesson 3-1

Solving Two-Step Equations

Lesson Objectives	**NAEP 2005 Strand:** Algebra; Geometry
▼ Solve two-step equations	**Topics:** Equations and Inequalities; Mathematical Reasoning
▼ Use deductive reasoning	**Local Standards:** _____

Key Concepts

Solving Two-Step Equations

Step 1 Use the Addition or Subtraction Property of Equality to get the term with a variable alone on one side of the equation.

Step 2 Use the Multiplication or Division Property of Equality to write an equivalent equation in which the variable has a coefficient of ☐ .

Example

❶ Solving a Two-Step Equation Solve $21 = -p + 8$.

$21 - \boxed{} = -p + 8 - \boxed{}$ **Subtract** ☐ **from each side.**

$\boxed{} = -p$ **Simplify.**

$\boxed{}(13) = \boxed{}(-p)$ **Use the Multiplication Property of Equality. Multiply each side by** ☐ .

$\boxed{} = p$ **Simplify.**

Check $21 = -p + 8$

$21 \overset{?}{=} -\left(\boxed{}\right) + 8$ **Substitute** ☐ **for p.**

$21 = \boxed{}$ ✓

Quick Check

1. Solve each equation. Check your answer.

a. $7 = 2y - 3$

b. $\dfrac{x}{9} - 15 = 12$

c. $-x + 15 = 12$

Examples

❷ Solving Two-Step Equations You order iris bulbs from a catalog. Iris bulbs cost $.90 each. The shipping charge is $2.50. If you have $18.50 to spend, how many iris bulbs can you order?

Relate ┌─────────┐ times ┌─────────────┐ plus ┌──────────┐ equals ┌──────────┐
        │ cost   │   │ number of   │   │ shipping │   │ amount   │
        │ per iris│   │ iris bulbs │   │   │   │ to spend │
        └─────────┘   └─────────────┘   └──────────┘   └──────────┘

Define Let $\boxed{b}$ = the number of bulbs you can order.

Write $\boxed{} \cdot \boxed{} + \boxed{} = \boxed{}$

$$0.9b + \boxed{} = 18.50$$

$0.9b + 2.50 - \boxed{} = 18.50 - \boxed{}$ **Subtract** $\boxed{}$ **from each side.**

$$0.9b = \boxed{}$$ **Simplify.**

$$\frac{0.9b}{\boxed{}} = \frac{16}{\boxed{}}$$ **Divide each side by** $\boxed{}$.

$$b = \boxed{}$$ **Simplify.**

Check Is the solution reasonable? You can only order whole iris bulbs. Since 18 bulbs would cost 18 · $.90 = $16.20 plus $2.50 for shipping, which is more than $\boxed{}$, you can only order $\boxed{}$ bulbs.

❸ Using Deductive Reasoning Solve $3 - 5z = 18$. Justify each step.

$3 - 5z \boxed{}\boxed{} = 18 \boxed{}\boxed{}$ **Subtraction Property of Equality**

$-5z = \boxed{}$ **Simplify.**

$\dfrac{-5z}{\boxed{}} = \dfrac{15}{\boxed{}}$ $\boxed{}$ **Property of Equality**

$z = \boxed{}$ **Simplify.**

Quick Check

2. Suppose your high school's baseball team scored 5 runs in Saturday's game. This was four more than $\frac{1}{2}$ the runs scored by the opposing team. How many runs did the opposing team score?

┌──────────────────┐
│   │
└──────────────────┘

3. Solve $-9 - 4m = 3$. Justify each step.

┌───┐
│   │
│   │
│   │
│   │
│   │
└───┘

Lesson 3-2

Solving Multi-Step Equations

Lesson Objectives	**NAEP 2005 Strand:** Algebra
▼ **1** Use the Distributive Property when combining like terms	**Topics:** Variables, Expressions, and Operations; Equations and Inequalities
▼ **2** Use the Distributive Property when solving equations	**Local Standards:** _____

Key Concepts

Steps for Solving a Multi-Step Equation

Step 1 Clear the equation of fractions and decimals.

Step 2 Use the Distributive Property to remove parentheses on each side.

Step 3 Combine like terms on each side.

Step 4 Undo addition or ☐ .

Step 5 Undo multiplication or ☐ .

Example

① **Combining Like Terms** Solve $3a + 6 + a = 90$.

$4a + 6 = 90$ **Combine like terms.**

$4a + 6 - \boxed{} = 90 - \boxed{}$ **Subtract** ☐ **from each side.**

$4a = \boxed{}$ **Simplify.**

$\dfrac{4a}{\boxed{}} = \dfrac{\boxed{}}{\boxed{}}$ **Divide each side by** ☐ **.**

$a = \boxed{}$ **Simplify.**

Quick Check

1. Solve each equation.

a. $3x - 4x + 6 = -2$

b. $7 = 4m - 2m + 1$

c. $-2y + 5 + 5y = 14$

d. $-3z + 8 + (-2z) = -12$

Examples

❷ Applying Multi-Step Equations You need to build a rectangular pen in your backyard for your dog. One side of the pen will be against the house. Two sides of the pen have a length of x ft and the width will be 25 ft. What is the greatest length the pen can be if you have 63 ft of fencing?

Relate | length of side | plus | 25 ft | plus | length of side | equals | amount of fencing |

Define Let $\boxed{x}$ = length of a side adjacent to the house.

Write $\boxed{} + \boxed{} + \boxed{} = \boxed{}$

$x + 25 + x = \boxed{}$

$\boxed{}x + 25 = \boxed{}$ **Combine like terms.**

$\boxed{} + 25 - \boxed{} = \boxed{} - \boxed{}$ **Subtract** $\boxed{}$ **from each side.**

$2x = \boxed{}$ **Simplify.**

$\dfrac{2x}{\boxed{}} = \dfrac{\boxed{}}{\boxed{}}$ **Divide each side by** $\boxed{}$.

$x = \boxed{}$

The pen can be $\boxed{}$ feet long.

❸ Solving an Equation With Grouping Symbols Solve $2(x - 3) = 8$.

$\boxed{} - \boxed{} = 8$ **Use the** $\boxed{}$ **Property.**

$\boxed{} - \boxed{} + \boxed{} = 8 + \boxed{}$ **Add** $\boxed{}$ **to each side.**

$2x = \boxed{}$ **Simplify.**

$\dfrac{2x}{\boxed{}} = \dfrac{\boxed{}}{\boxed{}}$ **Divide each side by** $\boxed{}$.

$x = \boxed{}$ **Simplify.**

Check $2(x - 3) = 8$

$2(\boxed{} - 3) \stackrel{?}{=} 8$ **Substitute** $\boxed{}$ **for** x.

$2(\boxed{}) \stackrel{?}{=} 8$

$\boxed{} = 8$ ✓

④ Solving an Equation That Contains Fractions Solve $\frac{3x}{2} + \frac{x}{5} = 17$.

$$\frac{3x}{2} + \frac{x}{5} = 17$$

$\boxed{}\left(\frac{3x}{2} + \frac{x}{5}\right) = \boxed{}(17)$ **Multiply each side by** $\boxed{}$ **, a common multiple of 2 and 5.**

$\boxed{}\left(\frac{3x}{2}\right) + \boxed{}\left(\frac{x}{5}\right) = 10(17)$ **Use the Distributive Property.**

$\boxed{}x + \boxed{}x = \boxed{}$ **Multiply.**

$17x = 170$ **Combine like terms.**

$\dfrac{17x}{\boxed{}} = \dfrac{170}{\boxed{}}$ **Divide each side by** $\boxed{}$ **.**

$x = \boxed{}$ **Simplify.**

Quick Check

2. A carpenter is building a rectangular fence for a playground. One side of the playground is the wall of a building 70 ft wide. He plans to use 340 ft of fencing material. What is the length of the playground if the width is 70 ft?

Solve each equation.

3. a. $3(k + 8) = 21$ **b.** $15 = -3(x - 1) + 9$

4. a. $\dfrac{m}{4} + \dfrac{m}{2} = \dfrac{5}{8}$

b. $\dfrac{2}{3}x - \dfrac{5}{8}x = 26$

Lesson 3-3

Equations With Variables on Both Sides

Lesson Objectives	NAEP 2005 Strand: Algebra
▼1 Solve equations with variables on both sides ▼2 Identify equations that are identities or have no solution	**Topics:** Variables, Expressions, and Operations; Equations and Inequalities **Local Standards:** _____

Vocabulary

An identity is _____

Example

1 **Variables on Both Sides** You can buy a skateboard for $60 from a friend and rent the safety equipment for $1.50 per hour. Or you can rent all items you need for $5.50 per hour. How many hours must you use the skateboard to justify buying your friend's skateboard?

Relate | cost of friend's skateboard | plus | equipment rental | equals | skateboard and equipment rental |

Define Let $\boxed{h}$ = the number of hours you must skateboard.

Write

$$\boxed{} + \boxed{} = \boxed{}$$

$$60 + \boxed{}h = \boxed{}h$$

$$60 + 1.5h - \boxed{}h = 5.5h - \boxed{}h \quad \textbf{Subtract } \boxed{}h \textbf{ from each side.}$$

$$60 = \boxed{}h \quad \textbf{Combine like terms.}$$

 $$\frac{60}{\boxed{}} = \frac{4h}{\boxed{}} \quad \textbf{Divide each side by } \boxed{}.$$

 $$\boxed{} = h \quad \textbf{Simplify.}$$

Quick Check

1. A hairdresser is considering ordering a certain shampoo. Company A charges $4 per 8-oz bottle plus a $10 handling fee per order. Company B charges $3 per 8-oz bottle plus a $25 handling fee per order. How many bottles must the hairdresser buy to justify using Company B?

Example

❷ Identities and Equations With No Solutions Solve each equation.

a. $-6z + 8 = z + 10 - 7z$

$-6z + 8 = -\boxed{}z + 10$ **Combine like terms.**

$-6z + 8 + \boxed{} = -6z + 10 + \boxed{}$ **Add** $\boxed{}$ **to each side.**

$\boxed{} = \boxed{}$ $\boxed{}$ **true for any value of z!**

The equation has $\boxed{}$ solution.

b. $4 - 4y = -2(2y - 2)$

$4 - 4y = -\boxed{}y + \boxed{}$ **Use the Distributive Property.**

$4 - 4y + \boxed{} = -4y + 4 + \boxed{}$ **Add** $\boxed{}$ **to each side.**

$\boxed{} = \boxed{}$ $\boxed{}$ **true!**

The equation is true for every value of *y*, so the equation is an _____

Quick Check

2. Determine whether each equation is an *identity* or whether it has *no solution*.

a. $9 + 5n = 5n - 1$

b. $9 + 5x = 7x + 9 - 2x$

3. Solve each equation.

a. $-6d = d + 4$

b. $7k - 4 = 5k + 16$

Lesson 3-4

Ratio and Proportion

Lesson Objectives	**NAEP 2005 Strand:** Number Properties and Operations; Measurement
▼1 Find ratios and rates	**Topics:** Ratios and Proportional Reasoning; Measuring Physical Attributes
▼2 Solve proportions	**Local Standards:** _____

Vocabulary and Key Concepts

Cross Products of a Proportion

If $\frac{a}{b} = \frac{c}{d}$ then $ad = \boxed{}$.

Example $\frac{2}{3} = \frac{8}{12}$, so $2 \cdot 12 = 3 \cdot 8$

A ratio is _____

_____

A rate is _____

_____

A unit rate is _____

_____

Unit analysis is _____

_____

A proportion is _____

_____

In the proportion $\frac{a}{b} = \frac{c}{d}$, the extremes of proportion are _____

In the proportion $\frac{a}{b} = \frac{c}{d}$, the means of a proportion are _____

In the proportion $\frac{a}{b} = \frac{c}{d}$, the cross products are _____

Examples

❶ Using Unit Rates A brand of grapefruit juice costs $1.56 for 48 oz. Find the unit rate.

$$\frac{\text{cost} \rightarrow \boxed{}}{\text{ounces} \rightarrow \boxed{}\text{oz}} = \$\boxed{}/\text{oz}$$

The unit rate is $\boxed{}$ per oz.

❷ Applying Proportions In 2000, Lance Armstrong completed the 3,630-km Tour de France course in 92.5 hours. Traveling at his average speed, how long would it take Lance Armstrong to ride 295 km?

Define Let $\boxed{t}$ = time needed to ride 295 km.

Relate $\boxed{\text{Tour de France average speed}}$ equals $\boxed{\text{295-km trip average speed}}$

Write

$$\frac{\boxed{}}{\boxed{}} = \frac{\boxed{} \leftarrow \text{kilometers}}{\boxed{} \leftarrow \text{hours}}$$

$$\frac{\boxed{}}{\boxed{}} = \frac{\boxed{}}{\boxed{t}}$$

$$\boxed{}\,t = \boxed{}\left(\boxed{}\right) \qquad \text{Write cross products.}$$

$$t = \frac{\boxed{}\left(\boxed{}\right)}{\boxed{}} \qquad \text{Divide each side by } \boxed{}.$$

$$t \approx \boxed{} \qquad \text{Simplify. Round to the nearest tenth.}$$

Traveling at his average speed, it would take Lance approximately

$\boxed{}$ hours to cycle 295 km.

❸ Converting Rates The fastest recorded speed for an eastern gray kangaroo is 40 mi per hour. What is the kangaroo's speed in feet per second?

$$\frac{\boxed{}\text{ mi}}{1\text{ h}} \cdot \frac{\boxed{}\text{ ft}}{1\text{ mi}} \cdot \frac{1\text{ h}}{\boxed{}\text{ min}} \cdot \frac{1\text{ min}}{\boxed{}\text{ s}} \qquad \text{Use appropriate conversion factors.}$$

$$= \frac{\boxed{}\text{ mi}}{1\text{ h}} \cdot \frac{\boxed{}\text{ ft}}{1\text{ mi}} \cdot \frac{1\text{ h}}{\boxed{}\text{ min}} \cdot \frac{1\text{ min}}{\boxed{}\text{ s}} \qquad \text{Divide the common units.}$$

$$= \boxed{}\text{ ft/s} \qquad \text{Simplify.}$$

The kangaroo's speed is about $\boxed{}$ ft/s.

Quick Check

1. Main Street Florist sells two dozen roses for $24.60. Flowers for You Florist sells six roses for $7.50. Find the unit rate for each. Which florist has the lower cost per rose?

Example

4 Solving Multi-Step Proportions Solve the proportion.

$$\frac{z + 3}{4} = \frac{z - 4}{6}$$

$(z + 3)\left(\boxed{}\right) = 4\left(\boxed{}\right)$ **Write cross products.**

$6z + \boxed{} = \boxed{} - 16$ **Use the Distributive Property.**

$\boxed{} + 18 = -16$ **Subtract** $\boxed{}$ **from each side.**

$2z = -\boxed{}$ **Subtract** $\boxed{}$ **from each side.**

    Divide each side by $\boxed{}$.

$z = \boxed{}$ **Simplify.**

Quick Check

2. Suppose you walk 2 miles in 35 minutes.

   a. Find the average walking speed. Write a rule to describe the distance d you walk as a function of the time t you walk.

   b. Use the function to find how far you would walk in an hour.

3. A sloth travels 0.15 miles per hour. Convert this speed to feet per minute.

4. Solve each proportion.

   a. $\frac{x + 2}{14} = \frac{x}{10}$

   b. $\frac{y - 15}{y + 4} = \frac{35}{7}$

   c. $\frac{3}{w + 6} = \frac{5}{w - 4}$

Lesson 3-5

Proportions and Similar Figures

Lesson Objectives	NAEP 2005 Strand: Number Properties and Operations; Geometry; Measurement
▼ Find missing measures of similar figures	**Topics:** Ratios and Proportional Reasoning; Transformation of Shapes and Preservation of Properties; Measuring Physical Attributes
▼ Use similar figures when measuring indirectly	**Local Standards:** _____

Vocabulary

Similar (~) figures are _____

_____

A scale drawing is _____

_____

A scale is _____

The scale factor is _____

_____

A dilation is _____

_____

Example

① **Finding the Length of a Side** In the figure at the right, $\triangle ABC \sim \triangle DEF$. Find AB.

Relate $\dfrac{\boxed{}}{BC} = \dfrac{DE}{\boxed{}}$ Write a proportion comparing the lengths of the corresponding sides.

Define Let $\boxed{x} = AB$.

Write $\dfrac{\boxed{}}{\boxed{}} = \dfrac{\boxed{}}{\boxed{}}$ Substitute $\boxed{}$ for *EF*, $\boxed{}$ for *BC*, $\boxed{}$ for *DE*, and $\boxed{}$ for *AB*.

$\boxed{}\boxed{} = 9\left(\boxed{}\right)$ Write cross products.

$\dfrac{\boxed{}}{\boxed{}} = \dfrac{\boxed{}}{\boxed{}}$ Divide each side by $\boxed{}$.

$x = \boxed{}$ Simplify.

AB is $\boxed{}$ mm.

Name_____ Class_____ Date _____

Quick Check

1. In the figure, $\triangle FGH \sim \triangle KLM$. Find LM.

Examples

❷ **Applying Similarity** A flagpole casts a shadow 102 feet long. A 6-ft tall man casts a shadow 17 ft long. How tall is the flagpole?

$$\frac{\boxed{}}{17} = \frac{x}{\boxed{}}$$ **Write a proportion.**

$\boxed{} x = \boxed{} \cdot \boxed{}$ **Write cross products.**

$\boxed{} x = \boxed{}$ **Simplify.**

$\dfrac{\boxed{}\,x}{\boxed{}} = \dfrac{\boxed{}}{\boxed{}}$ **Divide each side by** $\boxed{}$.

$x = \boxed{}$ **Simplify.**

The flagpole is $\boxed{}$ ft tall.

❸ **Finding Distances on Maps** The scale of the map is 1 inch : 10 miles. The map distance from Valkaria to Gifford is 2.375 inches. How far is the actual distance?

map $\longrightarrow$ $\dfrac{1}{\boxed{}}$ $=$ $\dfrac{\boxed{}}{x}$ $\longleftarrow$ map
actual $\longrightarrow$ $\longleftarrow$ actual   **Write a proportion.**

$1 \cdot x = \boxed{} \cdot \boxed{}$ **Write cross products.**

$x = \boxed{}$ **Simplify.**

The actual distance from Valkaria to Gifford is $\boxed{}$ mi.

Quick Check

2. A tree casts a 26-ft shadow. A boy standing nearby casts a 12-ft shadow. His height is 4.5 ft. How tall is the tree?

3. a. On the map in Example 3, measure the map distance from Grant to Gifford. Find the actual distance.

b. Critical Thinking If another map showed the distance from Valkaria to Wabasso but had a scale of 1 inch : 5 miles, what would the map distance be between the two locations?

Lesson 3-6

Equations and Problem Solving

Lesson Objectives	**NAEP 2005 Strand:** Algebra; Measurement
▼ Define a variable in terms of another variable	**Topics:** Equations and Inequalities; Measuring Physical Attributes
▼ Model distance-rate-time problems	**Local Standards:** _____

Vocabulary

Consecutive integers are _____

_____

An object in uniform motion is _____

_____

Examples

❶ **Consecutive Integer Problem** The sum of three consecutive integers is 72. Find the integers.

Relate | first integer | plus | second integer | plus | third integer | is | 72 |

Define Let | x | = the first integer.

Then | $x + 1$ | = the second integer,

and | | = the third integer.

Write | | + | | + | | = | |

$x +$ | | $+$ | | $= 72$

| | $x +$ | | $= 72$ **Combine like terms.**

$3x + 3 -$ | | $= 72 -$ | | **Subtract** | | **from each side.**

$3x =$ | | **Simplify.**

$\dfrac{3x}{\boxed{}} = \dfrac{\boxed{}}{\boxed{}}$ **Divide each side by** | | **.**

$x =$ | | **Simplify.**

If $x = 23$, then $x + 1 =$ | | , and $x + 2 =$ | | . The three integers are

| | , | | , and | | .

❷ Same-Direction Travel An airplane left an airport flying at 180 mi/h. A jet that flies at 330 mi/h left 1 hour later. The jet follows the same route as the airplane on parallel altitudes. How many hours will it take the jet to catch up with the airplane?

Define Let $\boxed{t}$ = the time the airplane travels.

Then $\boxed{t-1}$ = the time the jet travels.

Relate

Aircraft	Rate	Time	Distance Traveled
Airplane		t	$180t$
Jet	330		$330(t-1)$

Write

$180t = 330\left(\boxed{}\right)$ The distances traveled are equal.

$180t = \boxed{}\,t - \boxed{}$ Use the Distributive Property.

$180t - \boxed{} = 330t - 330 - \boxed{}$ Subtract $\boxed{}$ from each side.

$\boxed{}\,t = -330$ Combine like terms.

$\dfrac{-150t}{\boxed{}} = \dfrac{-330}{\boxed{}}$ Divide each side by $\boxed{}$.

$t = \boxed{}\dfrac{\boxed{}}{\boxed{}}$ Simplify.

$t - 1 = \boxed{}\dfrac{\boxed{}}{\boxed{}}$

The jet will catch up with the airplane in $\boxed{}$ hours.

Quick Check

1. The sum of three consecutive integers is 48.

a. Define a variable for one of the integers.

b. Write expressions for the other two integers.

c. Write and solve an equation to find the three integers.

Example

❸ **Opposite-Direction Travel** Two jets leave Dallas at the same time and fly in opposite directions. One is flying west 50 mi/h faster than the other. After 2 hours, they are 2500 miles apart. Find the speed of each jet.

Define   Let $\boxed{x}$ = the speed of the jet flying east.

         Then $\boxed{}$ = the speed of the jet flying west.

Relate

Jet	Rate	Time	Distance Traveled
Eastbound	x		$2x$
Westbound		2	$2(x + 50)$

Write $2x + 2(\boxed{}) = 2500$

         $2x + 2x + \boxed{} = 2500$ **Use the Distributive Property.**

             $\boxed{} + 100 = 2500$ **Combine like terms.**

     $4x + 100 - \boxed{} = 2500 - \boxed{}$ **Subtract** $\boxed{}$ **from each side.**

               $4x = 2400$ **Simplify.**

             $\dfrac{4x}{\boxed{}} = \dfrac{2400}{\boxed{}}$ **Divide each side by** $\boxed{}$.

                 $x = \boxed{}$

        $x + 50 = \boxed{}$

The jet flying east is flying at $\boxed{}$ mi/h. The jet flying west is flying at $\boxed{}$ mi/h.

Quick Check

2. A group of campers and one group leader left a campsite in a canoe. They traveled at an average rate of 10 km/h. Two hours later, the other group leader left the campsite in a motorboat. He traveled at an average rate of 22 km/h.

   a. How long after the canoe left the campsite did the motorboat catch up?

   b. How long did the motorboat travel?

3. Sarah and John leave Perryville traveling in opposite directions on a straight road. Sarah drives 12 miles per hour faster than John. After 2 hours, they are 176 miles apart. Find Sarah's speed and John's speed.

Lesson 3-7

Percent of Change

<table>
<tr><td>Lesson Objectives
▼ Find percent of change
▼ Find percent error</td><td>NAEP 2005 Strand: Number Properties and Operations
Topics: Ratios and Proportional Reasoning

Local Standards: _____</td></tr>
</table>

Vocabulary

Percent of change is the ratio $\dfrac{\boxed{}}{\boxed{}}$ expressed as a $\boxed{}$.

Percent of increase is _____

_____

Percent of decrease is _____

_____

The greatest possible error in a measurement is _____

_____

Percent error is _____

_____

Examples

❶ **Finding Percent of Change** The price of a skirt decreased from $32.95 to $28.95. Find the percent of decrease.

$$\text{percent of decrease} = \frac{\text{amount of change}}{\text{original amount}}$$

$$= \frac{32.95 - \boxed{}}{32.95}$$ **Subtract to find the amount of change.**
Substitute the original amount.

$$= \frac{\boxed{}}{32.95}$$ **Simplify the numerator.**

$$\approx \boxed{} \text{ or } \boxed{}\%$$ **Write as a decimal and then as a percent.**

The price of the skirt decreased by about $\boxed{}$.

❷ Applying Percent of Change Between 1940 and 1980, the federal budget increased from $9.5 billion to $725.3 billion. What was the percent of increase in the federal budget?

percent of increase $= \dfrac{\text{amount of change}}{\text{original amount}}$

$= \dfrac{\boxed{} - 9.5}{\boxed{}}$ **Substitute.**

$= \dfrac{\boxed{}}{9.5}$ **Simplify the numerator.**

$\approx \boxed{}$ or $\boxed{}$% **Write as a decimal and then as a percent.**

The federal budget increased by nearly $\boxed{}$%.

Quick Check

1. a. Find the percent of change if the price of a CD increases from $12.99 to $13.99. Round to the nearest percent.

b. Find the percent of change if the CD is on sale, and its price decreases from $13.99 to $12.99. Round to the nearest percent.

2. The number of alpaca owners increased from 146 in 1991 to 2,919 in 2000. Find the percent of increase. Round to the nearest percent.

Examples

❸ **Finding the Greatest Possible Error** You read the bathroom scale as 122 lb. What is your greatest possible error?

The scale is read to the nearest [   ] lb, so the greatest possible error is one half of 1 lb, or [   ] lb.

❹ **Finding Percent Error in Calculating Volume** A small jewelry box measures 7.4 cm by 12.2 cm by 4.2 cm. Find the percent error in calculating its volume.

The measurements are to the nearest 0.1 cm. The greatest possible error is [   ] cm.

as measured	**maximum value**	**minimum value**
$V = \ell \cdot w \cdot h$	$V = \ell \cdot w \cdot h$	$V = \ell \cdot w \cdot h$
$= 7.4 \boxed{} \cdot 4.2$	$= \boxed{} 12.25 \cdot 4.25$	$= 7.35 \cdot 12.15 \cdot \boxed{}$
$\approx \boxed{}$ cm^3	$\approx \boxed{}$	$\approx \boxed{}$

Possible Error: **maximum – measured**   **measured – minimum**

$387.87 - 379.18 = \boxed{}$ $379.18 - 370.61 = \boxed{}$

Use the difference that shows the greatest possible error to find the percent error.

percent error $= \dfrac{\text{greatest possible error}}{\text{measurement}}$ **Use the percent error formula.**

$= \dfrac{387.87 - \boxed{}}{379.18}$ **Substitute.**

$= \dfrac{\boxed{}}{379.18}$ **Simplify the numerator.**

$\approx \boxed{}$ **Write as a decimal.**

$\approx \boxed{}$%   **Round and write as a percent.**

The percent error is about [   ] %.

Quick Check

3. You measure a picture for the yearbook and record its height as 9 cm. What is your greatest possible error?

4. Suppose you measured your math book and recorded the dimensions as
1 in. × 9 in. × 10 in. Find the percent error in calculating its volume.

Lesson 3-8

Finding and Estimating Square Roots

Lesson Objectives	**NAEP 2005 Strand:** Number Properties and Operations
▼1 Find square roots ▼2 Estimate and use square roots	**Topics:** Number Sense; Estimation **Local Standards:** _____

Vocabulary and Key Concepts

Square Root

The number a is a square root of b if $a^2 =$ ☐.

Example $4^2 =$ ☐ and $(-4)^2 =$ ☐, so 4 and -4 are square roots of ☐.

The principal square root is _____

The negative square root of b is ☐.

The radicand is _____

Perfect squares are _____

Examples

❶ Simplifying Square Root Expressions Simplify each expression.

a. $\sqrt{25}$ = [ ]   positive square root

b. $\pm\sqrt{\dfrac{9}{25}}$ = ± [ ]   The square roots are ☐ and ☐.

c. $-\sqrt{64}$ = [ ]   Negative square root

d. $\sqrt{-49}$ = [ ]   For real numbers, the square root of a negative number is [ ].

e. $\pm\sqrt{0}$ = [ ]   There is only one square root of 0.

❷ Rational and Irrational Square Roots Tell whether each expression is *rational* or *irrational*.

a. $\pm\sqrt{144}$ = [ ]   [ ]

b. $\sqrt{\dfrac{1}{5}}$ = 0.44721359...   [ ]

c. $-\sqrt{6.25}$ = [ ]   [ ]

d. $\sqrt{\dfrac{1}{9}}$ = $0.\overline{3}$ [ ]

e. $\sqrt{7}$ = [ ]   [ ]

❸ Estimating Square Roots Between what two consecutive integers is $\sqrt{28.34}$?

$\sqrt{\boxed{}} < \sqrt{28.34} < \sqrt{\boxed{}}$ **28.34 is between the two consecutive perfect squares** $\boxed{}$ **and** $\boxed{}$.

$\boxed{} < \sqrt{28.34} < \boxed{}$ **The square roots of 25 and 36 are** $\boxed{}$ **and** $\boxed{}$ **, respectively.**

$\sqrt{28.34}$ is between $\boxed{}$ and $\boxed{}$.

❹ Applying Square Roots Suppose a rectangular field has a length y three times its width x. The formula $d = \sqrt{x^2 + y^2}$ gives the length of the diagonal of a rectangle. Find the distance of the diagonal across the field if $x = 8$ ft.

$d = \sqrt{x^2 + (3x)^2}$ **Substitute 3x for** $\boxed{}$.

$d = \sqrt{\boxed{}^2 + \left(3 \cdot \boxed{}\right)^2}$ **Substitute** $\boxed{}$ **for x.**

$d = \sqrt{\boxed{} + \boxed{}}$ **Simplify.**

$d = \sqrt{\boxed{}}$

$d \approx \boxed{}$ **Use a calculator. Round to the nearest tenth.**

The diagonal is about $\boxed{}$ ft long.

Quick Check

1. Simplify each expression.

   a. $\sqrt{49}$ $\boxed{}$ **b.** $\pm\sqrt{36}$ $\boxed{}$ **c.** $-\sqrt{121}$ $\boxed{}$ **d.** $\sqrt{\frac{1}{25}}$ $\boxed{}$

2. Tell whether each expression is rational or irrational.

   a. $\sqrt{8}$ **b.** $\pm\sqrt{225}$ **c.** $-\sqrt{75}$ **d.** $\sqrt{\frac{1}{4}}$

   $\boxed{}$ $\boxed{}$ $\boxed{}$ $\boxed{}$

3. Between what two consecutive integers is $-\sqrt{105}$?

4. Using the formula from Example 4, suppose $x = 10$ ft. How long is the diagonal across the field? Round to the nearest tenth of a foot.

Name_____ Class_____ Date _____

Lesson 3-9   The Pythagorean Theorem

Lesson Objectives	**NAEP 2005 Strand:** Geometry
▼ Solve problems using the Pythagorean Theorem ▼ Identify right triangles	**Topic:** Relationships Among Geometric Figures **Local Standards:** _____

Vocabulary and Key Concepts

The Pythagorean Theorem

In any right triangle, the sum of the squares of the lengths of the legs is equal to the square of the length of the hypotenuse.

$$\boxed{}^2 + \boxed{}^2 = \boxed{}^2$$

The Converse of the Pythagorean Theorem

If a triangle has sides of lengths a, b, and c, and $a^2 + b^2 = c^2$, then the triangle is a $\boxed{}$ with hypotenuse of length c.

The hypotenuse is _____

_____

The legs are _____

A conditional is _____

A hypothesis is _____

A conclusion is _____

A converse is _____

_____

Examples

① Using the Pythagorean Theorem What is the length of the hypotenuse of this triangle?

$a^2 + b^2 = c^2$ **Use the Pythagorean Theorem.**

$\boxed{}^2 + \boxed{}^2 = c^2$ **Substitute** $\boxed{}$ **for** *a* **and** $\boxed{}$ **for** *b*.

$\boxed{} + \boxed{} = c^2$ **Simplify.**

$\sqrt{\boxed{}} = \sqrt{c^2}$ **Find the principal square root of each side.**

$\boxed{} = c$ **Simplify.**

The length of the hypotenuse is 17 m.

8 m, c, 15 m triangle shown.

❷ Using the Converse of the Pythagorean Theorem Determine whether the given lengths are sides of a right triangle.

a. 5 in., 5 in., and 7 in.

$\boxed{}^2 + \boxed{}^2 \overset{?}{=} \boxed{}^2$ **Determine whether $a^2 + b^2 = c^2$, where c is the longest side.**

$\boxed{} + \boxed{} \overset{?}{=} \boxed{}$ **Simplify.**

$\boxed{} \neq \boxed{}$

This triangle $\boxed{}$ a right triangle.

b. 10 cm, 24 cm, and 26 cm

$\boxed{}^2 + \boxed{}^2 \overset{?}{=} \boxed{}^2$ **Determine whether $a^2 + b^2 = c^2$, where c is the longest side.**

$\boxed{} + \boxed{} \overset{?}{=} \boxed{}$ **Simplify.**

$\boxed{} = \boxed{}$

This triangle $\boxed{}$ a right triangle.

❸ Physics If two forces pull at right angles to each other, the resultant force is represented as the diagonal of a rectangle, as shown in the diagram. The diagonal forms a right triangle with two of the perpendicular sides of the rectangle.

For a 50-lb force and a 120-lb force, the resultant force is 130 lb. Are the forces pulling at right angles to each other?

$\boxed{}^2 + \boxed{}^2 \overset{?}{=} \boxed{}^2$ **Determine whether $a^2 + b^2 = c^2$, where c is the greatest force.**

$\boxed{} + \boxed{} \overset{?}{=} \boxed{}$

$\boxed{} = \boxed{}$

The forces of 50 lb and 120 lb $\boxed{}$ at right angles to each other.

Quick Check

1. What is the length of the hypotenuse of a right triangle with legs of lengths 7 cm and 24 cm?

$\boxed{}$

2. A triangle has sides of lengths 10 m, 24 m, and 26 m. Is the triangle a right triangle?

$\boxed{}$

3. Physics Consider Example 3. For a 70-lb force and a 60-lb force, the resultant force is 100 lb. Are the forces pulling at right angles to each other?

$\boxed{}$

Lesson 4-1

Inequalities and Their Graphs

Lesson Objectives	**NAEP 2005 Strand:** Algebra
▼ Identify solutions of inequalities	**Topics:** Variables, Expressions, and Operations; Equations and Inequalities
▼ Graph and write inequalities	
	Local Standards: _____

Vocabulary

A solution of an inequality is _____

_____

Examples

❶ Identifying Solutions by Evaluating Is each number a solution of $3 + 2x < 8$?

a. -2

$$3 + 2x < 8$$

$$3 + 2\left(\boxed{}\right) < 8 \qquad \leftarrow \textbf{Substitute for } \textbf{\textit{x}}. \rightarrow$$

$$3 - \boxed{} < 8 \qquad \leftarrow \textbf{Simplify.} \rightarrow$$

$$\boxed{} < 8 \qquad \leftarrow \textbf{Compare.} \rightarrow$$

-2 is a solution.

b. 3

$$3 + 2x < 8$$

$$3 + 2\left(\boxed{}\right) < 8$$

$$3 + \boxed{} < 8$$

$$\boxed{} < 8$$

3 is not a solution.

❷ Graphing Inequalities

a. Graph $d < 3$.

The solutions of $d < 3$ are all the points to the

$\boxed{}$ of 3.

b. Graph $-3 \geq g$.

The solutions of $-3 \geq g$ are $\boxed{}$ and all the

points to the $\boxed{}$ of -3.

❸ Writing an Inequality From a Graph Write an inequality for each graph.

a. $x < \boxed{}$ Numbers $\boxed{}$ 2 are graphed.

b. $x \leq \boxed{}$ Numbers $\boxed{}$ -3 are graphed.

Name_____ Class_____ Date _____

Quick Check

1. Is each number a solution of $6x - 3 > 10$?

   a. 1

   b. 2

   c. 3

   d. 4

2. Graph each inequality.

   a. $a < 1$

   b. $n \geq -3$

   c. $2 > p$

3. Write an inequality for each graph.

   a.

   b.

Name_____ Class_____ Date_____

Lesson 4-2

Lesson Objectives	NAEP 2005 Strand: Algebra
▼ Use addition to solve inequalities	**Topic:** Equations and Inequalities
▼ Use subtraction to solve inequalities	**Local Standards:** _____

Vocabulary and Key Concepts

Addition Property of Inequality

For every real number a, b, and c,

if $a > b$, then [   ] ;   if $a < b$, then [   ] .

Examples

$3 > 1$, so $3 + 2$ [ ] $1 + 2$. $-5 < 4$, so $-5 + 2$ [ ] $4 + 2$.

This property is also true for $\geq$ and $\leq$.

Subtraction Property of Inequality

For every real number a, b, and c,

if $a > b$, then [   ] ;   if $a < b$, then [   ] .

Examples

$3 > -1$, so $3 - 2$ [ ] $-1 - 2$. $-5 < 4$, so $-5 - 2$ [ ] $4 - 2$.

This property is also true for $\geq$ and $\leq$.

Equivalent inequalities are _____

_____

Examples

❶ **Using the Addition Property of Inequality** Solve $8 \geq d - 2$. Graph and check your solution.

$8 + \boxed{} \geq d - 2 + \boxed{}$ Add $\boxed{}$ to each side.

$\boxed{} \geq d$, or $d \leq 10$ Simplify.

Check $8 = d - 2$ Check the computation.

$8 \overset{?}{=} \boxed{} - 2$ Substitute $\boxed{}$ for *d*.

$8 = 8$ ✓

$8 \geq d - 2$ Check the direction of the inequality.

$8 \geq 9 - 2$ Substitute 9 for *d*.

$8 \geq 7$ $\boxed{}$

❷ Using the Subtraction Property of Inequality To receive a B in your literature class, you must earn more than 350 points of reading credits. Last week you earned 120 points. This week you earned 90 points. How many more points must you earn to receive a B?

Relate | points earned | plus | points needed | is more than | points required | .

Define Let $\boxed{p}$ = the number of points needed.

Write

$$\boxed{} \; + \; \boxed{} \quad \boxed{} \quad \boxed{}$$

$$120 \; + \; 90 \; + \; \boxed{}\boxed{}\boxed{}$$

$$\boxed{} \; + \; p \; \boxed{} \; 350 \qquad \textbf{Combine like terms.}$$

$$\boxed{} \; + \; p \; - \; \boxed{} \; \boxed{} \; 350 \; - \; \boxed{} \qquad \textbf{Subtract } \boxed{} \textbf{ from each side.}$$

$$p \; \boxed{} \; 140 \qquad \textbf{Simplify.}$$

You must earn 141 more points.

Quick Check

1. a. Solve $m - 6 > -4$. Graph your solution.

b. Solve $n - 7 \le -2$. Graph and check your solution.

2. a. Solve $t + 3 \ge 8$. Graph and check your solution.

b. Your baseball team has a goal to collect at least 160 blankets for a shelter. Team members brought 42 blankets on Monday and 65 blankets on Wednesday. How many blankets must the team donate on Friday to meet or exceed their goal?

Lesson 4-3

Lesson Objectives	**NAEP 2005 Strand:** Algebra
✔ Use multiplication to solve inequalities	**Topics:** Equations and Inequalities
✔ Use division to solve inequalities	**Local Standards:** _____

Key Concepts

Multiplication Property of Inequality

For every real number a and b, and for $c > 0$,

   if $a > b$, then ac ☐ bc;   if $a < b$, then ac ☐ bc.

Examples

$4 > -1$, so $4(5)$ ☐ $-1(5)$. $-6 < 3$, so $-6(5)$ ☐ $3(5)$.

For every real number a and b, and for $c < 0$,

   if $a > b$, then ac ☐ bc;   if $a < b$, then ac ☐ bc.

Examples

$4 > -1$, so $4(-2)$ ☐ $-1(-2)$. $-6 < 3$, so $-6(-2)$ ☐ $3(-2)$.

This property is also true for $\geq$ and $\leq$.

Division Property of Inequality

For every real number a and b, and for $c > 0$,

   if $a > b$, then $\frac{a}{c}$ ☐ $\frac{b}{c}$;   if $a < b$, then $\frac{a}{c}$ ☐ $\frac{b}{c}$.

Examples

$6 > 4$, so $\frac{6}{2}$ ☐ $\frac{4}{2}$. $2 < 8$, so $\frac{2}{2}$ ☐ $\frac{8}{2}$.

For every real number a and b, and for $c < 0$,

   if $a > b$, then $\frac{a}{c}$ ☐ $\frac{b}{c}$;   if $a < b$, then $\frac{a}{c}$ ☐ $\frac{b}{c}$.

Examples

$6 > 4$, so $\frac{6}{-2}$ ☐ $\frac{4}{-2}$. $2 < 8$, so $\frac{2}{-2}$ ☐ $\frac{8}{-2}$.

This property is also true for $\geq$ and $\leq$.

Examples

❶ Multiplying to Solve an Inequality Solve $3 \le -\frac{3}{5}x$. Graph and check the solutions.

$$\left(\square\frac{\square}{\square}\right)(3) \ge \left(\square\frac{\square}{\square}\right)\left(-\frac{3}{5}x\right)$$

Multiply each side by the reciprocal of $-\frac{3}{5}$, which is $\boxed{}$, and reverse the inequality symbol.

$-5 \ge x$, or $x \le -5$ **Simplify.**

Check $3 = -\frac{3}{5}x$ **Check the computation.**

$3 = -\frac{3}{5}\left(\boxed{}\right)$ **Substitute** $\boxed{}$ **for x.**

$3 = \boxed{}$ ✓

$3 \le -\frac{3}{5}x$ **Check the direction of the inequality.**

$3 \le -\frac{3}{5}\left(\boxed{}\right)$ **Substitute −10 for x.**

$3 \le 6$ $\boxed{}$

❷ Dividing to Solve an Inequality Solve $-4c < 24$. Graph the solutions.

$$\frac{-4c}{\boxed{}} > \frac{24}{\boxed{}}$$ **Divide each side by** $\boxed{}$. **Reverse the inequality symbol.**

$c > -6$ **Simplify.**

❸ Applying Inequalities Your family budgets $160 to spend on fuel for a trip. How many times can they fill the car's gas tank if it costs $25 each time?

Relate $\boxed{\text{cost per tank}}$ times $\boxed{\text{number of tanks}}$ $\boxed{\text{is at most}}$ $\boxed{\text{total fuel budget}}$.

Define   Let $\boxed{t}$ = the number of tanks of gas.

Write $\boxed{}$ · $\boxed{}$ $\boxed{}$ $\boxed{}$

$25t \le 160$

$$\frac{25t}{\boxed{}} \le \frac{160}{\boxed{}}$$ **Divide each side by** $\boxed{}$.

$t \le \boxed{}$ **Simplify.**

Your family can fill the car's gas tank at most 6 times.

Quick Check

Solve each inequality. Graph and check your solutions.

1. a. $\frac{b}{4} > \frac{1}{2}$

b. $\frac{y}{0.5} \le -3$

c. $\frac{-k}{4} > -1$

d. $-t < \frac{1}{2}$

2. a. $-3w \ge 12$

b. $0.6 > -0.2n$

3. Students in the school band are selling calendars. They earn $.40 on each calendar they sell. Their goal is to earn more than $327. Write and solve an inequality to find the least number of calendars they can sell and still reach their goal.

Lesson 4-4

Solving Multi-Step Inequalities

<table>
<tr><td>

Lesson Objectives

▼ Solve multi-step inequalities with variables on one side

▼ Solve multi-step inequalities with variables on both sides

</td><td>

NAEP 2005 Strand: Algebra

Topics: Equations and Inequalities

Local Standards: _____

</td></tr>
</table>

Example

1 Using More Than One Step Solve $5 + 4b < 21$.

$5 + 4b - \boxed{} < 21 - \boxed{}$ Subtract $\boxed{}$ from each side.

$4b < \boxed{}$ Simplify.

$\dfrac{4b}{\boxed{}} < \dfrac{16}{\boxed{}}$ Divide each side by $\boxed{}$.

$b < \boxed{}$ Simplify.

Check $5 + 4b = 21$ Check the computation.

$5 + 4\left(\boxed{}\right) \overset{?}{=} 21$ Substitute $\boxed{}$ for b.

$21 = 21$ ✓

$5 + 4b < 21$ Check the direction of the inequality.

$5 + 4\left(\boxed{}\right) < 21$ Substitute 3 for b.

$17 < 21$ $\boxed{}$

Quick Check

Solve each inequality. Check your solutions.

1. a. $-3x - 4 \leq 14$

b. $5 < 7 - 2t$

c. $-8 < 5n - 23$

Daily Notetaking Guide

Name_____ Class_____ Date _____

❷ Using the Distributive Property Solve $3x + 4(6 - x) < 2$.

$3x + $ ☐ $- $ ☐ < 2 Use the Distributive Property.

☐ $+ 24 < 2$ Combine like terms.

$-x + 24 - $ ☐ $< 2 - $ ☐   Subtract ☐ from each side.

$-x < $ ☐   Simplify.

$\dfrac{-x}{☐} > \dfrac{-22}{☐}$ Divide each side by ☐. Reverse the inequality symbol.

x ☐ ☐   Simplify.

❸ Multi-Step Inequalities Solve $5(-3 + d) \le 3(3d - 2)$.

☐ $+ $ ☐ $d \le $ ☐ $d - $ ☐   Use the Distributive Property.

$-15 + 5d - $ ☐ $\le 9d - 6 - $ ☐   Subtract ☐ from each side.

$-15 - $ ☐ ≤ -6 Combine like terms.

$-15 - 4d + $ ☐ $\le -6 + $ ☐   Add ☐ to each side.

$-4d \le $ ☐   Simplify.

$\dfrac{-4d}{☐} \ge \dfrac{9}{☐}$ Divide each side by ☐. Reverse the inequality symbol.

d ☐ ☐   Simplify.

Quick Check

2. a. $4p + 2(p + 7) < 8$

b. $15 \le 5 - 2(4m + 7)$

3. Solve each inequality. Check your solutions.

a. $3b + 12 > 27 - 2b$

b. $-6(x - 4) \ge 7(2x - 3)$

Name_____ Class_____ Date_____

Lesson 4-5   Compound Equalities

Lesson Objectives	NAEP 2005 Strand: Algebra
▼ Solve and graph inequalities containing *and*	**Topics:** Variables, Expressions, and Operations; Equations and Inequalities
❷ Solve and graph inequalities containing *or*	**Local Standards:** _____

Vocabulary

A compound inequality is _____

Examples

❶ **Writing a Compound Inequality** Write two compound inequalities that represent each situation. Graph the solutions.

a. all real numbers that are at least −1 and at most 3

$b \geq -1$ and $b \leq \boxed{}$

$-1 \leq b \leq 3$

b. all real numbers that are less than 31 but greater than 25

$31 \boxed{} n$ and $n \boxed{} 25$

$31 \boxed{} n \boxed{} 25$

❷ **Solving a Compound Inequality Containing And** Solve $5 > 5 - f > 2$. Graph the solutions.

Write the compound inequality as two inequalities joined by $\boxed{}$.

$$5 > 5 - f \qquad\qquad 5 - f > 2$$
$$5 - 5 > 5 - f - 5 \qquad 5 - f - 5 > 2 - 5$$
$$\boxed{} > -f \qquad\qquad -f > \boxed{}$$
$$\frac{0}{-1} \boxed{} \frac{-f}{-1} \qquad\qquad \frac{-f}{-1} \boxed{} \frac{-3}{-1}$$
$$0 < \boxed{} \qquad\qquad f < \boxed{}$$

$\boxed{} < f < \boxed{}$

❸ **Writing Compound Inequalities** Write an inequality that represents the situation. Graph the solutions.

all real numbers that are less than 0 or greater than 3

$n < \boxed{}$ or $n > \boxed{}$

Name_____ Class_____ Date _____

❹ Solving a Compound Inequality Containing *Or* Solve the compound inequality $3x + 2 < -7$ or $-4x + 5 < 1$. Graph the solutions.

$$3x + 2 < -7 \qquad \text{or} \qquad -4x + 5 < 1$$

$$3x + 2 - \boxed{} < -7 - \boxed{} \qquad\qquad -4x + 5 - \boxed{} < 1 - \boxed{}$$

$$3x < \boxed{} \qquad\qquad\qquad -4x < \boxed{}$$

$$\frac{3x}{\boxed{}} < \frac{-9}{\boxed{}} \qquad\qquad\qquad \frac{-4x}{\boxed{}} \boxed{} \frac{-4}{\boxed{}}$$

$$x < \boxed{} \qquad \text{or} \qquad x > \boxed{}$$

-5 -4 -3 -2 0 1 2 3 4 5

Quick Check

1. Write a compound inequality that represents each situation. Graph the solutions.

a. all real numbers greater than –2 but less than 9

b. The books were priced between \$3.50 and \$6.00, inclusive.

2. Solve each inequality. Graph your solutions.

a. $-6 \le 3x < 15$

b. $-3 < 2x - 1 < 7$

3. Write an inequality that represents all real numbers that are at most -5 or at least 3. Graph the solutions.

4. Solve the compound inequality $-2x + 7 > 3$ or $3x - 4 \ge 5$. Graph the solutions.

Lesson 4-6

Absolute Value Equations and Inequalities

Lesson Objectives	NAEP 2005 Strand: Number Properties and Operations; Algebra
▼ Solve equations that involve absolute value ▼ Solve inequalities that involve absolute value	**Topics:** Number Sense; Equations and Inequalities **Local Standards:** _____

Key Concepts

Solving Absolute Value Equations

To solve an equation in the form $|A| = b$, where A represents a variable expression and $b > 0$, solve _____

Solving Absolute Value Inequalities

To solve an inequality in the form $|A| < b$, where A is a variable expression and $b > 0$, solve _____

To solve an inequality in the form $|A| > b$, where A is a variable expression and $b > 0$, solve _____

Similar rules are true for $|A| \leq b$ and $|A| \geq b$.

Examples

1 Solving an Absolute Value Equation Solve and check $|a| - 3 = 5$.

$|a| - 3 + \boxed{} = 5 + \boxed{}$ Add $\boxed{}$ to each side.

$|a| = \boxed{}$ Simplify.

$a = \boxed{}$ or $a = -\boxed{}$ Definition of absolute value.

Check $|a| - 3 = 5$

$\boxed{} - 3 \stackrel{?}{=} 5$ ← Substitute $\boxed{}$ and $\boxed{}$ for a. → $\boxed{} - 3 \stackrel{?}{=} 5$

$\boxed{} - 3 = 5$ ✓ $\boxed{} - 3 = 5$ ✓

❷ Solving an Absolute Value Equation Solve $|3c - 6| = 9$.

$$3c - 6 = 9 \qquad \leftarrow \textbf{Write two equations.} \rightarrow \qquad 3c - 6 = -9$$

$$3c - 6 + \boxed{} = 9 + \boxed{} \quad \leftarrow \textbf{Add } \boxed{} \textbf{ to each side.} \rightarrow \quad 3c - 6 + \boxed{} = -9 + \boxed{}$$

$$3c = \boxed{} \qquad\qquad\qquad\qquad\qquad\qquad\qquad 3c = \boxed{}$$

$$\frac{3c}{\boxed{}} = \frac{\boxed{}}{\boxed{}} \quad \leftarrow \textbf{Divide each side by } \boxed{}. \rightarrow \quad \frac{3c}{\boxed{}} = \frac{\boxed{}}{\boxed{}}$$

$$c = \boxed{} \qquad\qquad\qquad\qquad\qquad\qquad\qquad c = \boxed{}$$

The value of c is $\boxed{}$ or $\boxed{}$.

❸ Solving an Absolute Value Inequality Solve $|y - 5| \leq 2$. Graph the solutions.

$$y - 5 \geq -2 \qquad \text{and} \quad y - 5 \leq 2 \qquad \textbf{Write a compound inequality.}$$

$$y - 5 + \boxed{} \geq -2 + \boxed{} \quad\Big|\quad y - 5 + \boxed{} \leq 2 + \boxed{} \qquad \textbf{Add } \boxed{} \textbf{ to each side.}$$

$$y \geq \boxed{} \qquad \text{and} \quad y \leq \boxed{} \qquad \textbf{Simplify.}$$

$$\boxed{} \leq y \leq \boxed{}$$

$$\begin{array}{ccccccccccccc} \leftarrow\!\!\!\!&\!\!\!\!|\!\!\!\!&\!\!\!\!|\!\!\!\!&\!\!\!\!|\!\!\!\!&\!\!\!\!|\!\!\!\!&\!\!\!\!|\!\!\!\!&\!\!\!\!|\!\!\!\!&\!\!\!\!|\!\!\!\!&\!\!\!\!|\!\!\!\!&\!\!\!\!|\!\!\!\!&\!\!\!\!|\!\!\!\!&\!\!\!\!|\!\!\!\!&\!\!\!\!\rightarrow \\ &-1&0&1&2&3&4&5&6&7&8&9&10 \end{array}$$

❹ Manufacturing The ideal diameter of a piston for one type of car is 88.000 mm. The actual diameter can vary from the ideal diameter by at most 0.007 mm. Find the range of acceptable diameters for the piston.

Relate $\boxed{\begin{array}{c}\text{greatest difference between}\\ \text{actual and ideal}\end{array}}$ $\boxed{\text{is at most}}$ $\boxed{0.007}$ mm.

Define Let $\boxed{d}$ = actual diameter in millimeters of the piston.

Write $\Big|\boxed{} - \boxed{}\Big| \qquad \boxed{} \qquad \boxed{}$

$$|d - 88.000| \leq 0.007$$

$$-0.007 \leq \qquad d - 88.000 \qquad \leq 0.007 \quad \textbf{Write a compound inequality.}$$

$$-0.007 + \boxed{} \leq d - 88.000 + \boxed{} \leq 0.007 + \boxed{} \quad \textbf{Add } \boxed{}.$$

$$\boxed{} \leq \qquad d \qquad \leq \boxed{} \qquad \textbf{Simplify.}$$

The actual diameter must be between 87.993 mm and 88.007 mm, inclusive.

Quick Check

1. Solve each equation. Check your solutions.

    a. $|t| - 2 = -1$ **b.** $3|n| = 15$ **c.** $4 = 3|w| - 2$

    d. Is there a solution of $2|n| = -15$? Explain.

2. Solve each equation. Check your solutions.

    a. $|c - 2| = 6$ **b.** $-5.5 = |t + 2|$ **c.** $|7d| = 14$

3. a. Solve and graph $|w + 2| > 5$.

    b. What are the solutions of $|w + 2| > -5$?

4. The ideal weight of one type of model airplane engine is 33.86 ounces. The actual weight may vary from the ideal by at most 0.05 ounce. Find the range of acceptable weights for this engine.

Lesson 5-1

Lesson Objective	NAEP 2005 Strand: Algebra
▼ Interpret, sketch, and analyze graphs from situations	Topic: Algebraic Representations
	Local Standards: _____

Examples

❶ Interpreting Graphs This graph shows someone taking a walk in the neighborhood. Describe what it shows by labeling each part.

Walk in Neighborhood

❷ Sketching a Graph A pelican flies above the water searching for fish. Sketch a graph of its altitude from takeoff from shore to diving to the water to catch a fish. Label each section.

Pelican Searching for Fish

❸ Relating Graphs to Situations Suppose you pour water into the container at a steady rate. Which graph shows the change in the height of the liquid in the container over time? Explain.

I   II   III

Quick Check

1. The graph shows a trip from home to school and back. The trip involves walking and getting a ride from a neighbor. Label each section of the graph.

Daily Commute

2. Sketch a graph of the distance from a child's feet to the ground as the child jumps rope. Label each section.

3. The graph at the right shows the time and distance of a moving object. Which of the following situations could be described by the graph?

   A. A car travels at a steady speed.
   B. A cyclist slows down as she rides up a hill and speeds up as she peddles over the top.
   C. A train slows down as it arrives at the station.
   D. A plane accelerates steadily down the runway until it takes off.

Lesson 5-2

Relations and Functions

Lesson Objectives	NAEP 2005 Strand: Algebra
▼ Identify relations and functions ▼ Evaluate functions	**Topic:** Patterns, Relations, and Functions **Local Standards:** _____

Vocabulary

A function is _____

_____

A relation is _____

The domain of a relation is _____

The range of a relation is _____

The vertical-line test says that, on the graph of a relation, _____

_____

_____

A function rule is _____

Function notation is _____

_____

Example

❶ **Using a Mapping Diagram** Determine whether each relation is a function.

$\{(4, 3), (2, -1), (-3, -3), (2, 4)\}$

The domain value 2 corresponds
to two range values, ☐ and ☐ .
The relation ☐ a function.

Quick Check

1. Use a mapping diagram to determine whether each relation is a function.

   a. $\{(3, -2), (8, 1), (9, 2), (3, 3), (-4, 0)\}$ **b.** $\{(6.5, 0), (7, -1), (6, 2), (2, 6), (5, -1)\}$

Examples

❷ **Using the Vertical-Line Test** Determine whether the relation
$\{(0, -2), (1, -2), (-3, 1), (-2, 0), (-1, -1), (3, 2), (2, -3)\}$ is a function.

Graph the ordered pairs on a coordinate plane

[box] vertical line passes through more than one point.

The relation [box] a function.

❸ **Making a Table From a Function Rule**

Make a table for $f(x) = -5x + 25$. Use $-2, 0, 2$, and 4 as domain values.

x	−5x + 25	f(x)
−2	−5([box]) + 25	[box]
0	−5([box]) + 25	[box]
2	−5([box]) + 25	[box]
4	−5([box]) + 25	[box]

❹ **Finding the Range** Evaluate the function rule $f(g) = -2g + 4$ to find the range for the domain $\{-1, 3, 5\}$.

$f(g) = -2g + 4$ $f(g) = -2g + 4$ $f(g) = -2g + 4$

$f(\boxed{}) = -2(\boxed{}) + 4$ $f(\boxed{}) = -2(\boxed{}) + 4$ $f(\boxed{}) = -2(\boxed{}) + 4$

$f(\boxed{}) = \boxed{} + 4$ $f(\boxed{}) = \boxed{} + 4$ $f(\boxed{}) = \boxed{} + 4$

$f(\boxed{}) = \boxed{}$ $f(\boxed{}) = \boxed{}$ $f(\boxed{}) = \boxed{}$

The range is $\left\{\boxed{}\right\}$.

Quick Check

2. Use the vertical-line test to determine whether the relation
$\{(0,2),(1,-1),(-1,4),(0,-3),(2,1)\}$ is a function.

3. Make a table for $f(x) = 8 - 3x$. Use $1, 2, 3$, and 4 as domain values.

4. Find the range of each function for the domain $\{-2, 0, 5\}$.

a. $f(x) = x - 6$

b. $y = -4x$

c. $g(t) = t^2 + 1$

Lesson 5-3

Function Rules, Tables, and Graphs

Lesson Objective	NAEP 2005 Strand: Algebra
▼ Model functions using rules, tables, and graphs	**Topic:** Algebraic Representations
	Local Standards: _____

Vocabulary

An independent variable is _____

_____

A dependent variable is _____

_____

Example

❶ **Three Views of a Function** At the local video store you can rent a video game for $3. It costs you $5 a month to operate your video game player. The total monthly cost $C(v)$ depends on the number of video games v you rent.

Use the function rule $C(v) = 5 + 3v$ to make a table of values and a graph.

v	$C(v) = 5 + 3v$	$(v, C(v))$
0	$C(\boxed{}) = 5 + 3(\boxed{}) = \boxed{}$	$(\boxed{}, \boxed{})$
1	$C(\boxed{}) = 5 + 3(\boxed{}) = \boxed{}$	$(\boxed{}, \boxed{})$
2	$C(\boxed{}) = 5 + 3(\boxed{}) = \boxed{}$	$(\boxed{}, \boxed{})$

Number of video games

Quick Check

1. Model the rule $f(x) = 3x + 4$ with a table of values and a graph.

x	$f(x)$

Example

2 **Graphing Functions**

a. Make a table of values and graph the function $y = |x| + 2$.

x	$y = |x| + 2$	(x, y)
−3	y = ☐ + 2 = ☐	(☐),(☐)
−1	y = ☐ + 2 = ☐	(☐),(☐)
0	y = ☐ + 2 = ☐	(☐),(☐)
1	y = ☐ + 2 = ☐	(☐),(☐)
3	y = ☐ + 2 = ☐	(☐),(☐)

b. Make a table of values and graph the function $f(x) = x^2 + 2$.

x	$f(x) = x^2 + 2$	(x, f(x))
−2	f(☐) = ☐ + 2 = ☐	(☐),(☐)
−1	f(☐) = ☐ + 2 = ☐	(☐),(☐)
0	f(☐) = ☐ + 2 = ☐	(☐),(☐)
1	f(☐) = ☐ + 2 = ☐	(☐),(☐)
2	f(☐) = ☐ + 2 = ☐	(☐),(☐)

Quick Check

2. Make a table of values and graph each function.

a. $f(x) = |x| - 1$ **b.** $f(x) = x^2 - 1$

x	f(x)

x	f(x)

Lesson 5-4

Lesson Objective	**NAEP 2005 Strand:** Algebra
▼ Write a function rule given a table or a real-world situation	**Topics:** Patterns, Relations, and Functions; Algebraic Representations; Variables, Expressions, and Operations
	Local Standards: _____

Example

❶ Writing a Rule from a Table Write a function rule for the table.

x	y
1	2
2	5
3	10
4	17

Ask yourself, "What can I do to 1 to get 2, 2 to get 5, . . . ?" You multiply each *x*-value times [   ] and add [ ] to get the *y*-value.

Relate [y] equals [*x* times itself] plus [1]

Write [ ]   =   [   ]   +   [ ]

A rule for the function is [   ].

Quick Check

1. Write a function rule for each table.

a.

x	f(x)
1	−1
2	0
3	1
4	2

b.

x	y
1	2
2	4
3	6
4	8

c.

x	y
1	3
2	4
3	5
4	6

Example

❷ **Writing a Function Rule** The journalism class makes $25 per ad sold in the yearbook. If the class sells *n* ads, how much money will it earn?

   a. Write a function rule to describe this relationship.

   Relate $\boxed{\text{money earned}}$ is $\boxed{25}$ times $\boxed{\text{number of ads sold}}$

   Define   Let $\boxed{n}$ = number of ads sold.

   Let $\boxed{P(n)}$ = money earned.

   Write $\boxed{}$ = $\boxed{}$ · $\boxed{}$

   The function rule $\boxed{}$ = $\boxed{}$ describes the relationship between the number of ads sold and the money earned.

   b. The class sold 6 ads. How much money did the class make?

   $P(n)$ =   25 · $\boxed{}$

   $P(\boxed{})$ =   25 · $\boxed{}$ **Substitute 6 for *n*.**

   $P(\boxed{})$ = $\boxed{}$ **Simplify.**

   The class made $\$\boxed{}$.

Quick Check

   2. a. A carpenter buys finishing nails by the pound. Each pound of nails costs $1.19. Write a function rule to describe this relationship.

   b. How much does 12 lb of finishing nails cost?

   c. Suppose you buy a word-processing software package for $199. You charge $15 per hour for word processing. Write a rule to describe your profit as a function of the number of hours you work.

Lesson 5-5   Direct Variation

Lesson Objectives	NAEP 2005 Strand: Algebra
▼ Write an equation of a direct variation ▼ Use ratios and proportions with direct variations	**Topics:** Patterns, Relations, and Functions; Algebraic Representations **Local Standards:** _____

Key Concepts

Direct Variation

A function in the form $y = kx$, where $k \neq 0$, is a [_____].

The constant of variation k is the coefficient of x. The variables y and x

are said to vary [_____] with each other.

Examples

❶ **Is an Equation a Direct Variation?** Is each equation a direct variation?
If it is, find the constant of variation.

a. $2x - 3y = 1$

$-3y = 1 - \boxed{}$ **Subtract** $\boxed{}$ **from each side.**

$y = -\boxed{} + \boxed{} x$ **Divide each side by** $\boxed{}$.

The equation $\boxed{}$ have the form $y = kx$. It $\boxed{}$ a direct variation.

b. $2x - 3y = 0$

$-3y = \boxed{}$ **Subtract** $\boxed{}$ **from each side.**

$y = \boxed{} x$ **Divide each side by** $\boxed{}$.

The equation $\boxed{}$ the form $y = kx$, so the equation $\boxed{}$ a direct

variation. The constant of variation is $\boxed{}$.

❷ **Writing an Equation Given a Point** Write an equation for the direct variation
that includes the point $(-3, 2)$.

$y = kx$ **Use the general form of a direct variation.**

$\boxed{} = k\left(\boxed{}\right)$ **Substitute** $\boxed{}$ **for x and** $\boxed{}$ **for y.**

$-\boxed{} = k$ **Divide each side by** $\boxed{}$ **to solve for k.**

$y = \boxed{} x$ **Write an equation. Substitute** $\boxed{}$ **for k in $y = kx$.**

The equation of the direct variation is $\boxed{}$.

❸ Weight and Mass The weight an object exerts on a scale varies directly with the mass of the object. If a bowling ball has a mass of 6 kg, the scale reads 59. Write an equation for the relationship between weight and mass.

Relate The weight varies directly with the mass. When $x = 6$, $y = 59$.

Define Let $\boxed{x}$ = the mass of an object.

Let $\boxed{y}$ = the weight of an object.

Write

$\boxed{} = k \boxed{}$ **Use the general form of a direct variation.**

$\boxed{} = k\left(\boxed{}\right)$ **Solve for *k*. Substitute** $\boxed{}$ **for *x* and** $\boxed{}$ **for *y*.**

$\dfrac{\boxed{}}{\boxed{}} = k$ **Divide each side by** $\boxed{}$ **to solve for *k*.**

$y = \dfrac{\boxed{}}{\boxed{}} x$ **Write an equation. Substitute** $\dfrac{\boxed{}}{\boxed{}}$ **for *k* in** $y = kx$**.**

The equation $\boxed{}$ relates the weight of an object to its mass.

Quick Check

1. Is each equation a direct variation? If it is, find the constant of variation.

   a. $7y = 2x$ **b.** $3y + 4x = 8$ **c.** $y - 7.5x = 0$

2. Write the equation of the direct variation that includes the point $(-3, -6)$.

3. A recipe for a dozen corn muffins calls for 1 cup of flour. The number of muffins varies directly with the amount of flour used. Write a direct variation for the relationship between the number of cups of flour and the number of muffins.

Examples

❹ Direct Variations and Tables For the data in the table at the right, tell whether y varies directly with x. If it does, write an equation for the direct variation.

The ratio $\frac{y}{x}$ is [_____] for each pair of data, so y [_____] vary directly with x.

x	y	$\frac{y}{x}$
-1	2	$\frac{2}{-1} =$ [____]
1	2	$\frac{\square}{\square} =$ [____]
2	-4	$\frac{\square}{\square} =$ [____]

❺ Physics Suppose a windlass requires 0.75 lb of force to lift an object that weighs 48 lb. How much force would you need to lift 210 lb?

Relate   The force of [_____] lb lifts [____] lb.

The force of [__] lb lifts [_____] lb.

Define   Let $\boxed{n}$ = the force you need to lift 210 lb.

Write $\dfrac{\boxed{\text{force}_1}}{\boxed{\text{weight}_1}} = \dfrac{\boxed{\text{force}_2}}{\boxed{\text{weight}_2}}$ Use a proportion.

$\dfrac{\square}{\square} = \dfrac{n}{\square}$ Substitute [_____] for force_1, [_____] for weight_1, and [_____] for weight_2.

$\boxed{}\left(\boxed{}\right) = \boxed{} n$ Use cross products.

$n \approx \boxed{}$ Solve for n.

You need about [____] lb of force to lift 210 lb.

Quick Check

4. For the equation in each table, tell whether y varies directly with x. If it does, write an equation for the direct variation.

a.

x	y
-2	3.2
1	2.4
4	1.6

b.

x	y
4	6
8	12
10	15

5. Recall Example 5. Suppose a second windlass requires 0.5 lb of force to lift an object that weighs 32 lb. How much force would you need to lift 160 lb?

Lesson 5-6   **Inverse Variation**

Lesson Objectives	**NAEP 2005 Strand:** Algebra
▼ Solve inverse variations	**Topic:** Patterns, Relations, and Functions
▼ Compare direct and inverse variation	**Local Standards:** _____

Vocabulary and Key Concepts

Direct and Inverse Variation

y varies [   ] with x.

y is [   ] proportional to x.

The [   ] $\frac{y}{x}$ is constant.

y varies [   ] with x.

y is [   ] proportional to x.

The [   ] xy is constant.

An equation in the form $xy = k$ or $y = \frac{k}{x}$, where $k \neq 0$, is an [   ].

The [   ] is k.

Examples

❶ **Finding the Missing Coordinate** The points $(5, 6)$ and $(3, y)$ are two points on the graph of an inverse variation. Find the missing value.

$x_1 \cdot y_1 = x_2 \cdot y_2$ Use the equation $x_1 \cdot y_1 = x_2 \cdot y_2$ since you know coordinates but not the constant of variation.

[   ]([   ]) = [   ]y_2 Substitute [   ] for x_1, [   ] for y_1, and [   ] for x_2.

[   ] = [   ]y_2 Simplify.

[   ] = y_2 Solve for y_2.

The missing value is [   ]. The point $(3, [   ])$ is on the graph of the

inverse variation that includes the point $(5, 6)$.

② Applying Inverse Variation to Physics Jeff weighs 130 pounds and is 5 ft from the lever's fulcrum. If Tracy weighs 93 pounds, how far from the fulcrum should she sit in order to balance the lever?

Relate A weight of [ ] lb is 5 ft from the fulcrum.

A weight of [ ] lb is [ ] ft from the fulcrum.
Weight and distance vary inversely.

Define Let $weight_1 = $ [ ] lb

Let $weight_2 = 93$ lb

Let $distance_1 = $ [ ] ft

Let $distance_2 = x$ ft

Write $weight_1 \cdot distance_1 = weight_2 \cdot distance_2$

[ ] $\cdot$ [ ] $=$ [ ] $\cdot \; x$ **Substitute.**

[ ] $=$ [ ]x **Simplify.**

$\dfrac{[\quad\quad]}{[\quad]} = x$ **Solve for x.**

[ ] $\approx x$ **Simplify.**

Tracy should sit about [ ] ft from the fulcrum to balance the lever.

③ Determining Direct or Inverse Variation Decide whether each data set represents a direct variation or an inverse variation. Then write an equation to model the data.

a.

x	y
3	10
5	6
10	3

The values of y seem to vary [ ] with the values of x. Check each product xy.

xy: $3(10) = 30$ $5(6) = 30$ $10(3) = 30$

The product of xy is the same for all pairs of data.

So, this is an [ ] variation, and $k = $ [ ].

The equation is [ ].

b.

x	y
2	3
4	6
8	12

The values of y seem to vary [ ] with the values of x. Check each ratio $\frac{y}{x}$.

$\dfrac{y \rightarrow}{x \rightarrow}$ $\dfrac{3}{2} = 1.5$ $\dfrac{6}{4} = 1.5$ $\dfrac{12}{8} = 1.5$

The ratio $\frac{y}{x}$ is the same for all pairs of data. So, this is a

[ ] variation, and $k = $ [ ].

The equation is [ ].

Quick Check

1. Each pair of points is on the graph of an inverse variation. Find the missing values.

   a. $(3, y)$ and $(5, 9)$

   b. $(75, 0.2)$ and $(x, 3)$

2. a. **Physics** A 100-lb weight is placed 4 ft from a fulcrum. How far from the fulcrum should a 75-lb weight be placed to balance the lever if weight and distance vary inversely?

   b. An 80-lb weight is placed 9 ft from a fulcrum. What weight should you put 6 ft from the fulcrum to balance the lever?

3. Determine whether the data in each table represent a direct variation or an inverse variation. Write an equation to model the data in each table.

a.

x	y
3	12
6	6
9	4

b.

x	y
3	12
5	20
8	32

4. Explain whether each situation represents a direct variation or an inverse variation.

   a. You are a discount store. All sweaters are on sale for $15 each.

   b. You walk 5 miles every day. Your speed and time vary from day to day.

Lesson 5-7

Describing Number Patterns

Lesson Objectives	NAEP 2005 Strand: Algebra
▼ Use inductive reasoning in continuing number patterns ▼ Write rules for arithmetic sequences	**Topic:** Patterns, Relations, and Functions **Local Standards:** _____

Vocabulary and Key Concepts

Arithmetic Sequence

$$\underline{A(n)} = a + (n - 1)d$$

A sequence is _____

A term of a sequence is _____

An arithmetic sequence is _____

_____

A common difference is _____

Inductive reasoning is _____

A conjecture is _____

Examples

❶ **Extending Number Patterns** Use inductive reasoning to describe the pattern. Then find the next two numbers in the pattern.

a. 1,   3,   9, . . .

[ ]   [ ]

The pattern is "multiply the previous term by [ ]." To find the next two

numbers, you [_____]: $9 \times$ [ ] $= 27$ and

$27 \times$ [ ] $= 81$.

b. 1, 9, 25, 49, . . .

The pattern is "squares of consecutive odd integers." To find the next two

numbers, square the next two consecutive odd integers: $9^2 =$ [ ] and

[ ] $^2 =$ [ ] .

❷ Finding the Common Difference Find the common difference of each arithmetic sequence.

a. 5,   2,   −1,   −4, . . .

The common difference is $\boxed{}$.

b. 8,   11,   14,   17, . . .

The common difference is $\boxed{}$.

❸ Finding Terms of a Sequence Find the first, fifth, and tenth terms of the sequence that has the rule $A(n) = 15 + (n − 1)(5)$.

first term: $A\left(\boxed{}\right) = 15 + \left(\boxed{} − 1\right)(5) = 15 + \boxed{}(5) = \boxed{}$

fifth term: $A\left(\boxed{}\right) = 15 + \left(\boxed{} − 1\right)(5) = 15 + \boxed{}(5) = \boxed{}$

tenth term: $A\left(\boxed{}\right) = 15 + \left(\boxed{} − 1\right)(5) = 15 + \boxed{}(5) = \boxed{}$

Quick Check

1. Use inductive reasoning to describe each pattern. Then find the next two numbers in each pattern.

a. 3, 9, 27, 81, . . .

b. 9, 15, 21, 27, . . .

c. 2, −4, 8, −16, . . .

2. Find the common difference of each sequence.

a. 11, 23, 35, 47, . . .

b. 8, 3, −2, −7, . . .

3. Find the first, sixth, and twelfth terms of each sequence.

a. $A(n) = −5 + (n − 1)(3)$

b. $A(n) = 6.3 + (n − 1)(5)$

Lesson 6-1

Rate of Change and Slope

Lesson Objectives	NAEP 2005 Strand: Algebra
▼ Find rates of change from tables and graphs	**Topic:** Algebraic Representations
▼ Find slope	**Local Standards:** _____

Vocabulary and Key Concepts

Slope

Slope is _____

$$\text{slope} = \frac{\text{vertical change}}{\text{horizontal change}} = \frac{\text{rise}}{\text{run}} = \frac{y_2 - y_1}{x_2 - x_1}, \text{ where } x_2 - x_1 \neq 0$$

Slopes of Lines

A line with [＿＿] slope slants upward from left to right.

A line with [＿＿] slope slants downward from left to right.

A line with a slope of 0 is [＿＿].

A line with an undefined slope is [＿＿].

$$\text{Rate of change} = \frac{\text{change in the } [\quad] \text{ variable}}{\text{change in the } [\quad] \text{ variable}}$$

Name_____ Class_____ Date _____

Examples

① **Finding Rate of Change Using a Table** For the data in the table, is the rate of change the same for each pair of consecutive mileage amounts?

Find the rate of change for each pair of consecutive mileage amounts.

$$\frac{\text{rate of}}{\text{change}} = \frac{\text{change in cost}}{\text{change in number of miles}}$$ **Cost depends on the number of miles.**

Fee for Miles Driven	
Miles	**Fee**
100	$30
150	$42
200	$54
250	$66

$$\frac{42 - 30}{150 - 100} = \frac{\boxed{}}{\boxed{}} = \frac{\boxed{}}{\boxed{}}$$

$$\frac{\boxed{} - 42}{200 - \boxed{}} = \frac{\boxed{}}{\boxed{}} = \frac{\boxed{}}{\boxed{}}$$

$$\frac{66 - \boxed{}}{\boxed{} - 200} = \frac{\boxed{}}{\boxed{}} = \frac{\boxed{}}{\boxed{}}$$

The rate of change for each pair of consecutive mileage amounts is

$\boxed{}$ per $\boxed{}$ miles. The rate of change is the same for all the data.

② **Finding Slope Using a Graph** Find the slope of each line.

a.

b.

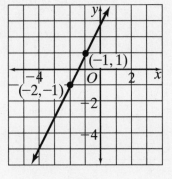

$$\text{slope} = \frac{\text{rise}}{\text{run}}$$

$$= \frac{\boxed{} - 1}{0 - \boxed{}}$$

$$= \frac{\boxed{}}{\boxed{}} = -\frac{\boxed{}}{\boxed{}}$$

The slope of the line is $\boxed{}$.

$$\text{slope} = \frac{\text{rise}}{\text{run}}$$

$$= \frac{-1 - \boxed{}}{\boxed{} - (-1)}$$

$$= \frac{\boxed{}}{\boxed{}} = \boxed{}$$

The slope of the line is $\boxed{}$.

❸ Finding Slope Using Points Find the slope of the line through $E(3, -2)$ and $F(-2, -1)$.

$$\text{slope} = \frac{\boxed{} - y_1}{\boxed{} - x_1}$$

$$= \frac{\boxed{} - (-2)}{-2 - \boxed{}} \qquad \textbf{Substitute} \left(\boxed{}, \boxed{}\right) \textbf{for } (x_2, y_2) \textbf{ and}$$
$$\left(\boxed{}, \boxed{}\right) \textbf{for } (x_1, y_1).$$

$$= \frac{1}{\boxed{}} = -\frac{\boxed{}}{\boxed{}} \qquad \textbf{Simplify.}$$

The slope of $\overleftrightarrow{EF}$ is $\boxed{}$.

Quick Check

1. Using the table in Example 1, find the rate of change using mileage amounts 100 and 200.

2. Find the slope of each line.

a.

b.

3. Find the slope of the line through each pair of points.

a. $C(2, 5)$ and $D(4, 7)$

b. $P(-1, 4)$ and $Q(3, -2)$

c. $M(a, b)$ and $N(c, d)$

Daily Notetaking Guide

Lesson 6-2

Lesson Objectives	**NAEP 2005 Strand:**
▼ Write linear equations in slope-intercept form	**Topics:** Patterns, Relations, and Functions; Equations and Inequalities
▼ Graph linear equations	**Local Standards:** _____

Vocabulary and Key Concepts

Slope-Intercept Form of a Linear Equation

The slope-intercept form of a linear equation is $y = mx + b$.

A linear equation is _____

_____

The y-intercept is _____

_____

Example

❶ **Identifying Slope and y-Intercept** What are the slope and y-intercept of $y = 2x - 3$?

$y = \quad mx \ + \quad b$ **Use slope-intercept form.**

$y = \boxed{}x + \boxed{}$

The slope is $\boxed{}$; the y-intercept is $\boxed{}$.

Quick Check

1. Find the slope and y-intercept of each equation.

   a. $y = -2x + 1$ **b.** $y = \frac{7}{6}x - \frac{3}{4}$ **c.** $y = -\frac{4}{5}x$

Name_____ Class_____ Date _____

Examples

❷ Writing an Equation From a Graph Write the equation for the line.

Step 1 Find the slope. Two points on the line are $(0, 1)$ and $(3, -1)$.

$$\text{slope} = \frac{\boxed{}}{\boxed{}}$$

$$= \boxed{}$$

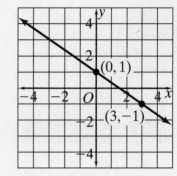

Step 2 Write an equation in slope-intercept form. The y-intercept is $\boxed{}$.

$y = mx + b$

$y = \boxed{}x + \boxed{}$ **Substitute** $\boxed{}$ **for m and** $\boxed{}$ **for b.**

❸ Graphing Equations Graph $y = \frac{1}{3}x - 2$.

Step 1 The y-intercept is $\boxed{}$. So plot a point at $\left(\boxed{}, \boxed{}\right)$.

Step 2 The slope is $\boxed{}$. Use the slope to plot a second point.

Step 3 Draw a line through the two points.

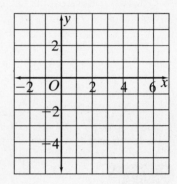

Quick Check

2. Write the equation of the line.

3. Graph $y = \frac{3}{2}x - 2$.

Example

❹ **Applying Slope-Intercept Form** The base pay for a used-car salesperson is $300 per week. The salesperson also earns 15% commission on sales made. The equation $t = 300 + 0.15s$ relates total earnings t to sales s. Graph the equation.

Step 1 Identify the slope and y-intercept.

$t = 300 + 0.15s$

$t = $ [ ] $+$ [ ]   **Rewrite the equation in slope-intercept form.**

     ↑   ↑

   slope y-intercept

Step 2 Plot two points. First plot a point at the y-intercept. Then use the slope to plot a second point.

The slope is [ ], which equals $\dfrac{[\ ]}{100}$. Plot a

second point [ ] units above and [ ] units to the right of the y-intercept.

Step 3 Draw a line through the points.

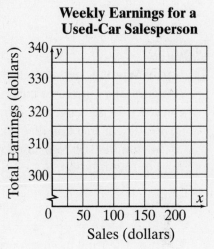

Weekly Earnings for a Used-Car Salesperson

Quick Check

4. Suppose the base pay of a delivery person is $150, and his commission on each sale is 30%. The equation relating his total earnings t to sales s is $t = 150 + 0.3s$. Graph the equation.

Lesson 6-3

Applying Linear Functions

Lesson Objectives	NAEP 2005 Strand: Algebra
▼ Interpret Linear Graphs	**Topic:** Algebraic Representations, Variables, Expressions and Operations, Equations and Inequalities
	Local Standards: _____

Example

1 **Social Science** In the aftermath of a hurricane, a tent city houses 1045 refugees. They are to be moved by bus to better accommodations. Each bus can carry 55 passengers. Assuming that every bus departs with a full load, write a linear function that relates the number of busloads already departed to the number still remaining at the tent city. Graph the function that models the situation.

Relate [_____] equals [____] minus [____] times [_____]

Define The total <u>number of refugees remaining</u> depends on <u>the number of busloads departed</u>. So <u>number of refugees remaining</u> is the dependent variable and <u>number of busloads departed</u> is the independent variable.

Let $x =$ [_____]   Let $y =$ [_____]

Write $y =$ [____] $-$ [____] $\cdot x$

The domain is the whole numbers 0 through 19 because the number of refugees remaining cannot [_____].

Quick Check

1. A sporting goods store sells cans of tennis balls. There are 3 tennis balls in each can. The coach of the tennis team is buying supplies. Write a linear function that relates the number of cans to the total number of tennis balls. Graph the function that models the situation.

$t =$ [_____] $n =$ [_____]

The function is [_____] .

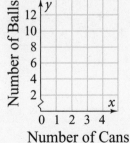

Name_____ Class_____ Date _____

Example

❷ Engineering One factor in the ability of soil to support the weight of man-made structures is the amount of water below the soil surface. The graph illustrates the changing water table in an urban area, due to water being pumped from drilled wells. The present time is designated as time $t = 0$.

a. What do the slope and the y-intercept mean for the given situation?

The slope is ⬚. This means that the water level is ⬚

at a rate of ⬚ inches per year.

The y-intercept is ⬚. This means that at present the level is

⬚ the minimum.

b. If the graph had the same slope but a y-intercept of 26, what could you conclude about the water table?

_____

_____

c. If the graph had a slope of -4.5 in./yr, what could you conclude about the water table?

_____

_____

Quick Check

2. a. Suppose you drew the following graph to represent how far you ride your bike at a steady rate. What is your rate?

b. If the graph had a slope of 10, what could you conclude about your bike ride?

Distance Traveled

Daily Notetaking Guide

Algebra 1 Lesson 6-3

Lesson 6-4

Standard Form

Lesson Objectives	NAEP 2005 Strand: Algebra
▼ Graph equations using intercepts	Topic: Patterns, Relations, and Functions
▼ Write equations in standard form	Local Standards: _____

Vocabulary and Key Concepts

Standard Form of a Linear Equation

The standard form of a linear equation is [   ] , where
A, B, and C are real numbers, and A and B are not both zero.

The x-intercept is _____

_____

Example

❶ **Finding x- and y-Intercepts** Find the x- and y-intercepts of $2x + 5y = 6$.

Step 1 To find the x-intercept,
substitute 0 for y and solve for x.

$2x + 5y = 6$

$2x + 5(0) = 6$

[   ]$x =$ [   ]

$x =$ [   ]

The x-intercept is [   ].

Step 2 To find the y-intercept,
substitute 0 for x and solve for y.

$2x + 5y = 6$

$2(0) + 5y = 6$

[   ]$y =$ [   ]

$y =$ [   ]

The y-intercept is [   ].

Quick Check

1. Find the x- and y-intercepts of $4x - 9y = -12$.

Name_____ Class_____ Date _____

Examples

❷ **Graphing Lines Using Intercepts** Graph $3x + 5y = 15$ using intercepts.

Step 1 Find the intercepts.

$3x + 5y = 15$

$3x + 5\left(\boxed{}\right) = 15$ **Substitute** $\boxed{}$ **for y.**

$\boxed{}x = \boxed{}$ **Solve for x.**

$x = \boxed{}$

$3x + 5y = 15$

$3\left(\boxed{}\right) + 5y = 15$ **Substitute** $\boxed{}$ **for x.**

$\boxed{}y = \boxed{}$ **Solve for y.**

$y = \boxed{}$

Step 2 Plot $\left(\boxed{}, 0\right)$ and $\left(0, \boxed{}\right)$.
Draw a line through the points.

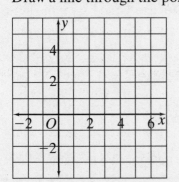

❸ **Transforming to Standard Form** Write $y = \frac{2}{3}x + 6$ in standard form using integers.

$y = \frac{2}{3}x + 6$

$\boxed{}y = \boxed{}\left(\frac{2}{3}x + 6\right)$ **Multiply each side by** $\boxed{}$.

$\boxed{}y = \boxed{}x + \boxed{}$ **Use the Distributive Property.**

$\boxed{} + 3y = \boxed{}$ **Subtract** $\boxed{}$ **from each side.**

The equation in standard form is $\boxed{}$.

Quick Check

2. Graph $5x + 2y = -10$ using the x- and y-intercepts.

3. Write $y = -\frac{2}{5}x + 1$ in standard form using integers.

Example

❹ Applying Standard Form Write an equation in standard form to find the number of hours you would need to work at each job to make a total of $130.

Job	Amount Paid per hour
Mowing Lawns	$12
Delivering Newspapers	$5

Define   Let x = the hours mowing lawns.

Let y = the hours delivering newspapers.

Relate | $12 per h mowing | plus | $5 per h delivering | equals | $130 |

Write   [ ]   +   [ ]   =   [ ]

The equation in standard form is [   ].

Quick Check

4. Data Analysis Write an equation in standard form to find the number of minutes someone who weighs 150 lb would need to bowl and walk to burn 250 calories.

Activity by a 150-lb Person	Calories Burned per Minute
Bicycling	10
Bowling	4
Hiking	7
Running 5.2 mi/h	11
Swimming Laps	12
Walking 3.5 mi/h	5

Name_____ Class_____ Date_____

Lesson 6-5   Point-Slope Form and Writing Linear Equations

Lesson Objectives	NAEP 2005 Strand:
▼ Graph and write linear equations using point-slope form	**Topics:** Patterns, Relations, and Functions; Variables, Expressions, and Operations
▼ Write a linear equation using data	**Local Standards:** _____

Key Concepts

Point-Slope Form of a Linear Equation

The point-slope form of the equation of a nonvertical line that passes through the point (x_1, y_1) with slope m is $\boxed{}$.

Linear Equations

Slope-Intercept Form	**Standard Form**	**Point-Slope Form**
$y = \boxed{} + \boxed{}$	$Ax + By = \boxed{}$	$\left(y - \boxed{}\right) = m\left(x - \boxed{}\right)$
m is the slope and b is the y-intercept.	A and B are not both 0.	(x_1, y_1) lies on the graph of the equation, and m is the slope.

Examples

$y = -\frac{2}{3}x + \frac{5}{3}$ $2x + 3y = 5$ $y - 1 = -\frac{2}{3}(x - 1)$

Examples

❶ Graphing Using Point-Slope Form Graph the equation $y - 2 = \frac{1}{3}(x - 1)$.

The equation shows that the line passes through $\left(\boxed{}, \boxed{}\right)$ with slope $\boxed{}$.

Start at $\left(\boxed{}, \boxed{}\right)$.

Using the slope, go up $\boxed{}$ unit and right $\boxed{}$ units to $\left(\boxed{}, \boxed{}\right)$.

Draw a line through the two points.

❷ Writing an Equation in Point-Slope Form Write the equation of the line with slope -2 that passes through the point $(3, -3)$.

$y - y_1 = m(x - x_1)$ Use point-slope form.

$y - \left(\boxed{}\right) = \boxed{}\left(x - \boxed{}\right)$ Substitute $\left(\boxed{}, \boxed{}\right)$ for (x_1, y_1) and $\boxed{}$ for m.

$y + \boxed{} = \boxed{}\left(x - \boxed{}\right)$ Simplify.

The equation is $\boxed{}$.

❸ Using Two Points to Write an Equation Write equations for the line in point-slope form and in slope-intercept form.

Step 1 Find the slope.

$$\frac{y_2 - y_1}{x_2 - x_1} = m$$

$$\frac{\boxed{} - \boxed{}}{\boxed{} - \boxed{}} = \boxed{}$$

The slope is $\boxed{}$.

Step 2 Use either point to write the equation in point-slope form.

Use $(-1, 4)$.

$$y - y_1 = m(x - x_1)$$

$$y - \boxed{} = \boxed{}\left(x - \left(\boxed{}\right)\right)$$

$$\boxed{}$$

Step 3 Rewrite the equation from Step 2 in slope-intercept form.

$$y - \boxed{} = \boxed{}(x + \boxed{})$$

$$y - \boxed{} = \boxed{}x - \boxed{}$$

$$\boxed{}$$

Quick Check

1. Graph the equation $y - 5 = -\frac{2}{3}(x + 2)$.

2. Write the equation of the line with slope $\frac{2}{5}$ that passes through the point $(10, -8)$.

Name_____ Class_____ Date _____

Example

❹ Writing an Equation Using a Table Is the relationship shown by the data linear? If so, model the data with an equation.

Step 1 Find the rate of change for consecutive ordered pairs.

$$\frac{\boxed{}}{-1} = \boxed{}$$

$$\frac{\boxed{}}{-3} = \boxed{}$$

$$\frac{\boxed{}}{-2} = \boxed{}$$

x	y
3	6
2	4
−1	−2
−3	−6

$-1\ (\qquad)\ \boxed{}$
$-3\ (\qquad)\ \boxed{}$
$-2\ (\qquad)\ \boxed{}$

The relationship $\boxed{}$ linear. The rate of change is $\boxed{}$.

Step 2 Use the slope and a point to write an equation.

$y - y_1 = m(x - x_1)$ **Use point-slope form.**

$y - \boxed{} = \boxed{}(x - \boxed{})$ **Substitute** $(\boxed{}, \boxed{})$ **for** (x_1, y_1) **and** $\boxed{}$ **for** m.

Quick Check

3. a. Write an equation for the line in Example 3 in point-slope form using point $(2, 3)$.

b. Write the equation you found in part (a) in slope-intercept form.

4. Is the relationship shown by the data in the table linear? If so, model the data with an equation.

Working Outdoors

Temperature	Calories Burned per Minute
68°F	3030
62°F	3130
56°F	3230
50°F	3330

Lesson 6-6

Parallel and Perpendicular Lines

Lesson Objectives	NAEP 2005 Strand: Geometry
▼ Determine whether lines are parallel	**Topics:** Algebraic Representations; Relationships Among Geometric Figures
▼ Determine whether lines are perpendicular	**Local Standards:** _____

Vocabulary and Key Concepts

Slopes of Parallel Lines

Nonvertical lines are parallel if _____

Any two vertical lines are parallel.

Example   The equations $y = \frac{2}{3}x + 1$ and $y = \frac{2}{3}x - 3$ have the same slope, $\frac{2}{3}$,

and different y-intercepts. The graphs of the two equations are parallel.

Slopes of Perpendicular Lines

Two lines are perpendicular if the product of their slopes is $\boxed{}$.
A vertical and a horizontal line are also perpendicular.

Example   The slope of $y = -\frac{1}{4}x - 1$ is $-\frac{1}{4}$. The slope of $y = 4x + 2$ is 4.

Since $-\frac{1}{4} \cdot 4 = -1$, the graphs of the two equations are perpendicular.

Parallel lines are _____

Perpendicular lines are _____

The product of a number and its negative reciprocal is _____

Examples

① **Writing Equations of Parallel Lines** Write an equation for the line that
contains $(-2, 3)$ and is parallel to $y = \frac{5}{2}x - 4$.

Step 1 Identify the slope of the given line. The slope of $y = \frac{5}{2}x - 4$ is $\boxed{}$.

Step 2 Write the equation of the line through $(-2, 3)$ using slope-intercept form.

$y - y_1 = m(x - x_1)$ **Use point-slope form.**

$y - \boxed{} = \boxed{}\left(x - \boxed{}\right)$ **Substitute** $\left(\boxed{}, \boxed{}\right)$ **for** (x_1, y_1) **and** $\boxed{}$ **for** m.

$y - \boxed{} = \boxed{}x - \boxed{}\left(\boxed{}\right)$ **Use the Distributive Property.**

$y - \boxed{} = \boxed{}x + \boxed{}$ **Simplify.**

$y = \boxed{}x + \boxed{}$ **Add** $\boxed{}$ **to each side and simplify.**

Daily Notetaking Guide

❷ Writing Equations for Perpendicular Lines The line in the graph represents the street in front of a house. The sidewalk from the front door is perpendicular to the street. Write an equation representing the sidewalk.

Step 1 Find the slope m of the street.

$$m = \frac{y_2 - y_1}{x_2 - x_1} = \frac{\boxed{} - \boxed{}}{\boxed{} - \boxed{}} = \frac{\boxed{}}{\boxed{}} = -\frac{\boxed{}}{\boxed{}}$$

Points (0, 2) and (3, 0) are on the street.

Step 2 Find the negative reciprocal of the slope.

The negative reciprocal of $-\frac{2}{3}$ is $\boxed{}$, so the slope of the

sidewalk is $\boxed{}$.

The y-intercept is $\boxed{}$.

The equation for the sidewalk is $\boxed{}$.

Quick Check

1. Write an equation for the line that contains $(2, -6)$ and is parallel to $y = 3x + 9$.

2. Write an equation of the line that contains $(1, 8)$ and is perpendicular to $y = \frac{3}{4}x + 1$.

3. Using the diagram in Example 2, write an equation in slope-intercept form for a new sidewalk perpendicular to the street from a front door at $(-1, -1)$.

Lesson 6-7

Scatter Plots and Equations of Lines

Lesson Objectives	NAEP 2005 Strand: Algebra; Data Analysis and Probability
▼ Write an equation for a trend line and use it to make predictions ▼ Write an equation for a line of best fit and use it to make predictions	**Topics:** Algebraic Representations; Characteristics of Data Sets **Local Standards:** _____

Vocabulary

The line of best fit is _____

_____

The correlation coefficient, r, tells you _____

_____

Examples

❶ **Trend Line** Make a scatter plot to represent the data. Draw a trend line and write an equation for the trend line. Use the equation to predict the time needed to travel 32 miles on a bicycle.

Speed on a Bicycle Trip

Miles	5	10	14	18	22
Time (min)	27	46	71	78	107

Step 1 Draw a scatter plot of the data.
Use a straightedge to draw a trend line.
Estimate two points on the line.
Two points are ($\boxed{}$, $\boxed{}$) and ($\boxed{}$, $\boxed{}$).

Step 2 Write an equation of the trend line.

$$m = \frac{y_2 - y_1}{x_2 - x_1} = \frac{\boxed{} - \boxed{}}{\boxed{} - \boxed{}} = \frac{\boxed{}}{\boxed{}} \approx \boxed{}$$

$y - y_1 = m(x - x_1)$ **Use point-slope form.**

$y - \boxed{} = \boxed{}\left(x - \boxed{}\right)$ **Substitute** $\boxed{}$ **for** m **and** $\left(\boxed{}, \boxed{}\right)$ **for** (x_1, y_1).

Step 3 Predict the time needed to travel 32 miles.

$y - \boxed{} = \boxed{}\left(\boxed{} - \boxed{}\right)$ **Substitute** $\boxed{}$ **for** x.

$y - \boxed{} = \boxed{}\left(\boxed{}\right)$ **Simplify within the parentheses.**

$y - \boxed{} = \boxed{}$ **Multiply.**

$y = \boxed{}$ **Add** $\boxed{}$ **to each side.**

The time needed to travel 32 miles is about $\boxed{}$ minutes.

Name_____ Class_____ Date _____

❷ Line of Best Fit Use a graphing calculator to find the equation of the line of best fit for the data at right. What is the correlation coefficient?

Use the EDIT feature of the STAT screen on your graphing calculator. Let 95 correspond to 1995. Enter the data for years and then enter the data for crimes.

LinReg

$y = ax + b$	
$a = -248.55$	**slope**
$b = 28945.07$	**y-intercept**
$r^2 = .9711922459$	
$r = -.9854908654$	**correlation coefficient**

**U.S. Crime Rate
(per 100,000 inhabitants)**

Year	No. of Crimes
1995	5275.9
1996	5086.6
1997	4930.0
1998	4619.3
1999	4266.8

Source: *Crime in the United States*

Use the CALC feature of the STAT screen. Find the equation for the line of best fit.

The equation for the line of best fit is ⎡_____⎤

for values a and b rounded to the nearest hundredth. The value of the correlation coefficient is ⎡_____⎤.

Quick Check

1. Graph the data below and draw a trend line. Find an equation for the trend line. Estimate the number of calories in a fast-food meal that has 14 g of fat.

Calories and Fat in Selected Fast-Food Meals

Fat (g)	6	7	10	19	20	27	36
Calories	276	260	220	388	430	550	633

2. Find the equation of the line of best fit. Let 91 correspond to 1991. What is the correlation coefficient?

Yearly Box Office Gross for Movies (billions)

1991 $4.8	1992 $4.9	1993 $5.2	1994 $5.4	1995 $5.5	1996 $6.0	1997 $6.4	1998 $7.0	1999 $7.4

Lesson 6-8

Graphing Absolute Value Equations

Lesson Objective	NAEP 2005 Strand: Algebra
▼ Translate the graph of an absolute value equation	**Topic:** Algebraic Representations
	Local Standards: _____

Vocabulary

The graph of an absolute value equation forms a _____

_____

A translation is _____

_____

Examples

❶ **Vertical Translations** Describe how the graphs of $y = |x|$ and $y = |x| + 1$ are the same and how they are different.

The graphs are the same shape. The y-intercept of $y = |x|$ is [ ]. The y-intercept of $y = |x| + 1$ is [ ].

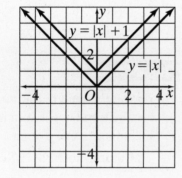

❷ **Graphing Vertical Translation** Graph $y = |x| - 3$ by translating $y = |x|$.

Start with a graph of $y = |x|$. Translate the graph down [ ] units.

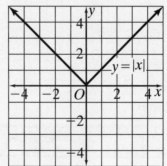

❸ **Writing an Absolute Value Equation** Write an equation for each translation of $y = |x|$.

a. 9 units down

The equation is [_____].

b. 13 units up

The equation is [_____].

❹ **Graphing a Horizontal Translation** Graph each equation by translating $y = |x|$.

a. $y = |x + 2.5|$

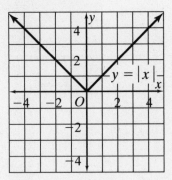

b. $y = |x - 2.5|$

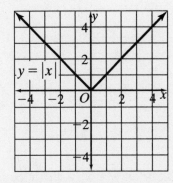

Start with a graph of $y = |x|$.

Translate the graph [   ] 2.5 units.

Start with a graph of $y = |x|$.

Translate the graph [   ] 2.5 units.

❺ **Writing an Absolute Value Equation** Write an equation for each translation of $y = |x|$.

a. 10 units left

The equation is [   ].

b. 7 units right

The equation is [   ].

Quick Check

1. Describe how each graph below is like $y = |x|$ and how it is different.

a.

[   ]

b.

[   ]

2. Graph each function by translating $y = |x|$.

    a. $y = |x| + 4$ **b.** $y = |x| - 5$

3. For each translation of $y = |x|$, write an equation.

    a. 2 units up   **b.** 5 units down

4. Graph each function by translating $y = |x|$.

    a. $y = |x - 4|$ **b.** $y = |x + 1|$

5. Write an equation for each translation of $y = |x|$.

    a. 5 units right   **b.** 7 units left

Lesson 7-1

Solving Systems by Graphing

Lesson Objectives	**NAEP 2005 Strand:** Algebra
▼ Solve systems by graphing	**Topics:** Equations and Inequalities
▼ Analyze special types of systems	**Local Standards:** _____

Vocabulary and Key Concepts

Numbers of Solutions of Systems of Linear Equations

different slopes

The lines ☐
so there is

☐ solution.

same slope
different *y*-intercepts

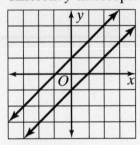

The lines ☐
so there are

☐ solutions.

same slope
same *y*-intercept

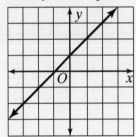

The lines are ☐
so there are

☐
solutions.

A system of linear equations is _____

_____

A solution of a system of linear equations is _____

_____

No solution means _____

_____

A system of equations has infinitely many solutions when _____

_____

Examples

❶ Solving a System of Equations Suppose you plan to start taking an aerobics class. Nonmembers pay $4 per class, while members pay $10 a month plus an additional $2 per class. What system of equations models the cost of the class to members and nonmembers?

Define Let $\boxed{c}$ = number of classes.

Let $\boxed{T(c)}$ = total cost of the classes.

Relate $\boxed{\text{cost}}$ is $\boxed{\begin{array}{c}\text{membership}\\\text{fee}\end{array}}$ plus $\boxed{\begin{array}{c}\text{cost of classes}\\\text{attended}\end{array}}$

Write member $\boxed{}$ = 10 + 2$\boxed{}$

nonmember $\boxed{}$ = 0 + 4$\boxed{}$

❷ Solve the system from the preceding Example. What does the solution mean in terms of the original situation?

$T(c) = 2c + 10$ The slope is $\boxed{}$. The intercept on the vertical axis is $\boxed{}$.

$T(c) = 4c$ The slope is $\boxed{}$. The intercept on the vertical axis is $\boxed{}$.

Graph the equations $T(c) = 2c + 10$ and $T(c) = 4c$.

The lines intersect at $\left(\boxed{}, \boxed{}\right)$. After $\boxed{}$ classes, both will cost $\boxed{}$.

❸ Systems With No Solution Solve by graphing. $y = 3x + 2$
$y = 3x - 2$

Graph both equations on the same coordinate plane.

$y = 3x + 2$ The slope is $\boxed{}$. The y-intercept is $\boxed{}$.

$y = 3x - 2$ The slope is $\boxed{}$. The y-intercept is $\boxed{}$.

The lines are $\boxed{}$. There is $\boxed{}$ solution.

❹ Systems With Infinitely Many Solutions Solve by graphing.
$3x + 4y = 12$

$y = -\frac{3}{4}x + 3$

Graph both equations on the same coordinate plane.

$3x + 4y = 12$ The y-intercept is $\boxed{}$. The x-intercept is $\boxed{}$.

$y = -\frac{3}{4}x + 3$ The slope is $\boxed{}$. The y-intercept is $\boxed{}$.

The graphs are the same line. The solutions are an infinite number of ordered pairs (x, y), such that $y = -\frac{3}{4}x + 3$.

Name_____ Class_____ Date _____

Quick Check

1. You are testing two fertilizers on bamboo plants C and D. Plant C is 5 cm tall and growing at a rate of 3 cm/day. Plant D is 11 cm tall and growing at a rate of 4 cm/day. Write a system of equations that models the height $H(d)$ of each plant as a function of days d.

2. Two friends are walking around a quarter-mile track. One person has completed six laps before the second one starts. The system below models the distance $d(t)$ in miles each walker covers as a function of time t in hours.

   $d(t) = 3t + 1.5$ $d(t) = 4t$

   a. Find the solution of the system by graphing.

Second Walker's Time (h)

   b. What does the solution mean in terms of the original situation?

3. Without graphing, how can you tell if a system has no solution? Give an example.

Lesson 7-2

Lesson Objective	**NAEP 2005 Strand:** Algebra
▼ Solve systems using substitution	**Topics:** Equations and Inequalities
	Local Standards: _____

Vocabulary

The substitution method is _____

_____

_____

Example

1 Using Substitution and the Distributive Property Solve using substitution. $-2x + y = -1$
$4x + 2y = 12$

Step 1 Solve the first equation for y because it has a coefficient of 1.

$-2x + y = -1$

$y = \boxed{}$ **Add** $\boxed{}$ **to each side.**

Step 2 Write an equation containing only one variable and solve.

$4x + 2y = 12$ **Start with the other equation.**

$4x + 2\left(\boxed{}\right) = 12$ **Substitute** $\boxed{}$ **for y in that equation.**

$4x + \boxed{} = 12$ **Use the Distributive Property.**

$\boxed{} = \boxed{}$ **Combine like terms and add** $\boxed{}$ **to each side.**

$x = \boxed{}$ **Divide each side by** $\boxed{}$.

Step 3 Solve for y in the other equation.

$-2\left(\boxed{}\right) + y = -1$ **Substitute** $\boxed{}$ **for x.**

$\boxed{} + y = -1$ **Simplify.**

$y = \boxed{}$ **Add** $\boxed{}$ **to each side.**

Since $x = \boxed{}$ and $y = \boxed{}$, the solution is $\left(\boxed{}\right)$.

Quick Check

1. Solve using substitution. Check your solution.

a. $y = 2x$
$7x - y = 15$

b. $6y + 8x = 28$
$3 = 2x - y$

Name_____ Class_____ Date _____

Example

❷ **Using Substitution** A class with 26 students is going to the zoo. Five chaperones will each drive a van or a car. Each van seats 7 persons, including the driver. Each car seats 5 persons, including the driver. How many vans and cars will be needed?

Let $\boxed{v}$ = number of vans and $\boxed{c}$ = number of cars.

drivers $\quad \boxed{v} + \boxed{c} = 5$

people $\ 7\boxed{v} + 5\boxed{c} = 31$

Solve using substitution.

Step 1 Write an equation containing only one variable.

$v + c = 5$ **Solve the first equation for c.**

$c = \boxed{} + 5$

Step 2 Write and solve an equation containing the variable v.

$7v + 5c = 31$

$7v + 5\left(\boxed{} + \boxed{}\right) = 31$ **Substitute $\boxed{}$ for c in the second equation.**

$7v - \boxed{} + \boxed{} = 31$ **Solve for v.**

$\boxed{} + \boxed{} = 31$

$\boxed{} = \boxed{}$

$v = \boxed{}$

Step 3 Solve for c in either equation.

$\boxed{} + c = 5$ **Substitute 3 for v in the first equation.**

$c = \boxed{}$

$\boxed{}$ vans and $\boxed{}$ cars are needed to transport 31 persons.

Quick Check

2. A rectangle is 4 times longer than it is wide. The perimeter of the rectangle is 30 cm. Find the dimensions of the rectangle.

Lesson 7-3

Solving Systems Using Elimination

Lesson Objectives	NAEP 2005 Strand: Algebra
▼ Solve systems by adding or subtracting	**Topics:** Equations and Inequalities
▼ Multiply first when solving systems	**Local Standards:** _____

Vocabulary

The elimination method is _____

_____

_____

Examples

❶ Adding Equations Solve by elimination. $2x + 3y = 11$

$-2x + 9y = 1$

Step 1 Eliminate x because the sum of the coefficients is 0.

$$2x + 3y = 11$$
$$-2x + 9y = 1$$

$\boxed{} + \boxed{} = \boxed{}$ **Addition Property of Equality**

$y = \boxed{}$ **Solve for y.**

Step 2 Solve for the eliminated variable x using either original equation.

$2x + 3y = 11$ **Choose the first equation.**

$2x + 3\left(\boxed{}\right) = 11$ **Substitute** $\boxed{}$ **for y.**

$2x + \boxed{} = 11$ **Solve for x.**

$2x = \boxed{}$

$x = \boxed{}$

Since $x = \boxed{}$ and $y = \boxed{}$, the solution is $\left(\boxed{}, \boxed{}\right)$.

Check See if $(4, 1)$ makes the equation *not* used in Step 2 true.

$-2\left(\boxed{}\right) + 9\left(\boxed{}\right) \stackrel{?}{=} 1$ **Substitute** $\boxed{}$ **for x and** $\boxed{}$ **for y into the second equation.**

$\boxed{} + \boxed{} \stackrel{?}{=} 1$

$\boxed{} = 1 ✔$

❷ Multiplying One Equation Suppose the school band is selling cans of popcorn for $5 per can and cans of mixed nuts for $8 per can. The band sells a total of 240 cans and receives a total of $1,614. Find the number of each type of can.

Define Let ⟨p⟩ = number of cans of popcorn sold.

Let ⟨n⟩ = number of cans of nuts sold.

Relate | total number of cans | | total amount of sales |

Write ☐ + ☐ = 240   5☐ + 8☐ = 1,614

Step 1 Eliminate one variable.

| **Start with the given system.** | **To prepare to eliminate *p*, multiply the first equation by ☐.** | **Subtract the equations to eliminate *p*.** |

$$p + n = 240 \quad \rightarrow \quad ☐(p + n = 240) \quad \rightarrow \quad 5p + 5n = 1{,}200$$
$$5p + 8n = 1{,}614 \quad \rightarrow \quad 5p + 8n = 1{,}614 \quad \rightarrow \quad 5p + 8n = 1{,}614$$

☐ − ☐ = ☐

Step 2 Solve for *n*.

☐ n = ☐

n = ☐

Step 3 Solve for the eliminated variable using either of the original equations.

$p + n = 240$ **Choose the first equation.**

$p +$ ☐ $= 240$ **Substitute** ☐ **for *n*.**

$p = 102$ **Solve for *p*.**

The band sold ☐ cans of popcorn and ☐ cans of mixed nuts.

Quick Check

1. Suppose a band at another school sells erasers for $2 per package and pencils for $5 per package. The band sells 220 packages in all and earns a total of $695. Find the number of each type of package sold.

Example

❸ **Multiplying Both Equations** Solve by elimination. $3x + 5y = 10$
$5x + 7y = 10$

Step 1 Eliminate one variable.

Start with the given system.		To prepare to eliminate x, multiply one equation by ☐ and the other equation by ☐.		Subtract the equations to eliminate x.

$3x + 5y = 10$ → ☐$(3x + 5y = 10)$ → $15x + 25y = 50$

$\underline{5x + 7y = 10}$ → ☐$(5x + 7y = 10)$ → $\underline{15x + 21y = 30}$

☐ + ☐ = ☐

Step 2 Solve for y.

☐y = ☐

y = ☐

Step 3 Solve for the eliminated variable x using either of the original equations.

$3x + 5y = 10$ **Use the first equation.**

$3x + 5($☐$) = 10$ **Substitute** ☐ **for** y.

$3x +$ ☐ $= 10$

$3x =$ ☐

$x =$ ☐

The solution is ☐.

Quick Check

2. Solve by elimination.

  a. $6x - 3y = 3$
        $-6x + 5y = 3$

  b. $15x + 3y = 9$
        $10x + 7y = -4$

Lesson 7-4

Applications of Linear Systems

Lesson Objective	**NAEP 2005 Strand:** Algebra
▼ Write systems of linear equations	**Topics:** Equations and Inequalities
	Local Standards: _____

Key Concepts

Methods for Solving Systems of Linear Equations

Graphing   Use graphing for solving systems that are easily graphed. If the point of intersection does not have integers for coordinates, find the exact solution by using one of the methods below or by using a graphing calculator.

Substitution   Use substitution when one variable has a coefficient of 1 or -1.

Elimination   Use elimination for solving any system.

Examples

❶ Writing Systems A chemist has one solution that is 50% acid. She has another solution that is 25% acid. How many liters of each type of acid solution should she combine to get 10 liters of a 40% acid solution?

Define Let $\boxed{a}$ = volume of the 50% solution.

Let $\boxed{b}$ = volume of the 25% solution.

Relate volume of solution   amount of acid

Write $\boxed{} + \boxed{} = 10$ $\boxed{}a + \boxed{}b = \boxed{}(10)$

Step 1 Choose one of the equations and solve for a variable.

$a + b = 10$ **Solve for a.**

$a = 10 - \boxed{}$ **Subtract** $\boxed{}$ **from each side.**

Step 2 Find b.

$\boxed{}a + \boxed{}b = \boxed{}(10)$

$0.5\left(\boxed{}\right) + 0.25b = 0.4(10)$ **Substitute** $\boxed{}$ **for a. Use parentheses.**

$5 - \boxed{} + 0.25b = 0.4(10)$ **Use the Distributive Property.**

$5 - \boxed{} = \boxed{}$ **Simplify.**

$-0.25b = \boxed{}$ **Subtract** $\boxed{}$ **from each side.**

$b = \boxed{}$ **Divide each side by** $\boxed{}$.

Step 3 Find a. Substitute $\boxed{}$ for b in either equation.

$a + \boxed{} = 10$ **Solve for a.**

$a = \boxed{}$ **Subtract** $\boxed{}$ **from each side.**

To make 10 L of 40% acid solution, you need $\boxed{}$ L of 50% solution and $\boxed{}$ L of 25% solution.

Name_____ Class_____ Date_____

❷ Finding a Break-Even Point Suppose you have a typing service. You buy a personal computer for $1,750 on which to do your typing. You charge $5.50 per page for typing. Expenses are $.50 per page for ink, paper, electricity, and other expenses. How many pages must you type to break even?

Define Let $\boxed{p}$ = the number of pages.

Let $\boxed{d}$ = the amount of dollars of expenses or income.

Relate

Expenses are per-page expenses plus computer purchase.	Income is price times pages typed.

Write $\boxed{} = 0.5\boxed{} + 1,750$ $\boxed{} = 5.5\boxed{}$

Choose a method to solve this system. Use substitution since it is easy to substitute for d with these equations.

$d = 0.5p + 1,750$ **Start with one equation.**

$\boxed{} = 0.5p + 1,750$ **Substitute** $\boxed{}$ **for** *d*.

$\boxed{} = 1,750$ **Solve for** *p*.

$p = \boxed{}$

To break even, you must type 350 pages.

Quick Check

1. Suppose a chemist combines a 25% acid solution and a 50% acid solution to make 40 L of 45% acid solution. How many liters of each solution did she use?

2. Suppose an antique car club publishes a newsletter. Expenses are $.35 for printing and mailing each copy, plus $770 total for research and writing. The price of the newsletter is $.55 per copy. How many copies of the newsletter must the club sell to break even?

Example

❸ Finding Speed Suppose it takes you 6.8 hours to fly about 2,800 miles from Miami, Florida, to Seattle, Washington. At the same time, a friend flies from Seattle to Miami. His plane travels with the same average airspeed, but his flight only takes 5.6 hours. Find the average airspeed of the planes. Find the average wind speed.

Define Let $\boxed{A}$ = the airspeed.   Let $\boxed{W}$ = the wind speed.

Relate with tail wind   with head wind

(rate)(time) = distance   (rate)(time) = distance

$\boxed{(A + W)}$ (time) = distance $\boxed{(A - W)}$ (time) = distance

Write $\boxed{}$ 5.6 = $\boxed{}$ $\boxed{}$ 6.8 = $\boxed{}$

Solve by elimination. First divide to get the variables on the left side of each equation with coefficients of 1 or −1.

$(A + W)5.6 = 2{,}800 \rightarrow A + W = \boxed{}$ **Divide each side by** $\boxed{}$.

$(A - W)6.8 = 2{,}800 \rightarrow A - W \approx \boxed{}$ **Divide each side by** $\boxed{}$.

Step 1 Eliminate W.

$$A \; + \; W \; = \; 500$$
$$A \; - \; W \; = \; 412$$

Add the equations to eliminate W.

$\boxed{} + \boxed{} = \boxed{}$

Step 2 Solve for A.

$A = \boxed{}$ **Divide each side by** $\boxed{}$.

Step 3 Solve for W using either of the original equations.

$A + W = 500$ **Use the first equation.**

$\boxed{} + W = 500$ **Substitute** $\boxed{}$ **for A.**

$W = \boxed{}$ **Solve for W.**

The average airspeed of the planes is $\boxed{}$ mi/h. The average wind speed is $\boxed{}$ mi/h.

Quick Check

3. A plane takes about 6 hours to fly you 2,400 miles from New York City to Seattle, Washington. At the same time, your friend flies from Seattle to New York City. His plane travels with the same average airspeed, but his flight takes 5 hours. Find the average airspeed of the planes. Find the average wind speed.

Name_____ Class_____ Date_____

Lesson 7-5

Linear Inequalities

Lesson Objectives	NAEP 2005 Strand: Algebra
▼1 Graph linear inequalities	**Topics:** Variables, Expressions, and Operations; Equations and Inequalities
▼2 Write and use linear inequalities when modeling real-world situations	**Local Standards:** _____

Vocabulary

A linear inequality is _____

_____

Each point in the region is a [_____] of the inequality.

The solutions of an inequality are _____

_____

Each point on a *dashed* boundary line is not a solution.

Each point on a *solid* boundary line is a solution.

Example

1 **Rewriting to Graph an Inequality** Graph $4x - 3y \geq 6$.
Solve $4x - 3y \geq 6$ for y.

$4x - 3y \geq 6$

$-3y \geq \boxed{} + 6$ **Subtract** $\boxed{}$ **from each side.**

$y \boxed{} \boxed{} x - 2$ **Divide each side by** $\boxed{}$**. Reverse the inequality symbol.**

Graph $y = \boxed{} x - \boxed{}$. The coordinates of the points on the

boundary line make the inequality true. So, use a $\boxed{}$ line.

Since $y \leq \boxed{} x - \boxed{}$, shade $\boxed{}$ the boundary line.

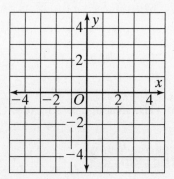

Quick Check

1. a. Graph $y \geq 3x - 1$.

b. Graph $6x + 8y \geq 12$.

Name_____ Class_____ Date _____

Example

② **Making a Budget** Suppose your budget allows you to spend no more than $24 for decorations for a party. Streamers cost $2 a roll and tablecloths cost $6 each. Use intercepts to graph the inequality that represents the situation. Find three possible combinations of streamers and tablecloths you can buy.

Relate | cost of streamers | plus | cost of tablecloths | is less than or equal to | total budget |

Define Let $\boxed{s}$ = the number of rolls of streamers.

Let $\boxed{t}$ = the number of tablecloths.

Write $2\boxed{}$ + $6\boxed{}$ ≤ $\boxed{}$

Graph $2s + 6t = 24$ by graphing the intercepts $\left(\boxed{},\boxed{}\right)$

and $\left(\boxed{},\boxed{}\right)$. The coordinates of the points on the boundary

line make the inequality true. So, use a $\boxed{}$ line.

Graph only in Quadrant I, since you cannot buy a negative amount of decorations.

Test the point $(0, 0)$.

$$2s + 6t \le 24$$

$2\left(\boxed{}\right) + 6\left(\boxed{}\right) \le 24$ **Substitute (0, 0) for (s, t).**

$\boxed{} \le 24$ **Since the inequality is true, (0, 0) is a solution.**

Shade the region containing $(0, 0)$.

Since the boundary line is included in the graph, the intercepts are also solutions

to the inequality. The solution $(9, 1)$ means that if you buy $\boxed{}$ rolls of streamers,

you can buy $\boxed{}$ tablecloth. Three solutions are $(9, 1)$, $\left(\boxed{},\boxed{}\right)$, and $\left(\boxed{},\boxed{}\right)$.

Quick Check

2. Suppose you plan to spend no more than $24 on meat for a cookout. Hamburger costs $3.00/lb and chicken wings cost $2.40/lb. Write and graph an equation to find three possible combinations of hamburger and chicken wings you can buy.

Name_____ Class_____ Date_____

Lesson 7-6

Systems of Linear Inequalities

Lesson Objectives	NAEP 2005 Strand: Algebra
✔1 Solve systems of linear inequalities by graphing	**Topics:** Equations and Inequalities
✔2 Model real-world situations using systems of linear inequalities	**Local Standards:** _____

Vocabulary

A system of linear inequalities is _____

_____

A solution of a system of linear inequalities is _____

_____

Example

1 **Writing a System of Inequalities From a Graph** Write a system of inequalities using the shaded regions below.

boundary: $y = -\frac{1}{2}x + 2$

The region lies [   ] the boundary line, so the inequality is $y\ \boxed{}\ -\frac{1}{2}x + 2$.

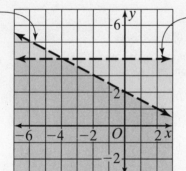

boundary: $y = 4$

The region lies [   ] the boundary line, so the inequality is $y\ \boxed{}\ 4$.

system for the darkened region: $y < -\frac{1}{2}x + 2$
$y < 4$

Quick Check

1. Write a system of inequalities for the dark region of each of the graphs.

a. [   ]

b. [   ]

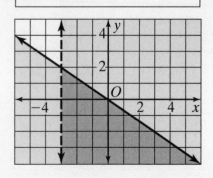

Daily Notetaking Guide

Name_____ Class_____ Date _____

Example

❷ **Writing and Using Inequalities** You need to make a fence for a dog run. The length of the run can be no more than 60 ft, and you have 136 feet of fencing that you can use. What are the possible dimensions of the dog run?

Define Let $\boxed{\ell}$ = length of the dog run.

Let $\boxed{w}$ = width of the dog run.

Relate $\boxed{\begin{array}{c}\text{the}\\\text{length}\end{array}}$ is no more than $\boxed{60}$ ft $\boxed{\begin{array}{c}\text{the}\\\text{perimeter}\end{array}}$ is no more than $\boxed{136}$ ft

Write $\boxed{}$ ≤ $\boxed{}$ 2$\boxed{}$ + 2$\boxed{}$ ≤ $\boxed{}$

Solve by graphing. $\ell \leq \boxed{}$

$2\ell + 2w \leq \boxed{}$

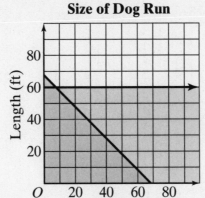

Size of Dog Run

$\ell \leq 60$

Shade $\boxed{}$
$\ell = 60$.

$2\ell + 2w \leq 136$

Graph the intercepts

$\left(\boxed{}, \boxed{}\right)$ and $\left(\boxed{}, \boxed{}\right)$.

Test $(0, 0)$.

$2\left(\boxed{}\right) + 2\left(\boxed{}\right) \leq 136$

$\left(\boxed{}\right) \leq 136$

Shade $\boxed{}$ $2\ell + 2w = 136$.

The solutions are the coordinates of the points that lie in the darkened region and on the lines $\ell = 60$ and $2\ell + 2w = 136$.

Quick Check

2. Suppose you want to fence a rectangular garden plot. You want the length of the garden to be at least 50 ft and the perimeter to be no more than 140 ft. Solve by graphing to show all of the possible dimensions of the garden.

Dimensions of Garden

Width (ft)

Name_____ Class_____ Date_____

Example

❸ Graphing Inequalities Suppose you have two jobs, babysitting for $5 per hour and sacking groceries for $6 per hour. You can work no more than 20 hours each week, but you need to earn at least $90 per week. How many hours can you work at each job?

Define Let $\boxed{b}$ = hours of babysitting.

Let $\boxed{s}$ = hours of sacking groceries.

Relate | the number of hours worked | is less than or equal to | $\boxed{20}$ | | the amount earned | is at least | $\boxed{90}$ |

Write $\boxed{} + \boxed{}$ $\leq$ $\boxed{}$ $5\boxed{} + 6\boxed{}$ $\geq$ $\boxed{}$

Solve by graphing. $b + s \leq 20$
$5b + 6s \geq 90$

Jobs

Sacking Groceries (h) — vertical axis: 4, 8, 12, 16, 20

Babysitting (h) — horizontal axis: O, 4, 8, 12, 16, 20

The solutions are all the coordinates of the points that are nonnegative numbers in the shaded region and on the lines $b + s = 20$ and $5b + 6s = 90$.

Quick Check

3. a. Give two solutions from the graph in Example 3.

b. Critical Thinking Why are the solutions to the problem only nonnegative numbers?

Daily Notetaking Guide

Lesson 8-1

Zero and Negative Exponents

Lesson Objectives	NAEP 2005 Strand: Number Properties and Operations
☑ Simplify expressions with zero and negative exponents	**Topics:** Number Sense; Properties of Number and Operations
☑ Evaluate exponential expressions	**Local Standards:** _____

Key Concepts

Zero as an Exponent

For every nonzero number a, $\boxed{}$.

Examples $5^0 = 1$ $(-2)^0 = 1$ $(1.02)^0 = 1$ $\left(\frac{1}{3}\right)^0 = 1$

Negative Exponent

For every nonzero number a and integer n, $a^{-n} = \boxed{}$.

Examples $6^{-4} = \frac{1}{6^4}$ $(-8)^{-1} = \frac{1}{(-8)^1}$

Examples

❶ Simplifying a Power Simplify:

a. $3^{-2} = \boxed{}$ **Use the definition of negative exponent.**

$= \boxed{}$ **Simplify.**

b. $(-22.4)^0 = \boxed{}$ **Use the definition of zero as an exponent.**

❷ Simplifying an Exponential Expression Simplify each expression.

$\frac{1}{x^{-3}} = 1 \div x^{-3}$ **Rewrite using a division symbol.**

$= 1 \div \dfrac{1}{\boxed{}}$ **Use the definition of negative exponent.**

$= 1 \cdot \boxed{}$ **Multiply by the reciprocal of $\frac{1}{x^3}$, which is $\boxed{}$.**

$= \boxed{}$ **Identity Property of Multiplication**

Quick Check

1. Simplify each expression.

a. 3^{-4}

b. $(-7)^0$

c. $(-4)^{-3}$

$\boxed{}$ $\boxed{}$ $\boxed{}$

Name_____ Class_____ Date _____

Example

③ Evaluating an Exponential Expression Evaluate $4x^2y^{-3}$ for $x = 3$ and $y = -2$.

$$4x^2y^{-3} = 4\left(\boxed{}\right)^2\left(\boxed{}\right)^{-3}$$ **Substitute** $\boxed{}$ **for** x **and** $\boxed{}$ **for** y.

$$= \frac{4\left(\boxed{}\right)^2}{\left(\boxed{}\right)^3}$$ **Use the definition of negative exponent.**

$$= \frac{36}{-8} = \boxed{}$$ **Simplify.**

Quick Check

2. Simplify each expression.

   a. $11m^{-5}$

         b. $7s^{-4}t^2$

   c. $\dfrac{2}{a^{-3}}$

         d. $\dfrac{n^{-5}}{v^2}$

3. Evaluate each expression for $n = -2$ and $w = 5$.

   a. $n^{-3}w^0$

         b. $\dfrac{n^{-1}}{w^2}$

   c. $\dfrac{w^0}{n^4}$

         d. $\dfrac{1}{nw^{-2}}$

Lesson 8-2

Scientific Notation

Lesson Objectives	**NAEP 2005 Strand:** Number Properties and Operations
▼ Write numbers in scientific and standard notation	**Topics:** Number Sense; Estimation
▼ Use scientific notation	**Local Standards:** _____

Key Concepts

Scientific Notation

A number in scientific notation is written as the product of two factors in the form $a \times 10^n$, where n is an integer and $1 \le a < 10$.

Examples 3.4×10^6 5.43×10^{13} 2.1×10^{-10}

Examples

❶ Recognizing Scientific Notation Is each number written in scientific notation? If not, explain.

a. 0.46×10^4 [   ] ; 0.46 is less than [   ].

b. 3.25×10^{-2} [   ]

c. 13.2×10^6 [   ] ; [   ] is greater than [   ].

❷ Writing a Number in Scientific Notation Write each number in scientific notation.

a. 234,000,000

$234{,}000{,}000 = $ [   ] $\times 10^{[\;]}$ **Move the decimal point** [ ] **places to the left and use** [ ] **as an exponent. Drop the zeros after the 4.**

b. 0.000063

$0.000063 = $ [   ] $\times 10^{[\;]}$ **Move the decimal point** [ ] **places to the right and use** [ ] **as an exponent. Drop the zeros before the 6.**

Quick Check

1. Is each number written in scientific notation? If not, explain.

a. 3.42×10^{-7}

[   ]

b. 52×10^4

[   ]

c. 0.04×10^{-5}

[   ]

Example

❸ Writing a Number in Standard Notation Write each number in standard notation.

a. elephant's mass: 8.8×10^4 kg

$$8.8 \times 10^4 = \boxed{}$$

$$= \boxed{} \text{ kg}$$

A positive exponent indicates a number greater than 10. Move the decimal point $\boxed{}$ **places to the right.**

b. ant's mass: 7.3×10^{-5} kg

$$7.3 \times 10^{-5} = \boxed{}$$

$$= \boxed{} \text{ kg}$$

A negative exponent indicates a number between 0 and 1. Move the decimal point $\boxed{}$ **places to the left.**

Quick Check

2. Write each number in scientific notation.

a. 267,000

b. 46,205,000

c. 0.0000325

d. 0.000000009

3. Write each number in standard notation.

a. 3.2×10^{12}

b. 5.07×10^4

c. 5.6×10^{-4}

d. 8.3×10^{-2}

Examples

❹ Using Scientific Notation to Order Numbers Order 0.0063×10^5, 6.03×10^4, 6103, and 63.1×10^3 from least to greatest.

Write each number in scientific notation.

$$6.3 \times 10^{\square} \qquad 6.03 \times 10^{\square} \qquad 6.103 \times 10^{\square} \qquad 6.31 \times 10^{\square}$$

Order the powers of 10. Arrange the decimals with the same power of 10 in order.

$$\boxed{} \times 10^{\square} \qquad \boxed{} \times 10^{\square} \qquad \boxed{} \times 10^{\square} \qquad \boxed{} \times 10^{\square}$$

Write the original numbers in order.

❺ Multiplying a Number in Scientific Notation Simplify. Write each answer using scientific notation.

a. $6(8 \times 10^{-4}) = (\boxed{} \cdot \boxed{}) \times 10^{-4}$ **Associative Property of Multiplication**

$\qquad = \boxed{} \times 10^{-4}$ **Simplify inside the parentheses.**

$\qquad = \boxed{} \times 10^{\square}$ **Write the product in scientific notation.**

b. $0.3(1.3 \times 10^3) = (\boxed{} \cdot \boxed{}) \times 10^3$ **Associative Property of Multiplication**

$\qquad = \boxed{} \times 10^3$ **Simplify inside the parentheses.**

$\qquad = \boxed{} \times 10^{\square}$ **Write the product in scientific notation.**

Quick Check

4. Order 60.2×10^{-5}, 63×10^4, 0.067×10^3, 61×10^{-2} from least to greatest.

5. Simplify. Write each answer using scientific notation.

    a. $2.5(6 \times 10^3)$ **b.** $0.4(2 \times 10^{-9})$

Lesson 8-3   Multiplication Properties of Exponents

Lesson Objectives	NAEP 2005 Strand: Number Properties and Operations
▼ Multiply powers	Topics: Number Sense; Estimation
▼ Work with scientific notation	Local Standards: _____

Key Concepts

Multiplying Powers With the Same Base

For every nonzero number a and integers m and n, $a^m \cdot a^n = \boxed{}$.

Example $3^5 \cdot 3^4 = 3^{5+4} = 3^9$

Example

❶ Multiplying Powers Rewrite each expression using each base only once.

a. $7^3 \cdot 7^2 = 7^{3\boxed{}2}$ $\boxed{}$ exponents of powers with the same base.

     $= \boxed{}$ Simplify the sum of the exponents.

b. $6^8 \cdot 6^{-8} = 6^{8\boxed{}(-8)}$ $\boxed{}$ exponents of powers with the same base.

     $= \boxed{}$ Simplify the sum of the exponents.

     $= \boxed{}$ Use the definition of zero as an exponent.

Quick Check

1. Rewrite each expression using each base only once.

a. $5^3 \cdot 5^6$ **b.** $2^4 \cdot 2^{-3}$ **c.** $7^{-3} \cdot 7^2 \cdot 7^6$

Example

❷ Multiplying Powers in an Algebraic Expression Simplify each expression.

a. $4x^6 \cdot 5x^{-4} = (\boxed{} \cdot \boxed{})(x^6 \cdot x^{-4})$ $\boxed{}$ **Property of Multiplication**

$= \boxed{}\left(x^{\boxed{}} + (\boxed{})\right)$ **Add exponents of powers with the same base.**

$= \boxed{}$ **Simplify.**

b. $2q \cdot 3p^3 \cdot 4q^4 = \left(2 \cdot \boxed{} \cdot 4\right)(p^3)\left(q \cdot \boxed{}\right)$ **Commutative and Associative Properties of Multiplication**

$= \boxed{}(p^3)\left(\boxed{} \cdot \boxed{}\right)$ **Multiply the coefficients. Write q as $\boxed{}$.**

$= \boxed{}(p^3)\left(q^{\boxed{}}\right)$ **Add exponents of powers with the same base.**

$= \boxed{}$ **Simplify.**

Quick Check

2. Simplify each expression.

a. $n^2 \cdot n^3 \cdot 7n$

b. $2y^3 \cdot 7x^2 \cdot 2y^4$

c. $m^2 \cdot n^{-2} \cdot 7m$

Example

❸ Multiplying Numbers in Scientific Notation Simplify $(3 \times 10^{-3})(7 \times 10^{-5})$. Write the answer in scientific notation.

$(3 \times 10^{-3})(7 \times 10^{-5}) = \left(3 \cdot \boxed{}\right)\left(10^{\boxed{}} \cdot 10^{\boxed{}}\right)$ **Commutative and Associative Properties of Multiplication**

$= \boxed{} \times 10^{\boxed{}}$ **Simplify.**

$= 2.1 \times 10^{\boxed{}} \cdot 10^{\boxed{}}$ **Write 21 in scientific notation.**

$= 2.1 \times 10^{\boxed{} + \boxed{}}$ **Add exponents of powers with the same base.**

$= 2.1 \times 10^{\boxed{}}$ **Simplify.**

Quick Check

3. Simplify each expression. Write each answer in scientific notation.

a. $(2.5 \times 10^8)(6 \times 10^3)$

b. $(1.5 \times 10^{-2})(3 \times 10^4)$

c. $(9 \times 10^{-6})(7 \times 10^{-9})$

Example

❹ **Applying Multiplication Properties of Exponents** The speed of light is 3×10^8 m/s. If there are 1×10^{-3} km in 1 m, and 3.6×10^3 s in 1 h, find the speed of light in km/h.

Speed of light $= \dfrac{\text{meters}}{\text{seconds}} \cdot \dfrac{\text{kilometers}}{\text{meters}} \cdot \dfrac{\text{seconds}}{\text{hour}}$ **Use dimensional analysis.**

$= \left(\square \times 10^{\square}\right)\frac{m}{s} \cdot \left(\square \times 10^{\square}\right)\frac{km}{m} \cdot \left(\square \times 10^{\square}\right)\frac{s}{h}$ **Substitute.**

$= \left(\square \cdot \square \cdot \square\right) \times \left(10^{\square} \cdot 10^{-3} \cdot 10^{\square}\right)$ **Commutative and Associative Properties of Multiplication**

$= \square \times \left(10^{\square + \square + \square}\right)$ **Simplify.**

$= 10.8 \times 10^{\square}$ **Add exponents.**

$= 1.08 \times 10^{\square} \cdot 10^{\square}$ **Write 10.8 in scientific notation.**

$= \square \times 10^{\square}$ **Add the exponents.**

Quick Check

4. A human body contains about 3.2×10^4 microliters of blood for each pound of body weight. Each microliter of blood contains about 5×10^6 red blood cells. Find the approximate number of red blood cells in the body of a 160-lb person.

Name_____ Class_____ Date_____

Lesson 8-4

More Multiplication Properties of Exponents

Lesson Objectives	**NAEP 2005 Strand:** Number Properties and Operations
▼ Raise a power to a power	**Topic:** Properties of Number and Operations
▼ Raise a product to a power	**Local Standards:** _____

Key Concepts

Raising a Power to a Power

For every nonzero number a and integers m and n, $(a^m)^n = $ ☐ .

Examples $(5^4)^2 = 5^{4 \cdot 2} = 5^8$ $(n^2)^5 = n^{2 \cdot 5} = n^{10}$

Raising a Product to a Power

For every nonzero number a and b and integer n, $(ab)^n = $ ☐ .

Example $(3x)^4 = 3^4 x^4 = 81x^4$

Examples

❶ Simplifying a Power Raised to a Power Simplify $(a^3)^4$.

$(a^3)^4 = a^{3\,☐\,4}$ ☐ **exponents when raising a power to a power.**

$= a^{☐}$ **Simplify.**

❷ Simplifying an Expression With Powers Simplify $b^2(b^3)^{-2}$.

$b^2(b^3)^{-2} = b^2 \cdot b^{3\,☐\,(-2)}$ ☐ **exponents in $(b^3)^{-2}$.**

$= b^2 \cdot b^{☐}$ **Simplify.**

$= b^{2\,☐\,(-6)}$ ☐ **exponents when multiplying powers of the same base.**

$= b^{☐}$ **Simplify.**

$= ☐$ **Write using only positive exponents.**

Quick Check

1. Simplify.

a. $(a^4)^7$

b. $(a^{-4})^7$

2. Simplify.

a. $t^2(t^7)^{-2}$

b. $(a^4)^2 \cdot (a^2)^5$

Examples

❸ Simplifying a Product Raised to a Power Simplify $(4xy^3)^2(x^3)^{-3}$.

$(4xy^3)^2(x^3)^{-3} = 4^{\square}x^{\square}(y^3)^{\square} \cdot (x^3)^{-3}$ **Raise the three factors to the second power.**

$= 4^2 \cdot x^2 \cdot y^{\square} \cdot x^{\boxed{}}$ $\boxed{}$ **exponents of a power raised to a power.**

$= 4^2 \cdot x^2 \cdot x^{\boxed{}} \cdot y^{\square}$ **Use the Commutative Property of Multiplication.**

$= 4^2 \cdot x^{\boxed{}} \cdot y^6$ **Add exponents of powers with the same base.**

$= \boxed{}$ **Simplify.**

❹ Applying Multiplication Properties of Exponents An object has a mass of 10^2 kg. The expression $10^2 \cdot (3 \times 10^8)^2$ describes the amount of resting energy in joules the object contains. Simplify the expression.

$10^2 \cdot (3 \times 10^8)^2 = 10^{\square} \cdot 3^{\square} \cdot (10^8)^{\square}$ **Raise each factor within parentheses to the second power.**

$= 10^{\square} \cdot 3^{\square} \cdot 10^{\boxed{}}$ **Simplify $(10^8)^2$.**

$= 3^{\square} \cdot 10^{\square} \cdot 10^{\boxed{}}$ **Use the Commutative Property of Multiplication.**

$= 3^{\square} \cdot 10^{\square +\boxed{}}$ **Add exponents of powers with the same base.**

$= \boxed{} \times 10^{\boxed{}}$ **Simplify. Write in scientific notation.**

Quick Check

3. Simplify each expression.

a. $(2z)^4$ **b.** $(4g^5)^{-2}$ **c.** $(2a^3)^5(3ab^2)^3$ **d.** $(6mn)^3(5m^{-3})^2$

4. An hour of television use consumes 1.45×10^{-1} kWh (kilowatt-hour) of electricity. Each kilowatt-hour of electricity use is equivalent to 3.6×10^6 joules of energy. Simplify the expression $(1.45 \times 10^{-1})(3.6 \times 10^6)$ to find how many joules a television uses in 1 hour.

Lesson 8-5

Division Properties of Exponents

Lesson Objectives	NAEP 2005 Strand: Number Properties and Operations
▼ Divide powers with the same base	Topic: Properties of Number and Operations
▼ Raise a quotient to a power	Local Standards: _____

Key Concepts

Dividing Powers With the Same Base

For every nonzero number a and integers m and n, $\dfrac{a^m}{a^n} = $ ☐ .

Example $\dfrac{3^7}{3^3} = 3^{7-3} = 3^4$

Raising a Quotient to a Power

For every nonzero number a and b and integer n, $\left(\dfrac{a}{b}\right)^n = $ ☐ .

Example $\left(\dfrac{4}{5}\right)^3 = \dfrac{4^3}{5^3} = \dfrac{64}{125}$

Examples

❶ Simplifying an Algebraic Expression Simplify.

$\dfrac{p^3 j^{-4}}{p^{-3} j^6} = p^{3-\left(\boxed{}\right)} j^{-4\boxed{}6}$ ☐ exponents when dividing powers with the same base.

$= p^{\boxed{}} j^{\boxed{}}$ **Simplify.**

$= \boxed{}$ **Rewrite using positive exponents.**

❷ Applying Division Properties of Exponents A small dog's heart beats about 64 million beats in a year. If there are about 530 thousand minutes in a year, what is the dog's average heart rate in beats per minute?

$\dfrac{64 \text{ million beats}}{530 \text{ thousand min}} = \dfrac{6.4 \times 10^{\boxed{}} \text{beats}}{5.3 \times 10^{\boxed{}} \text{min}}$ **Write in scientific notation.**

$= \dfrac{6.4}{\boxed{}} \times 10^{7-\boxed{}}$ ☐ exponents when dividing powers with the same base.

$= \dfrac{6.4}{\boxed{}} \times 10^{\boxed{}}$ **Simplify the exponent.**

$\approx 1.21 \times 10^{\boxed{}}$ **Divide. Round to the nearest hundredth.**

$= \boxed{} \dfrac{\text{beats}}{\text{min}}$ **Write in standard notation.**

❸ **Raising a Quotient to a Power** Simplify $\left(\frac{3}{y^3}\right)^4$.

$\left(\frac{3}{y^3}\right)^4 = \dfrac{3^{\boxed{}}}{(y^3)^{\boxed{}}}$ 　**Raise the numerator and the denominator to the** $\boxed{}$ **power.**

$= \dfrac{3^4}{y^{\boxed{}}}$ 　**Multiply the exponent in the denominator.**

$= \boxed{}$ 　**Simplify.**

Quick Check

1. Simplify each expression.

 a. $\dfrac{b^4}{b^9}$ 　　　　 b. $\dfrac{a^2b}{a^4b^3}$ 　　　 c. $\dfrac{m^{-1}n^2}{m^3n}$ 　　　 d. $\dfrac{x^2y^{-1}z^4}{xy^4z^{-3}}$

2. Find each quotient. Write each answer in scientific notation.

 a. $\dfrac{2 \times 10^3}{8 \times 10^8}$ 　　　　　　　 b. $\dfrac{7.5 \times 10^{12}}{2.5 \times 10^{-4}}$

 c. In 2000 the total amount of glass recycled in the United States was 2.7 million tons. The population of the United States in 2000 was 281.4 million people. On average, about how many tons of glass were recycled per person?

3. Simplify each expression.

 a. $\left(\frac{3}{x^2}\right)^2$ 　　　　 b. $\left(\frac{x}{y^2}\right)^3$ 　　　 c. $\left(\frac{t^7}{2^3}\right)^2$

Example

④ Simplifying an Exponential Expression

a. Simplify $\left(\frac{2}{3}\right)^{-3}$.

$\left(\frac{2}{3}\right)^{-3} = \left(\boxed{}\right)^{\boxed{}}$ **Rewrite using the reciprocal of $\frac{2}{3}$.**

$= \dfrac{3^{\boxed{}}}{2^{\boxed{}}}$ **Raise the numerator and the denominator to the** $\boxed{}$ **power.**

$= \boxed{}$ or $\boxed{}$ **Simplify.**

b. Simplify $\left(-\frac{4b}{c}\right)^{-2}$.

$\left(-\dfrac{4b}{c}\right)^{-2} = \left(\boxed{}\right)^{2}$ **Rewrite using the reciprocal of $-\dfrac{4b}{c}$.**

$= \left(\dfrac{\boxed{}}{4b}\right)^{2}$ **Write the fraction with a negative numerator.**

$= \dfrac{(-c)^{\boxed{}}}{(4b)^{\boxed{}}}$ **Raise the numerator and denominator to the** $\boxed{}$ **power.**

$= \boxed{}$ **Simplify.**

Quick Check

4. Simplify each expression.

a. $\left(\frac{3}{4}\right)^{-3}$

b. $\left(\frac{-1}{2}\right)^{-5}$

c. $\left(\frac{2r}{s}\right)^{-1}$

d. $\left(\frac{7a}{m}\right)^{-2}$

Name_____ Class_____ Date_____

Lesson 8-6   Geometric Sequences

Lesson Objectives	NAEP 2005 Strand: Algebra
▼ Form geometric sequences ▼ Use formulas when describing geometric sequences	Topic: Patterns, Relations, and Functions Local Standards: _____

Vocabulary and Key Concepts

Geometric Sequence

$$A(n) = a \cdot r^{n-1}$$

nth term | first term | common ratio | term number

A geometric sequence is _____

_____

A common ratio is _____

_____

Example

1 Finding the Common Ratio Find the common ratio of each sequence.

a. $3, -15, 75, -375, \ldots$

3   −15   75   −375

×(☐) ×(☐) ×(☐)

The common ratio is ☐.

b. $3, \dfrac{3}{2}, \dfrac{3}{4}, \dfrac{3}{8}, \ldots$

3      $\dfrac{3}{2}$ $\dfrac{3}{4}$ $\dfrac{3}{8}$

× ☐   × ☐   × ☐

The common ratio is ☐.

Quick Check

1. Find the common ratio of each sequence.

a. $750, 150, 30, 6, \ldots$

☐

b. $-3, -6, -12, -24, \ldots$

☐

c. $4, 6, 9, 13.5, \ldots$

☐

Examples

❷ Arithmetic or Geometric Sequence Determine whether each sequence is arithmetic or geometric.

a. $162, 54, 18, 6, \ldots$

The sequence has a [_____]

ratio. The sequence is [_____].

b. $98, 101, 104, 107, \ldots$

The sequence has a [_____]

difference. The sequence is [_____].

❸ Finding Terms of a Sequence Find the first, fifth, and tenth terms of the sequence that has the rule $A(n) = -3(2)^{n-1}$.

first term: $A(1) = -3(2)^{\square - 1} = -3(2)^{\square} = -3(1) = \boxed{}$

fifth term: $A(5) = -3(2)^{\square - 1} = -3(2)^{\square} = -3(16) = \boxed{}$

tenth term: $A(10) = -3(2)^{\square - 1} = -3(2)^{\square} = -3(512) = \boxed{}$

Quick Check

2. Determine whether each sequence is arithmetic or geometric.

a. $2, 4, 6, 8, \ldots$

b. $2, 4, 8, 16, \ldots$

c. $1, 3, 5, 7, \ldots$

3. Find the first, sixth, and twelfth terms of each sequence.

a. $A(n) = 4 \cdot 3^{n-1}$

b. $A(n) = -2 \cdot 5^{n-1}$

Example

④ Applying Geometric Sequences Suppose you drop a tennis ball from a height of 2 meters. On each bounce, the ball reaches a height that is 75% of its previous height. Write a rule for the height the ball reaches on each bounce. In centimeters, what height will the ball reach on its third bounce?

The first term is 2 meters, which is [   ] cm.

Use a diagram to help understand the problem.

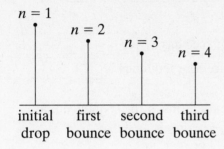

$n = 1$

$n = 2$

$n = 3$

$n = 4$

| initial | first | second | third |
| drop | bounce | bounce | bounce |

The ball drops from an initial height, for which there is no bounce. The initial height is 200 cm, when $n = 1$. The third bounce is $n = 4$. The common ratio is 75%, or 0.75.

A rule for the sequence is $A(n) = 200 \cdot 0.75^{n-1}$.

$A(n) = 200 \cdot 0.75^{n-1}$ **Use the sequence to find the height of the third bounce.**

$A(\boxed{}) = 200 \cdot 0.75^{\boxed{}-1}$ **Substitute** $\boxed{}$ **for n to find the height of the third bounce.**

$= 200 \cdot 0.75^{\boxed{}}$ **Simplify exponents.**

$= 200 \cdot \boxed{}$ **Evaluate powers.**

$= \boxed{}$ **Simplify.**

The height of the third bounce is $\boxed{}$ cm.

Quick Check

4. Using the information from Example 4, suppose you drop a tennis ball from a height of 3 meters. In centimeters, what height will the ball reach on its second bounce?

Lesson 8-7

Exponential Functions

Lesson Objectives	NAEP 2005 Strand: Algebra
▼ 1 Evaluate exponential functions ▼ 2 Graph exponential functions	**Topics:** Patterns, Relations, and Functions **Local Standards:** _____

Key Concepts

Exponential Function

An exponential function is a function in the form of $y = \boxed{}$, where a is a nonzero constant, b is greater than 0 and not equal to 1, and x is a real number.

Examples $y = 0.5 \cdot 2^x$ $f(x) = -2 \cdot 0.5^x$

Examples

❶ Evaluating an Exponential Function Evaluate the exponential function $y = 3^x$ for $x = 2, 3, 4$.

x	$y = 3^x$	y
2	$3^{\boxed{}} = 9$	$\boxed{}$
3	$3^{\boxed{}} = 27$	$\boxed{}$
4	$3^{\boxed{}} = 81$	$\boxed{}$

❷ Applying Exponential Functions Suppose two mice live in a barn. The number of mice quadruples every 3 months. The function $f(x) = 2 \cdot 4^x$ models this situation. How many mice will be in the barn after 2 years?

$f(x) = \boxed{} \cdot \boxed{}^x$

$f(x) = \boxed{} \cdot \boxed{}^{\boxed{}}$ **In two years, there are** $\boxed{}$ **three-month time periods.**

$f(x) = 2 \cdot \boxed{}$ **Simplify powers.**

$f(x) = \boxed{}$ **Simplify.**

Algebra 1 Lesson 8-7 **151**

❸ **Applying Exponential Functions** The function $f(x) = 1.25^x$ models the increase in size of an image being copied over and over at 125% on a photocopier. Graph the function.

x	$f(x) = 1.25^x$	(x, f(x))
1	$1.25^{\square} = 1.25 \approx \boxed{}$	$(\boxed{}, \boxed{})$
2	$1.25^{\square} = 1.5625 \approx \boxed{}$	$(\boxed{}, \boxed{})$
3	$1.25^{\square} \approx 1.9531 \approx \boxed{}$	$(\boxed{}, \boxed{})$
4	$1.25^{\square} \approx 2.4414 \approx \boxed{}$	$(\boxed{}, \boxed{})$
5	$1.25^{\square} \approx 3.0518 \approx \boxed{}$	$(\boxed{}, \boxed{})$

Quick Check

1. Evaluate each exponential function for the domain $\{-2, 0, 3\}$.

   a. $y = 4^x$
               b. $f(x) = 10 \cdot 5^x$
               c. $g(x) = -2 \cdot 3^x$

2. Suppose the population of 10 animals quadruples every year. Use the function $f(x) = 10 \cdot 4^x$. How many animals would there be after 6 years?

3. a. Consider Example 3. You can also make images that are smaller than the original. The function $y = 0.9^x$ models the new size of an image being copied over and over at 90%. Graph the function.

   b. Critical Thinking In both models, what does $f(0)$ represent?

Lesson 8-8

Lesson Objectives	NAEP 2005 Strand: Algebra
▼ Model exponential growth	Topic: Algebraic Representations
▼ Model exponential decay	Local Standards: _____

Vocabulary and Key Concepts

Exponential Growth

Exponential growth can be modeled with the function [＿＿＿＿＿＿] for $a > 0$ and $b > 1$.

starting amount (when $x = 0$)
↓
$y = a \cdot b^x$ ← exponent
↑

The [＿＿＿＿], which is greater than 1, is the [＿＿＿＿＿＿] factor.

Exponential Decay

The function [＿＿＿＿＿＿] models exponential decay for $a > 0$ and $0 < b < 1$.

starting amount (when $x = 0$)
↓
$y = a \cdot b^x$ ← exponent
↑

The [＿＿＿＿], which is between 0 and 1, is the [＿＿＿＿＿＿] factor.

Compound interest is _____

_____

The interest period is the _____

Examples

❶ **Compound Interest** Suppose you deposit $1000 in a fund that pays 7.2% interest compounded annually. Find the account balance after 5 years.

Relate   [y]   =   [a]   ·   [b^x]   **Use an exponential function.**

Define   Let [x] = the number of interest periods.

Let [y] = the balance.

Let [a] = the [＿＿＿＿＿＿] deposit, $1000.

Let [b] = 100% + 7.2% = 107.2% = [＿＿＿＿＿] .

Write y =   [＿＿＿＿] · [＿＿＿＿]^x

=   [＿＿＿＿] · [＿＿＿＿]$^{[\ ]}$ **Once a year for [ ] years is [ ] interest periods. Substitute [ ] for x.**

≈   [＿＿＿＿]

Use a calculator. Round to the nearest cent.

The balance after 5 years will be $[＿＿＿＿] .

❷ **Compound Interest** Suppose the account in Example 1 paid interest
compounded quarterly instead of annually. Find the balance after 5 years.

Relate $\boxed{y}$ = $\boxed{a}$ · $\boxed{b^x}$ **Use an exponential function.**

Define   Let $\boxed{x}$ = the number of interest periods.

Let $\boxed{y}$ = the balance.

Let $\boxed{a}$ = the inital deposit, \$ $\boxed{}$.

Let $\boxed{b}$ =   100% + $\dfrac{\boxed{}\,\%}{\boxed{}}$.   There are $\boxed{}$ interest periods in 1 year, so divide the interest into $\boxed{}$ parts.

=   1   +   0.018 = $\boxed{}$

Write y = $\boxed{}$ · $\boxed{}^x$

= $\boxed{}$ · $1.018^{\boxed{}}$ **Four interest periods a year for 5 years is** $\boxed{}$ **interest periods. Substitute** $\boxed{}$ **for** x.

≈ $\boxed{}$ **Use a calculator. Round to the nearest cent.**

The balance after 5 years will be \$ $\boxed{}$.

Quick Check

1. Suppose the interest rate on the account in Example 1 was 8%. How much
   would be in the account after 18 years?

2. You deposit \$200 into an account earning 5%, compounded monthly. How
   much will be in the account after 1 year? After 2 years? After 5 years?

Example

❸ **Modeling Exponential Decay** Suppose the population of a certain endangered species has decreased 2.4% each year. Suppose there were 60 of these animals in a given area in 1999.

a. Write an equation to model the number of animals in this species that remain alive in that area.

Relate $\boxed{y}$ = $\boxed{a}$ · $\boxed{b^x}$ **Use an exponential function.**

Define Let $\boxed{x}$ = the number of years since 1999.

Let $\boxed{y}$ = the number of animals that remain.

Let $\boxed{a}$ = $\boxed{}$, the initial population in 1999.

Let $\boxed{b}$ = the decay factor, which is $100\% - 2.4\% = 97.6\% = \boxed{}$.

Write y = $\boxed{}$ · $\boxed{}^x$

b. Use your equation to find the approximate number of animals remaining in 2005.

$y = 60 \cdot 0.976^x$

$y = 60 \cdot 0.976^{\boxed{}}$ **2005 is** $\boxed{}$ **years after 1999, so substitute** $\boxed{}$ **for x.**

≈ 52 **Use a calculator. Round to the nearest whole number.**

The approximate number of animals of this endangered species remaining in the area in 2005 is $\boxed{}$.

Quick Check

3. Statistics In 1990, the population of Washington, D.C., was about 604,000 people. Since then the population has decreased about 1.8% per year.

a. Write an equation to model the population of Washington, D.C., since 1990.

b. Suppose the current trend in population change continues. Predict the population of Washington, D.C., in 2010.

Lesson 9-1

Adding and Subtracting Polynomials

Lesson Objectives	**NAEP 2005 Strand:** Algebra
▼ Describe polynomials	**Topic:** Variables, Expressions, and Operations
▼ Add and subtract polynomials	**Local Standards:** _____

Vocabulary

A monomial is _____

_____

The degree of a monomial is _____

_____

A polynomial is _____

_____

In the standard form of a polynomial, _____

_____

The degree of a polynomial is _____

_____

A binomial is _____

A trinomial is _____

Example

① Degree of a Monomial Find the degree of each monomial.

a. 18   Degree: ☐   The degree of a nonzero constant is ☐.

b. $3xy^3$ Degree: ☐   The exponents are ☐ and ☐. Their sum is ☐.

c. $6c$ Degree: ☐ $6c = 6c^1$. The exponent is ☐.

Quick Check

1. Critical Thinking What is the degree of $9x^0$? Explain.

_____

Examples

❷ Classifying Polynomials Write each polynomial in standard form combining like terms. Then name each polynomial by its degree and the number of its terms.

a. $-2 + 7x$

$7x - \boxed{}$

$\boxed{}$ $\boxed{}$

b. $3x^5 - 2 - 2x^5 + 7x$

$3x^5 - \boxed{} + 7x - \boxed{}$

$\boxed{} + 7x - 2$

$\boxed{}$ degree $\boxed{}$

❸ Adding Polynomials Simplify $(6x^2 + 3x + 7) + (2x^2 - 6x - 4)$.

Line up like terms. Then add the coefficients.

$$\begin{array}{cccccc} 6x^2 & + & 3x & + & 7 \\ 2x^2 & - & 6x & - & 4 \\ \hline \boxed{} & - & \boxed{} & + & \boxed{} \end{array}$$

❹ Subtracting Polynomials Simplify $(2x^3 + 4x^2 - 6) - (5x^3 + 2x - 2)$.

Method 1 Subtract vertically.

Line up like terms. Then add the coefficients.

$$\begin{array}{cccc} 2x^3 & + \boxed{} & - & 6 \\ -(5x^3 & + \boxed{} & - & 2) \\ \hline \end{array}$$ Line up like terms.

$$\begin{array}{cccc} 2x^3 & + \boxed{} & - & 6 \\ -5x^3 & \boxed{}\boxed{}\boxed{} & & 2 \\ \hline \boxed{} & + 4x^2 & - 2x & - \boxed{} \end{array}$$ Add the opposite.

Method 2 Subtract horizontally.

$(2x^3 + 4x^2 - 6) - (5x^3 + 2x - 2)$

$= 2x^3 + 4x^2 - 6 \boxed{} 5x^3 \boxed{} \boxed{} + 2$ Write the opposite of each term in the polynomial being subtracted.

$= \left(2x^3 - \boxed{}\right) + 4x^2 - 2x + \left(\boxed{} + 2\right)$ Group like terms.

$= \boxed{} + 4x^2 - \boxed{} - \boxed{}$ Simplify.

Name_____ Class_____ Date_____

Quick Check

2. Write each polynomial in standard form. Then name each polynomial based on its degree and the number of its terms.

a. $6x^2 + 7 - 9x^4$

b. $3y - 4 - y^3$

c. $8 + 7v - 11v$

3. Simplify each sum.

a. $(12m^2 + 4) + (8m^2 + 5)$

b. $(t^2 - 6) + (3t^2 + 11)$

c. $(9w^3 + 8w^2) + (7w^3 + 4)$

d. $(2p^3 + 6p^2 + 10p) + (9p^3 + 11p^2 + 3p)$

4. Simplify each difference.

a. $(v^3 + 6v^2 - v) - (9v^3 - 7v^2 + 3v)$

b. $(30d^3 - 29d^2 - 3d) - (2d^3 + d^2)$

c. $(4x^2 + 5x + 1) - (6x^2 + x + 8)$

Daily Notetaking Guide

Lesson 9-2

Multiplying and Factoring

Lesson Objectives	NAEP 2005 Strand: Algebra
▼ Multiply a polynomial by a monomial	Topic: Variables, Expressions, and Operations
▼ Factor a monomial from a polynomial	Local Standards: _____

Examples

❶ Multiplying a Monomial and a Trinomial Simplify $-2g^2(3g^3 + 6g - 5)$.

$-2g^2(3g^3 + 6g - 5)$

$= \boxed{}(3g^3) -2g^2\left(\boxed{}\right) -2g^2\left(\boxed{}\right)$ **Use the Distributive Property.**

$= -6g^{2+3} - 12g^{2+\boxed{}} + \boxed{}$ **Multiply the coefficients and add the exponents of powers with the same base.**

$= \boxed{} - \boxed{} + 10g^2$ **Simplify.**

❷ Finding the Greatest Common Factor Find the GCF of $2x^4 + 10x^2 - 6x$.

List the prime factors of each term. Identify the factors common to all terms.

$2x^4 = 2 \cdot x \cdot \boxed{} \cdot x \cdot \boxed{}$

$10x^2 = 2 \cdot \boxed{} \cdot x \cdot \boxed{}$

$6x = \boxed{} \cdot 3 \cdot x$

The GCF is $\boxed{}$.

❸ Factoring Out a Monomial Factor $4x^3 + 12x^2 - 16x$.

Step 1 Find the GCF.

$4x^3 = 2 \cdot \boxed{} \cdot x \cdot \boxed{} \cdot \boxed{}$

$12x^2 = 2 \cdot 2 \cdot \boxed{} \cdot x \cdot x$

$16x = 2 \cdot \boxed{} \cdot 2 \cdot \boxed{} \cdot x$

The GCF is $\boxed{}$.

Step 2 Factor out the GCF.

$4x^3 + 12x^2 - 16x$

$= 4x\left(\boxed{}\right) + \boxed{}(3x) + 4x(-4)$

$= \boxed{}\left(x^2 + \boxed{} - \boxed{}\right)$

Quick Check

1. Simplify each product.

a. $4b(5b^2 + b + 6)$

b. $-7h(3h^2 - 8h - 1)$

c. $2x(x^2 - 6x + 5)$

2. Find the GCF of the terms of each polynomial.

a. $5v^5 + 10v^3$

b. $3t^2 - 18$

c. $4b^3 - 2b^2 - 6b$

3. Use the GCF to factor each polynomial.

a. $8x^2 - 12x$

b. $5d^3 + 10d$

c. $6m^3 - 12m^2 - 24m$

Name_____ Class_____ Date _____

Lesson 9-3

Multiplying Binomials

Lesson Objectives	NAEP 2005 Strand: Algebra
▼ 1 Multiply binomials using FOIL ▼ 2 Multiply trinomials by binomials	**Topic:** Variables, Expressions, and Operations **Local Standards:** _____

Examples

❶ Multiplying Using FOIL Simplify $(4x + 2)(3x - 6)$.

First   Outer   Inner   Last

$(4x + 2)(3x - 6)$ = $(\boxed{})(3x)$ + $(4x)(\boxed{})$ + $(\boxed{})(3x)$ + $(2)(\boxed{})$

= $12x^2$ − $\boxed{}$ + $6x$ − $\boxed{}$

= $\boxed{}$ − $\boxed{}$ − $\boxed{}$

The product is $\boxed{}$.

❷ Applying Multiplication of Polynomials Find the area of the shaded region. Simplify.

area of outer rectangle = $(3x + 2)(\boxed{})$

area of hole = $x(\boxed{})$

area of shaded region = area of outer rectangle − area of hole

= $(3x + 2)(\boxed{})$ $\boxed{}$ $\boxed{}$ $(x + 3)$ **Substitute.**

= $\boxed{}$ − $3x$ + $\boxed{}$ − $2 - x^2 - \boxed{}$ **Use FOIL to simplify $(3x + 2)(2x − 1)$ and the Distributive Property to simplify $x(x + 3)$.**

= $6x^2 - \boxed{}$ − $3x$ + $\boxed{}$ − $3x - \boxed{}$ **Group like terms.**

= $\boxed{}$ − $\boxed{}$ − $\boxed{}$ **Simplify.**

Quick Check

1. Simplify each product using FOIL.

   a. $(3x + 4)(2x + 5)$

   b. $(3x − 4)(2x + 5)$

   c. $(3x + 4)(2x − 5)$

   d. $(3x − 4)(2x − 5)$

Example

❸ **Multiplying a Trinomial and a Binomial** Simplify the product $(3x^2 - 2x + 3)(2x + 7)$.

Method 1 Multiply using the vertical method.

$$
\begin{array}{ccccc}
3x^2 & - & 2x & + & 3 \\
 & & 2x & + & 7 \\
\hline
\boxed{} & - & 14x & + & \boxed{} \\
\boxed{} & - 4x^2 & + & \boxed{} \\
\hline
\boxed{} & + 17x^2 & - & \boxed{} & + & \boxed{}
\end{array}
$$

Multiply by $\boxed{}$.

Multiply by $\boxed{}$.

Add like terms.

Method 2 Multiply using the horizontal method.

$(2x + 7)(3x^2 - 2x + 3)$

$= \left(\boxed{}\right)(3x^2) - (2x)\left(\boxed{}\right) + \left(\boxed{}\right)(3) + (7)\left(\boxed{}\right) - \left(\boxed{}\right)(2x) + (7)\left(\boxed{}\right)$

$= \quad 6x^3 \quad - \quad \boxed{} \quad + \quad 6x \quad + \quad \boxed{} \quad - \quad 14x \quad + \quad \boxed{}$

$= \quad \boxed{} \quad + \quad 17x^2 \quad - \quad \boxed{} \quad + \quad 21$

The product is $\boxed{}$.

Quick Check

2. Find an expression for the area of each shaded region. Simplify.

a.   5x + 8

5x   6x + 2

x + 6

b.   x + 1

x   2x − 2

x − 2

3. Simplify $(6n - 8)(2n^2 + n + 7)$ using both methods shown in Example 3.

Lesson 9-4

Multiplying Special Cases

Lesson Objectives	NAEP 2005 Strand: Algebra
▼ Find the square of a binomial ▼ Find the difference of squares	**Topic:** Variables, Expressions, and Operations **Local Standards:** _____

Key Concepts

The Square of a Binomial

$(a + b)^2 = $ [   ]

$(a - b)^2 = $ [   ]

The square of a binomial is the square of the first term plus twice the product of the two terms plus the square of the last term.

The Difference of Squares

$(a + b)(a - b) = $ [   ]

The product of the sum and difference of the same two terms is the difference of their squares.

Example

❶ Squaring a Binomial

a. Find $(y + 11)^2$.

$(y + 11)^2 = y^2 + $ [   ] $(11) + 11^2$ **Square the binomial.**

$= $ [   ] $+ $ [   ] $+ $ [   ]   **Simplify.**

b. Find $(3w - 6)^2$.

$(3w - 6)^2 = ($[   ]$)^2 - $[   ]$(3w)($[   ]$) + 6^2$ **Square the binomial.**

$= $ [   ] $- $ [   ] $w + $ [   ]   **Simplify.**

Quick Check

1. Find each square.

a. $(t + 6)^2$

b. $(5y + 1)^2$

c. $(7m - 2p)^2$

d. $(9c - 8)^2$

Example

❷ **Applying the Square of a Binomial** Among guinea pigs, the black fur gene (B) is dominant and the white fur gene (W) is recessive. This means that a guinea pig with at least one dominant gene (BB or BW) will have black fur. A guinea pig with two recessive genes (WW) will have white fur.

	B	W
B	BB	BW
W		

The Punnett square models the possible combinations that parents who carry both genes can give to their offspring. Since WW is $\frac{1}{4}$ of the outcomes, the probability that a guinea pig has white fur is ☐ .

You can model the Punnett square probabilities with the expression $\left(\frac{1}{2}B + \frac{1}{2}W\right)^2$. Show that this product gives the same result as the Punnett square.

$$\left(\tfrac{1}{2}B + \tfrac{1}{2}W\right)^2 = \left(\tfrac{1}{2}B\right)^2 + 2\left(\boxed{}\right)\left(\tfrac{1}{2}W\right) + \left(\boxed{}\right)^2 \quad \textbf{Square the binomial.}$$

$$= \boxed{} + \boxed{} + \tfrac{1}{4}W^2 \quad \textbf{Simplify.}$$

The expressions $\frac{1}{4}B^2$ and $\boxed{}W^2$ show that the probability offspring will have either two dominant genes or two recessive genes is $\boxed{}$. The expression $\frac{1}{2}BW$ shows there is $\boxed{}$ chance that the offspring will inherit both genes. These are the $\boxed{}$ probabilities in the Punnett square.

Quick Check

2. When you play a game with two number cubes, you can find probabilities by squaring a binomial. Let A represent rolling 1 or 2 and B represent rolling 3, 4, 5, or 6. The probability of A is $\frac{1}{3}$, and the probability of B is $\frac{2}{3}$.

a. Find $\left(\frac{1}{3}A + \frac{2}{3}B\right)^2$

b. What is the probability that both number cubes you roll show 1 or 2?

c. What is the probability that one number cube shows a 1 or 2 and the other shows 3, 4, 5, or 6?

d. What is the probability that both number cubes show 3, 4, 5, or 6?

Name_____ Class_____ Date _____

Examples

❸ Mental Math

a. Find 81^2 using mental math.

$81^2 = \left(80 + \boxed{}\right)^2$

$= 80^2 + \boxed{}\left(\boxed{} \cdot 1\right) + \boxed{}^2$ **Square the binomial.**

$= \boxed{} + 160 + \boxed{} = \boxed{}$ **Simplify.**

b. Find 59^2 using mental math.

$59^2 = \left(60 - \boxed{}\right)^2$

$= \boxed{} - 2\left(\boxed{} \cdot 1\right) + 1^2$ **Square the binomial.**

$= \boxed{} - \boxed{} + 1 = \boxed{}$ **Simplify.**

❹ Finding the Difference of Squares Find $(p^4 - 8)(p^4 + 8)$.

$(p^4 - 8)(p^4 + 8) = (p^4)^{\boxed{}} - (\boxed{})^2$ **Find the difference of squares.**

$= \boxed{} - \boxed{}$ **Simplify.**

❺ Mental Math Find $43 \cdot 37$.

$43 \cdot 37 = \left(40 + \boxed{}\right)\left(40 - \boxed{}\right)$ **Express each factor using 40 and 3.**

$= \boxed{}^2 - \boxed{}$ **Find the difference of squares.**

$= \boxed{} - 9 = \boxed{}$ **Simplify.**

Quick Check

3. Use mental math.

a. 31^2

b. 29^2

c. 98^2

d. 203^2

4. Find each product.

a. $(d + 11)(d - 11)$

b. $(c^2 + 8)(c^2 - 8)$

c. $(9v^3 + w^4)(9v^3 - w^4)$

5. a. $18 \cdot 22$

b. $19 \cdot 21$

c. $50 \cdot 61$

d. $87 \cdot 93$

Lesson 9-5

Factoring Trinomials of the Type $x^2 + bx + c$

Lesson Objective	NAEP 2005 Strand: Algebra
▼ Factor trinomials	Topic: Variables, Expressions, and Operations
	Local Standards: _____

Examples

❶ **Factoring $x^2 + bx + c$** Factor $x^2 + 8x + 15$.

Find the factors of 15. Identify the pair that has a sum of 8.

$x^2 + 8x + 15 = (x + \boxed{})(x + \boxed{})$

Check $x^2 + 8x + 15 \stackrel{?}{=} (x + \boxed{})(x + \boxed{})$

$= \boxed{} + 5x + 3x + \boxed{}$

$= x^2 + 8x + 15$

Factors of 15	Sum of Factors
1 and $\boxed{}$	$\boxed{}$
$\boxed{}$ and 5	$\boxed{}$

❷ **Factoring $x^2 - bx + c$** Factor $c^2 - 9c + 20$.

Since the middle term is negative, find the negative factors of 20. Identify the pair that has a sum of -9.

$c^2 - 9c + 20 = (c - \boxed{})(c - \boxed{})$

Factors of 20	Sum of Factors
$\boxed{}$ and -20	$\boxed{}$
$\boxed{}$ and -10	$\boxed{}$
$\boxed{}$ and $\boxed{}$	$\boxed{}$

Quick Check

1. Factor each expression. Check your answer.

   a. $g^2 + 7g + 10$ **b.** $v^2 + 21v + 20$ **c.** $a^2 + 13a + 30$

2. **a.** $k^2 - 10k + 25$ **b.** $x^2 - 11x + 18$ **c.** $q^2 - 15q + 36$

Name_____ Class_____ Date _____

Examples

❸ Factoring Trinomials With a Negative *c*

a. Factor $x^2 + 13x - 48$.
Identify the pair of factors of -48
that has a sum of 13.

Factors of -48	Sum of Factors
☐ and -48	☐
48 and ☐	☐
☐ and -24	☐
24 and ☐	☐
☐ and -16	☐
16 and ☐	☐

$x^2 + 13x - 48 = \left(x + \boxed{}\right)\left(x - \boxed{}\right)$

b. Factor $n^2 - 5n - 24$.
Identify the pair of factors of -24
that has a sum of -5.

Factors of -24	Sum of Factors
☐ and -24	☐
24 and ☐	☐
☐ and -12	☐
12 and ☐	☐
☐ and -8	☐

$n^2 - 5n - 24 = \left(n + \boxed{}\right)\left(n - \boxed{}\right)$

❹ Factoring Trinomials With Two Variables
Factor $d^2 + 17dg - 60g^2$.

Find the factors of -60. Identify the pair that has
a sum of 17.

$d^2 + 17dg - 60g^2 = \left(d - \boxed{}g\right)\left(d + \boxed{}g\right)$

Factors of -60	Sum of Factors
☐ and -60	☐
60 and ☐	☐
☐ and -30	☐
30 and ☐	☐
☐ and -20	☐
20 and ☐	☐

Quick Check

3. Factor each expression.

a. $m^2 + 8m - 20$

b. $p^2 - 3p - 40$

c. $y^2 - y - 56$

4. a. $x^2 + 11xy + 24y^2$

b. $v^2 + 2vw - 48w^2$

c. $m^2 - 17mn - 60n^2$

Lesson 9-6

Factoring Trinomials
of the Type $ax^2 + bx + c$

Lesson Objective	**NAEP 2005 Strand:** Algebra
▼ Factor trinomials of the type $ax^2 + bx + c$	**Topic:** Variables, Expressions, and Operations
	Local Standards: _____

Key Concepts

FOIL = first, outer, inner, last

product is a product is c

$(\blacksquare x + \blacksquare)\ (\blacksquare x + \blacksquare)$

sum of products is b

Examples

❶ c Is Positive Factor $20x^2 + 17x + 3$.

$$20x^2 \qquad\qquad + 17x \qquad\qquad\qquad + 3$$

$$\boxed{\text{F}} \qquad\qquad \boxed{\text{O}} \qquad \boxed{\text{I}} \qquad\qquad \boxed{\text{L}}$$

factors of a $\boxed{} \cdot 20$ $\qquad 1 \cdot 3 + 1 \cdot 20 = \boxed{}$ $\qquad 1 \cdot 3$ factors of c

$\qquad\qquad\qquad\qquad\qquad 1 \cdot 1 + 3 \cdot 20 = \boxed{}$ $\qquad 3 \cdot 1$

$\qquad\qquad 2 \cdot \boxed{}$ $\qquad 2 \cdot \boxed{} + \boxed{} \cdot 10 = \boxed{}$ $\qquad 1 \cdot 3$

$\qquad\qquad\qquad\qquad\qquad 2 \cdot 1 + 3 \cdot 10 = \boxed{}$ $\qquad 3 \cdot 1$

$\qquad\qquad \boxed{} \cdot 5$ $\qquad \boxed{} \cdot 3 + 1 \cdot 5 = \boxed{}$ $\qquad 1 \cdot 3$

$$20x^2 + 17x + 3 = (\boxed{} + 1)(\boxed{} + 3)$$

❷ c Is Negative Factor $3n^2 - 7n - 6$.

$$3n^2 \qquad\qquad -7n \qquad\qquad\qquad -6$$

$(1)(3)$ $\qquad (1)(-6) + (\boxed{})(3) = \boxed{}$ $\qquad (1)(-6)$

$\qquad\qquad (\boxed{})(1) + (-6)(3) = \boxed{}$ $\qquad (-6)(1)$

$\qquad\qquad (1)(-3) + (\boxed{})(3) = \boxed{}$ $\qquad (2)(-3)$

$\qquad\qquad (1)(\boxed{}) + (-3)(3) = \boxed{}$ $\qquad (-3)(2)$

$$3n^2 - 7n - 6 = (\boxed{} - 3)(\boxed{} + 2)$$

Daily Notetaking Guide

❸ Factoring Out a Monomial First Factor $18x^2 + 33x - 30$ completely.

$18x^2 + 33x - 30 = \boxed{}\left(6x^2 + \boxed{}x - \boxed{}\right)$ **Factor out the GCF.**

Factor $6x^2 + 11x - 10$.

$6x^2$	$+ 11x$	$- 10$
$(2)(3)$	$(2)(-10) + (1)\left(\boxed{}\right) = \boxed{}$	$(1)(-10)$
	$\left(\boxed{}\right)(1) + (-10)(3) = \boxed{}$	$(-10)(1)$
	$(2)(-5) + \left(\boxed{}\right)(3) = \boxed{}$	$(2)(-5)$
	$(2)(2) + (-5)(3) = \boxed{}$	$(-5)(2)$
	$(2)\left(\boxed{}\right) + (5)\left(\boxed{}\right) = \boxed{}$	$(5)(-2)$

$6x^2 + 11x - 10 = \left(\boxed{} + 5\right)\left(\boxed{} - 2\right)$

$18x^2 + 33x - 30 = \boxed{}\left(2x + \boxed{}\right)\left(3x - \boxed{}\right)$ **Include the GCF in your final answer.**

Quick Check

1. Factor each expression.

a. $2y^2 + 5y + 2$

b. $6n^2 - 23n + 7$

c. $2y^2 - 5y + 2$

2. a. $5d^2 - 14d - 3$

b. $2n^2 + n - 3$

c. $20p^2 - 31p - 9$

3. a. $2v^2 - 12v + 10$

b. $4y^2 + 14y + 6$

c. $18k^2 - 12k - 6$

Lesson 9-7

Lesson Objectives	**NAEP 2005 Strand:** Algebra
V1 Factor perfect-square trinomials	**Topic:** Variables, Expressions, and Operations
V2 Factor the difference of squares	**Local Standards:** _____

Vocabulary and Key Concepts

Perfect-Square Trinomials

For every real number a and b:

$a^2 + 2ab + b^2 = (a + b)(a + b) = $ ⬚

$a^2 - 2ab + b^2 = (a - b)(a - b) = $ ⬚

Examples

$x^2 + 10x + 25 = (x + 5)(x + 5) = (x + 5)^2$ $x^2 - 10x + 25 = (x - 5)(x - 5) = (x - 5)^2$

Difference of Two Squares

For every real number a and b:

$a^2 - b^2 = $ ⬚

Examples

$x^2 - 81 = (x + 9)(x - 9)$ $16x^2 - 49 = (4x + 7)(4x - 7)$

You can factor a perfect-square trinomial into _____

Example

① **Factoring a Perfect-Square Trinomial with $a = 1$** Factor $m^2 - 6m + 9$.

$m^2 - 6m + 9 = m \cdot m - 6m + 3 \cdot 3$ **Rewrite first and last terms.**

$= m \cdot m - \boxed{}\left(m \cdot \boxed{}\right) + 3 \cdot 3$ **Does the middle term equal 2ab? 6m =** ⬚ .

$= \left(m - \boxed{}\right)^2$ **Write the factors as the square of a binomial.**

Quick Check

1. Factor each expression.

a. $x^2 + 8x + 16$ **b.** $n^2 + 16n + 64$ **c.** $n^2 - 16n + 64$

Examples

❷ Factoring a Perfect-Square Trinomial with $a \neq 1$ The area of a square is $(16h^2 + 40h + 25)$ in.^{2}. Find the length of a side.

$16h^2 + 40h + 25 = \left(\boxed{}\right)^2 + 40h + \boxed{}^2$ Write $16h^2$ as $\left(\boxed{}\right)^2$ and 25 as $\boxed{}^2$.

Does the middle term equal $2ab$?

$= (4h)^2 + 2\left(\boxed{}\right)(5) + 5^2$ $40h = 2\left(\boxed{}\right)(5)$ ✔

$= \left(\boxed{} + \boxed{}\right)^2$ Write the factors as the square of a binomial.

The side of the square has a length of $\boxed{}$ in.

❸ The Difference of Two Squares for $a = 1$ Factor $a^2 - 16$.

$a^2 - 16 = a^2 - \boxed{}^2$ Rewrite 16 as $\boxed{}^2$.

$= \left(a + \boxed{}\right)\left(a - \boxed{}\right)$ Factor.

Check Use FOIL to multiply.

$(a + \boxed{})(a - \boxed{})$

$a^2 - \boxed{} + 4a - \boxed{}$

$a^2 - \boxed{}$ ✔

Quick Check

2. Factor each expression.

   a. $9g^2 - 12g + 4$

   b. $4t^2 + 36t + 81$

   c. $4t^2 - 36t + 81$

3. Factor each expression. Check your answer.

   a. $x^2 - 36$

   b. $m^2 - 100$

   c. $p^2 - 49$

Examples

❹ The Difference of Two Squares for *a ≠ 1* Factor $9b^2 - 25$.

$9b^2 - 25 = \left(\boxed{}\right)^2 - \boxed{}^2$ **Rewrite $9b^2$ as $\left(\boxed{}\right)^2$ and 25 as $\boxed{}^2$.**

$ = \left(3b + \boxed{}\right)\left(\boxed{} - 5\right)$ **Factor.**

❺ Factoring Out a Common Factor Factor $5x^2 - 80$.

$5x^2 - 80 = \boxed{}\left(x^2 - \boxed{}\right)$ **Factor out the GCF of $\boxed{}$.**

$ = \boxed{}\left(x + \boxed{}\right)\left(x - \boxed{}\right)$ **Factor ($x^2 - 16$).**

Check   Use FOIL to multiply the binomials. Then multiply by the GCF.

$\boxed{}\left(x + \boxed{}\right)\left(x - \boxed{}\right)$

$5\left(x^2 - \boxed{}\right)$

$5x^2 - 80$ ✔

Quick Check

4. Factor each expression.

   a. $9v^2 - 4$ **b.** $25x^2 - 64$ **c.** $4w^2 - 49$

5. Factor each expression.

   a. $8y^2 - 50$ **b.** $3c^2 - 75$ **c.** $28k^2 - 7$

Lesson 9-8

Factoring by Grouping

Lesson Objectives	**NAEP 2005 Strand:** Algebra
▼ Factor polynomials with four terms ▼ Factor trinomials by grouping	**Topic:** Variables, Expressions, and Operations **Local Standards:** _____

Vocabulary and Key Concepts

Factoring Polynomials

1. Factor out the greatest common factor (GCF).
2. If the polynomial has two terms or three terms, look for a difference of two squares, a product of two squares, or a pair of binomial factors.
3. If there are four or more terms, group terms and factor to find common binomial factors.
4. As a final check, make sure there are no common factors other than 1.

Factor by grouping is _____

_____

Examples

❶ Factoring a Four-Term Polynomial Factor $6x^3 + 3x^2 - 4x - 2$.

$6x^3 + 3x^2 - 4x - 2 = \boxed{}(2x + 1) - 2\left(\boxed{}\right)$ Factor the GCF from each group of two terms.

$= \left(\boxed{}\right)(3x^2 - 2)$ Factor out $\left(\boxed{}\right)$.

Check $6x^3 + 3x^2 - 4x - 2 \stackrel{?}{=} \left(\boxed{}\right)(3x^2 - 2)$

$= 6x^3 - \boxed{} + \boxed{} - 2$ Use FOIL.

$= 6x^3 + 3x^2 - 4x - 2$ ✔   Write in standard form.

❷ Factoring Completely Factor $8t^4 + 12t^3 + 16t + 24$.

$8t^4 + 12t^3 + 16t + 24 = \boxed{}\left(2\boxed{} + 3t^3 + \boxed{} + 6\right)$ Factor out the GCF, $\boxed{}$.

$= 4\left[\boxed{}\left(2t + \boxed{}\right) + 2\left(\boxed{} + 3\right)\right]$ Factor by grouping.

$= 4(2t + 3)\left(\boxed{} + 2\right)$ Factor again.

❸ **Finding the Dimensions of a Rectangular Prism** A rectangular prism has
a volume of $36x^3 + 51x^2 + 18x$. Factor to find the possible expressions for
the length, width, and height of the prism.

Factor $36x^3 + 51x^2 + 18x$.

Step 1 $\boxed{}(12x^2 + \boxed{} + 6)$ Factor out the GCF, $\boxed{}$.

Step 2 $12 \cdot 6 = \boxed{}$ Find the product ac.

Step 3 Factors   →   Sum

$4 \cdot \boxed{}$ → $4 + \boxed{} = \boxed{}$ Find two factors of ac that have sum b.

$\boxed{} \cdot 12$ → $\boxed{} + 12 = \boxed{}$ Use mental math to determine a good place to start.

$8 \cdot \boxed{}$ → $8 + \boxed{} = \boxed{}$

Step 4 $3x\left(12x^2 + \boxed{} + 9x + \boxed{}\right)$ Rewrite the trinomial.

Step 5 $3x\left[\boxed{}(3x + 2) + \boxed{}(3x + 2)\right]$ Factor by grouping.

$3x\left(\boxed{} + 3\right)\left(3x + \boxed{}\right)$ Factor again.

The possible dimensions of the prism are $\boxed{}$, $\boxed{}$, and $\boxed{}$.

Quick Check

1. Factor each expression. Check your answer.

a. $5t^4 + 20t^3 + 6t + 24$ **b.** $2w^3 + w^2 - 14w - 7$ **2.** $45m^4 - 9m^3 + 30m^2 - 6m$

3. Find expressions for the possible dimensions of each rectangular prism.

a.

$6g^3 + 20g^2 + 16g$

b.

$3m^3 + 10m^2 + 3m$

Name_____ Class_____ Date_____

Lesson 10-1

Exploring Quadratic Graphs

Lesson Objectives

▼ Graph quadratic functions of the form $y = ax^2$

▼ Graph quadratic functions of the form $y = ax^2 + c$

NAEP 2005 Strand: Algebra

Topics: Patterns, Relations, and Functions; Algebraic Representations

Local Standards: _____

Vocabulary and Key Concepts

Standard Form of a Quadratic Function

A quadratic function is a function that can be written in the form

$y = $ [_____], where $a \neq 0$. This form is called the

[_____] form of a quadratic function.

Examples $y = 5x^2$ $y = x^2 + 7$ $y = x^2 - x - 3$

A parabola is _____

The axis of symmetry is _____

_____

A vertex is _____

The minimum is _____

_____

The maximum is _____

_____

Examples

❶ **Identifying a Vertex** Identify the vertex of each graph. Tell whether it is a minimum or a maximum.

a.

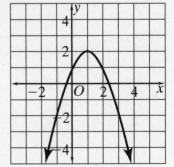

The vertex is [_____].

It is a [_____].

b.

The vertex is [_____].

It is a [_____].

❷ Graphing $y = ax^2 + c$ Graph the quadratic functions $y = 3x^2$ and $y = 3x^2 - 2$. Compare the graphs.

x	$y = 3x^2$	$y = 3x^2 - 2$
2	12	☐
1	☐	1
0	0	☐
−1	☐	1
−2	12	☐

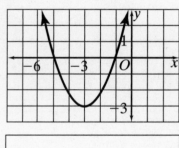

The graph of $y = 3x^2 - 2$ has the same shape as the graph of $y = 3x^2$, but is shifted down ☐ units.

Quick Check

1. Identify the vertex of each graph. Tell whether it is a minimum or maximum.

a.

☐

b.

☐

2. a. Graph $y = x^2$ and $y = x^2 - 4$. Compare the graphs.

b. Critical Thinking Describe what positive and negative values of c do to the position of the vertex of $y = x^2$.

Example

❸ Applying Graphs of Quadratic Functions A monkey drops an orange from a branch 26 ft above ground. The force of gravity causes the orange to fall toward Earth. The function $h = -16t^2 + 26$ gives the height of the orange, h, in feet after t seconds. Graph this quadratic function.

t	$h = -16t^2 + 26$
0	26
0.25	
0.5	
0.75	
1	
1.25	

Time (seconds)

Height h is dependent on time t. Graph t on the x-axis and h on the y-axis. Use nonnegative values for t.

Quick Check

3. a. Suppose a squirrel is in a tree 24 ft above the ground. She drops an acorn. The function $h = -16t^2 + 24$ gives the height of the acorn, h, in feet after t seconds. Graph this quadratic function.

b. Critical Thinking Describe a reasonable domain and range for the function in Example 3.

Lesson 10-2

Quadratic Functions

<table>
<tr><td>

Lesson Objectives

▼**1** Graph quadratic functions of the form $y = ax^2 + bx + c$

▼**2** Graph quadratic inequalities

</td><td>

NAEP 2005 Strand: Algebra

Topics: Patterns, Relations, and Functions; Algebraic Representations; Equations and Inequalities

Local Standards: _____

</td></tr>
</table>

Key Concepts

Graph of a Quadratic Function

The graph of $y = ax^2 + bx + c$, where $a \neq 0$, has the line $x = \boxed{}$ as its axis of symmetry. The x-coordinate of the vertex is $\boxed{}$.

Examples

❶ **Graphing $y = ax^2 + bx + c$** Graph the function $y = 2x^2 + 4x - 3$.

Step 1 Find the equation of the axis of symmetry and the coordinates of the vertex.

$$x = -\frac{b}{2a} = -\frac{\boxed{}}{2\left(\boxed{}\right)} = \boxed{}$$ **Find the equation of the axis of symmetry.**

The x-coordinate of the vertex is $\boxed{}$.

$y = 2x^2 + 4x - 3$

$y = 2\left(\boxed{}\right)^2 + 4\left(\boxed{}\right) - 3$ **To find the y-coordinate of the vertex, substitute $\boxed{}$ for x.**

$= \boxed{}$

The vertex is $\boxed{}$.

Step 2 Find two other points.
Use the y-intercept.

For $x = 0$, $y = \boxed{}$, so one point is $\boxed{}$.

Choose a value for x on the same side of the vertex.

Let $x = 1$

$y = 2(\boxed{})^2 + 4(\boxed{}) - 3$ **Find the y-coordinate for $x = 1$.**

$= \boxed{}$

For $x = 1$, $y = \boxed{}$, so another point is $\boxed{}$.

Step 3 Reflect $(0, -3)$ and $(1, 3)$ across the axis of symmetry to get two more points. Then draw the parabola.

❷ Graphing Quadratic Inequalities Graph the quadratic inequality
$y > -x^2 + 6x - 5$.

Graph the boundary curve, $y \boxed{} -x^2 + 6x - 5$.

Use a $\boxed{}$ curve because the solution of the inequality
$y > -x^2 + 6x - 5$ does not include the boundary.

Shade $\boxed{}$ the curve.

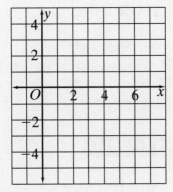

Quick Check

1. Graph $f(x) = x^2 - 6x + 9$. Label the axis of symmetry and the vertex.

2. Graph each quadratic inequality.

   a. $y \le x^2 + 2x - 5$

   b. $y > x^2 + x + 1$

Lesson 10-3

Solving Quadratic Equations

Lesson Objectives	**NAEP 2005 Strand:** Algebra
▼ Solve quadratic equations by graphing	**Topic:** Equations and Inequalities
▼ Solve quadratic equations using square roots	**Local Standards:** _____

Key Concepts

Standard Form of a Quadratic Equation

A quadratic equation is an equation that can be written in the form [   ]

where $a \neq 0$. This form is called the [   ] form of a quadratic equation.

Example

1 **Solving by Graphing** Solve each equation by graphing the related function.

a. $2x^2 = 0$

Graph $y = 2x^2$

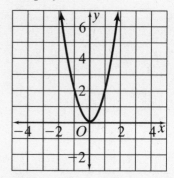

There is one solution,

$x = $ [   ].

b. $2x^2 + 2 = 0$

Graph $y = 2x^2 + 2$

There is [   ] solution.

c. $2x^2 - 2 = 0$

Graph $y = 2x^2 - 2$

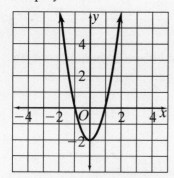

There are two solutions,

$x = $ [   ] and $x = $ [   ].

Quick Check

1. Solve each equation by graphing the related function.

a. $x^2 - 1 = 0$

b. $2x^2 + 4 = 0$

c. $x^2 - 16 = -16$

Daily Notetaking Guide

Examples

❷ Using Square Roots Solve $3x^2 - 75 = 0$.

$3x^2 - 75 + \boxed{} = 0 + \boxed{}$ **Add** $\boxed{}$ **to each side.**

$3x^2 = \boxed{}$

$x^2 = \boxed{}$ **Divide each side by** $\boxed{}$.

$x = \pm\sqrt{\boxed{}}$ **Find the square roots.**

$x = \boxed{}$ **Simplify.**

❸ Applying Quadratic Equations A museum is planning an exhibit that will contain a large globe. The surface area of the globe will be 315 ft^2. Find the radius of the sphere. Use the equation $S = 4\pi r^2$, where S is the surface area and r is the radius.

$S = 4\pi r^2$

$\boxed{} = 4\pi r^2$ **Substitute** $\boxed{}$ **for S.**

$\dfrac{\boxed{}}{4\pi} = r^2$ **Put in calculator-ready form.**

$\sqrt{\dfrac{\boxed{}}{4\pi}} = r$ **Find the principal square root.**

$\boxed{} \approx r$ **Use a calculator.**

The radius of the sphere is about $\boxed{}$ ft.

Quick Check

2. Solve each equation.

   a. $t^2 - 25 = 0$ **b.** $3n^2 + 12 = 12$ **c.** $2g^2 + 32 = 0$

3. A city is planning a circular fountain. The depth of the fountain will be 3 ft. The maximum volume will be 1800 ft.^{3} Find the radius of the fountain using the equation $V = \pi r^2 h$, where V is the volume, r is the radius, and h is the depth.

Lesson 10-4

Factoring to Solve Quadratic Equations

Lesson Objective	NAEP 2005 Strand: Algebra
▼ Solve quadratic equations by factoring	**Topic:** Equations and Inequalities
	Local Standards: _____

Key Concepts

Zero-Product Property

For every real number a and b, if $ab = 0$, then $a = \boxed{}$ or $b = \boxed{}$.

Example If $(x + 3)(x + 2) = 0$, then $x + 3 = 0$ or $x + 2 = 0$.

Examples

❶ **Using the Zero-Product Property** Solve $(2x + 3)(x - 4) = 0$ by using the Zero-Product Property.

$(2x + 3)(x - 4) = 0$

$2x + 3 = 0$ or $x - 4 = 0$ **Use the Zero-Product Property.**

$2x = \boxed{}$ **Solve for x.**

$x = \boxed{}$ or $x = \boxed{}$

Check Substitute $\boxed{}$ for x.   Substitute $\boxed{}$ for x.

$(2x + 3)(x - 4) = 0$ $(2x + 3)(x - 4) = 0$

$[2\left(\boxed{}\right) + 3]\left(\boxed{} - 4\right) \stackrel{?}{=} 0$ $[2\left(\boxed{}\right) + 3]\left(\boxed{} - 4\right) \stackrel{?}{=} 0$

$(0)\left(-5\tfrac{1}{2}\right) = 0 ✓$ $\left(\boxed{}\right)(0) = 0 ✓$

❷ **Solving by Factoring** Solve $x^2 + x - 42 = 0$ by factoring.

$x^2 + x - 42 = 0$

$\left(x + \boxed{}\right)\left(x - \boxed{}\right) = 0$ **Factor $x^2 + x - 42$.**

$x + \boxed{} = 0$ or $x - \boxed{} = 0$ **Use the Zero-Product Property.**

$x = \boxed{}$ or $x = \boxed{}$ **Solve for x.**

❸ Applying the Zero-Product Property The diagram shows a pattern for an open-top box. The total area of the sheet of material used to make the box is 130 in.^{2}. The height of the box is 1 in. Therefore, 1 in. × 1 in. squares are cut from each corner. Find the dimensions of the box.

Define   Let $\boxed{x}$ = width of a side of the box.

Then the width of the material = $x + 1 + 1 = \boxed{}$.

Then the length of the material = $x + 3 + 1 + 1 = \boxed{}$.

Relate   width $\times$ length $=$ area of the sheet

Write $(x + 2) \quad (x + 5) \quad = \quad \boxed{}$

$x^2 + \boxed{} + 10 = 130$ **Find the product** $\left(x + \boxed{}\right)\left(x + \boxed{}\right)$.

$x^2 + 7x - \boxed{} = 0$ **Subtract** $\boxed{}$ **from each side.**

$\left(x - \boxed{}\right)\left(x + \boxed{}\right) = 0$ **Factor** $x^2 + 7x - \boxed{}$.

$x - \boxed{} = 0$ or $x + \boxed{} = 0$ **Use the Zero-Product Property.**

$x = \boxed{}$ or $x = \boxed{}$ **Solve for x.**

The only reasonable solution is $\boxed{}$. So the dimensions of the box are

$\boxed{}$ in. $\times$ $\boxed{}$ in. $\times$ $\boxed{}$ in.

Quick Check

1. Solve each equation.

   a. $(x + 7)(x - 4) = 0$ **b.** $(3y - 5)(y - 2) = 0$ **2.** Solve $x^2 - 8x - 48 = 0$ by factoring.

3. Suppose that a box has a base with a width of x, a length of $x + 1$, and a height of 2 in. It is cut from a rectangular sheet of material with an area of 182 in.^{2}. Find the dimensions of the box.

Lesson 10-5

Completing the Square

Lesson Objective ▼ Solve quadratic equations by completing the square	**NAEP 2005 Strand:** Algebra **Topic:** Equations and Inequalities **Local Standards:** _____

Vocabulary

Completing the square is _____

_____

Examples

❶ Finding n to Complete the Square Find the value of c to complete the square for $x^2 - 16x + c$.

The value of b in the expression $x^2 - 16x + c$ is [   ].

The term to add to $x^2 - 16x$ is [   ].

❷ Solving $x^2 + bx = c$ Solve the equation $x^2 + 5x = 50$ by completing the square.

Step 1 Write the left side of $x^2 + 5x = 50$ as a perfect square.

$x^2 + 5x = 50$

$x^2 + 5x + \left(\boxed{} \right)^2 = 50 + \left(\boxed{} \right)^2$ Add $\left(\boxed{} \right)^2$, or $\frac{25}{4}$, to each side.

$\left(x + \frac{5}{2} \right)^2 = \dfrac{\boxed{}}{4} + \dfrac{\boxed{}}{4}$ Write $x^2 + 5x + \left(\frac{5}{2} \right)^2$ as a square.

$\left(x + \frac{5}{2} \right)^2 = \dfrac{\boxed{}}{4}$ Simplify.

Step 2 Solve the equation.

$\left(x + \frac{5}{2} \right) = \pm \sqrt{\frac{225}{4}}$ Find the square root of each side.

$x + \frac{5}{2} = \pm \dfrac{\boxed{}}{2}$ Simplify.

$x + \frac{5}{2} = \boxed{}$ or $x + \frac{5}{2} = \boxed{}$ Write as two equations.

$x = \boxed{}$ or $x = \boxed{}$ Solve for x.

Quick Check

1. Find the value of n such that $x^2 + 22x + n$ is a perfect square trinomial.

Example

❸ **Solving $x^2 + bx + c = 0$** Solve $x^2 + 10x - 16 = 0$ by completing the square. Round to the nearest hundredth.

Step 1 Rewrite the equation in the form $x^2 + bx = c$ and complete the square.

$$x^2 + 10x - 16 = 0$$

$x^2 + 10x = \boxed{}$ **Add** $\boxed{}$ **to each side of the equation.**

$x^2 + 10x + \boxed{} = 16 + \boxed{}$ **Add** $\left(\boxed{}\right)^2$**, or** $\boxed{}$**, to each side of the equation.**

$\left(x + \boxed{}\right)^2 = \boxed{}$ **Write** $x^2 + 10x + 25$ **as a square.**

Step 2 Solve the equation.

$x + 5 = \pm \sqrt{\boxed{}}$ **Find the square root of each side.**

$x + 5 \approx \pm \boxed{}$ **Use a calculator.**

$x + 5 \approx \boxed{}$ or $x + 5 \approx \boxed{}$ **Write as two equations.**

$x \approx \boxed{} - \boxed{}$ or $x \approx \boxed{} - \boxed{}$ **Subtract** $\boxed{}$ **from each side.**

$x \approx \boxed{}$ or $x \approx \boxed{}$ **Simplify.**

Quick Check

2. Solve the equation $m^2 - 6m = 247$.

3. Solve each equation. Round to the nearest hundredth.

a. $x^2 + 5x + 3 = 0$

b. $x^2 - 14x + 16 = 0$

Example

❹ Applying the Complete-the-Square Method Suppose you wish to section off a soccer field as shown in the diagram to run a variety of practice drills. If the area of the field is 6,000 yd², what is the value of x?

Define | width | $= x + 10 + 10 =$ | _____ |.

| length | $= x + x + 10 + 10 =$ | _____ |.

Relate | Length | $\times$ | width | $=$ | area |.

Write $\left(\boxed{}\right)\left(\boxed{}\right) = \boxed{}$

$2x^2 + \boxed{} + \boxed{} = \boxed{}$

Step 1 Rewrite the equation in the form $x^2 + bx = c$.

$2x^2 + \boxed{} + \boxed{} = \boxed{}$

$2x^2 + \boxed{} = \boxed{}$ Subtract $\boxed{}$ from each side.

$x^2 + \boxed{} = \boxed{}$ Divide each side by $\boxed{}$.

Step 2 Complete the square.

$x^2 + 30x + \boxed{} = 2{,}800 + \boxed{}$ Add $\left(\frac{30}{2}\right)^2$, or $\boxed{}$, to each side.

$\left(x + \boxed{}\right)^2 = \boxed{}$ Write $x^2 + 30x + \boxed{}$ as a square.

Step 3 Solve the equation.

$(x + 15) = \pm\sqrt{\boxed{}}$ Take the square root of each side.

$x + 15 = \pm\boxed{}$ Use a calculator.

$x + 15 = \boxed{}$ or $x + 15 = \boxed{}$ Write as two equations.

$x = \boxed{}$ or $x = \boxed{}$ Use the positive answer for this problem.

The value of x is $\boxed{}$ yd.

Quick Check

4. Solve each equation. Round to the nearest hundredth.

a. $4a^2 + 8a = 24$

b. $5n^2 - 3n - 15 = 10$

Lesson 10-6

Lesson Objectives	NAEP 2005 Strand: Algebra
❶ Use the quadratic formula when solving quadratic equations	**Topic:** Equations and Inequalities
❷ Choose an appropriate method for solving a quadratic equation	**Local Standards:** _____

Key Concepts

Quadratic Formula

If $ax^2 + bx + c = 0$, and $a \neq 0$, then $x = \dfrac{-b\,\square \pm \sqrt{\square^2 - 4\,\square\,\square}}{2\,\square}$.

Example

❶ **Using the Quadratic Formula** Solve $x^2 + 2 = -3x$ using the quadratic formula.

$x^2 + 3x + 2 = 0$ **Add** ☐ **to each side and write in standard form.**

$x = \boxed{}$ **Use the quadratic formula.**

$x = \dfrac{-\square \pm \sqrt{(\square)^2 - 4(\square)(\square)}}{2(\square)}$ **Substitute** ☐ **for** *a*, ☐ **for** *b*, **and** ☐ **for** *c*.

$x = \dfrac{\square \pm \sqrt{\square}}{\square}$ **Simplify.**

$x = \dfrac{-3 + \square}{2}$ or $x = \dfrac{-3 - \square}{2}$ **Write two solutions.**

$x = \boxed{}$ or $x = \boxed{}$ **Simplify.**

Check   for $x = \boxed{}$ for $x = \boxed{}$

$(\boxed{})^2 + 3(\boxed{}) + 2 \stackrel{?}{=} 0$ $(\boxed{})^2 + 3(\boxed{}) + 2 \stackrel{?}{=} 0$

$\quad\quad 1 - 3 + 2 \stackrel{?}{=} 0$ $\quad\quad 4 - 6 + 2 \stackrel{?}{=} 0$

$\quad\quad\quad\quad 0 = 0 \checkmark$ $\quad\quad\quad\quad 0 = 0 \checkmark$

Quick Check

1. Use the quadratic formula to solve each equation.

   a. $x^2 - 2x - 8 = 0$ **b.** $x^2 - 4x = 117$

Examples

❷ Applying the Quadratic Formula A child throws a ball upward with an initial upward velocity of 15 ft/s from a height of 2 ft. If no one catches the ball, after how many seconds will it land? Use the vertical motion formula $h = -16t^2 + vt + c$, where $h = 0$, v = velocity, c = starting height, and t = time to land. Round to the nearest hundredth of a second.

Step 1 Use the vertical motion formula.

$$h = -16t^2 + vt + c$$

$$0 = -16t^2 + \boxed{}t + \boxed{} \quad \text{Substitute } \boxed{} \text{ for } h, \boxed{} \text{ for } v, \text{ and } \boxed{} \text{ for } c.$$

Step 2 Use the quadratic formula.

$$x = \frac{-\boxed{} \pm \sqrt{\boxed{}^{\boxed{}} - \boxed{}}}{\boxed{}}$$

$$t = \frac{-\boxed{} \pm \sqrt{\boxed{}^2 - 4(\boxed{})(\boxed{})}}{2(\boxed{})} \quad \begin{array}{l}\text{Substitute } \boxed{} \text{ for } a, \boxed{} \text{ for } b, \\ \boxed{} \text{ for } c, \text{ and } t \text{ for } x.\end{array}$$

$$t = \frac{-\boxed{} \pm \sqrt{\boxed{} + \boxed{}}}{\boxed{}} \quad \text{Simplify.}$$

$$t = \frac{-\boxed{} \pm \sqrt{\boxed{}}}{\boxed{}}$$

$$t \approx \frac{-\boxed{} + \boxed{}}{-32} \quad \text{or} \quad t \approx \frac{-\boxed{} - \boxed{}}{-32} \quad \text{Write two solutions.}$$

$$t \approx \boxed{} \quad \text{or} \quad t \approx \boxed{} \quad \begin{array}{l}\text{Simplify. Use the positive answer} \\ \text{because it is the only reasonable solution.}\end{array}$$

The ball will land in about $\boxed{}$ seconds.

❸ Choosing an Appropriate Method Which method(s) would you choose to solve each equation? Justify your reasoning.

a. $5x^2 + 8x - 14 = 0$ $\boxed{}$; the equation

$\boxed{}$ be factored easily.

b. $25x^2 - 169 = 0$ Square $\boxed{}$; there is no x term.

c. $x^2 - 2x - 3 = 0$ $\boxed{}$; the equation $\boxed{}$

easily factorable.

d. $x^2 - 5x + 3 = 0$ $\boxed{}$, completing

the square, or graphing; the x^2 term is 1, but

the equation $\boxed{}$ factorable.

Quick Check

2. A football player kicks a ball with an initial upward velocity of 38.4 ft/s from a starting height of 3.5 ft.

   a. Substitute the values into the vertical motion formula from Example 2. Let $h = 0$.

   b. Solve the equation. If no one catches the ball, how long will it be in the air? Round to the nearest tenth of a second.

3. Which method(s) would you choose to solve each equation? Justify your reasoning.

   a. $13x^2 - 5x + 21 = 0$ **b.** $x^2 - x - 30 = 0$ **c.** $144x^2 = 25$

4. Solve each equation. Round to the nearest hundredth.

   a. $-3x^2 + 5x - 2 = 0$ **b.** $7x^2 - 2x - 8 = 0$

Lesson 10-7

Using the Discriminant

Lesson Objective	NAEP 2005 Strand: Algebra
▼ Find the number of solutions of a quadratic equation	**Topic:** Equations and Inequalities
	Local Standards: _____

Vocabulary and Key Concepts

Property of the Discriminant

For the quadratic equation $ax^2 + bx + c = 0$, where $a \neq 0$, you can use the value of the discriminant to determine the number of solutions.

If $b^2 - 4ac > 0$, there are [　　　] solutions.

If $b^2 - 4ac = 0$, there is [　　　] solution.

If $b^2 - 4ac < 0$, there are [　　　] solutions.

The discriminant is _____

_____

Example

❶ Using the Discriminant Find the number of solutions of $x^2 = -3x - 7$ using the discriminant.

$x^2 + 3x + 7 = 0$ **Write in standard form.**

$b^2 - 4ac = [\ ]^2 - 4([\ ])([\ ])$ **Evaluate the discriminant. Substitute for a, b, and c.**

$= 9 - [\ ]$ **Use the order of operations.**

$= [\ ]$ **Simplify.**

Since [　　] < 0, the equation has [　　] solution.

Quick Check

1. Find the number of solutions for each equation.

  a. $x^2 = 2x - 3$ **b.** $3x^2 - 4x = 7$ **c.** $5x^2 + 8 = 2x$

Example

❷ **Applying the Discriminant** A football is kicked from a starting height of 3 ft with an initial upward velocity of 40 ft/s. Will the football ever reach a height of 30 ft? Use the vertical motion formula $h = -16t^2 + vt + c$, where $h = 30$, $v = $ velocity, $c = $ starting height, and $t = $ time to land.

$$h = -16t^2 + vt + c$$ **Use the vertical motion formula.**

$$\boxed{} = -16t^2 + \boxed{}\,t + 3$$ **Substitute** $\boxed{}$ **for** h, $\boxed{}$ **for** v, **and** $\boxed{}$ **for** c.

$$0 = -16t^2 + 40t - \boxed{}$$ **Write in standard form.**

$$b^2 - 4ac = (40)^2 - 4\left(\boxed{}\right)\left(\boxed{}\right)$$ **Evaluate the discriminant.**

$$= \boxed{} - 1{,}728$$ **Use the order of operations.**

$$= \boxed{}$$ **Simplify.**

The discriminant is $\boxed{}$. The football $\boxed{}$ reach a height of 30 ft.

Quick Check

2. A construction worker on the ground tosses an apple to a fellow worker who is 20 ft above the ground. The starting height of the apple is 5 ft with an initial upward velocity of 32 ft/s. Will the apple reach the worker? Use the vertical motion formula.

Lesson 10-8

Lesson Objective	NAEP 2005 Strand: Algebra
▼ Choose a linear, quadratic, or exponential model for data	**Topic:** Algebraic Representations
	Local Standards: _____

Key Concepts

Linear, Quadratic, and Exponential Functions

Linear

$y =$ [____]

Quadratic

$y =$ [____]

Exponential

$y =$ [____]

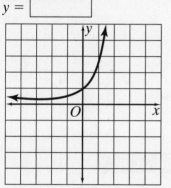

Examples

❶ **Choosing a Model by Graphing** Graph each set of points. Which model is most appropriate for each set?

a. $(-2, 2.25), (0, 3),$ $(1, 4), (2, 6)$

b. $(-2, -2), (0, 2),$ $(1, 4), (2, 6)$

c. $(-1, 5), (2, 11), (0, 3),$ $(1, 5), (-2, 11)$

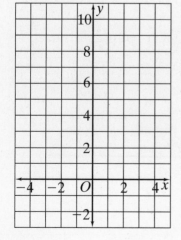

[_____]   [_____]   [_____]

Name_____ Class_____ Date _____

❷ Applying Graphing Models A local conservation organization collected the data in the table. It indicates the number of deer estimated to be living in the area over a five-year period. Determine which kind of function best models the data. Write an equation to model the data.

Year	Estimated Population
0	90
1	69
2	52
3	40
4	31

Step 1 Graph the data to decide which model is most appropriate.

The graph curves, and it does not

look quadratic. It may be

[   ].

Step 2: Test for a common ratio.

Year	Estimated Population
0	90
1	69
2	52
3	40
4	31

$69 \div 90 \approx 0.766$

$52 \div 69 \approx$ [   ]

$40 \div 52 \approx$ [   ]

$31 \div 40 =$ [   ]

There is a common ratio, about [   ].

The population of deer each year is about

[   ] times its value the previous year.

Step 3 Write an exponential model.

Relate $y = \boxed{a} \cdot \boxed{b}^x$

Define Let $\boxed{a}$ = the initial value, 90.

Let $\boxed{b}$ = the decay factor,

[   ].

Write $y = $ [   ] $\cdot$ [   ]^x

Step 4 Test x values 1 and 2.

$y = $ [   ] $\cdot$ [   ]^1 $y = $ [   ] $\cdot$ [   ]^2

$y \approx $ [   ] $y \approx $ [   ]

The predicted value $(1,$ [   ]$)$

matches the corresponding data point.

The point $(2,$ [   ]$)$ is close to the

data point $(2,$ [   ]$)$. The equation

$y = $ [   ] $\cdot$ [   ]^x models the data.

Quick Check

1. a. Graph this set of points: $(-1.5, -2), (0, 2), (1, 4), (2, 6)$.
Which model is most appropriate?

b. Which kind of function best models the data in the table? Write an equation to model the data.

x	y
0	4
1	4.4
2	4.84
3	5.324
4	5.8564

2. The profits of a small company are shown in the table at the right. Let $x = 0$ correspond to year 0.

a. Graph the data to determine which kind of function best models the data.

Year	Profit (dollars)
0	0
1	5,000
2	20,000
3	44,000
4	79,000

b. Write an equation to model the data.

Lesson 11-1

Simplifying Radicals

Lesson Objectives	**NAEP 2005 Strand:** Algebra
▼ Simplify radicals involving products ▼ Simplify radicals involving quotients	**Topic:** Variables, Expressions, and Operations **Local Standards:** _____

Key Concepts

Multiplication Property of Square Roots

For every number $a \geq 0$ and $b \geq 0$, $\sqrt{ab} = \boxed{} \cdot \boxed{}$.

Example $\sqrt{54} = \boxed{} \cdot \boxed{} = \boxed{} \cdot \sqrt{6} = 3\sqrt{6}$

Division Property of Square Roots

For every number $a \geq 0$ and $b > 0$, $\sqrt{\dfrac{a}{b}} = \dfrac{\boxed{}}{\boxed{}}$.

Example $\sqrt{\dfrac{16}{25}} = \dfrac{\boxed{}}{\boxed{}} = \dfrac{4}{5}$

Simplest Radical Form

A radical expression is in simplest radical form when all three statements are true.

• The radicand has no $\boxed{}$.

• The radicand has no $\boxed{}$.

• The $\boxed{}$ has no radical.

A radical expression is _____

Rationalize means _____

_____

_____

Examples

❶ Removing Variable Factors Simplify $\sqrt{28x^7}$.

$\sqrt{28x^7} = \sqrt{\boxed{}^{\boxed{}} \cdot 7x}$ $\boxed{}^{\boxed{}}$ is a perfect square and a factor of $28x^7$.

$= \sqrt{\boxed{}^{\boxed{}}} \cdot \sqrt{7x}$ Use the Multiplication Property of Square Roots.

$= \boxed{}^{\boxed{}} \sqrt{7x}$ Simplify $\sqrt{\boxed{}^{\boxed{}}}$.

② **Multiplying Two Radicals** Simplify each radical expression.

a. $\sqrt{12} \cdot \sqrt{32} = \sqrt{\boxed{} \cdot \boxed{}}$ Use the Multiplication Property of Square Roots.

$= \sqrt{\boxed{}}$ Simplify under the radical.

$= \sqrt{\boxed{} \cdot 6}$ $\boxed{}$ is a perfect square and a factor of 384.

$= \sqrt{\boxed{}} \cdot \sqrt{6}$ Use the Multiplication Property of Square Roots.

$= \boxed{}\sqrt{6}$ Simplify $\sqrt{\boxed{}}$.

b. $7\sqrt{5x} \cdot 3\sqrt{8x} = \boxed{}\sqrt{\boxed{}x^2}$ Multiply the whole numbers and use the Multiplication Property of Square Roots.

$= 21\sqrt{\boxed{}^{\boxed{}} \cdot 10}$ $\boxed{}^{\boxed{}}$ is a perfect square and a factor of $40x^2$.

$= 21\sqrt{\boxed{}^{\boxed{}}} \cdot \sqrt{10}$ Use the Multiplication Property of Square Roots.

$= 21 \cdot \boxed{}\sqrt{10}$ Simplify $\sqrt{\boxed{}^{\boxed{}}}$.

$= \boxed{}\sqrt{10}$ Simplify.

③ **Simplifying Radicals by Dividing** Simplify $\sqrt{\dfrac{75x^5}{48x}}$.

$\sqrt{\dfrac{75x^5}{48x}} = \sqrt{\dfrac{\boxed{}^{\boxed{}}}{\boxed{}}}$ Divide the numerator and denominator by $\boxed{}$.

$= \dfrac{\sqrt{\boxed{}^{\boxed{}}}}{\sqrt{\boxed{}}}$ Use the Division Property of Square Roots.

$= \dfrac{\sqrt{\boxed{}} \cdot \sqrt{\boxed{}}}{\sqrt{16}}$ Use the Multiplication Property of Square Roots.

$= \dfrac{\boxed{}^{\boxed{}}}{\boxed{}}$ Simplify $\sqrt{\boxed{}}, \sqrt{\boxed{}}$, and $\sqrt{\boxed{}}$.

Name_____ Class_____ Date _____

❹ Rationalizing a Denominator Simplify by rationalizing the denominator.

a. $\dfrac{3}{\sqrt{7}} = \dfrac{3}{\sqrt{7}} \cdot \dfrac{\boxed{}}{\boxed{}}$ Multiply by $\dfrac{\boxed{}}{\boxed{}}$ to make the denominator a perfect square.

$ = \dfrac{\boxed{}}{\boxed{}}$ Use the Multiplication Property of Square Roots.

$ = \dfrac{3\sqrt{7}}{7}$ Simplify $\boxed{}$.

b. $\dfrac{\sqrt{11}}{\sqrt{12x^3}} = \dfrac{\sqrt{11}}{\sqrt{12x^3}} \cdot \dfrac{\boxed{}}{\boxed{}}$ Multiply by $\dfrac{\boxed{}}{\boxed{}}$ to make the denominator a perfect square.

$ = \dfrac{\boxed{}}{\boxed{}}$ Use the Multiplication Property of Square Roots.

$ = \dfrac{\sqrt{33x}}{6x^2}$ Simplify $\boxed{}$.

Quick Check

Simplify each radical expression.

1. $-a\sqrt{60a^7}$

2. a. $\sqrt{13} \cdot \sqrt{52}$

b. $5\sqrt{3c} \cdot \sqrt{6c}$

3. $\sqrt{\dfrac{27x^3}{3x}}$

4. a. $\dfrac{3}{\sqrt{3}}$

b. $\dfrac{\sqrt{5}}{\sqrt{18t}}$

Lesson 11-2   **Operations With Radical Expressions**

Lesson Objectives	NAEP 2005 Strand: Algebra
▼ Simplify sums and differences	**Topic:** Variables, Expressions and Operations
▼ Simplify products and quotients	**Local Standards:** _____

Vocabulary

Like radicals are _____

_____

Unlike radicals are _____

_____

Conjugates are _____

_____

Examples

❶ Combining Like Radicals Simplify $4\sqrt{3} + \sqrt{3}$.

$4\sqrt{3} + \sqrt{3} = \boxed{}\sqrt{3} + \boxed{}\sqrt{3}$ **Both terms contain** $\sqrt{\boxed{}}$.

$= (\boxed{} + \boxed{})\sqrt{3}$ **Use the Distributive Property to combine like radicals.**

$= \boxed{}\sqrt{3}$ **Simplify.**

❷ Simplifying to Combine Like Radicals Simplify $8\sqrt{5} - \sqrt{45}$.

$8\sqrt{5} - \sqrt{45} = 8\sqrt{5} - \sqrt{\boxed{} \cdot 5}$ $\boxed{}$ **is a perfect square and a factor of 45.**

$= 8\sqrt{5} - \sqrt{\boxed{}} \cdot \sqrt{5}$ **Use the Multiplication Property of Square Roots.**

$= \boxed{}\sqrt{5} - \boxed{}\sqrt{5}$ **Simplify** $\sqrt{\boxed{}}$.

$= (\boxed{} - \boxed{})\sqrt{5}$ **Use the Distributive Property to combine like terms.**

$= \boxed{}\sqrt{5}$ **Simplify.**

Quick Check

1. Simplify each expression.

   a. $-3\sqrt{5} - 4\sqrt{5}$ **b.** $\sqrt{10} - 5\sqrt{10}$

Examples

❸ Using the Distributive Property Simplify $\sqrt{5}\left(\sqrt{8}+9\right)$.

$\sqrt{5}\left(\sqrt{8}+9\right)=\sqrt{\boxed{}}+\boxed{}\sqrt{5}$ Use the Distributive Property.

$=\sqrt{\boxed{}}\cdot\sqrt{\boxed{}}+\boxed{}\sqrt{5}$ Use the Multiplication Property of Square Roots.

$=\boxed{}\sqrt{\boxed{}}+\boxed{}\sqrt{5}$ Simplify.

❹ Simplifying Using FOIL Simplify $\left(\sqrt{6}-3\sqrt{21}\right)\left(\sqrt{6}+\sqrt{21}\right)$.

$\left(\sqrt{6}-3\sqrt{21}\right)\left(\sqrt{6}+\sqrt{21}\right)$

$=\sqrt{\boxed{}}+\sqrt{\boxed{}}-3\sqrt{\boxed{}}-3\sqrt{\boxed{}}$ Use FOIL.

$=\boxed{}-\boxed{}\sqrt{126}-3\left(\boxed{}\right)$ Combine like radicals and simplify $\sqrt{36}$ and $\sqrt{441}$.

$=\boxed{}-2\sqrt{\boxed{}\cdot 14}-\boxed{}$ $\boxed{}$ is a perfect-square factor of 126.

$=\boxed{}-2\sqrt{\boxed{}}\cdot\sqrt{\boxed{}}-63$ Use the Multiplication Property of Square Roots.

$=\boxed{}-\boxed{}\sqrt{\boxed{}}-63$ Simplify $\sqrt{9}$.

$=\boxed{}-\boxed{}\sqrt{14}$ Simplify.

Quick Check

Simplify each expression.

2. a. $3\sqrt{20}+2\sqrt{5}$

3. a. $\sqrt{5}(2+\sqrt{10})$

4. a. $(2\sqrt{6}+3\sqrt{3})(\sqrt{6}-5\sqrt{3})$

b. $3\sqrt{3}-2\sqrt{27}$

b. $\sqrt{2x}(\sqrt{6x}-11)$

b. $(\sqrt{7}+4)^2$

Example

5 **Art** A painting has a length : width ratio approximately equal to the golden ratio $(1 + \sqrt{5}) : 2$. The length of the painting is 51 in. Find the exact width of the painting in simplest radical form. Then find the approximate width to the nearest inch.

Relate $(1 + \sqrt{5}) : 2 =$ length : width

Define $\boxed{51}$ = length of painting

$\boxed{x}$ = width of painting

Write $\dfrac{(1 + \sqrt{5})}{2} = \dfrac{\boxed{}}{\boxed{}}$

$\boxed{}(1 + \sqrt{5}) = \boxed{}$ **Cross multiply.**

$x\left(\dfrac{1 + \sqrt{5}}{\boxed{}}\right) = \dfrac{102}{\boxed{}}$ **Solve for x.**

$x = \dfrac{102}{1 + \sqrt{5}} \cdot \dfrac{\boxed{}}{\boxed{}}$ **Multiply the numerator and denominator by the $\boxed{}$ of the denominator.**

$x = \dfrac{102(1 - \sqrt{5})}{\boxed{} - \boxed{}} = \dfrac{102(1 - \sqrt{5})}{\boxed{}}$ **Multiply and simplify the denominator.**

$x = \dfrac{\boxed{}(1 - \sqrt{5})}{\boxed{}}$ **Divide 102 and -4 by the common factor $\boxed{}$.**

$x = \boxed{}$ **Use a calculator.**

$x \approx \boxed{}$ **Round.**

The exact width of the painting is $\boxed{}$ inches. The approximate width of the painting is $\boxed{}$ inches.

Quick Check

5. Another painting has a length : width ratio approximately equal to the golden ratio $(1 + \sqrt{5}) : 2$. Find the length of the painting if the width is 34 inches.

Lesson 11-3

Solving Radical Equations

Lesson Objectives	NAEP 2005 Strand: Algebra
❶ Solve equations containing radicals ❷ Identify extraneous solutions	**Topic:** Variables, Expressions, and Operations **Local Standards:** _____

Vocabulary

A radical equation is _____

_____

An extraneous solution is _____

_____

Example

❶ **Solving by Isolating the Radical** Solve the equation and check your solution.

$\sqrt{x} - 5 = 4$

$\sqrt{x} = \boxed{}$ **Isolate the radical on the left side of the equation.**

$(\sqrt{x})^2 = \boxed{}^2$ **Square each side.**

$x = \boxed{}$

Check $\sqrt{x} - 5 = 4$

$\sqrt{\boxed{}} - 5 \overset{?}{=} 4$ **Substitute** $\boxed{}$ **for x.**

$\boxed{} - 5 \overset{?}{=} 4$

$4 = 4 \checkmark$

Quick Check

1. Solve each equation. Check your solutions.

  a. $\sqrt{x} + 7 = 12$ **b.** $\sqrt{a} - 4 = 5$ **c.** $\sqrt{c - 2} = 6$

Name_____ Class_____ Date _____

Examples

2 Riding a Roller Coaster On a roller coaster ride, your speed in a loop depends on the height of the hill you have just come down and the radius of the loop in feet. The equation $v = 8\sqrt{h - 2r}$ gives the velocity v in feet per second of a car at the top of the loop.

The loop on a roller coaster ride has a radius of 18 ft. Your car has a velocity of 120 ft/s at the top of the loop. How high is the hill you have just come down before going into the loop?

Solve $v = 8\sqrt{h - 2r}$ for h when $v = \boxed{}$ and $r = \boxed{}$.

$\boxed{} = 8\sqrt{h - 2(\boxed{})}$ Substitute $\boxed{}$ for v and $\boxed{}$ for r.

$\dfrac{120}{\boxed{}} = \dfrac{8\sqrt{h - 2(18)}}{\boxed{}}$ Divide each side by $\boxed{}$ to isolate the radical.

$\boxed{} = \sqrt{h - \boxed{}}$ Simplify.

$\left(\boxed{}\right)^2 = \left(\sqrt{h - \boxed{}}\right)^2$ Square both sides.

$\boxed{} = h - 36$

$\boxed{} = h$

The hill is $\boxed{}$ ft high.

3 Solving with Radical Expressions on Both Sides Solve $\sqrt{3x - 4} = \sqrt{2x + 3}$.

$\left(\sqrt{3x - 4}\right)^2 = \left(\sqrt{2x + 3}\right)^2$ Square both sides.

$3x - 4 = 2x + 3$ Simplify.

$3x = 2x + \boxed{}$ Add $\boxed{}$ to each side.

$\boxed{} = 7$ Subtract $\boxed{}$ from each side.

Check $\sqrt{3x - 4} = \sqrt{2x + 3}$

$\sqrt{3(\boxed{}) - 4} \overset{?}{=} \sqrt{2(\boxed{}) + 3}$ Substitute $\boxed{}$ for x.

$\sqrt{\boxed{}} = \sqrt{\boxed{}}$ ✓

The solution is $\boxed{}$.

❹ **Identifying Extraneous Solutions** Solve $x = \sqrt{x + 12}$.

$$(x)^2 = \left(\sqrt{x + 12}\right)^2 \qquad \text{Square both sides.}$$

$$x^2 = x + 12$$

$$x^2 - \boxed{} - \boxed{} = 0 \qquad \text{Simplify.}$$

$$\left(x - \boxed{}\right)\left(x + \boxed{}\right) = 0 \qquad \text{Solve the quadratic equation by factoring.}$$

$$\left(x - \boxed{}\right) = 0 \text{ or } \left(x + \boxed{}\right) = 0 \qquad \text{Use the Zero-Product Property.}$$

$$x = \boxed{} \text{ or } x = \boxed{} \qquad \text{Solve for } x.$$

Check $\quad x = \sqrt{x + 12}$

$$\boxed{} \overset{?}{=} \sqrt{\boxed{} + 12} \qquad \boxed{} \overset{?}{=} \sqrt{\boxed{} + 12}$$

$$\boxed{} = \boxed{} \checkmark \qquad \boxed{} \neq 3$$

The solution to the original equation is $\boxed{}$. The value $\boxed{}$ is an extraneous solution.

Quick Check

2. Use the formula from Example 2. Find the height of the hill when the velocity at the top of the loop is 35 ft/s, and the radius of the loop is 24 ft.

3. Solve $\sqrt{3t + 4} = \sqrt{5t - 6}$. Check your answer.

4. Critical Thinking In Example 4, how could you determine that -3 was not a solution of $x = \sqrt{x + 12}$ without going through all the steps of the check?

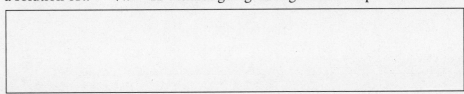

Lesson 11-4

Graphing Square Root Functions

Lesson Objectives	**NAEP 2005 Strand:** Algebra
▼ Graph square root functions	**Topic:** Algebraic Representations
▼ Translate graphs of square root functions	**Local Standards:** _____

Vocabulary

A square root function is _____

_____

Examples

1 **Finding the Domain of a Square Root Function** Find the domain of each function.

a. $y = \sqrt{x + 5}$

$x + \boxed{} \geq 0$ **Make the radicand greater than or equal to 0.**

$x \geq \boxed{}$

The domain is the set of all numbers greater than or equal to $\boxed{}$.

b. $y = 6\sqrt{4x - 12}$

$4x - 12 \geq \boxed{}$ **Make the radicand greater**

$4x \geq \boxed{}$ **than or equal to $\boxed{}$.**

$x \geq \boxed{}$

The domain is the set of all numbers greater than or equal to $\boxed{}$.

2 **Measurement** The size of a television screen is the length of the screen's diagonal d in inches. The equation $d = \sqrt{2A}$ estimates the length of a diagonal of a television with screen area A. Graph the function.

Domain
$2A \geq 0$

$A \geq 0 \rightarrow$

Screen Area (sq. in.)	Length of Diagonal (in.)
0	
50	
100	
200	
300	
400	

Quick Check

1. Find the domain of $y = \sqrt{x - 7}$.

[_____]

Examples

❸ Graphing a Vertical Translation Graph $y = \sqrt{x} + 4$
by translating the graph of $y = \sqrt{x}$.

For the graph $y = \sqrt{x} + 4$, the graph of
$y = \sqrt{x}$ is shifted ☐ units ☐.

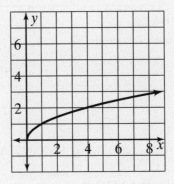

❹ Graphing a Horizontal Translation Graph
$f(x) = \sqrt{x + 3}$ by translating the graph of $y = \sqrt{x}$.

For the graph $f(x) = \sqrt{x + 3}$, the graph of
$y = \sqrt{x}$ is shifted ☐ units to the ☐.

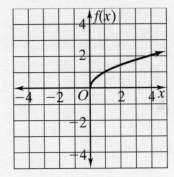

Quick Check

2. Critical Thinking What is the area of a television screen with a diagonal length of
45 inches?

3. Graph $f(x) = \sqrt{x} - 4$ by translating
the graph of $f(x) = \sqrt{x}$.

4. Graph $f(x) = \sqrt{x - 3}$ by translating
the graph of $f(x) = \sqrt{x}$.

Lesson 11-5

Trigonometric Ratios

Lesson Objective	NAEP 2005 Strand: Measurement
▼ Find trigonometric ratios	**Topic:** Measuring Physical Attributes
	Local Standards: _____

Vocabulary

Ratios of the sides of a right triangle are called [＿＿＿＿＿＿] ratios.

$\sin A = \dfrac{\text{length of leg } [\qquad] \angle A}{\text{length of } [\qquad]} = \dfrac{[\ ]}{[\ ]}$

$\cos A = \dfrac{\text{length of leg } [\qquad] \text{ to } \angle A}{\text{length of } [\qquad]} = \dfrac{[\ ]}{[\ ]}$

$\tan A = \dfrac{\text{length of leg } [\qquad] \angle A}{\text{length of leg } [\qquad] \text{ to } \angle A} = \dfrac{[\ ]}{[\ ]}$

Example

❶ Finding Trigonometric Ratios Use the triangle. Find sin A, cos A, and tan A.

$\sin A = \dfrac{\text{opposite leg}}{\text{hypotenuse}} = \dfrac{[\ ]}{[\ ]} = \dfrac{3}{[\ ]}$

$\cos A = \dfrac{\text{adjacent leg}}{\text{hypotenuse}} = \dfrac{[\ ]}{[\ ]} = \dfrac{[\ ]}{[\ ]}$

$\tan A = \dfrac{\text{opposite leg}}{\text{adjacent leg}} = \dfrac{[\ ]}{[\ ]} = \dfrac{[\ ]}{[\ ]}$

Quick Check

1. Use the triangle in Example 1. Find sin B, cos B, and tan B.

Example

❷ **Finding Missing Side Lengths** Find the value of x in the triangle.

Step 1 Decide which trigonometric ratio to use.

You know the angle and the length of the [_____].

You are trying to find the [_____] side.

Use the [_____].

Step 2 Write an equation and solve.

$$\cos 30° = \frac{\boxed{}}{\boxed{}}$$

$$\cos 30° = \frac{\boxed{}}{\boxed{}}$$ **Substitute** $\boxed{}$ **for adjacent leg and** $\boxed{}$ **for hypotenuse.**

$$x = \boxed{}\left(\cos \boxed{}°\right)$$ **Solve for x.**

$\boxed{}$ ☒ COS $\boxed{}$ ENTER 12.99038106   **Use a calculator.**

$$x \approx \boxed{}$$ **Round to the nearest tenth.**

The value of x is about $\boxed{}$.

Quick Check

2. Find the value of x in each triangle. Round to the nearest tenth.

a.

b.

Lesson 11-6

Angles of Elevation and Depression

Lesson Objective	**NAEP 2005 Strand:** Measurement
▼ Use trigonometric ratios	**Topic:** Measuring Physical Attributes
	Local Standards: _____

Vocabulary

An angle of elevation is an _____

_____

An angle of depression is measured _____

_____

Examples

❶ Using Angle of Elevation Suppose the angle of elevation from a rowboat to the top of a lighthouse is 70°. The lighthouse is 70 ft tall. How far from the lighthouse is the rowboat? Round your answer to the nearest foot.

Relate You know the [＿＿＿＿＿] and the

[＿＿＿＿＿]. You are trying to find the

[＿＿＿＿＿]. Use the [＿＿＿].

Define Let $\boxed{x}$ = the distance from the boat to the lighthouse.

Write

$$\tan A = \frac{\rule{3cm}{0.4pt}}{\rule{3cm}{0.4pt}}$$

$$\tan 70° = \frac{\boxed{}}{\boxed{}}$$ Substitute for the angle and the sides.

$$x = \frac{\boxed{}}{\boxed{}}$$ Solve for **x**.

$$x \approx \boxed{}$$ Use a calculator.

$$x \approx \boxed{}$$ Round to the nearest unit.

The rowboat is about [＿＿] feet from the lighthouse.

Daily Notetaking Guide

Name_____ Class_____ Date_____

2 **Using Angle of Depression**

A pilot is flying a plane 15,000 ft above the ground. The pilot begins a 3° descent to an airport runway. How far is the airplane from the start of the runway (in ground distance)?

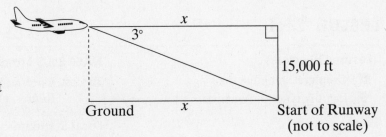

Ground x Start of Runway (not to scale)

$$\tan A = \frac{\boxed{}}{\boxed{}}$$

$$\tan \boxed{}° = \frac{\boxed{}}{\boxed{}}$$ **Substitute for the angle and the sides.**

$$\boxed{}(\tan \boxed{}°) = \boxed{}$$ **Multiply each side by** $\boxed{}$ **.**

$$x = \frac{15{,}000}{\boxed{}}$$ **Divide each side by** $\boxed{}$ **.**

$$x \approx \boxed{}$$ **Use a calculator.**

$$x \approx \boxed{}$$ **Round to the nearest 10,000 feet.**

The airplane is about $\boxed{}$ ft (about $\boxed{}$ mi) from the start of the runway.

Quick Check

1. The angle of elevation from a point on the ground 300 ft from a tower is 42°. How tall is the tower?

   $\boxed{}$

2. Suppose the pilot in Example 2 is at an altitude of 26,000 ft when the airplane begins a 2° descent. How far is the airplane from the start of the runway?

   $\boxed{}$

Lesson 12-1

Lesson Objectives	NAEP 2005 Strand: Algebra
▼1 Graph rational functions ▼2 Identify types of functions	Topics: Patterns, Relations, and Functions; Algebraic Representations Local Standards: _____

Vocabulary and Key Concepts

A rational function can be written in the form $f(x) = $ _____.

A [____] is an asymptote of a graph if the [____] of the function gets [____] to the line as x or y gets [____] in [_____].

Families of Functions

[_____] **function**

$y = mx + b$

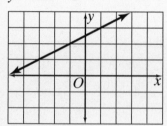

slope = [__]

y-intercept = [__]

The greatest exponent is 1.

[_____] **value function**

$y = |x - a| + b$

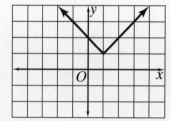

shift $y = |x|$ horizontally [__] units

shift $y = |x|$ vertically [__] units

vertex at [__]

The greatest exponent is [__].

[_____] **function**

$y = ax^2 + bx + c$

[_____] with axis of symmetry at $x = $ [__]

The greatest exponent is [__].

[_____] **function**

$y = ab^x$

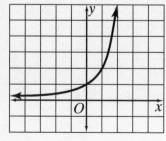

growth for $b > $ [__]

decay for [__] $< b < $ [__]

The variable is the [_____].

[_____] **function**

$y = \sqrt{x - b} + c$

shift $y = \sqrt{x}$ horizontally [__] units

shift $y = \sqrt{x}$ vertically [__] units

The variable is under the [_____].

[_____] **function**

$y = \dfrac{a}{x - b} + c$

vertical asymptote at $x = $ [__]

horizontal asymptote at $y = $ [__]

The variable is in the [_____].

Example

1 **Using a Vertical Asymptote** Identify the vertical asymptote of $y = \frac{4}{x-3}$. Then graph the function.

Step 1 Find the vertical asymptote.

$x - 3 = \boxed{}$ The numerator and denominator have $\boxed{}$ common factors. Find any value(s) where the denominator equals $\boxed{}$.

$x = \boxed{}$ This is the equation of the $\boxed{}$ asymptote.

Step 2 Make a table of values. Use values of x near $\boxed{}$, the asymptote.

x	y
2	
1	
0	
−1	
4	
5	
6	

Step 3 Graph the function.

Quick Check

1. Identify the vertical asymptote of each function. Then graph the function.

a. $f(x) = \frac{1}{x+2}$

b. $h(x) = \frac{2}{x-3}$

Example

❷ **Using Vertical and Horizontal Asymptotes** Identify the asymptotes of
$y = \frac{4}{x + 4} + 3$. Then graph the function.

Step 1 From the form of the function, you can see that there is a vertical

asymptote at $x = $ ⬚ and a ⬚ asymptote

at $y = $ ⬚. Sketch the asymptotes.

Step 2 Make a table of values. **Step 3** Graph the function.
Use values of x near -4.

x	y
−10	$2\frac{1}{3}$
−8	
−6	
−5	
−3	
−2	
−1	
2	

Quick Check

2. Identify the asymptotes of each function. Then graph the function.

   a. $f(x) = \frac{1}{x + 2} - 3$ **b.** $y = \frac{1}{x - 4} + 1$

Example

❸ **Identifying Functions** Describe the graph of each function.

a. $y = \frac{x}{6}$

The graph is a line with slope ☐ and y-intercept ☐.

b. $y = 6^x$

The graph is of [_____] growth.

c. $y = 6x^2$

The graph is a [_____] with axis of symmetry at [_____].

d. $y = |x - 6|$

The graph is an [_____] function with a vertex at (☐, ☐).

e. $y = \frac{6}{x}$

The graph is a [_____] with vertical asymptote at [_____] and horizontal asymptote at [_____].

f. $y = \sqrt{x - 6}$

The graph is the [_____] function [_____] shifted right ☐ units.

Quick Check

3. Describe the graph of each function.

a. $g(x) = |x + 4|$

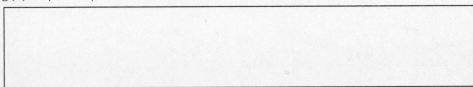

b. $f(x) = 8 \cdot 2^x$

c. $h(x) = \frac{2}{x + 1}$

Lesson 12-2

Simplifying Rational Expressions

Lesson Objective ▼ Simplify rational expressions	**NAEP 2005 Strand:** Algebra **Topic:** Variables, Expressions, and Operations **Local Standards:** _____

Vocabulary

A rational expression is _____

Examples

❶ **Simplifying a Rational Expression** Simplify $\dfrac{4x - 20}{x^2 - 9x + 20}$.

$$\dfrac{4x - 20}{x^2 - 9x + 20} = \dfrac{\boxed{}(x - 5)}{\left(x - \boxed{}\right)\left(\boxed{} - \boxed{}\right)}$$ Factor the numerator and the denominator.

$$= \dfrac{4(x - 5)^{\boxed{}}}{(x - 4)(x - 5)_{\boxed{}}}$$ Divide out the common factor $\boxed{}$.

$$= \dfrac{\boxed{}}{\boxed{}}$$ Simplify.

❷ **Recognizing Opposite Factors** Simplify $\dfrac{3x - 27}{81 - x^2}$.

$$\dfrac{3x - 27}{81 - x^2} = \dfrac{3\left(\boxed{}\right)}{(9 - x)\left(\boxed{}\right)}$$ Factor the numerator and the denominator.

$$= \dfrac{3(x - 9)}{-1\left(\boxed{}\right)(9 + x)}$$ Factor $\boxed{}$ from $9 - x$.

$$= \dfrac{3(x - 9)^{\boxed{}}}{-1_{\boxed{}}(x - 9)(9 + x)}$$ Divide out the common factor $\boxed{}$.

$$= -\dfrac{\boxed{}}{\boxed{}}$$ Simplify.

Name_____ Class_____ Date _____

❸ Evaluating a Rational Expression The baking time for bread depends, in part, on its size and shape. A good approximation for the baking time, in minutes, of a cylindrical loaf is $\frac{60 \cdot \text{volume}}{\text{surface area}}$, or $\frac{30rh}{r + h}$, where the radius r and the length h of the baked loaf are in inches. Find the baking time for a loaf that is 8 inches long and has a radius of 3 inches. Round your answer to the nearest minute.

$\frac{30rh}{r + h} = \frac{30(\boxed{})(\boxed{})}{\boxed{} + \boxed{}}$ Substitute $\boxed{}$ for r and $\boxed{}$ for h.

$= \dfrac{\boxed{}}{\boxed{}}$ **Simplify.**

$\approx \boxed{}$ **Round to the nearest whole number.**

The baking time is approximately $\boxed{}$ minutes.

Quick Check

1. Simplify each expression.

a. $\frac{12c^2}{3c + 6}$

$\boxed{}$

b. $\frac{c^2 - c - 6}{c^2 + 5c + 6}$

$\boxed{}$

2. Simplify each expression.

a. $\frac{x - 4}{4 - x}$

$\boxed{}$

b. $\frac{8 - 4r}{r^2 + 2r - 8}$

$\boxed{}$

3. a. Find the baking time for a loaf that is 4 inches long and has a radius of 3 inches. Round your answer to the nearest minute.

$\boxed{}$

b. Critical Thinking The ratio $\frac{60 \cdot \text{volume}}{\text{surface area}}$ for a cylinder is $\frac{60\pi r^2 h}{2\pi r^2 + 2\pi rh}$. Simplify this expression to show that it is the same as the expression evaluated in Example 3.

$\boxed{}$

Name_____ Class_____ Date_____

Lesson 12-3   Multiplying and Dividing Rational Expressions

Lesson Objectives	NAEP 2005 Strand: Algebra
▼ Multiply rational expressions	Topic: Variables, Expressions, and Operations
▼ Divide rational expressions	Local Standards: _____

Examples

① Using Factoring Multiply $\frac{3x + 1}{4}$ and $\frac{8x}{9x^2 - 1}$.

$$\frac{3x + 1}{4} \cdot \frac{8x}{9x^2 - 1} = \frac{3x + 1}{4} \cdot \frac{8x}{(3x - 1)(\boxed{} + \boxed{})}$$ **Factor the denominator.**

$$= \frac{\overset{3x+1}{\cancel{3x+1}}\boxed{}}{\underset{4}{\boxed{}}} \cdot \frac{\overset{8}{\cancel{8}}x}{(3x - 1)\underset{\boxed{}}{\cancel{(3x+1)}}}$$ **Divide out the common factors:** $\left(\boxed{}\right)$ **and 4.**

$$= \frac{\boxed{}}{3x - 1}$$ **Simplify.**

② Multiplying a Rational Expression by a Polynomial

Multiply $\frac{5x + 1}{3x + 12}$ and $x^2 + 7x + 12$.

$$\frac{5x + 1}{3x + 12} \cdot (x^2 + 7x + 12) = \frac{5x + 1}{3\left(\boxed{}\right)} \cdot \frac{\left(\boxed{}\right)\left(\boxed{}\right)}{1}$$ **Factor.**

$$= \frac{5x + 1}{3\underset{\boxed{}}{\cancel{(x+4)}}} \cdot \frac{(x + 3)\overset{\boxed{}}{\cancel{(x+4)}}}{1}$$ **Divide out the common factor** $\boxed{}$.

$$= \frac{(5x + 1)(x + 3)}{\boxed{}}$$ **Leave in factored form.**

③ Dividing Rational Expressions Divide $\frac{x^2 + 13x + 40}{x - 7}$ by $\frac{x + 8}{x^2 - 49}$.

$$\frac{x^2 + 13x + 40}{x - 7} \div \frac{x + 8}{x^2 - 49}$$

$$= \frac{x^2 + 13x + 40}{x - 7} \cdot \frac{\boxed{}}{x + 8}$$ **Multiply by** $\frac{x^2 - 49}{x + 8}$, **the** $\boxed{}$ **of** $\frac{x + 8}{x^2 - 49}$.

$$= \frac{\left(\boxed{}\right)(x + 8)}{x - 7} \cdot \frac{\left(\boxed{}\right)(x - 7)}{x + 8}$$ **Factor.**

$$= \frac{\overset{\boxed{}}{\cancel{(x+8)}}(x + 5)}{\underset{\boxed{}}{\cancel{x-7}}} \cdot \frac{(x + 7)\overset{\boxed{}}{\cancel{(x-7)}}}{\underset{\boxed{}}{\cancel{x+8}}}$$ **Divide out the common factors** $\boxed{}$ **and** $\boxed{}$.

$$= \left(\boxed{}\right)\left(\boxed{}\right)$$ **Leave in factored form.**

Name_____ Class_____ Date _____

❹ Dividing a Rational Expression by a Polynomial

Divide $\dfrac{x^2 + 9x + 14}{11x}$ by $(8x^2 + 16x)$.

$$\dfrac{x^2 + 9x + 14}{11x} \div \dfrac{8x^2 + 16x}{1}$$

$$= \dfrac{x^2 + 9x + 14}{11x} \cdot \dfrac{1}{\boxed{}}$$

Multiply by the $\boxed{}$ of $8x^2 + 16x$.

$$= \dfrac{(x + 7)\left(\boxed{}\right)}{11x} \cdot \dfrac{1}{\boxed{}(x + 2)}$$

Factor.

$$= \dfrac{(x + 7)\cancel{(x + 2)}^{\boxed{}}}{11x} \cdot \dfrac{1}{8x\cancel{(x + 2)}_{\boxed{}}}$$

Divide out the common factor $\boxed{}$.

$$= \dfrac{\boxed{}}{\boxed{}}$$

Simplify.

Quick Check

Multiply.

1. $\dfrac{x - 2}{8x} \cdot \dfrac{-8x - 16}{x^2 - 4}$

2. $\dfrac{3}{c} \cdot (c^3 - c)$

Divide.

3. $\dfrac{a - 2}{ab} \div \dfrac{a - 2}{a}$

4. $\dfrac{z^2 + 2z - 15}{z^2 + 9z + 20} \div (z - 3)$

Lesson 12-4

Dividing Polynomials

Lesson Objective	NAEP 2005 Strand: Algebra
▼ Divide polynomials	**Topic:** Variables, Expressions, and Operations
	Local Standards: _____

Key Concepts

Dividing a Polynomial by a Polynomial

Step 1 Arrange the terms of the dividend and divisor in [　　　　] form.

Step 2 Divide the first term of the dividend by the first term of the divisor. This is the first term of the [　　　　].

Step 3 Multiply the first term of the quotient by the divisor and place the [　　　　] under the dividend.

Step 4 Subtract this product from the [　　　　].

Step 5 Bring down the next term.
Repeat Steps 2–5 as necessary until the degree of the remainder is less than the degree of the divisor.

Examples

❶ Dividing a Polynomial by a Monomial Divide $18x^3 + 9x^2 - 15x$ by $3x^2$.

$(18x^3 + 9x^2 - 15x) \div 3x^2 = (18x^3 + 9x^2 - 15x) \cdot \dfrac{1}{\boxed{}}$ **Multiply by the reciprocal of** [　　　] **.**

$= \dfrac{18x^3}{\boxed{}} + \dfrac{9x^2}{\boxed{}} - \dfrac{15x}{\boxed{}}$ **Use the [　　　　　] Property.**

$= 6x^1 + \boxed{}x^{\boxed{}} - \dfrac{5}{x}$ **Use the division rules for exponents.**

$= \boxed{}$ **Simplify.**

❷ Dividing a Polynomial by a Binomial Divide $5x^2 + 2x - 3$ by $x + 2$.

Step 1   Begin the long division process.

Align terms by their degrees.
Put 5x above 2x of the dividend.

$$\begin{array}{r} \boxed{}\,x \\ x + 2 \overline{)\,5x^2 + \boxed{}\,x - 3} \\ 5x^2 + \boxed{}\,x \\ \hline \boxed{}\,x - 3 \end{array}$$

Divide: Think $5x^2 \div x = \boxed{}$.

Multiply: $5x(x + 2) = \boxed{}$. Then subtract.

Bring down −3.

Step 2   Repeat the process: Divide, multiply, subtract, bring down.

$$\begin{array}{r} 5x - \boxed{} \\ x + 2 \overline{)\,5x^2 + 2x - 3} \\ 5x^2 + 10x \\ \hline -8x - 3 \\ -8x - \boxed{} \\ \hline 13 \end{array}$$

Divide: $-8x \div x = \boxed{}$.

Multiply: $-8(x + 2) = \boxed{}$. Then subtract.

The remainder is $\boxed{}$.

The answer is $\boxed{} - \boxed{} + \dfrac{\boxed{}}{\boxed{}}$.

❸ Dividing Polynomials With a Zero Coefficient The width and area of a rectangle are shown in the figure. What is the length?

$w = 2x + 3$ in.

$A = (6x^3 + 5x^2 + 9)$ in.^{2}

Since $A = \ell w$, divide the area by the width to find the length.

$$\begin{array}{r} 3x^{\boxed{}} - \boxed{} + 3 \\ 2x + 3 \overline{)\,6x^3 + 5x^2 + 0x + 9} \\ \boxed{}\,x^3 + \boxed{}\,x^2 \\ \hline -\boxed{}\,x^2 + \boxed{} \\ -4x^2 - \boxed{} \\ \hline 6x + \boxed{} \\ \boxed{} + \boxed{} \\ \hline \boxed{} \end{array}$$

Rewrite the dividend with 0x.

The length of the rectangle is $\left(\boxed{} - \boxed{} + \boxed{}\right)$ in.

④ Reordering Terms and Dividing Polynomials Divide $-8x - 2 + 6x^2$ by $-1 + x$.

Rewrite $-8x - 2 + 6x^2$ as $6x^2 - 8x - 2$ and $-1 + x$ as $x - 1$. Then divide.

The answer is $\boxed{}$ – $\boxed{}$ – $\dfrac{\boxed{}}{\boxed{}}$.

Quick Check

Divide.

1. $(3m^3 - 6m^2 + m) \div 3m^2$

2. $(2b^2 - b - 3) \div (b + 1)$

3. $(t^4 + t^2 + t - 3) \div (t - 1)$

4. $(9 - 6a^2 - 11a) \div (3a - 2)$

Lesson 12-5

Adding and Subtracting Rational Expressions

Lesson Objectives	NAEP 2005 Strand: Algebra
1 Add and subtract rational expressions with like denominators	**Topic:** Variables, Expressions, and Operations
2 Add and subtract rational expressions with unlike denominators	**Local Standards:** _____

Examples

1 Subtracting Expressions With Like Denominators

Subtract $\dfrac{3x+5}{3x^2+2x-8}$ from $\dfrac{4x+7}{3x^2+2x-8}$.

$\dfrac{4x+7}{3x^2+2x-8} - \dfrac{3x+5}{3x^2+2x-8} = \dfrac{4x+7\;\boxed{}\;(3x+5)}{3x^2+2x-8}$ Subtract the numerators.

$= \dfrac{4x+7\;-3x-\boxed{}}{3x^2+2x-8}$ Use the $\boxed{}$ Property.

$= \dfrac{\boxed{}\;\boxed{}}{\big(\boxed{}\big)(x+2)\;\boxed{}}$ Simplify the numerator.
Factor the denominator.
Divide out the common factor $\boxed{}$.

$= \dfrac{\boxed{}}{\boxed{}}$ Simplify.

2 Adding Expressions With Monomial Denominators Add $\dfrac{3}{4x}+\dfrac{1}{8}$.

Step 1 Find the LCD of $\dfrac{3}{4x}$ and $\dfrac{1}{8}$.

$4x = 2 \cdot 2 \cdot \boxed{}$

$8 = 2 \cdot 2 \cdot \boxed{}$ Factor each denominator.

$LCD = 2 \cdot 2 \cdot 2 \cdot x = \boxed{}$

Step 2 Rewrite using the LCD and add.

$\dfrac{3}{4x}+\dfrac{1}{8} = \dfrac{\boxed{} \cdot 3}{\boxed{} \cdot 4x} + \dfrac{1 \cdot \boxed{}}{8 \cdot x}$ Rewrite each fraction using the LCD.

$= \dfrac{\boxed{}}{8x} + \dfrac{x}{\boxed{}}$ Simplify numerators and denominators.

$= \dfrac{\boxed{}}{\boxed{}}$ Add the numerators.

❸ Adding Expressions With Polynomial Denominators

Add $\dfrac{7}{x+4}$ and $\dfrac{3}{x-5}$.

Step 1 Find the LCD of $x + 4$ and $x - 5$. Since there are no common factors, the LCD is $(x+4)\left(\boxed{}\right)$.

Step 2 Rewrite using the LCD, and add.

$$\dfrac{7}{x+4} + \dfrac{3}{x-5} = \dfrac{7\left(\boxed{}\right)}{(x+4)(x-5)} + \dfrac{3\left(\boxed{}\right)}{(x+4)(x-5)} \qquad \text{Rewrite the fractions using the } \boxed{}.$$

$$= \dfrac{7x - \boxed{}}{(x+4)(x-5)} + \dfrac{\boxed{} + \boxed{}}{(x+4)(x-5)} \qquad \text{Simplify each numerator.}$$

$$= \dfrac{7x - 35 + \boxed{} + \boxed{}}{(x+4)(x-5)} \qquad \text{Add the numerators.}$$

$$= \dfrac{\boxed{} - \boxed{}}{(x+4)(x-5)} \qquad \text{Simplify the numerator.}$$

❹ Air Travel The distance between Seattle, Washington, and Miami, Florida, is about 5415 miles. The ground speed for jet traffic from Seattle to Miami can be about 14% faster than the ground speed from Miami to Seattle. Use r for the jet's ground speed. Write and simplify and expression for the round-trip air time.

Miami to Seattle time: $\dfrac{5415}{r}$ 　　time $= \dfrac{\text{distance}}{\text{rate}}$

Seattle to Miami time: $\dfrac{\boxed{}}{\boxed{}\,r}$ 　　time $= \dfrac{\text{distance}}{\text{rate}}$ 　　**14% more than a number is 114% of the number.**

An expression for the total time is $\dfrac{5415}{r} + \dfrac{5415}{1.14r}$.

$$\dfrac{5415}{r} + \dfrac{5415}{1.14r} = \dfrac{6173.1}{\boxed{}\,r} + \dfrac{5415}{1.14r} \qquad \text{Rewrite using the LCD } \boxed{}.$$

$$= \dfrac{\boxed{}}{1.14r} \qquad \text{Add the numerators.}$$

$$= \dfrac{\boxed{}}{r} \qquad \text{Simplify.}$$

Name_____ Class_____ Date _____

Quick Check

Add or subtract.

1. a. $\dfrac{4}{t-2} - \dfrac{5}{t-2}$

b. $\dfrac{2c+1}{5m+2} - \dfrac{3c-4}{5m+2}$

2. a. $\dfrac{3}{7y^4} + \dfrac{2}{3y^2}$

b. $\dfrac{5}{12b} + \dfrac{15}{36b^2}$

3. a. $\dfrac{5}{t+4} + \dfrac{3}{t-1}$

b. $\dfrac{-2}{a+2} + \dfrac{3a}{2a-1}$

4. **Air Travel** The distance between Atlanta, Georgia, and Albuquerque, New Mexico, is about 1,270 miles. The ground speed for jet traffic from Atlanta to Albuquerque can be about 12% faster than the ground speed from Albuquerque to Atlanta. Use r for a jet's ground speed. Write and simplify an expression for the round-trip air time.

Lesson 12-6

Solving Rational Equations

Lesson Objectives	NAEP 2005 Strand: Algebra
▼ Solve rational equations	**Topics:** Algebraic Representations; Equations
▼ Solve proportions	and Inequalities
	Local Standards: _____

Vocabulary

A rational equation is _____

Example

1 **Solving by Factoring** Solve $\frac{6}{x^2} = \frac{5}{x} - 1$. Check the solution.

$$\boxed{}\left(\frac{6}{x^2}\right) = \boxed{}\left(\frac{5}{x} - 1\right) \qquad \text{Multiply each side by the LCD, } \boxed{}.$$

$$\frac{\boxed{}}{\boxed{}}\left(\frac{6}{x^2}\right) = \frac{\boxed{}}{\boxed{}}\left(\frac{5}{x}\right) - \boxed{}(1) \qquad \text{Use the } \boxed{} \text{ Property.}$$

$$6 = \boxed{}x - \boxed{} \qquad \text{Simplify.}$$

$$x^2 - \boxed{} + \boxed{} = 0 \qquad \text{Collect terms on one side.}$$

$$\left(\boxed{}\right)\left(\boxed{}\right) = 0 \qquad \text{Factor the } \boxed{} \text{ expression.}$$

$$\boxed{} - \boxed{} = 0 \text{ or } \boxed{} - \boxed{} = 0 \qquad \text{Use the } \boxed{} \text{ Property.}$$

$$x = \boxed{} \text{ or } \qquad x = \boxed{} \qquad \text{Solve.}$$

Check $\frac{6}{\boxed{}^2} \stackrel{?}{=} \frac{5}{\boxed{}} - 1$ $\qquad$ $\frac{6}{\boxed{}^2} \stackrel{?}{=} \frac{5}{\boxed{}} - 1$

$\frac{\boxed{}}{\boxed{}} = \frac{\boxed{}}{\boxed{}}$ ✓ $\qquad$ $\frac{\boxed{}}{\boxed{}} = \frac{\boxed{}}{\boxed{}}$ ✓

Quick Check

1. Solve each equation. Check your solution.

a. $\frac{1}{3} + \frac{1}{3x} = \frac{1}{6}$ $\qquad\qquad\qquad$ **b.** $\frac{5}{m} = \frac{2}{m^2} + 2$

Example

❷ Work-Rate Problem Renee can mow the lawn in 20 minutes. Joanne can do the same job in 30 minutes. How long will it take them if they work together?

Define Let n = the time to complete the job if they work together (in minutes).

Person	Work Rate (part of job/min.)	Time Worked (min.)	Part of job done
Renee	$\dfrac{\boxed{}}{\boxed{}}$	n	$\dfrac{\boxed{}}{\boxed{}}$
Joanne	$\dfrac{\boxed{}}{\boxed{}}$	n	$\dfrac{\boxed{}}{\boxed{}}$

Relate Renee's part done + Joanne's part done = complete job

Write $\dfrac{n}{\boxed{}} \quad + \quad \dfrac{n}{\boxed{}} \quad = \quad 1$

$\boxed{}\left(\dfrac{n}{\boxed{}} + \dfrac{n}{\boxed{}}\right) = \boxed{}(1)$ **Multiply each side by the LCD, $\boxed{}$.**

$3n + 2n = \boxed{}$ **Use the $\boxed{}$ Property.**

$\boxed{} = \boxed{}$ **Simplify.**

$\boxed{} = \boxed{}$ **Simplify.**

It will take them $\boxed{}$ minutes to mow the lawn together.

Quick Check

2. Peggy can pick a bushel of apples in 45 min. Peter can pick a bushel of apples in 75 min. How long will it take them to pick a bushel if they work together?

Name_____ Class_____ Date _____

Example

❸ **Checking to Find an Extraneous Solution** Solve $\frac{x+3}{x-1}=\frac{4}{x-1}$.

$(x+3)(\boxed{}-\boxed{})=\boxed{}(x-1)$ **Write cross products.**

$\boxed{}-x+\boxed{}-3=4x-\boxed{}$ **Use the** $\boxed{}$ **Property.**

$x^2+\boxed{}-\boxed{}=4x-\boxed{}$ **Combine** $\boxed{}$ **terms.**

$x^2-\boxed{}+\boxed{}=\boxed{}$ **Subtract** $\boxed{}$ **from each side.**

$(x-\boxed{})(x-\boxed{})=0$ **Factor.**

$\boxed{}-\boxed{}=0$ **Use the Zero-Product Property.**

$\boxed{}=\boxed{}$ **Simplify.**

Check $\frac{\boxed{}+3}{\boxed{}-1}\overset{?}{=}\frac{4}{\boxed{}-1}$

$\frac{\boxed{}}{\boxed{}}=\frac{\boxed{}}{\boxed{}}$ **Undefined! There is no division by** $\boxed{}$.

The equation has no solution because $\boxed{}$ makes the denominator equal $\boxed{}$.

Quick Check

3. Solve each equation. Check your solution.

a. $\frac{3}{a}=\frac{5}{a-2}$

b. $\frac{n}{5}=\frac{4}{n+1}$

c. $\frac{2}{c^2}=\frac{2}{c^2+1}$

d. $\frac{w^2}{w-1}=\frac{1}{w-1}$

Lesson 12-7

Counting Methods and Permutations

Lesson Objectives	NAEP 2005 Strand: Data Analysis and Probability
☑ Use the multiplication counting principle	**Topic:** Probability
☑ Find permutations	**Local Standards:** _____

Vocabulary and Key Concepts

Multiplication Counting Principle

If there are *m* ways to make a first selection and *n* ways to make a

second selection, there are [   ] ways to make the two selections.

Example For 5 shirts and 8 pairs of shorts, the number of possible outfits is [ ] · [ ] = [   ].

Permutation Notation

The expression $_nP_r$ represents the number of permutations of *n* objects arranged *r* at a time.

n will be the first factor.

$$_nP_r = \underbrace{n(n-1)(n-2) \ldots}$$

Stop when you have *r* factors.

Example $_8P_3$ represents 8 objects (players) chosen 3 at a time, or [ ] · [ ] · [ ] = [   ].

A permutation is _____

Examples

❶ **Using a Tree Diagram** Suppose you have three shirts and three ties that coordinate. Make a tree diagram to find the number of possible outfits you have.

There are [   ] possible outfits.

Shirts	Ties	Outfits
Shirt 1	Tie 1 →	[ ]
	Tie 2 →	[ ]
	Tie 3 →	[ ]
Shirt 2	Tie 1 →	[ ]
	Tie 2 →	[ ]
	Tie 3 →	[ ]
Shirt 3	Tie 1 →	[ ]
	Tie 2 →	[ ]
	Tie 3 →	[ ]

❷ **Using the Multiplication Counting Principle** Suppose there are two routes you can drive to get from Austin, Texas, to Dallas, Texas, and four routes from Dallas, Texas, to Tulsa, Oklahoma. How many possible routes are there from Austin to Tulsa through Dallas?

$$\boxed{} \cdot \boxed{} = \boxed{} \leftarrow \text{Routes from Austin to Tulsa through Dallas}$$

Routes from Austin to Dallas **Routes from Dallas to Tulsa**

There are $\boxed{}$ possible routes from Austin to Tulsa.

❸ **Counting Permutations** In how many ways can 11 students enter a classroom?

There are 11 choices for the first student, $\boxed{}$ for the second, $\boxed{}$ for the third, and so on.

$11 \cdot \boxed{} \cdot \boxed{} \cdot \boxed{} \cdot \boxed{} \cdot \boxed{} \cdot \boxed{} \cdot \boxed{} \cdot \boxed{} \cdot \boxed{}$ **Use a calculator.**

$= \boxed{}$

There are $\boxed{}$ possible ways in which the students can enter the classroom.

❹ **Using Permutation Notation** Simplify $_8P_5$.

Method 1 Use pencil and paper.

$_8P_5 = \boxed{} \cdot \boxed{} \cdot \boxed{} \cdot \boxed{} \cdot \boxed{}$ **The first factor is** $\boxed{}$**, and there are** $\boxed{}$ **factors.**

$= \boxed{}$ **Simplify.**

Method 2 Use a graphing calculator.

Use **MATH** to select **nPr** in the **PRB** screen.

$_8P_5 = \boxed{}$

❺ **Computers** Suppose you use five different letters from the 26 letters of the alphabet to make a password. Find the number of possible five-letter passwords.

There are 26 letters in the alphabet. You are finding the number of permutations of $\boxed{}$ letters arranged $\boxed{}$ at a time.

$\boxed{}P\boxed{} = 26 \cdot \boxed{} \cdot \boxed{} \cdot \boxed{} \cdot \boxed{}$ **Use a calculator.**

$= \boxed{}$

There are $\boxed{}$ five-letter passwords in which letters do not repeat.

Quick Check

1. Suppose you have two T-shirts and four pairs of shorts you could bring for gym class. Make a tree diagram to find the number of possible outfits for the gym.

2. At the neighborhood pizza shop, there are five vegetable toppings and three meat toppings for a pizza. How many different pizzas can you order with one meat and one vegetable topping?

3. A swimming pool has eight lanes. In how many ways can eight swimmers be assigned lanes for a race?

4. Simplify each expression.
   a. $_9P_3$

   b. $_7P_3$

   c. $_5P_2$

5. Suppose your cousin needs to choose a four-digit number to use with a new debit card. Find the number of possible four-digit numbers without a repeating digit.

Lesson 12-8

Combinations

Lesson Objectives	NAEP 2005 Strand: Data Analysis and Probability
▼ Find combinations	Topic: Probability
▼ Find probability with counting techniques	Local Standards: _____

Vocabulary and Key Concepts

Combination Notation

The expression $\boxed{}$ represents the number of combinations of n objects arranged r at a time.

$$_nC_r = \frac{_nP_r}{_rP_r} = \frac{n(n-1)(n-2)...}{r(r-1)(r-2)...} \begin{array}{l} \leftarrow r \text{ factors, starting with } \boxed{} \\ \leftarrow r \text{ factors, starting with } \boxed{} \end{array}$$

Example $\quad _4C_3 = \frac{_4P_3}{_3P_3} = \frac{4 \cdot \boxed{} \cdot \boxed{}}{3 \cdot \boxed{} \cdot \boxed{}} = \boxed{}$

A combination is _____ _____

_____

Examples

❶ **Counting Combinations** Eighteen people enter a talent contest. Awards will be given to the top ten finishers. How many different groups of ten winners can be chosen?

The order in which the top ten winners are listed once they are chosen does not distinguish one group of winners from another. You need the number of combinations of 18 potential winners chosen 10 at a time.

$_{18}C_{10} = \dfrac{\boxed{}}{_{10}P_{10}}$ **Write using permutation notation.**

$= \dfrac{18 \cdot \boxed{} \cdot \boxed{} \cdot \boxed{} \cdot \boxed{} \cdot \boxed{} \cdot \boxed{} \cdot \boxed{} \cdot \boxed{} \cdot \boxed{}}{10 \cdot \boxed{} \cdot \boxed{} \cdot \boxed{} \cdot \boxed{} \cdot \boxed{} \cdot \boxed{} \cdot \boxed{} \cdot \boxed{} \cdot \boxed{}}$

$= \boxed{}$ **Use a calculator.**

Daily Notetaking Guide

❷ Using Permutations in Probability Suppose you have eight new CDs (three rock, two jazz, and three country). If you choose the CDs at random, what is the probability that the first one is country and the second one is jazz?

probability the first choice is country $= \dfrac{\boxed{}}{8}$ $\boxed{}$ **of the eight CDs are country.**

probability the second choice is jazz $= \dfrac{\boxed{}}{7}$ $\boxed{}$ **of the remaining CDs are jazz.**

$P(\text{country, then jazz}) = \dfrac{3}{8} \cdot \dfrac{2}{7}$ **Multiply the probabilities.**

$= \dfrac{\boxed{}}{\boxed{}}$ **Multiply.**

$= \dfrac{\boxed{}}{\boxed{}}$ **Simplify.**

The probability that you choose country, then jazz is $\dfrac{\boxed{}}{\boxed{}}$.

Quick Check

1. a. For your history report, you can choose to write about two of a list of five presidents of the United States. Use $_nC_r$ notation to write the number of combinations possible for your report.

$\boxed{}$

b. Calculate the number of combinations of presidents on whom you could report.

$\boxed{}$

c. Critical Thinking Explain why you should model this situation with combinations, not permutations.

$\boxed{}$

2. Suppose you have three novels and two history books to read over the summer. If you choose books at random, what is the probability that you first choose a novel, and then a history book?

$\boxed{}$

Example

❸ Using Combinations in Probability Suppose you have eight red pens and four black pens in a box. You choose five pens without looking. What is the probability that all the pens you choose are red?

There are 12 pens in all. Eight of the pens are red.

number of favorable outcomes = $_8C_\boxed{}$ **number of ways to choose 5 pens from the** $\boxed{}$ **red pens**

number of possible outcomes = $_\boxed{}C_5$ **number of ways to choose 5 pens from the** $\boxed{}$ **possible pens**

$P(5 \text{ red pens}) = \dfrac{\text{number of } \boxed{} \text{ outcomes}}{\text{total number of outcomes}}$ **Use the definition of probability.**

$= \dfrac{\boxed{}}{_{12}C_5}$ **Substitute.**

$= \dfrac{56}{\boxed{}} = \dfrac{\boxed{}}{\boxed{}}$ **Simplify each expression. Simplify the fractions.**

The probability that you will choose five red pens is $\dfrac{\boxed{}}{\boxed{}}$, or about $\boxed{}$%.

Quick Check

3. a. Suppose you have the pens in Example 3. You choose eight pens at random. How many combinations are possible?

b. How many combinations have only red pens?

c. What is the probability that all of the pens are red?

A Note to the Student:

This section of your workbook contains a series of pages that support your mathematics understandings for each chapter and lesson presented in your student edition.

- Practice pages provide additional practice for every lesson.

- Guided Problem Solving pages lead you through a step-by-step solution to an application problem in each lesson.

- Vocabulary pages contain a variety of activities to increase your reading and math understanding, ranging from graphic organizers to vocabulary review puzzles.

Practice 1-1

Write an algebraic expression for each phrase.

1. 7 increased by x

2. p multiplied by 3

3. 10 decreased by m

4. n less than 7

5. the product of 2 and q

6. 3 more than m

Write a phrase for each algebraic expression.

7. $\frac{8}{a}$

8. $s - 10$

9. $x + 13$

10. $ab + 2$

Define a variable and write an algebraic expression for each phrase.

11. the difference of 8 and a number

12. the sum of 4 and a number

13. the product of 2 and a number

14. 3 increased by a number

15. 10 plus the quotient of a number and 15

16. 12 less than a number

Define a variable and write an algebraic equation to model each situation.

17. What is the total cost of buying several shirts at $24.95 each?

18. The number of gal of water used to water trees is 30 times the number of trees.

19. What is the amount of money in a bank containing only dimes?

20. What is the number of marbles left in a 48-marble bag after some marbles have been given away?

21. The total cost equals the price of the tickets multiplied by eight people.

22. What is the cost of buying several pairs of pants at $32.95 per pair?

Define variables and write an equation to model the relationship in each table.

23.

Number of Tickets	Total Cost
2	$7
4	$14
6	$21

24.

Number of Hours	Distance Traveled
1	55 mi
3	165 mi
5	275 mi

25.

Number of Hours	Total Pay
8	$40
12	$60
16	$80

26.

Total Cost	Change From $10
$10.00	$0
$9.00	$1.00
$7.50	$2.50

27.

Number of Days	Length
1	0.45 in.
4	1.80 in.
8	3.60 in.

28.

Miles Traveled	Miles Remaining
0	500
125	375
350	150

1-1 • Guided Problem Solving

GPS **Student Page 7, Exercise 42**

Multiple Choice Which equation best describes the relationship between the amount of money a in a bag of quarters and the number of quarters q?

A. $a = 0.25q$ **B.** $a = 0.25 + q$ **C.** $q = 0.25a$ **D.** $q = 0.25 + q$

Read and Understand

1. What two quantities are related? _____

Plan and Solve

2. How much money is 1 quarter worth? _____

3. How much money are 2 quarters worth? _____

4. Explain how you would determine the amount of money 5 quarters are worth.

   _____

5. How would you express the amount of money q quarters are worth? _____

6. Write an equation that describes the relationship between the amount of money a in a bag of quarters and the number of quarters q. _____

Look Back and Check

7. Check the reasonableness of your answer by explaining why the other answer choices do not make sense.

   _____

Solve Another Problem

8. Mark has a pocket full of nickels. Which equation best describes the relationship between the amount of money a in his pocket and the number of nickels n?

   A. $a = n + 0.05$ **B.** $a = 0.05n$ **C.** $n = 0.05 + a$ **D.** $n = 0.05a$

Practice 1-2

Exponents and Order of Operations

Simplify each expression.

1. $4 + 6(8)$

2. $\dfrac{4(8-2)}{3+9}$

3. $4 \times 3^2 + 2$

4. $40 \div 5(2)$

5. $2.7 + 3.6 \times 4.5$

6. $3[4(8-2)+5]$

7. $4 + 3(15 - 2^3)$

8. $17 - [(3+2) \times 2]$

9. $6 \times (3+2) \div 15$

Evaluate each expression.

10. $\dfrac{a+2b}{5}$ for $a = 1$ and $b = 2$

11. $\dfrac{5m+n}{5}$ for $m = 6$ and $n = 15$

12. $x + 3y^2$ for $x = 3.4$ and $y = 3$

13. $7a - 4(b+2)$ for $a = 5$ and $b = 2$

Simplify each expression.

14. $\dfrac{100-15}{9+8}$

15. $\dfrac{2(3+4)}{7}$

16. $\dfrac{3(4+12)}{2(7-3)}$

17. $14 + 3 \times 4$

18. $8 + 3(4+3)$

19. $3 + 4[13 - 2(6-3)]$

20. $8(5 + 30 \div 5)$

21. $(3.4)(2.7) + 5$

22. $50 \div 2 + 15 \times 4$

23. $7(9-5)$

24. $2(3^2) - 3(2)$

25. $4 + 8 \div 2 + 6 \times 3$

26. $(7+8) \div (4-1)$

27. $5[2(8+5) - 15]$

28. $(6+8) \times (8-4)$

29. $12\left(\dfrac{6+30}{9-3}\right)$

30. $14 + 6 \times 2^3 - 8 \div 2^2$

31. $\dfrac{7(14) - 3(6)}{2}$

32. $14 \div [3(8-2) - 11]$

33. $3\left(\dfrac{9+13}{6}\right)$

34. $\dfrac{4(8-3)}{3+2}$

35. $5 + 4^2 \times 8 - 2^3 \div 2^2$

36. $4^2 + 5^2(8-3)$

37. $5(3^2 + 2) - 2(6^2 - 5^2)$

Evaluate each expression for $a = 2$ and $b = 6$.

38. $2(7a - b)$

39. $(a^3 + b^2) \div a$

40. $3b \div (2a - 1) + b$

41. $\dfrac{5a+2}{b}$

42. $\dfrac{3(b-2)}{4(a+1)}$

43. $9b + a^4 \div 8$

Use the expression $r + 0.12m$ to calculate the cost of renting a car. The basic rate is r. The number of miles driven is m.

44. The basic rate is \$15.95. The car is driven 150 mi.

45. The basic rate is \$32.50. The car is driven 257 mi.

Evaluate each expression for $s = 3$ and $t = 9$.

46. $8(4s - t)$

47. $(2t - 3s) \div 4$

48. $t^2 - s^4$

49. $s(3t + 6)$

50. $\dfrac{5s^2}{t}$

51. $\dfrac{2t^2}{s^3}$

1-2 • Guided Problem Solving

GPS Student Page 14, Exercise 63

a. **Geometry** The formula for the volume of a cylinder is $V = \pi r^2 h$.
   What is the volume of the cylinder? Round your answer to the
   nearest hundredth of a cubic inch.

b. **Critical Thinking** About how many cubic inches does an ounce of
   juice fill? Round your answer to the nearest tenth of a cubic inch.

c. The formula for the surface area of a cylinder is $SA = 2\pi r(r + h)$.
   What is the surface area of the cylinder? Round your answer to the
   nearest hundredth of a square inch.

Read and Understand

1. What are the two formulas that you will need to use? _____

2. What information is given in the picture? _____

Plan and Solve

3. What is the value you will use for r? _____

4. What is the value you will use for h? _____

5. What is the decimal approximation for π? _____

6. What is the volume of the cylinder? _____

7. What is the surface area of the cylinder? _____

8. About how many cubic inches does an ounce of juice fill? _____

Look Back and Check

9. Round your volume to the nearest cubic inch. Check the reasonableness
   of your answer by dividing your volume by 2. Your answer should be
   close to 12, which is the number of ounces of juice in the cylinder.

Solve Another Problem

10. What is the volume of a cylinder if the radius is 2.0 inches and the
    height is 2.5 inches?

    _____

Practice 1-3

Name the set(s) of numbers to which each number belongs.

1. -0.002 **2.** $12\frac{1}{2}$ **3.** 8   **4.** 5π

5. $\sqrt{7}$ **6.** -22 **7.** -3.4 **8.** $\sqrt{36}$

Is each statement *true* or *false*? If the statement is false, give a counterexample.

9. Every whole number is an integer.   **10.** Every integer is a whole number.

11. Every rational number is a real number.   **12.** Every multiple of 7 is odd.

Use <, =, or > to compare.

13. $-10.98 \ \blacksquare \ -10.99$ **14.** $-\frac{1}{3} \ \blacksquare \ -0.3$ **15.** $-\frac{11}{5} \ \blacksquare \ -\frac{4}{5}$

16. $-\frac{1}{2} \ \blacksquare \ -\frac{5}{10}$ **17.** $-\frac{3}{8} \ \blacksquare \ -\frac{7}{16}$ **18.** $\frac{3}{4} \ \blacksquare \ \frac{13}{16}$

Order the numbers in each group from least to greatest.

19. $-\frac{8}{9}, -\frac{7}{8}, -\frac{22}{25}$ **20.** $-3\frac{4}{9}, -3.45, -3\frac{12}{25}$ **21.** $-\frac{1}{4}, -\frac{1}{5}, -\frac{1}{3}$

22. $-1.7, -1\frac{3}{4}, -1\frac{7}{9}$ **23.** $-\frac{3}{4}, -\frac{7}{8}, -\frac{2}{3}$ **24.** $2\frac{3}{4}, 2\frac{5}{8}, 2.7$

Determine which set of numbers is most reasonable for each situation.

25. the number of dolphins in the ocean

26. the height of a basketball player

27. the number of pets you have

28. the circumference of a compact disk

Find each absolute value.

29. $\left|\frac{3}{10}\right|$ **30.** $|-327|$ **31.** $|-3.46|$ **32.** $\left|-\frac{1}{2}\right|$

33. Name the sets(s) of numbers to which each number in the table belongs. Choose among: whole numbers, integers, rational numbers, irrational numbers, and real numbers.

Type of Account	Principal	Rate	Time (years)	Interest
Checking	$154.23	0.0375	$\frac{30}{365}$	$.48
Savings	$8000	0.055	$3\frac{1}{2}$	$1540

1-3 • Guided Problem Solving

GPS **Student Page 21, Exercise 64**

Multiple Choice Use the number line. If *R* and *T* are opposites, what is the value of *Q*?

A. 7   **B.** 0   **C.** −3   **D.** −7

$$Q \quad P \quad R \quad S \quad T$$

Read and Understand

1. Give an example of two numbers that are opposites. ———————————————

Plan and Solve

2. On the number line above, mark the location of the number 0.

3. On the number line above, label the points *R* and *T* with their values.

4. What is the value of *Q*? ———————————————————

Look Back and Check

5. Check that your answer is correct by labeling all the remaining points on the number line.

Solve Another Problem

6. Use the number line. If *P* and *T* are opposites, what is the value of *R*?

   A. 0   **B.** 2   **C.** −2   **D.** −6

$$Q \quad P \quad R \quad S \quad T$$

Practice 1-4

The relationships in the tables below are functions. Write a function rule for each.

1.

Number of Baseball Teams	Number of Players Required
1	9
2	18
3	27
4	36

2.

Number of CDs Purchased	Total Cost
1	$13
2	$26
3	$39
4	$52

3.

Number of Homework Questions	Number of Minutes for Homework
1	25
2	30
3	35
4	40

4.

Number of Rides Taken	Cost of Fair
1	$10.00
2	$12.50
3	$15.00
4	$17.50

Identify the independent and dependent quantity in each situation.

5. The amount of money earned babysitting increases with the number of hours spent babysitting.

6. The cost of a skating party increases with the number of people attending the party.

7. The volume of water in a bathtub decreases with the number of minutes it has been draining.

8. The number of people attending the event decreases with the total cost for tickets.

Complete each table. Then write a function rule for each relationship.

9.

Number of Cases of Water	Number of Bottles of Water
1	24
2	48
3	72
4	
5	

10.

Number of Minutes	Cost of Phone Call
1	$.60
2	$.70
3	$.80
4	
5	

Function Rule: _____

Function Rule: _____

1-4 • Guided Problem Solving

GPS **Student Page 30, Exercise 13**

Each side of the first figure is one unit. Find a function rule for the relationship between a figure's number and its perimeter.

Figure 1   Figure 2

Figure 3   Figure 4

Read and Understand

1. How do you find the perimeter of a figure? _____

Plan and Solve

2. Determine the perimeter of each figure above and complete the table.

3. By how much is the perimeter changing each time?

_____

Figure Number	Perimeter
1	▨
2	▨
3	▨
4	▨

4. Write a function rule for the relationship between the figure's number and its perimeter.

_____

Look Back and Check

5. Check that your function rule is correct by substituting $n = 3$ to verify that the rule gives the correct perimeter.

_____

Solve Another Problem

6. Each side of the first figure is one unit. Draw and complete a table that shows the figure number and its perimeter. Then find a function rule for the relationship between a figure's number and its perimeter.

Figure 1   Figure 2   Figure 3   Figure 4

Figure Number	1	2	3	4
Perimeter				

Practice 1-5

Make a scatter plot for each set of data below.

1. Height and Hourly Pay of Ten People

Height (inches)	Hourly Pay	Height (inches)	Hourly Pay
62	$6.00	72	$8.00
65	$8.50	72	$6.00
68	$6.50	73	$7.50
70	$6.00	74	$6.25
70	$7.50	74	$8.00

2. Speed of Winds in Some U.S. Cities

Station	Average Speed (mi/h)	Highest Speed (mi/h)
Atlanta, GA	9.1	60
Casper, WY	12.9	81
Dallas, TX	10.7	73
Mobile, AL	9.0	63
St. Louis, MO	9.7	60

Source: National Climatic Data Center

Describe the trend in each scatter plot below.

3.

4.

5.

6. In Exercise 1, is there a *positive correlation*, a *negative correlation*, or *no correlation* between height and hourly pay?

7. In Exercise 2, is there a *positive correlation*, a *negative correlation*, or *no correlation* between average wind speed and highest wind speed?

Would you expect a *positive correlation*, a *negative correlation*, or *no correlation* between the two data sets? Explain why.

8. a person's age and the number of pets he or she has

9. the number of times you brush your teeth and the number of cavities you get

10. the number of days it rains per year and the number of umbrellas sold

11. a. In the scatter plot on the right, what does a point represent?

b. How can you tell if some infants weighed the same?

c. How can you tell which infants were weighed at the same age?

d. Is there a correlation between age and weight? Explain.

Age and Weight for 9 Infants

1-5 • Guided Problem Solving

GPS **Student Page 36, Exercise 16**

a. **Transportation** In the scatter plot at the right, what does a point represent?

b. How can you tell if some vehicles traveled the same distance?

c. How can you tell which vehicles paid the same toll charge?

d. Is there a correlation between distance traveled and toll charges? Explain.

Toll Charges for 9 Vehicles on the Indiana Toll Road

SOURCE: Indiana Department of Highways

Read and Understand

1. What two quantities are related in the scatter plot?

_____

2. What is the scale on the horizontal axis?

_____

Plan and Solve

3. Explain what a point represents on the scatter plot. _____

4. How can you tell if some vehicles traveled the same distance? _____

_____

5. How can you tell which vehicles paid the same toll charge? _____

_____

6. Is there a correlation between distance traveled and toll charges? Explain. _____

_____

_____

Look Back and Check

7. Circle two points that represent two vehicles that paid the same toll charge. Put a square around two vehicles that traveled the same distance. Check the reasonableness of your answer by comparing these pairs of points with your responses above.

Solve Another Problem

8. In the scatter plot above, what are the approximate maximum and minimum toll charges paid by these 9 vehicles?

_____

Practice 1-6

Find the mean, median, and mode. Which measure of central tendency best describes the data?

1. number of cars sold in the past 10 days
   1 5 3 2 1 0 4 2 6 1

2. utility bills for the past 6 months
   $90 $120 $140 $135 $112 $126

3. prices of a sweater in 5 different stores
   $31.25 $27.50 $28.00 $36.95 $32.10

4. scores on a 10-point quiz
   7 9 10 8 4 2 6 10 8

Find the range.

5. hourly wages
   $7.25 $6.75 $8.10 $9.56 $7.10 $7.75

6. ages of students on the quiz team
   15 15 14 16 17 16 16 15

Write and solve an equation to find the value of x.

7. $4.8, 1.6, 5.2, x$; mean 3.7

8. $40, 98, 94, 102, 21, x$; mean 88

9. $100, 172, 85, 92, x$; mean 115

10. $25.6, 19.3, 19, x$, mean 24

11. A coffee machine is considered reliable if the range of amounts of coffee that it dispenses is less than 2 fluid ounces (fl oz). In eight tries, a particular machine dispensed the following amounts: 7.1, 6.8, 7.6, 7.1, 7.4, 6.8, 7, and 6.7 fl oz. Is the machine reliable? Explain

12. To test the exhaust fumes of a car, an inspector took six samples. The exhaust samples contained the following amounts of gas in parts per million (ppm): 8, 5, 7, 6, 9, and 5. If the maximum allowable mean is 6 ppm, did the car pass the test? Explain.

13. Randy had grades of 85, 92, 96, and 89 on his last four math tests. What grade does he need on his next test to have an average of 92?

14. **a.** A bakery collected the following data about the number of loaves of fresh bread sold on each of 24 business days. Make a stem-and-leaf plot for the data.

| 43 | 39 | 17 | 38 | 50 | 42 | 34 | 28 | 37 | 42 | 40 | 33 |
| 72 | 36 | 45 | 21 | 29 | 44 | 41 | 37 | 40 | 35 | 51 | 54 |

   b. Find the mean, median, mode(s), and range of the data.

15. The back-to-back stem-and-leaf plot shows the number of calls made to each of two police departments in the last 14 days. Find the mean, median, mode(s), and range of each side of the stem-and-leaf plot.

    Dept. A   Dept. B

    | 9 5 2 | 3 | 1 4 |
    | 8 6 2 1 | 4 | 7 9 9 |
    | 8 8 8 2 | 5 | 0 2 2 2 4 |
    | 3 2 1 | 6 | 1 1 3 |
    | | 7 | 1 |

16. The back-to-back stem-and-leaf plot shows the average daytime temperature (in °F) at two different locations for each of the past 15 weeks. Find the mean, median, mode, and range of each side of the stem-and-leaf plot.

    Locn. A   Locn. B

    | 9 8 7 | 6 | 5 6 6 7 9 |
    | 7 5 1 0 | 7 | 2 4 5 6 8 |
    | 9 4 3 3 1 | 8 | 0 4 7 9 |
    | 1 0 0 | 9 | 1 |

1-6 • Guided Problem Solving

GPS **Student Page 44, Exercise 25**

Manufacturing Two manufacturing plants create sheets of steel for medical instruments. The back-to-back stem-and-leaf plot at the right shows data collected from the two plants.

a. Find the mean, median, mode, and range of each set of data.

b. Which measure of central tendency best describes each set of data? Explain.

c. **Reasoning** Which plant has the better quality control? Explain.

Width of Steel (millimeters)	
Manufacturing Plant A	Manufacturing Plant B
	4 | 3 5 9
8 7 4 4 2 | 5 | 2 7
4 3 1 | 6 | 3 4
	7 | 2

means 6.1 ← 1 \| 6 \| 3 → means 6.3

Read and Understand

1. Describe how to determine the mean, median, mode, and range.

_____

Plan and Solve

2. Find the mean, median, mode, and range of each set of data. Record the results in the table.

	Mean	Median	Mode	Range
Plant A				
Plant B				

3. Which measure of central tendency best describes each set of data? Explain.

_____

4. Which plant has the better quality control? Justify your answer.

_____

Look Back and Check

5. Check the reasonableness of your mean values. Are they between the minimum and maximum data values?

Solve Another Problem

6. If 7.5 is added to the data for Plant A, would the same plant have the better quality control? Explain.

_____

1A: Graphic Organizer

Study Skill Always write down your assignments. Do not rely on your memory to recall all assignments from all your classes.

Write your answers.

1. What is the chapter title? _____

2. Find the Table of Contents page for this chapter at the front of the book. Name four topics you will study in this chapter.

   _____   _____

   _____   _____

3. Complete the graphic organizer as you work through the chapter.
   1. Write the title of the chapter in the center oval.
   2. When you begin a lesson, write the name of the lesson in a rectangle.
   3. When you complete that lesson, write a skill or key concept from that lesson in the outer oval linked to that rectangle.

   Continue with steps 2 and 3 clockwise around the graphic organizer.

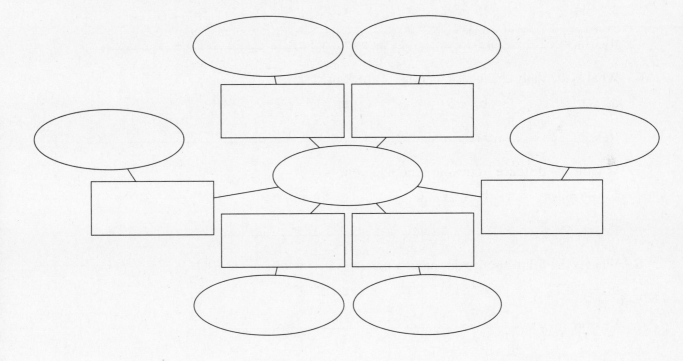

Vocabulary and Study Skills

1B: Reading Comprehension

Study Skill When finding the answer to a math problem, be sure your answer makes sense in the context of the problem.

For each exercise, you are given a question with three answer choices. Circle each choice that would be possible in some situation. Some questions may have more than one possible answer. If a choice is not possible, explain.

1. How many buses are needed?

   a. −3   **b.** 2.5   **c.** 3

   Reason: _____

2. What is the temperature?

   a. −5°   **b.** 0°   **c.** 75.5°

   Reason: _____

3. What is the class average on the test?

   a. −15   **b.** 78.4   **c.** 85

   Reason: _____

4. What is the daily change for a group of stock prices?

   a. −10.50   **b.** −5   **c.** 23

   Reason: _____

5. What is the distance from your school to your home?

   a. −6 miles   **b.** 0.25 mile   **c.** 4.4 miles

   Reason: _____

6. What is the total cost of your purchases?

   a. −$30.23   **b.** $13.00   **c.** $23.375

   Reason: _____

7. What is the profit?

   a. −$20.40   **b.** $0   **c.** $125.75

   Reason: _____

8. **High-Use Academic Words** What does *context* mean in the study skill?

   a. estimation   **b.** situation

1C: Reading/Writing Math Symbols

For use after Lesson 1-2

Study Skill When you take notes in class, keep up with what is being said by using abbreviations. Use abbreviations that you will be able to understand when you review your notes.

Mathematics is a language made up of symbols that represent words and amounts. For example, the mathematical expression 5 × 2 symbolizes five times two.

Explain the meaning of each mathematical expression using words.

1. $3 \cdot 7$ _____

_____

2. $5n$ _____

_____

3. $3 \div 4$ _____

_____

4. $\dfrac{7}{12}$ _____

_____

5. 2^x _____

_____

6. $6(7)$ _____

_____

Write each phrase with math symbols.

7. 7 minus 3 _____

8. p divided by 2 _____

9. 4 divided by x _____

10. y equals 9 _____

1D: Visual Vocabulary Practice

For use after Lesson 1-6

Study Skill The Glossary contains the key vocabulary for this course, as well as illustrated examples.

Concept List

absolute value	function rule	inequality
opposites	power	range
scatter plot	variable	whole numbers

Write the concept that best describes each exercise. Choose from the concept list above.

1. m _____	**2.** 5^3 _____	**3.** 12 23 54 81 69 _____
4. -12 and 12 _____	**5.** _____	**6.** $|-52|$ _____
7. $-4 < 10$ _____	**8.** $0, 1, 2, 3, \ldots$ _____	**9.** $P = 5 + 0.02n$ _____

1E: Vocabulary Check

Study Skill Strengthen your vocabulary. Use these pages and add cues and summaries by applying the Cornell Notetaking style.

Write the definition for each word at the right. To check your work, fold the paper back along the dotted line to see the correct answers.

_____

_____

_____

Algebraic Expression

_____

_____

Equation

_____

_____

Natural Numbers

_____

_____

_____

Integers

_____

_____

_____

Absolute Value

1E: Vocabulary Check (continued)

Write the vocabulary word for each definition. To check your work, fold the paper forward along the dotted line to see the correct answers.

A mathematical phrase that can include numbers, variables, and operation symbols.

_____

A mathematical sentence that uses an equal sign.

_____

The counting numbers.

_____

Whole numbers and their opposites.

_____

The distance that a number is from zero on a number line.

_____

Name_____ Class_____ Date_____

1F: Vocabulary Review

For use with Chapter Review

Study Skill Many words in English have more than one meaning. Often a word has one meaning in ordinary conversation, and a different specific meaning or exact definition when it is used in math or science or grammar. You can often figure out which meaning to use by looking at the sentence that contains the word. To help you decide what a word means, consider the surroundings, or context, in which you see the word.

Read the mathematical definition in the left column and the sentence in the right column. In the blank in the middle, write the one word from the list below that fits both the definition and the sentence.

base   like   origin   constant
power   function   open   term

Definition

Sentence

1. a term that has no variable   _____   That noise is _____.
                                                          It just never seems to stop.

2. a number that is multiplied   _____   Put this statue on its _____
   repeatedly   so it will not fall over.

3. the kind of terms that have   _____   I really _____ that kind
   exactly the same variable   of food. It is my favorite.
   factors

4. the kind of math sentence   _____   The door should be _____
   that has one or more variables   so the customers can come in.

5. the base and exponent of an   _____   Turn off the _____
   expression of the form a^n before you try to repair those
                                                          wires.

6. the point where the axes of   _____   What is the _____ of
   a coordinate plane intersect   that custom? I wonder how it began.

7. a number, a variable, or the   _____   He will come home from
   product of a number and one   college at the end of the
   or more variables   _____.

8. a relation that assigns exactly   _____   What is the _____ of that
   one value in the range to each   key on the keyboard?
   value of the domain

Practice 2-1

Simplify each expression.

1. $6 + (-4)$

2. $-2 + (-13)$

3. $-18 + 4$

4. $15 + (-32)$

5. $-27 + (-14)$

6. $8 + (-3)$

7. $-12.2 + 31.9$

8. $-2.3 + (-13.9)$

9. $19.8 + (-27.4)$

10. $\frac{1}{4} + \left(-\frac{3}{4}\right)$

11. $\frac{2}{3} + \left(-\frac{1}{3}\right)$

12. $-\frac{7}{12} + \frac{1}{6}$

13. $2\frac{2}{3} + (-1)$

14. $-3\frac{3}{4} + 1\frac{1}{2}$

15. $2\frac{1}{3} + \left(-4\frac{2}{3}\right)$

16. $-6.3 + 8.2$

17. $-3.82 + 2.83$

18. $-7.8 + 9$

19. $|-12| + |-21|$

20. $|-13 + 6|$

21. $-14 + |-7|$

Evaluate each expression for $m = 2.5$.

22. $-m + 1.6$

23. $-3.2 + m$

24. $-2.5 + (-m)$

Simplify.

25. $-3 + (-6) + 14$

26. $4 + (-8) + (-14)$

27. $2.7 + (-3.2) + 1.5$

28. $-2.5 + (-1.2) + (-2.3)$

29. $\frac{1}{2} + \left(-\frac{1}{3}\right) + \frac{1}{4}$

30. $-\frac{2}{3} + \left(-\frac{1}{3}\right) + \left(-1\frac{1}{3}\right)$

Simplify.

31. $\begin{bmatrix} 4 & -1 \\ 2 & 5 \end{bmatrix} + \begin{bmatrix} -1 & 2 \\ -2 & -3 \end{bmatrix}$

32. $\begin{bmatrix} -4.7 \\ 2.3 \\ -1.5 \end{bmatrix} + \begin{bmatrix} 5.1 \\ -2.7 \\ 2.6 \end{bmatrix}$

33. The temperature at 5:00 A.M. is $-38°$F. The temperature rises $20°$ by 11:00 A.M. What is the temperature at 11:00 A.M.?

34. A football team has possession of the ball on their own 15-yd line. The next two plays result in a loss of 7 yd and a gain of 3 yd, respectively. On what yard line is the ball after the two plays?

35. Suppose your opening checking account balance is $124.53. After you write a check for $57.49 and make a deposit of $103.49, what is your new balance?

36. During an emergency exercise, a submarine dives 37 ft, rises 16 ft, and then dives 18 ft. What is the net change in the submarine's position after the second dive?

2-1 • Guided Problem Solving

GPS **Student Page 62, Exercise 69**

Jobs Use the data in the tables.

a. Write the data in each table as a matrix.

b. Add the matrices to find the total number of workers in each pay category for each work shift.

c. How many weekend employees on the evening shift earn $6.50 per hour?

d. How many weekend employees work the night shift?

e. **Critical Thinking** Suppose all employees work 8-hour shifts both Saturday and Sunday. How would you use the matrix to find the total wages of the weekend employees?

f. Find the total wages of the weekend employees.

Number of Employees

Saturday Schedule
Hourly Wage

Shift	$6.25	$6.50	$7.00	$7.50
Day	8	3	5	1
Evening	10	2	2	1
Night	4	1	0	1

Sunday Schedule
Hourly Wage

Shift	$6.25	$6.50	$7.00	$7.50
Day	5	2	1	1
Evening	8	2	0	1
Night	2	1	0	1

Read and Understand

1. What information is given in the tables?

   _____

2. Write a matrix for the Saturday schedule and another for the Sunday schedule.

Plan and Solve

3. Add the matrices to find the total number of workers in each pay category for each work shift.

   _____

4. How many weekend employees on the evening shift earn $6.50 per hour? _____

5. Suppose all employees work 8-hour shifts both Saturday and Sunday. How would you use the matrix to find the total wages of the weekend employees? _____

   _____

6. Find the total wages of the weekend employees. _____

Look Back and Check

7. Explain why a matrix helped to make the information in the table more understandable.

   _____

Solve Another Problem

8. How many weekend night employees are there? _____

Guided Problem Solving

Practice 2-2

Subtracting Rational Numbers

Simplify.

1. $13 - 6$

2. $19 - 35$

3. $-4 - 8$

4. $-14 - (-6)$

5. $18 - (-25)$

6. $-32 - 17$

7. $-6.8 - 14.6$

8. $-9.3 - (-23.9)$

9. $-8.2 - 0.8$

10. $18.3 - (-8.1)$

11. $-3 - (-15)$

12. $6.4 - 17$

13. $\frac{3}{4} - 1\frac{1}{4}$

14. $-\frac{1}{3} - \frac{2}{3}$

15. $-\frac{1}{4} - \left(-\frac{3}{4}\right)$

16. $|-11| - |-29|$

17. $|-4 - 8|$

18. $|9.8| - |-15.7|$

19. $|-8 - (-32)|$

20. $|3.7 - (-6.8)|$

21. $2.83 - 3.82$

Evaluate each expression for $c = -3$ and $d = -6$.

22. $c - d$

23. $-c - d$

24. $-c - (-d)$

25. $|c + d|$

26. $-c + d$

27. $3c - 2d$

Simplify.

28. $8 - (-4) - (-5)$

29. $6 - 10 - 4$

30. $10 - 14 - 15$

31. $-6 - 3 - (-2)$

32. $-5 + 7 - 9$

33. $-2 - 2 - 4$

Subtract.

34. $\begin{bmatrix} -3 & -1 \\ 2 & 4 \end{bmatrix} - \begin{bmatrix} 5 & -2 \\ -3 & 8 \end{bmatrix}$

35. $\begin{bmatrix} 6.1 & -4 \\ -3.7 & -2.1 \end{bmatrix} - \begin{bmatrix} 7.0 & -2.3 \\ -1.6 & 4.2 \end{bmatrix}$

36. The temperature in the evening was 68°F. The following morning, the temperature was 39°F. What is the difference between the two temperatures?

37. What is the difference in altitude between Mt. Everest, which is about 29,028 ft above sea level, and Death Valley, which is about 282 ft below sea level?

38. Suppose the balance in your checking account was $234.15 when you wrote a check for $439.87. (This is known as overdrawing your account.) Describe the account's new balance.

39. After three plays in which a football team lost 7 yd, gained 3 yd, and lost 1 yd, respectively, the ball was placed on the team's own 30-yd line. Where was the ball before the three plays?

2-2 • Guided Problem Solving

GPS **Student Page 67, Exercise 55**

a. **Sports** Write the data in each table at right as a matrix.

b. Subtract the 2000 matrix from the 2005 matrix to find the changes in participation in sports activities.

c. **Writing** Suppose you invest in sporting goods. In which sport would you invest? Use elements from your matrix to explain.

City-Wide Participation in Sports Activities (thousands)

	Sport	Elementary	High School	College
2000	Basketball	5.5	8.2	4.9
	Tennis	1.4	3.2	3.9
	Soccer	4.2	3.8	1.3
	Volleyball	1.6	5.2	5.1

	Sport	Elementary	High School	College
2005	Basketball	6.8	7.9	4.9
	Tennis	1.0	1.8	1.7
	Soccer	5.6	4.1	1.3
	Volleyball	1.8	4.9	2.9

Read and Understand

1. What information is given in the tables?

   _____

2. Write a matrix for each table.

Plan and Solve

3. Subtract the 2000 matrix from the 2005 matrix to find the changes in participation in sports activities.

   _____

4. Suppose you invested in sporting goods. In which sport would you invest? Use elements from your matrix to explain.

   _____

Look Back and Check

5. Explain how organizing data into a matrix made it easier to learn more about the information in the tables.

   _____

Solve Another Problem

6. Use your two original matrices to determine which sport had the highest participation rate in 2000 and in 2005. Explain how you used your matrices to arrive at your answers.

   _____

Practice 2-3

Multiplying and Dividing Rational Numbers

Simplify each expression.

1. $(-2)(8)$

2. $(-6)(-9)$

3. $(-3)^4$

4. -2^5

5. $(6)(-8)$

6. $(-14)^2$

7. $2(-4)(-6)$

8. $-30 \div (-5)$

9. $\dfrac{-52}{-13}$

10. $(-8)(5)(-3)$

11. -7^2

12. -3^5

13. $\dfrac{-68}{17}$

14. $\dfrac{(-4)(-13)}{-26}$

15. $\dfrac{225}{(-3)(-5)}$

Evaluate each expression.

16. x^3 for $x = -5$

17. $s^2t \div 10$ for $s = -2$ and $t = 10$

18. $-2m + 4n^2$ for $m = -6$ and $n = -5$

19. $\dfrac{v}{w}$ for $v = \dfrac{2}{5}$ and $w = -\dfrac{1}{2}$

20. $-cd^2$ for $c = 2$ and $d = -4$

21. $(x + 4)^2$ for $x = -11$

22. $\left(\dfrac{a}{b}\right)^2 + b^3$ for $a = 24$ and $b = -6$

23. $4p^2 + 7q^3$ for $p = -3$ and $q = -2$

24. $(e + f)^4$ for $e = -3$ and $f = 7$

25. $5f^2 - z^2$ for $f = -1$ and $z = -4$

Simplify each expression.

26. $2^4 - 3^2 + 5^2$

27. $(-8)^2 - 4^3$

28. $32 \div (-7 + 5)^3$

29. $\dfrac{3}{4} \div \left(-\dfrac{3}{7}\right)$

30. $18 + 4^2 \div (-8)$

31. $26 \div [4 - (-9)]$

32. $4^3 - (2 - 5)^3$

33. $-(-4)^3$

34. $(-8)(-5)(-3)$

35. $(-3)^2 - 4^2$

36. $\dfrac{-45}{-15}$

37. $(-2)^6$

38. $\dfrac{-90}{6}$

39. $\dfrac{-15}{(7 - 4)}$

40. $\dfrac{195}{-13}$

Evaluate each expression.

41. $(a + b)^2$ for $a = 6$ and $b = -8$

42. $d^3 \div e$ for $d = -6$ and $e = -3$

43. $(m + 5n)^3$ for $m = 2$ and $n = -1$

44. $j^5 - 5k$ for $j = -4$ and $k = -1$

45. $xy + z$ for $x = -4, y = 3,$ and $z = -3$

46. $4s \div (-3t)$ for $s = -6$ and $t = -2$

47. $\dfrac{r^3}{s}$ for $r = -6$ and $s = -2$

48. $\dfrac{-h^5}{-4}$ for $h = 4$

259 *Algebra 1 Lesson 2-3*

2-3 • Guided Problem Solving

GPS Student Page 75, Exercise 83

Entertainment As riders plunge down the hill of a roller coaster, you can approximate the height h, in feet, above the ground of their roller coaster car. Use the function $h = 155 - 16t^2$ where t is the number of seconds since the start of the descent.

155 ft

a. How far is a rider from the bottom of the hill after 1 second? 2 seconds?

b. **Critical Thinking** Does it take more than or less than 4 seconds to reach the bottom? Explain.

Read and Understand

1. What do each of the variables in the function represent?

_____

2. What are the units that would be used for values of h and t? _____

Plan and Solve

3. How far is the rider from the bottom of the hill after 1 second? _____

4. How far is the rider from the bottom of the hill after 2 seconds? _____

5. What value would you use for h if the roller coaster car were at the bottom of the hill? _____

6. Does it take more than or less than 4 seconds to reach the bottom? Explain. _____

_____

Look Back and Check

7. Explain how you use order of operations when using the roller coaster function.

_____

Solve Another Problem

8. For a different roller coaster, the height h, in feet, above the ground of the roller coaster car is approximated by the function $h = 200 - 16t^2$. How far is a rider from the bottom of the hill on this roller coaster after 2 seconds?

Practice 2-4

Simplify each expression.

1. $2(x + 6)$ **2.** $-5(8 - b)$ **3.** $4(-x + 7)$

4. $(5c - 7)(-3)$ **5.** $-2.5(3a + 5)$ **6.** $-(3k - 12)$

7. $-\frac{3}{4}(12 - 16d)$ **8.** $\frac{2}{3}(6h - 1)$ **9.** $(-3.2x + 2.1)(-6)$

10. $3.5(3x - 8)$ **11.** $4(x + 7)$ **12.** $-2.5(2a - 4)$

13. $\frac{2}{3}(12 - 15d)$ **14.** $-2(k - 11)$ **15.** $-\frac{1}{3}(6h + 15)$

16. $(2c - 8)(-4)$ **17.** $-(4 - 2b)$ **18.** $2(3x - 9)$

19. $4(2r + 8)$ **20.** $-5(b - 5)$ **21.** $3(f + 2)$

22. $6h + 5(h - 5)$ **23.** $-5d + 3(2d - 7)$ **24.** $7 + 2(4x - 3)$

25. $2(3h + 2) - 4h$ **26.** $2(4 + y)$ **27.** $\frac{1}{2}(2n - 4) - 2n$

28. $-w + 4(w + 3)$ **29.** $0.4(3d - 5)$ **30.** $-4d + 2(3 + d)$

31. $2x + \frac{3}{4}(4x + 16)$ **32.** $2(3a + 2)$ **33.** $5(t - 3) - 2t$

34. $5(b + 4) - 6b$ **35.** $\frac{2}{5}(5k + 35) - 8$ **36.** $0.4(2s + 4)$

37. $\frac{2}{3}(9b - 27)$ **38.** $\frac{1}{2}(12n - 8)$ **39.** $0.5(2x - 4)$

40. $2(a - 4) + 15$ **41.** $13 + 2(5c - 2)$ **42.** $7 + 2(\frac{1}{5}a - 3)$

43. $5(3x + 12)$ **44.** $2(m + 1)$ **45.** $4(2a + 2) - 17$

46. $-4x + 3(2x - 5)$ **47.** $3(t - 12)$ **48.** $-6 - 3(2k + 4)$

Write an expression for each phrase.

49. 5 times the quantity x plus 6

50. twice the quantity y minus 8

51. the product of -15 and the quantity x minus 5

52. 32 divided by the quantity y plus 12

53. -8 times the quantity 4 decreased by w

54. the quantity x plus 9, times the quantity 7 minus x

2-4 • Guided Problem Solving

GPS **Student Page 84, Exercise 78**

Shopping Suppose you buy 4 cans of tomatoes at $1.02 each, 3 cans of tuna for $.99 each, and 3 boxes of pasta at $.52 each. Write an expression to model this situation. Then use the Distributive Property to find the total cost.

Read and Understand

1. What is the Distributive Property? _____

2. What type of information is given to you in the problem? _____

Plan and Solve

3. Write an expression that shows how to determine the total amount spent on tomatoes. _____

4. Write an expression that shows how to determine the total amount spent on tuna. _____

5. Write an expression that shows how to determine the total amount spent on pasta. _____

6. Write an expression that models the total amount of money you will spend. _____

7. Use the Distributive Property to find the total cost. _____

Look Back and Check

8. Check the reasonableness of your answer by rounding the cost of each item and estimating the total cost. _____

_____

Solve Another Problem

9. In order to paint your bedroom, you buy 2 gallons of paint that cost $10.50 each, 3 paint brushes that cost $2.99 each, and 2 paint rollers that cost $1.25 each. Write an expression to model this situation. Then use the Distributive Property to find the total cost.

_____

Practice 2-5

Name the property that each equation illustrates.

1. $83 + 6 = 6 + 83$

2. $8 + x = x + 8$

3. $1 \cdot 4y = 4y$

4. $15x + 15y = 15(x + y)$

5. $(8 \cdot 7) \cdot 6 = 8 \cdot (7 \cdot 6)$

6. $\frac{2}{3}\left(\frac{3}{2}\right) = 1$

7. $3(a + 2b) = 3a + 6b$

8. $7x + 2y = 2y + 7x$

9. $7 + (8 + 15) = (7 + 8) + 15$

10. $x + (-x) = 0$

11. $x + y = y + x$

12. $6 \cdot (x \cdot y) = (6 \cdot x) \cdot y$

13. $16 + 0 = 16$

14. $3w + 5y = 5y + 3w$

15. $7(3 + 4y) = 21 + 28y$

16. $0 = 30 \cdot 0$

17. $4a + (5b + 6c) = (4a + 5b) + 6c$

18. $ab + c = ba + c$

19. $wr = rw$

20. $20(a + b) = 20(b + a)$

Give a reason to justify each step.

21. a. $4c + 3(2 + c) = 4c + 6 + 3c$
   b. $\qquad\qquad = 4c + 3c + 6$
   c. $\qquad\qquad = (4c + 3c) + 6$
   d. $\qquad\qquad = (4 + 3)c + 6$
   e. $\qquad\qquad = 7c + 6$

22. a. $8w - 4(7 - w) = 8w - 28 + 4w$
   b. $\qquad\qquad = 8w + (-28) + 4w$
   c. $\qquad\qquad = 8w + 4w + (-28)$
   d. $\qquad\qquad = (8 + 4)w + (-28)$
   e. $\qquad\qquad = 12w + (-28)$
   f. $\qquad\qquad = 12w - 28$

23. a. $5(x + y) + 2(x + y) = 5x + 5y + 2x + 2y$
   b. $\qquad\qquad = 5x + 2x + 5y + 2y$
   c. $\qquad\qquad = (5 + 2)x + (5 + 2)y$
   d. $\qquad\qquad = 7x + 7y$

Use mental math to simplify each expression.

24. $48 + 27 + 2 + 3$

25. $10 \cdot 72 \cdot 5 \cdot 2$

26. $10 \cdot 8 \cdot 3 \cdot 10$

27. $8\frac{1}{2} + 4\frac{1}{3} + 2\frac{1}{2} + 2\frac{2}{3}$

28. Henry bought an apple for $0.75, some apricots for $1.50, some cherries for $3.25, and three bananas for $1.50. Find the total cost of the fruit.

29. Suppose you buy some camping supplies. You purchase waterproof matches for $3.95, a compass for $18.25, flashlight batteries for $3.75, and a map for $2.05. Find the total cost of the supplies.

30. You go to the video store and rent some DVDs for $8.50 and a video game for $3.69. While there, you buy a box of popcorn for $2.31 and a candy bar for $1.50. Find the total cost of the items.

2-5 • Guided Problem Solving

GPS Student Page 89, Exercise 31

Shopping Suppose you are buying soccer equipment: a pair of cleats for $31.50, a soccer ball for $14.97, and shin guards for $6.50. Use mental math to find the total cost.

Read and Understand

1. What is the problem asking you to do? _____

2. What two properties of real numbers will
   help you solve this problem using mental math? _____   _____

Plan and Solve

3. Explain what the Commutative Property of Addition states. _____
   _____

4. Explain what the Associative Property of Addition states. _____
   _____

5. How can you use the Commutative Property to rewrite the expression 31.50 + 14.97 + 6.50 in
   order to be able to use mental math? _____

6. How will you use the Associative Property to find the total cost? _____
   _____

7. What is your total cost? _____

Look Back and Check

8. Check the reasonableness of your answer by rounding the cost of each item and estimating the
   total cost. _____
   _____

Solve Another Problem

9. Suppose you are buying new clothes for school: a pair of pants for $24.50, a shirt for $13.99, and
   a pair of shoes for $12.50. Use mental math to find the total cost. _____
   _____

Practice 2-6

Theoretical and Experimental Probability

A driver collected data on how long it takes to drive to work.

Time in minutes	20	25	30
Number of trips	4	8	2

1. Find P(the trip will take 25 min).

2. Find P(the trip will take 20 min).

3. Find P(the trip will take at least 25 min).

Use the data in the line plot to find each probability.

Student Birth Months

					X						X
X		X			X				X		X
X		X			X	X		X	X		X
X	X	X	X		X	X	X	X	X	X	X
JAN	FEB	MAR	APR	MAY	JUN	JUL	AUG	SEP	OCT	NOV	DEC

4. P(June)

5. P(October)

6. P(first six months of year)

7. P(May)

8. P(not December)

9. P(last three months of year)

A cereal manufacturer selects 100 boxes of cereal at random. Ninety-nine of the boxes are the correct weight. Find each probability.

10. P(the cereal box is the correct weight)

11. P(the cereal box is not the correct weight)

12. There are 24,000 boxes of cereal. Predict how many of the boxes are the correct weight.

13. One letter is chosen at random from the word *ALGEBRA*. Find each probability.

   a. P(the letter is A)
   b. P(the letter is a vowel)

14. Patrice has a 40% chance of making a free throw. What is the probability that she will miss the free throw?

15. A box of animal crackers contains five hippos, two lions, three zebras, and four elephants. Find the probability if one animal cracker is chosen at random.

   a. P(a hippo)
   b. P(not an elephant)
   c. P(an elephant or a lion)

16. Anthony is making a collage for his art class by picking shapes randomly. He has five squares, two triangles, two ovals, and four circles. Find each probability.

   a. P(circle is chosen first)
   b. P(a square is not chosen first)
   c. P(a triangle or a square is chosen first)

        Algebra 1 Lesson 2-6   **265**

2-6 • Guided Problem Solving

GPS **Student Page 97, Exercise 42**

Birthdays Each day in the United States, about 753,000 people have a
birthday. Each day about 10,700 people celebrate their sixteenth birthday.
Find the probability that someone celebrating a birthday today will turn 16.
Round to the nearest percent.

Read and Understand

1. What information are you given in the problem? _____

2. What is the problem asking you to figure out? _____

3. How do you compute the probability of an event occurring? _____

_____

Plan and Solve

4. What is the number of favorable events in this situation? _____

5. What is the number of possible outcomes in this situation? _____

6. Find the exact probability that someone celebrating a birthday today will turn 16.

_____

7. Convert your answer to Step 6 to the nearest percent. _____

Look Back and Check

8. The average life expectancy is around 78 years. Check the reasonableness of your answer by
   assuming that each age from 0 to 78 has the same probability as the probability found in Step 6.
   Multiply this probability by 79 to account for the probability for each age. Round to the nearest
   percent. Is your answer near 100%? Did we overestimate or underestimate with our assumption?
   Explain.

_____

_____

Solve Another Problem

9. What is the probability that someone celebrating a birthday today is *not* turning 16? Round to
   the nearest percent.

_____

Practice 2-7

1. Suppose you have a dark closet containing seven blue shirts, five yellow shirts, and eight white shirts. You pick two shirts at random from the closet. Find each probability.

    a. P(blue then yellow) with replacing   **b.** P(blue then yellow) without replacing

    c. P(yellow then yellow) with replacing   **d.** P(yellow then yellow) without replacing

    e. P(yellow then white) with replacing   **f.** P(yellow then white) without replacing

    g. P(blue then blue) with replacing   **h.** P(blue then blue) without replacing

A and B are independent events. Find the missing probability.

2. $P(A) = \frac{3}{7}, P(A \text{ and } B) = \frac{1}{3}$. Find $P(B)$.

3. $P(B) = \frac{1}{5}, P(A \text{ and } B) = \frac{2}{13}$. Find $P(A)$.

4. $P(B) = \frac{15}{16}, P(A \text{ and } B) = \frac{3}{4}$. Find $P(A)$.

5. $P(A) = \frac{8}{15}, P(B) = \frac{3}{4}$. Find $P(A \text{ and } B)$.

6. Suppose you draw two tennis balls at random from a bag containing seven pink, four white, three yellow, and two striped balls. Find each probability.

    a. P(yellow then pink) with replacing   **b.** P(yellow then pink) without replacing

    c. P(pink then pink) with replacing   **d.** P(pink then pink) without replacing

    e. P(striped then striped) with replacing   **f.** P(striped then striped) without replacing

    g. P(pink then white) with replacing   **h.** P(pink then white) without replacing

A and B are independent events. Find the missing probability.

7. $P(A) = \frac{3}{4}, P(A \text{ and } B) = \frac{1}{2}$. Find $P(B)$.

8. $P(A) = \frac{3}{7}, P(B) = \frac{1}{6}$. Find $P(A \text{ and } B)$.

9. $P(B) = \frac{9}{10}, P(A \text{ and } B) = \frac{3}{5}$. Find $P(A)$.

10. $P(B) = \frac{1}{4}, P(A \text{ and } B) = \frac{3}{20}$. Find $P(A)$.

Use an equation to solve each problem.

11. A bag contains green and yellow color tiles. You pick two tiles at random without replacing the first one. The probability that the first tile is yellow is $\frac{3}{5}$. The probability of drawing two yellow tiles is $\frac{12}{35}$. Find the probability that the second tile you pick is yellow.

12. A bag contains red and blue marbles. You pick two marbles at random without replacing the first one. The probability of drawing a blue and then a red is $\frac{4}{15}$. The probability that your second marble is red if your first marble is blue is $\frac{2}{3}$. Find the probability that the first marble is blue.

2-7 • Guided Problem Solving

GPS **Student Page 105, Exercise 33**

a. Agriculture An acre of land in Indiana is chosen at random. What is the probability that it is cropland?

b. An acre of land is chosen at random from each of the three states listed. What is the probability that all three acres will be cropland?

Percent of Cropland	
Alabama	8%
Florida	7%
Indiana	58%

Read and Understand

1. What information is given in the table? _____

2. Are these events independent or dependent? _____

Plan and Solve

3. If an acre of land in Indiana is chosen at random, what is the probability that it is cropland?

   _____

4. If an acre of land in Florida is chosen at random, what is the probability that it is cropland?

   _____

5. If an acre of land in Alabama is chosen at random, what is the probability that it is cropland?

   _____

6. If an acre of land is chosen at random from each of the three states, what is the probability that all three acres will be cropland?

   _____

Look Back and Check

7. Explain why it is reasonable that the probability that all three acres are cropland is much smaller than the probability that the acre of land is cropland in any one state.

   _____

   _____

Solve Another Problem

8. If an acre of land is chosen at random from Alabama and Florida, what is the probability that both acres will be cropland? _____

2A: Graphic Organizer

For use before Lesson 2-1

Study Skill Keep notes as you work through each chapter to help you organize your thinking and to make it easier to review the material when you complete the chapter.

Write your answers.

1. What is the chapter title? _____

2. Find the Table of Contents page for this chapter at the front of the book. Name four topics you will study in this chapter.

   _____   _____

   _____   _____

3. Complete the graphic organizer as you work through the chapter.
   1. Write the title of the chapter in the center oval.
   2. When you begin a lesson, write the name of the lesson in a rectangle.
   3. When you complete that lesson, write a skill or key concept from that lesson in the outer oval linked to that rectangle.
   Continue with steps 2 and 3 clockwise around the graphic organizer.

2B: Reading Comprehension

Study Skill When you read a paragraph, it is a good idea to read it twice: once to get an overview, then again to find the essential information.

Read the passage below and answer the following questions.

> The blue whale is the largest animal on earth. A blue whale is about 100 million times larger than the krill, one of the smallest creatures it eats. The skeleton of a blue whale can weigh about 50,000 pounds. The heart of a blue whale can be the size of a small car. The largest recorded blue whale weighed 160 tons. About how much of that weight was *not* the skeleton?

1. What is the subject of this paragraph? _____

2. What are the numbers 50,000 and 160 in the paragraph referring to?

   _____

3. What question are you asked to answer? _____

   _____

4. What is the weight (and the units) for the skeleton? _____

5. What is the total weight (and the units) of the largest blue whale? _____

6. How can you convert 160 tons into pounds? _____

   _____

7. Write an expression for how much of the whale's weight is *not* the skeleton.

   _____

8. Simplify the expression to answer the question asked in the paragraph.

   _____

9. **High-Use Academic Words** What does *convert* mean for you to do in Step 6?

   a. measure   **b.** change

2C: Reading/Writing Math Symbols

For use after Lesson 2-3

Study Skill When you take notes in any subject, it helps if you learn to use abbreviations and symbols such as @ (at); #, #s (number, numbers); w/ (with); w/o (without); s/b (should be).

For Exercises 1–7, match the symbolic expression in Column A with its written expression in Column B by drawing a line between them.

Column A		Column B
1. $2 + x$	**A.**	one-third of x
2. $\frac{r}{3}$	**B.**	absolute value of negative 6
3. $-12 \div x$	**C.**	18 decreased by r
4. $18 - r$	**D.**	2 more than x
5. $\frac{1}{3}x$	**E.**	the sum of x and y
6. $|-6|$	**F.**	r divided into 3 parts
7. $x + y$	**G.**	negative 12 divided by x

For Exercises 8–14, match the symbolic expression in Column C with its written expression in Column D by drawing a line between them.

Column C		Column D
8. $h - 8$	**H.**	100 minus w
9. $12 + y$	**I.**	twice w
10. $-12x$	**J.**	12 greater than y
11. $2w$	**K.**	quotient of r and 32
12. $k - 14$	**L.**	negative 12 times x
13. $100 - w$	**M.**	14 subtracted from k
14. $\frac{r}{32}$	**N.**	8 less than h

2D: Visual Vocabulary Practice

For use after Lesson 2-6

• •

Study Skill If a word is not in the Glossary, use a dictionary to find its meaning.

Concept List

complement of an event	constant	event
like terms	matrix	Multiplication Property of Zero
odds	probability	reciprocal

Write the concept that best describes each exercise.
Choose from the concept list above.

1. $5:6$	**2.** $\dfrac{3}{5}$ and $\dfrac{5}{3}$	**3.** $-2x^2y$ and $8x^2y$
_____	_____	_____
4. 27	**5.** $\begin{bmatrix} 4 & -2 & 9 \\ 0 & 6 & -5 \end{bmatrix}$	**6.** tossing a 4 on a number cube
_____	_____	_____
7. For every real number n, $n \cdot 0 = 0$	**8.** $\dfrac{\text{number of favorable outcomes}}{\text{number of possible outcomes}}$	**9.** $1 - P(\text{event})$
_____	_____	_____

Vocabulary and Study Skills

2E: Vocabulary Check

Study Skill Strengthen your vocabulary. Use these pages and add cues and summaries by applying the Cornell Notetaking style.

Write the definition for each word at the right. To check your work, fold the paper back along the dotted line to see the correct answers.

_____

_____

_____

_____   Multiplicative Inverse

_____

_____

_____   Coefficient

_____

_____

_____   Like Terms

_____

_____

_____   Constant

_____

_____

_____   Matrix

_____

_____

2E: Vocabulary Check (continued)

Write the vocabulary word for each definition. To check your work, fold the paper forward along the dotted line to see the correct answers.

Given a nonzero rational number *a/b*, it is *b/a*.

_____

The numerical factor of a term.

_____

These have exactly the same variable factors in a variable expression.

_____

A term that has no variable factor.

_____

A rectangular arrangement of numbers in rows and columns.

_____

Vocabulary and Study Skills

2F: Vocabulary Review

For use with Chapter Review

Study Skill One of the most difficult things about reading a mathematics textbook is the new vocabulary you will encounter. Often you encounter several new terms in each section. It is important to learn the definitions of new terms as soon as they are introduced. Read aloud or recite the new terms as you read them. Reciting a rule, definition, or formula can help you to remember and recall it.

For Exercises 1–7, match each term in Column A with its definition in Column B by drawing a line between them.

Column A		Column B
1. experimental probability	A.	a process of reasoning logically from given facts to a conclusion
2. odds	B.	all possible outcomes of an event
3. dependent events	C.	describes the likelihood of an event by comparing favorale and unfavorable outcomes
4. deductive reasoning	D.	two events in which the occurrence of one event affects the probability of the second event
5. like terms	E.	the ratio of the number of times an event actually happens to the number of times the experiment is done
6. sample space	F.	the ratio of the number of favorable outcomes to the number of possible outcomes if all outcomes have the same chance of happening
7. theoretical probability	G.	terms with exactly the same variable factors in a variable expression

For Exercises 8–14, match each term in Column C with its definition in Column D by drawing a line between them.

Column C		Column D
8. coefficient	H.	any group of outcomes in a situation involving probability
9. independent events	I.	a number, variable, or the product or quotient of a number and one or more variables
10. term	J.	the result of a single trial in a probability experiment
11. event	K.	the numerical factor when a term has a variable
12. constant	L.	two events for which the outcome of one does not affect the other
13. probability	M.	how likely it is that an event will occur
14. outcome	N.	a term that has no variable factor

Practice 3-1

Solving Two-Step Equations

Solve each equation. Check your answer.

1. $5a + 2 = 7$

2. $2x + 3 = 7$

3. $3b + 6 = 12$

4. $9 = 5 + 4t$

5. $4a + 1 = 13$

6. $-t + 2 = 12$

Write an equation to model each situation. Then solve.

7. You want to buy a bouquet of yellow roses and baby's breath for $16. The baby's breath costs $3.50 per bunch, and the roses cost $2.50 each. You want one bunch of baby's breath and some roses for your bouquet. How many roses can you buy?

8. Suppose you walk at the rate of 210 ft/min. You need to walk 10,000 ft. How many more minutes will it take you to finish if you have already walked 550 ft?

9. Suppose you have shelled 6.5 lb of pecans, and you can shell pecans at a rate of 1.5 lb per hour. How many more hours will it take you to shell a total of 11 lb of pecans?

10. To mail a first class letter, the U.S. Postal Service charges $.34 for the first ounce and $.21 for each additional ounce. It costs $1.18 to mail your letter. How many ounces does your letter weigh?

11. Suppose you want to buy one pair of pants and several pairs of socks. The pants cost $24.95, and the socks are $5.95 per pair. How many pairs of socks can you buy if you have $50.00 to spend?

Solve each equation. Check your answer.

12. $5.8n + 3.7 = 29.8$

13. $67 = -3y + 16$

14. $-d + 7 = 3$

15. $\frac{m}{9} + 7 = 3$

16. $6.78 + 5.2x = -36.9$

17. $5z + 9 = -21$

18. $3x - 7 = 35$

19. $36.9 = 3.7b - 14.9$

20. $4s - 13 = 51$

21. $9f + 16 = 70$

22. $11.6 + 3a = -16.9$

23. $-9 = -\frac{h}{12} + 5$

24. $-c + 2 = 5$

25. $-67 = -8n + 5$

26. $22 = 7 - 3a$

27. $\frac{k}{3} - 19 = -26$

28. $-21 = \frac{n}{3} + 2$

29. $3x + 5.7 = 15$

30. $\frac{a}{5} - 2 = -13$

31. $2x + 23 = 49$

32. $\frac{x}{2} + 8 = -3$

Justify each step.

33. $\quad\quad 24 - x = -16$

   a. $24 - x - 24 = -16 - 24$

   b. $\quad\quad -x = -40$

   c. $\quad -1(-x) = -1(-40)$

   d. $\quad\quad\quad x = 40$

34. $\quad\quad \frac{x}{7} + 4 = 15$

   a. $\frac{x}{7} + 4 - 4 = 15 - 4$

   b. $\quad\quad \frac{x}{7} = 11$

   c. $\quad 7(\frac{x}{7}) = 7(11)$

   d. $\quad\quad x = 77$

35. $\quad\quad -8 = 2x - 5$

   a. $-8 + 5 = 2x - 5 + 5$

   b. $\quad\quad -3 = 2x$

   c. $\quad -\frac{3}{2} = \frac{2x}{2}$

   d. $\quad -\frac{3}{2} = x$

3-1 • Guided Problem Solving

GPS **Student Page 123, Exercise 45**

Insurance One health insurance policy pays people for claims by multiplying the claim amount by 0.8 and then subtracting $500. Write a rule that describes the insurance payment as a function of the claim amount. Then find the claim amount for an insurance payment of $4650.

Read and Understand

1. Describe in words how the insurance company determines how to pay people for their insurance claims. _____

2. What two quantities will be related by the function rule? _____

Plan and Solve

3. Define your two variables.

   _____   _____

4. Write your rule that describes the insurance payment as a function of the claim amount. _____

5. For which variable will you substitute the value $4650? _____

6. Substitute $4650 in and solve your equation for the claim amount. _____

Look Back and Check

7. Multiplying by 0.8 is equivalent to finding 80% of a number. Check the reasonableness of your answer by finding 80% of your claim amount. Your answer should be $500 more than $4650.

Solve Another Problem

8. What would the insurance payment be for a claim of $3000? _____

Practice 3-2

Solving Multi-Step Equations

Solve each equation. Check your answer.

1. $2n + 3n + 7 = -41$

2. $2x - 5x + 6.3 = -14.4$

3. $2z + 9.75 - 7z = -5.15$

4. $3h - 5h + 11 = 17$

5. $2t + 8 - t = -3$

6. $6a - 2a = -36$

7. $3c - 8c + 7 = -18$

8. $7g + 14 - 5g = -8$

9. $2b - 6 + 3b = 14$

10. $2(a - 4) + 15 = 13$

11. $7 + 2(a - 3) = -9$

12. $13 + 2(5c - 2) = 29$

13. $5(3x + 12) = -15$

14. $4(2a + 2) - 17 = 15$

15. $2(m + 1) = 16$

16. $-4x + 3(2x - 5) = 31$

17. $-6 - 3(2k + 4) = 18$

18. $3(t - 12) = 27$

19. $-w + 4(w + 3) = -12$

20. $4 = 0.4(3d - 5)$

21. $-4d + 2(3 + d) = -14$

22. $2x + \frac{3}{4}(4x + 16) = 7$

23. $2(3a + 2) = -8$

24. $5(t - 3) - 2t = -30$

25. $5(b + 4) - 6b = -24$

26. $\frac{2}{5}(5k + 35) - 8 = 12$

27. $0.4(2s + 4) = 4.8$

28. $\frac{2}{3}(9b - 27) = 36$

29. $\frac{1}{2}(12n - 8) = 26$

30. $0.5(2x - 4) = -17$

31. $18 = \frac{c + 5}{2}$

32. $\frac{2}{9}s = -6$

33. $\frac{1}{3}x = \frac{1}{2}$

34. $\frac{2}{3}g + \frac{1}{2}g = 14$

35. $\frac{3x + 7}{2} = 8$

36. $\frac{2x - 6}{4} = -7$

37. $\frac{2}{3}k + \frac{1}{4}k = 22$

38. $-\frac{4}{7}h = -28$

39. $-8 = \frac{4}{5}k$

40. $\frac{3}{4} - \frac{1}{3}z = \frac{1}{4}$

41. $-9 = \frac{3}{4}m$

42. $\frac{5}{6}c - \frac{2}{3}c = \frac{1}{3}$

43. $\frac{4}{5} = -\frac{4}{7}g$

44. $\frac{9x + 6 - 4x}{2} = 8$

45. $-\frac{1}{6}d = -4$

Write an equation to model each situation. Then solve.

46. The attendance at a baseball game was 400 people. Student tickets cost $2 and adult tickets cost $3. Total ticket sales were $1050. How many tickets of each type were sold?

47. The perimeter of a pool table is 30 ft. The table is twice as long as it is wide. What is the length of the pool table?

48. Lopez spent $\frac{1}{3}$ of his vacation money for travel and $\frac{2}{5}$ of his vacation money for lodging. He spent $1100 for travel and lodging. What is the total amount of money he spent on his vacation?

49. Victoria weighs $\frac{5}{7}$ as much as Mario. Victoria weighs 125 lb. How much does Mario weigh?

50. Denise's cell phone plan is $29.95 per month plus $.10 per minute for each minute over 300 minutes of call time. Denise's cell phone bill is $99.95. For how many minutes was she billed?

3-2 • Guided Problem Solving

GPS **Student Page 130, Exercise 58**

Cell Phones Jane's cell phone plan is $40 per month plus $.15 per minute for each minute over 200 minutes of call time. If Jane's cell phone bill is $58.00, for how many extra calling minutes was she billed?

Read and Understand

1. Explain how the amount of Jane's phone bill is determined? _____

2. What is the problem asking you to determine? _____

Plan and Solve

3. What would Jane's phone bill be if she talked for exactly 200 minutes? _____

4. What would Jane's phone bill be if she talked for 10 extra minutes? _____

5. Write an equation to model this situation. _____

6. Use your equation to determine how many extra calling minutes Jane was billed for if her phone bill was $58.00. _____

Look Back and Check

7. Is this a reasonable plan? How many minutes do you talk on the telephone each month? Is it reasonable to allow 200 minutes before charging extra? _____

_____

Solve Another Problem

8. Janet's cable company charges her a basic fee of $59. For each premium channel, she is charged an extra $12. How many premium channels does she have if her total bill is $107 each month?

_____

Practice 3-3

Equations With Variables on Both Sides

Solve each equation. Check your answer. If appropriate, write *identity* or *no solution*.

1. $7 - 2n = n - 14$

2. $2(4 - 2r) = -2(r + 5)$

3. $3d + 8 = 2d - 7$

4. $6t = 3(t + 4) - t$

5. $8z - 7 = 3z - 7 + 5z$

6. $7x - 8 = 3x + 12$

7. $3(n - 1) = 5n + 3 - 2n$

8. $2(6 - 4d) = 25 - 9d$

9. $4s - 12 = -5s + 51$

10. $8(2f - 3) = 4(4f - 8)$

11. $6k - 25 = 7 - 2k$

12. $3v - 9 = 7 + 2v - v$

13. $4(b - 1) = -4 + 4b$

14. $\frac{1}{4}x + \frac{1}{2} = \frac{1}{4}x - \frac{1}{2}$

15. $6 - 4d = 16 - 9d$

16. $\frac{2}{3}a - \frac{3}{4} = \frac{3}{4}a$

17. $2s - 12 + 2s = 4s - 12$

18. $3.6y = 5.4 + 3.3y$

19. $4.3v - 6 = 8 + 2.3v$

20. $4b - 1 = -4 + 4b + 3$

21. $\frac{2}{3}(6x + 3) = 4x + 2$

22. $6y + 9 = 3(2y + 3)$

23. $4g + 7 = 5g - 1 - g$

24. $2(n + 2) = 5n - 5$

25. $6 - 3d = 5(2 - d)$

26. $6.1h = 9.3 - 3.2h$

27. $-4.4s - 2 = -5.5s - 4.2$

28. $3(2f + 4) = 2(3f - 6)$

29. $\frac{3}{4}t - \frac{5}{6} = \frac{2}{3}t$

30. $3v + 8 = 8 + 2v + v$

31. $\frac{1}{2}d - \frac{3}{4} = \frac{3}{5}d$

32. $5(r + 3) = 2r + 6$

33. $8 - 3(p - 4) = 2p$

Write an equation to model each situation. Then solve. Check your answer.

34. Hans needs to rent a moving truck. Suppose Company A charges a rate of $40 per day and Company B charges a $60 fee plus $20 per day. For what number of days is the cost the same?

35. Suppose a video store charges nonmembers $4 to rent each video. A store membership costs $21 and members pay only $2.50 to rent each video. For what number of videos is the cost the same?

36. Suppose your club is selling candles to raise money. It costs $100 to rent a booth from which to sell the candles. If the candles cost your club $1 each and are sold for $5 each, how many candles must be sold to equal your expenses?

Find the value of x.

37.

$(4x - 2)°$ $(5x - 3)°$

38.

$\left(\frac{1}{4}x + 3\right)°$ $\left(\frac{3}{4}x - 7\right)°$

39.

$(1.15 + 0.8x)°$ $(2.3 - 1.5x)°$

3-3 • Guided Problem Solving

GPS Student Page 138, Exercise 40

Spreadsheet Don set up a spreadsheet to solve
$5(x - 3) = 4 - 3(x + 1)$.

a. Does Don's spreadsheet show a solution to the
   equation?

b. Between which two values of x is the solution to
   the equation? How do you know?

c. For what values of x is $4 - 3(x + 1)$ less than $5(x - 3)$?

	A	B	C
1	x	$5(x - 3)$	$4 - 3(x + 1)$
2	−5	−40	16
3	−3	−30	10
4	−1	−20	4
5	1	−10	−2
6	3	0	−8

Read and Understand

1. Describe what the values in each column represent. _____

_____

2. What is Don trying to use the spreadsheet for? _____

Plan and Solve

3. Explain what a solution to an equation is. _____

_____

4. Does Don's spreadsheet show a solution to the equation? _____

5. Between what two values of x is the solution to the equation? _____

   How do you know? _____

6. For what values of x is $4 - 3(x + 1)$ less than $5(x - 3)$? _____

Look Back and Check

7. Check the reasonableness of your answer by substituting a value
   between 1 and 3 into your equation to see if the sides are
   approximately equal to each other.

Solve Another Problem

8. Describe how Don could set up a spreadsheet to
   solve $2(x + 5) - 2 = 4(x - 7)$.

Practice 3-4

Ratio and Proportion

Find each unit rate.

1. $60 for 8 h

2. $\dfrac{\$3}{4 \text{ lb}}$

3. $\dfrac{861 \text{ bagels}}{3 \text{ d}}$

4. $\dfrac{850 \text{ cal}}{1.25 \text{ h}}$

5. An 8-ounce bottle of lotion costs $4.50. What is the cost per ounce?

6. A pound of coffee costs $14.99. What is the cost per ounce?

Which pairs of ratios could form a proportion? Justify your answer.

7. $\dfrac{10}{24}, \dfrac{7}{18}$

8. $\dfrac{6}{9}, \dfrac{10}{15}$

9. $\dfrac{3}{4}, \dfrac{18}{24}$

10. $\dfrac{16}{2}, \dfrac{8}{1}$

11. $-\dfrac{4.8}{4}, -\dfrac{6.4}{5}$

Solve each proportion.

12. $\dfrac{g}{5} = \dfrac{6}{10}$

13. $\dfrac{z}{4} = \dfrac{7}{8}$

14. $\dfrac{13.2}{6} = \dfrac{m}{12}$

15. $-\dfrac{m}{5} = -\dfrac{2}{5}$

16. $\dfrac{5.5}{11} = \dfrac{x}{5}$

17. $-\dfrac{2}{3} = -\dfrac{10}{t}$

18. $\dfrac{4}{6} = \dfrac{x}{24}$

19. $\dfrac{s}{3} = \dfrac{7}{10}$

20. $\dfrac{4}{9} = \dfrac{10}{r}$

21. $\dfrac{x}{4.8} = \dfrac{6}{3.2}$

22. $\dfrac{5}{4} = \dfrac{c}{12}$

23. $-\dfrac{32}{h} = -\dfrac{1}{3}$

24. $\dfrac{2}{6} = \dfrac{p}{9}$

25. $\dfrac{f}{6} = \dfrac{3}{4}$

26. $\dfrac{15}{a} = \dfrac{3}{8}$

27. $\dfrac{3}{4} = \dfrac{k}{24}$

28. $\dfrac{a}{6} = \dfrac{3}{9}$

29. $\dfrac{4}{5} = \dfrac{k}{9}$

30. $\dfrac{3}{y} = \dfrac{5}{8}$

31. $\dfrac{t}{7} = \dfrac{9}{21}$

32. $\dfrac{2}{9} = \dfrac{10}{x}$

33. $\dfrac{x}{15} = \dfrac{3}{4}$

34. $\dfrac{18}{11} = \dfrac{49.5}{x}$

35. $\dfrac{2}{1.2} = \dfrac{5}{x}$

36. $-\dfrac{x-1}{4} = \dfrac{2}{3}$

37. $\dfrac{3}{6} = \dfrac{x-3}{8}$

38. $\dfrac{2x-2}{14} = \dfrac{2x-4}{6}$

39. $\dfrac{x+2}{x-2} = \dfrac{4}{8}$

40. $\dfrac{x+2}{6} = \dfrac{x-1}{12}$

41. $-\dfrac{x+8}{10} = -\dfrac{x-3}{2}$

42. You are riding your bicycle. It takes you 28 min to go 8 mi. If you continue traveling at the same rate, how long will it take you to go 15 mi?

43. Suppose you traveled 84 mi in 1.5 h. Moving at the same speed, how many mi would you cover in $3\frac{1}{4}$ h?

44. A canary's heart beats 130 times in 12 s. Use a proportion to find how many times its heart beats in 50 s.

45. Your car averages 18 mi per gal on the highway. If gas costs $1.85 per gal, how much does it cost in dollars per mi to drive your car on the highway?

283

3-4 • Guided Problem Solving

GPS **Student Page 147, Exercise 56**

Bonnie and Tim do some yardwork for their neighbor. The ratio comparing
the amount of time each one works is 7 : 4. The neighbor pays them $88. If
Bonnie worked more, how much should each of them receive?

Read and Understand

1. What does the ratio 7 : 4 describe? _____

2. If an equation were used to solve this problem, what would x represent? _____

Plan and Solve

3. Write a verbal model for this problem. _____

4. Let b represent the amount of money Bonnie earns. Write an
   expression that represents how much money Tim will make. _____

5. Write an equation to model this situation. _____

6. Solve the equation to find b. _____

7. How much money did each person receive? _____

Look Back and Check

8. Check the amount each person earned to make sure Bonnie made
   more money than Tim. Why is this reasonable?

Solve Another Problem

9. If 2 tons of rock costs $15.50, then how many tons of rock can you buy for $45?

_____

Practice 3-5

Proportions and Similar Figures

Each pair of figures is similar. Find the length of *x*.

1.

2.

3.

4.

5.

6.

7.

8.

Use a proportion to solve.

9. △*ABC* is similar to △*XYZ*. The length *AB* is 10. The length *BC* is 7. Find the length *XY* if the length *YZ* is 14.

10. Marty has a scale model of a car. The scale is 1 in. : 32 in. If the model is 6.75 in. long, how long is the actual car?

11. A blueprint scale is 1 in. : 12 ft. The width of a building is 48 ft. What is the width of the building on the blueprint?

12. Angie is using similar triangles to find the height of a tree. A stick that is 5 ft tall casts a shadow that is 4 ft long. The tree casts a shadow that is 22 ft long. How tall is the tree?

13. △*ABC* is similar to △*XYZ*. The length *AC* is 10. The length *BC* is 16. What is the length *XZ* if the length *YZ* is 12?

14. A map has a scale of 1 in. : 25 mi. Two cities are 175 mi apart. How far apart are they on the map?

3-5 • Guided Problem Solving

GPS **Student Page 153, Exercise 23**

Architecture A blueprint scale is 1 in. : 9 ft. On the plan, the room measures 2.5 in. by 3 in. What are the actual dimensions of the room?

Read and Understand

1. What is the blueprint scale? _____

2. How large is the room on the plans? _____

3. What is the problem asking you to determine? _____

Plan and Solve

4. Write a proportion that can be used to determine the actual width of the room. _____

5. Write a proportion that can be used to determine the actual length of the room. _____

6. Solve your proportions to find the actual dimensions of the room. _____

Look Back and Check

7. The blueprint scale written as a ratio is $\frac{1}{9}$, and as a decimal is approximately 0.11. Check the reasonableness of your answers by checking to see if the ratios of each dimension reduce to $\frac{1}{9}$ or 0.11.

Solve Another Problem

8. What are the actual dimensions of the room if the scale is 1 in. : 6 ft?

Practice 3-6

Write and solve an equation for each situation.

1. A passenger train's speed is 60 mi/h, and a freight train's speed is 40 mi/h. The passenger train travels the same distance in 1.5 h less time than the freight train. How long does each train take to make the trip?

2. Lois rode her bike to visit a friend. She traveled at 10 mi/h. While she was there, it began to rain. Her friend drove her home in a car traveling at 25 mi/h. Lois took 1.5 h longer to go to her friend's than to return home. How many hours did it take Lois to ride to her friend's house?

3. May rides her bike the same distance that Leah walks. May rides her bike 10 km/h faster than Leah walks. If it takes May 1 h and Leah 3 h to travel that distance, how fast does each travel?

4. The length of a rectangle is 4 in. greater than the width. The perimeter of the rectangle is 24 in. Find the dimensions of the rectangle.

5. The length of a rectangle is twice the width. The perimeter is 48 in. Find the dimensions of the rectangle.

6. At 10:00 A.M., a car leaves a house at a rate of 60 mi/h. At the same time, another car leaves the same house at a rate of 50 mi/h in the opposite direction. At what time will the cars be 330 miles apart?

7. Marla begins walking at 3 mi/h toward the library. Her friend meets her at the halfway point and drives her the rest of the way to the library. The distance to the library is 4 miles. How many hours did Marla walk?

8. Fred begins walking toward John's house at 3 mi/h. John leaves his house at the same time and walks toward Fred's house on the same path at a rate of 2 mi/h. How long will it be before they meet if the distance between the houses is 4 miles?

9. A train leaves the station at 6:00 P.M. traveling west at 80 mi/h. On a parallel track, a second train leaves the station 3 hours later traveling west at 100 mi/h. At what time will the second train catch up with the first?

10. It takes 1 hour longer to fly to St. Paul at 200 mi/h than it does to return at 250 mi/h. How far away is St. Paul?

11. Find three consecutive integers whose sum is 126.

12. The sum of four consecutive odd integers is 216. Find the four integers.

13. A rectangular picture frame is to be 8 in. longer than it is wide. Dennis uses 84 in. of oak to frame the picture. What is the width of the frame?

14. Each of two congruent sides of an isosceles triangle is 8 in. less than twice the base. The perimeter of the triangle is 74 in. What is the length of the base?

3-6 • Guided Problem Solving

GPS **Student Page 164, Exercise 22**

At 12:00 P.M. a truck leaves Centerville traveling 45 mi/h. One hour later a train leaves Centerville traveling 60 mi/h. They arrive in Smithfield at the same time.

Time	Truck 45t	Train 60(t − 1)
1 P.M.	45 mi	0 mi
2 P.M.	90 mi	60 mi
3 P.M.	135 mi	120 mi
4 P.M.	180 mi	180 mi
5 P.M.	225 mi	240 mi

a. Use the table to find when the train and truck arrive in Smithfield.

b. **Critical Thinking** What piece of information can you get from the table that you would NOT get by solving the equation $45t = 60(t - 1)$?

Read and Understand

1. What information are you given in the problem? _____

2. What is the problem asking you to figure out? _____

Plan and Solve

3. Explain how you can use the table to determine when the train and truck arrive in Smithfield. _____

_____

4. At what time did the train and truck arrive in Smithfield? _____

5. What information would you have if you solved the equation for *t*? _____

6. What piece of information can you get from the table that you would *not* get by solving the equation? _____

Look Back and Check

7. The truck traveled for 4 hours, and the train traveled for 3 hours. Check the reasonableness of your answer by evaluating the appropriate expressions for each time to see if the distances are equal.

Solve Another Problem

8. A delivery van drives due east toward its destination at 55 mph. Another van drives due west at 60 mph. After 3 hours they are 345 miles apart. How far did each van travel?

_____

Practice 3-7

Find each percent of change. Describe the percent of change as an increase or decrease. Round to the nearest whole number.

1. 36 g to 27 g

2. 40 cm to 100 cm

3. 90 in. to 45 in.

4. 500 lb to 1500 lb

5. $90 to $84.50

6. $100 to $140

7. $15 to $5.50

8. 100 mi to 175 mi

9. 280 m to 320 m

10. 58 to 76

11. 60 to 150

12. 600 mi to 480 mi

13. 18 to 27

14. 290 yd to 261 yd

15. 26.2 to 22.8

16. $8.50 to $12.75

17. $36\frac{1}{2}$ to $29\frac{1}{4}$

18. $74\frac{3}{4}$ to $66\frac{1}{2}$

19. $6\frac{3}{4}$ to $8\frac{1}{4}$

20. $15\frac{1}{2}$ to $18\frac{1}{4}$

Find each percent of change. Describe the percent of change as an increase or decrease. Round to the nearest whole number.

21. In 1985, the average price for gasoline was $1.20/gal. In 2000, the average price for gasoline was $1.56. Find the percent of change.

22. In 1980, Texas had 27 U.S. Representatives. That number increased to 30 in 2000. Find the percent of change.

23. In 1980, the average annual tuition charge for a four-year public university was $840. The average annual tuition charge in 2000 was $3356. What is the percent of change?

24. The United States imported 6,909,000 barrels of oil per day in 1980. In 2000, the United States imported 11,459,000 barrels of oil per day. What is the percent of change?

25. In 1977, the average number of households with cable television was 16.6%. In 2000, the average number of households with cable television was 68%. What is the percent of change?

26. In 1989, there were 38,000 licensed drivers under the age of 16. In 1999, the total number of licensed drivers under 16 was 33,248. Find the percent of change.

27. In 1990, Atlanta, GA, failed to meet air quality standards on 42 days. In 1999, Atlanta failed to meet air quality standards on 61 days. What is the percent of change?

Find the greatest possible error and the percent error for each measurement.

28. 3 cm

29. 0.5 cm

30. 6 cm

31. 16 in.

32. 36.85 g

33. 0.9 cm

Find the minimum and maximum possible areas for rectangles with the following measurements.

34. 8 cm × 10 cm

35. 3 in. × 5 in.

36. 8 m × 12 m

Find the minimum and maximum possible volume for a rectangular solid with the following measurements.

37. 16 in. × 22 in. × 18 in.

38. 13 cm × 15 cm × 18 cm

39. 3 m × 4 m × 5 m

3-7 • Guided Problem Solving

GPS **Student Page 172, Exercise 50**

Sales Suppose that you are selling sweatshirts for a class fundraiser.
The wholesaler charges you $8 for each sweatshirt.

a. You charge $16 for each sweatshirt. Find the percent of increase.

b. Generalize your answer to part (a). Doubling a price is the same as a
   ___?___% of increase.

c. After the fundraiser is over, you reduce the price on the remaining
   sweatshirts to $8. Find the percent of decrease.

d. Generalize your answer to part (c). Cutting a price in half is the same
   as a ___?___% of decrease.

Read and Understand

1. What information is given in the problem? _____

2. Explain how to determine the percent of increase and the percent of decrease. _____

   _____

Plan and Solve

3. You charge $16 for each sweatshirt. What is the percent of increase? _____

4. Generalize your answer. Doubling a price is the same as a _____ %
   increase.

5. After the fundraiser is over, you reduce the price on the
   remaining sweatshirts to $8. Find the percent of decrease. _____

6. Generalize your answer. Cutting a price in half is the same as a _____ %
   decrease.

Look Back and Check

7. Explain why it is reasonable that doubling a price is the same as a 100%
   of increase and cutting a price in half is the same as a 50% of decrease. _____

   _____

Solve Another Problem

8. Ticket prices for the school yearbook have been
   raised from $15 to $30. What is the percent of increase? _____

Practice 3-8

Tell whether each expression is *rational* or *irrational*.

1. $-\sqrt{64}$ **2.** $\sqrt{1600}$ **3.** $\pm\sqrt{160}$ **4.** $\sqrt{144}$

5. $\sqrt{125}$ **6.** $-\sqrt{340}$ **7.** $\sqrt{1.96}$ **8.** $-\sqrt{0.09}$

Use a calculator to find each square root to the nearest hundredth.

9. $\sqrt{20}$ **10.** $\sqrt{73}$ **11.** $-\sqrt{38}$ **12.** $\sqrt{130}$

13. $\sqrt{149.3}$ **14.** $-\sqrt{8.7}$ **15.** $\sqrt{213.8}$ **16.** $-\sqrt{320.7}$

17. $\sqrt{113.9}$ **18.** $-\sqrt{840.6}$ **19.** $-\sqrt{1348.9}$ **20.** $\sqrt{928.2}$

Simplify each expression.

21. $\sqrt{49}$ **22.** $-\sqrt{2.25}$ **23.** $\sqrt{\dfrac{1}{16}}$ **24.** $\sqrt{400}$

25. $\sqrt{6.25}$ **26.** $\pm\sqrt{\dfrac{36}{25}}$ **27.** $\sqrt{196}$ **28.** $\sqrt{2.56}$

29. $\sqrt{0.25}$ **30.** $\pm\sqrt{\dfrac{9}{100}}$ **31.** $\sqrt{576}$ **32.** $\pm\sqrt{\dfrac{121}{36}}$

33. $\sqrt{1600}$ **34.** $-\sqrt{0.04}$ **35.** $\sqrt{2500}$ **36.** $\sqrt{4.41}$

Between what two consecutive integers is each square root?

37. $\sqrt{40}$ **38.** $\sqrt{139}$ **39.** $-\sqrt{75}$ **40.** $\sqrt{93}$

41. $-\sqrt{105.6}$ **42.** $-\sqrt{173.2}$ **43.** $\sqrt{1123.7}$ **44.** $\sqrt{216.9}$

Solve the following problems. Round to the nearest tenth if necessary.

45. You are to put a metal brace inside a square shipping container. The formula $d = \sqrt{2x^2}$ gives the length of the metal brace, where x is the length of the side of the container. Find the length of the brace for each container side length.

     a. $x = 3$ ft   **b.** $x = 4.5$ ft   **c.** $x = 5$ ft   **d.** $x = 8$ ft

46. You are designing a cone-shaped storage container. Use the formula $r = \sqrt{\dfrac{3V}{\pi h}}$ to find the radius of the storage container. Find the radius when $V = 10,000$ ft^3 and $h = 10$ ft.

3-8 • Guided Problem Solving

GPS Student Page 179, Exercise 52

Physics If you drop an object, the time t in seconds that it takes to fall d feet is given by the formula $t = \sqrt{\dfrac{d}{16}}$.

a. Find the time it takes an object to fall 400 ft.
b. Find the time it takes an object to fall 1600 ft.
c. **Critical Thinking** In part (b), the object falls four times as far as in part (a). Does it take four times as long to fall? Explain.

Read and Understand

1. What information is given in the problem? _____

2. Explain what each variable represents. _____

Plan and Solve

3. Find the time it takes an object to fall 400 ft. _____

4. Find the time it takes an object to fall 1600 ft. _____

5. Does it take four times as long for an object to fall four times as far? _____

Look Back and Check

6. Explain why it is reasonable that the time does not increase at the same rate as the distance.

   _____

   _____

Solve Another Problem

7. Find the time it takes an object to fall 800 ft. _____

Practice 3-9

Use the triangle at the right.
Find the length of the missing
side to the nearest tenth.

1. $a = 12, b = 35, c = \blacksquare$ **2.** $a = 10, b = \blacksquare, c = 26$ **3.** $a = 11, b = \blacksquare, c = 61$

4. $a = 36, b = 15, c = \blacksquare$ **5.** $a = 8, b = 15, c = \blacksquare$ **6.** $a = \blacksquare, b = 24, c = 40$

7. $a = 18, b = \blacksquare, c = 35$ **8.** $a = 17, b = \blacksquare, c = 49$ **9.** $a = 42, b = 37, c = \blacksquare$

10. $a = \blacksquare, b = 80, c = 90$ **11.** $a = 8, b = 8, c = \blacksquare$ **12.** $a = 19, b = \blacksquare, c = 26$

13. $a = \blacksquare, b = 27, c = 33$ **14.** $a = \blacksquare, b = 13, c = 24$ **15.** $a = 9, b = \blacksquare, c = 13$

16. $a = 19, b = 45, c = \blacksquare$ **17.** $a = \blacksquare, b = 24, c = 39$ **18.** $a = 14, b = 14, c = \blacksquare$

Determine whether the given lengths are sides of a right triangle.

19. 20, 21, 29   **20.** 16, 30, 34   **21.** 24, 60, 66   **22.** 23, 18, 14

23. 10, 24, 28   **24.** 45, 28, 53   **25.** $\frac{4}{5}, \frac{3}{5}, 1$ **26.** $\frac{2}{3}, \frac{4}{3}, \frac{1}{3}$

27. 3.5, 4.4, 5.5   **28.** 10.5, 11.3, 13.8   **29.** 3.3, 6.5, 5.6   **30.** 24, 70, 74

31. 4.2, 7.0, 5.6   **32.** 5.2, 6.5, 3.9   **33.** 2.1, 3.5, 2.8   **34.** 4.8, 7.5, 5.4

35. 7.5, 4.3, 6.7   **36.** $\frac{1}{9}, \frac{1}{15}, \frac{1}{18}$ **37.** $\frac{1}{2}, \frac{6}{5}, \frac{13}{10}$ **38.** $\frac{1}{5}, \frac{1}{4}, \frac{1}{3}$

Find the missing length to the nearest tenth.

39. A ladder is 25 ft long. The ladder needs to reach to a window that is
24 ft above the ground. How far away from the building should the
bottom of the ladder be placed?

40. Suppose you are making a sail in the shape of a right triangle for a
sailboat. The length of the longest side of the sail is 65 ft. The sail is to
be 63 ft high. What is the length of the third side of the sail?

41. Suppose you leave your house and travel 13 mi due west. Then you
travel 3 mi due south. How far are you from your house?

42. A wire is run between the tips of two poles. One pole is 23 ft taller than
the other pole. The poles are 37 ft apart. How long does the wire need
to be to reach between the two poles?

43. A 20-ft-long wire is used to support a television antenna. The wire is
connected to the antenna 15 ft above the ground. How far away from
the base of the tower will the other end of the wire be located?

3-9 • Guided Problem Solving

GPS **Student Page 185, Exercise 40**

Solar Power Solar cars use panels built out of photovoltaic cells, which convert sunlight into electricity. Consider a car like the one shown. Not counting the driver's "bubble," the panels form a rectangle.

a. The length of the rectangle is 13 ft and the diagonal is 14.7 ft. Find the width. Round to the nearest tenth of a foot.

b. Find the area of the rectangle.

c. The panels produce a maximum power of about 11 watts/ft^2. Find the maximum power produced by the panels on the car. Round to the nearest watt.

Read and Understand

1. Make a sketch and label it with the known information.

Plan and Solve

2. What relationship can be used to determine the width of the rectangle? _____

3. What is the width of the rectangle rounded to the nearest tenth of a foot? _____

4. Find the area of the rectangle. _____

5. The panels produce a maximum power of about 11 watts/ft^2. Find the maximum power produced by the panels on the car, rounded to the nearest watt. _____

Look Back and Check

6. Check the reasonableness of your answer by verifying that your numbers for the rectangle's dimensions satisfy the Pythagorean Theorem.

Solve Another Problem

7. If the maximum power of the panels is increased to 15 watts/ft^2, what will be the maximum power produced by the panels on the car? _____

3A: Graphic Organizer

For use before Lesson 3-1

Study Skill Keep notes as you work through each chapter to help you organize your thinking and to make it easier to review the material when you complete the chapter.

Write your answers.

1. What is the chapter title? _____

2. Find the Table of Contents page for this chapter at the front of the book. Name four topics you will study in this chapter.

   _____   _____

   _____   _____

3. Complete the graphic organizer as you work through the chapter.
   1. Write the title of the chapter in the center oval.
   2. When you begin a lesson, write the name of the lesson in a rectangle.
   3. When you complete that lesson, write a skill or key concept from that lesson in the outer oval linked to that rectangle.
   Continue with steps 2 and 3 clockwise around the graphic organizer.

3B: Reading Comprehension

Study Skill Some math problems have many steps and can be confusing. Sometimes, if you hurry through a problem, you leave out important steps. Think carefully about what the next step to solving a problem might be.

The equations and justification statements given below are the correct ones to find the length of *b* in the right triangle.

Steps	Justifications	Thoughts for Organizing Steps
$a^2 + b^2 = c^2$		Use the Pythagorean Theorem.
$5^2 + b^2 = 13^2$	Substitute 5 for *a* and 13 for *c*.	Replace variables with any known values.
$25 + b^2 = 169$	Simplify by squaring each number.	Perform existing calculations.
$b^2 = 144$	Simplify.	
$\sqrt{b^2} = \sqrt{144}$	Find the principal square root of each side.	More work is needed to isolate the variable.
$b = 12$	Simplify.	

Find the length of the missing side of each right triangle shown.

1.

2.

3. **High-Use Academic Words** What does it mean to *isolate*, as mentioned in the last sentence in the thoughts for organizing steps?
   a. rewrite the equation so that the variable is by itself
   b. replace the variable with a known value

Vocabulary and Study Skills

3C: Reading/Writing Math Symbols

For use after Lesson 3-4

Study Skill There are many symbols that are abbreviations for longer words. Using these symbols when taking notes helps you keep up with the person giving the notes. Learn these symbols for quicker note taking.

Write what each abbreviated math symbol means.

1. ¢/oz _____

2. mi/h _____

3. ft/min _____

4. km/h _____

5. ft/mi _____

6. $/yr _____

7. $/lb _____

8. ft/wk _____

9. gal/wk _____

10. mi/gal _____

11. $lb/in.^2$ _____

12. ft/sec^2 _____

13. m/sec^2 _____

14. $/oz _____

Write each phrase in symbol form.

15. miles per gallon _____

16. dollars per pound _____

17. kilometers per hour _____

18. feet per minute _____

3D: Visual Vocabulary Practice
High-Use Academic Words

For use after Lesson 3-4

• •

Study Skills If a word is not in the Glossary, use a dictionary to find its meaning.

Concept List

approximate	compare	convert
define	describe	evaluate
explain	identify	model

Write the concept that best describes each exercise. Choose from the concept list above.

1. Let n = number of CDs.	**2.** $a = -5$ $3 \cdot a + 4 = 3 \cdot (-5) + 4$ $= -15 + 4$ $= -11$	**3.** $\pi \approx \frac{22}{7}$
4. x-coordinate $(-2, 4)$ y-coordinate	**5.** $2 + (-5)$ -3 $2 + (-5) = -3$	**6.** The graph is a function because there is exactly one range value for each domain value.
7. $-6 < 5$	**8.** To plot $(-2, 3)$, move 2 units to the left of the origin. Then move 3 units up.	**9.** $10 \text{ gal} \cdot \dfrac{4 \text{ qt}}{1 \text{ gal}} = 40 \text{ qt}$

3E: Vocabulary Check

Study Skill Strengthen your vocabulary. Use these pages and add cues and summaries by applying the Cornell Notetaking style.

Write the definition for each word at the right. To check your work, fold the paper back along the dotted line to see the correct answers.

_____

_____

_____   Identity

_____

_____   Ratio

_____

_____

_____   Unit Analysis

_____

_____

_____   Proportion

_____

_____

_____   Cross Products

_____

_____

3E: Vocabulary Check (continued)

Write the vocabulary word for each definition. To check your work, fold the paper forward along the dotted line to see the correct answers.

An equation that is true for every value of the variable.

_____

A comparison of two numbers by division.

_____

The process of selecting conversion factors to produce appropriate units.

_____

An equation that states that two ratios are equal.

_____

In a proportion, $\frac{a}{b} = \frac{c}{d}$, the products ad and bc. These products are equal.

_____

3F: Vocabulary Review Puzzle

For use with Chapter Review

Study Skill When you complete a puzzle such as a word search, read the list of words carefully and completely. As you identify each word in the word search, circle it and then cross off the word from the list. Pay special attention to the spelling of each word.

Complete the word search.

rate	proportion	leg	hypotenuse
theorem	dilation	percent	identity
scale drawing	square root	similar figures	Pythagorean
equation	conditional	ratio	equivalent

```
L  E  G  Z  X  D  I  L  A  T  I  O  N  M  P
A  N  E  P  Y  T  H  A  G  O  R  E  A  N  T
N  P  E  R  C  E  N  T  D  Y  C  S  P  A  H
O  D  E  O  M  Z  G  I  N  E  K  C  Q  H  E
I  O  S  P  O  D  E  N  R  T  Y  A  U  Y  O
T  E  I  O  N  J  K  L  E  A  R  L  D  P  R
I  W  D  R  A  T  I  O  N  R  O  E  U  O  E
D  H  T  T  F  Y  L  O  M  F  D  D  M  T  M
N  V  D  I  L  A  I  I  O  N  K  R  A  E  J
O  T  R  O  S  T  C  F  U  N  B  A  T  N  S
C  F  Y  N  A  W  O  R  D  S  X  W  H  U  T
E  E  Q  U  I  V  A  L  E  N  T  I  W  S  F
C  S  Q  U  A  R  E  R  O  O  T  N  B  E  L
X  E  I  D  E  N  T  I  T  Y  D  G  S  T  U
S  I  M  I  L  A  R  F  I  G  U  R  E  S  C
```

Practice 4-1

Inequalities and Their Graphs

Determine whether each number is a solution of the given inequality.

1. $x \leq -8$ **a.** -10 **b.** 6 **c.** -8

2. $-1 > x$ **a.** 0 **b.** -3 **c.** -6

3. $w < \frac{18}{7}$ **a.** 5 **b.** -2 **c.** $3\frac{1}{2}$

4. $0.65 \geq y$ **a.** 0.43 **b.** -0.65 **c.** 0.56

5. $2y + 1 > -5$ **a.** -4 **b.** -2 **c.** 4

6. $7x - 14 \leq 6x - 16$ **a.** 0 **b.** -4 **c.** 2

7. $n(n - 6) \geq -4$ **a.** 3 **b.** -2 **c.** 5

Write an inequality for each graph.

8.

9.

10.

11.

Graph each inequality.

12. $x > 6$ **13.** $y \leq -10$ **14.** $8 \geq b$

15. $-4 < w$ **16.** $x < -7$ **17.** $x \geq 12$

Define a variable and write an inequality to model each situation.

18. The temperature in a refrigerated truck must be kept at or below 38°F. _____

19. The maximum weight on an elevator is 2000 pounds. _____

20. A least 20 students were sick with the flu. _____

21. The maximum occupancy in an auditorium is 250 people. _____

22. The maximum speed on the highway is 55 mi/h. _____

23. A student must have at least 450 out of 500 points to earn an A. _____

24. The circumference of an official major league baseball is at least 9.00 inches. _____

Match the inequality with its graph.

25. $6 < x$ **26.** $-6 \geq x$ **27.** $4 > x$ **28.** $x \leq -4$

A.

B.

C.

D.

4-1 • Guided Problem Solving

GPS Student Page 204, Exercise 65

Air Travel Your travel agent is making plans for you to go from Chicago to New Orleans. A direct flight costs too much. Option A consists of flights from Chicago to Dallas to New Orleans. Option B consists of flights from Chicago to Orlando to New Orleans. Write an inequality comparing the mileage of these two options.

Read and Understand

1. Describe option A. _____

2. Describe option B. _____

3. The problem asks you to write an inequality for what? _____

Plan and Solve

4. What is the mileage between each of the cities in option A?

   Chicago to Dallas _____   Dallas to New Orleans _____

5. What is the total mileage for option A? _____

6. What is the mileage between each of the cities in option B?

   Chicago to Orlando _____   Orlando to New Orleans _____

7. What is the total mileage for option B? _____

8. Write an inequality comparing the mileage for option A and option B. _____

Look Back and Check

9. Write a sentence to describe the relationship between the mileage for option A and option B. Check that this sentence matches your inequality written above.

_____

Solve Another Problem

10. An office supply store sells a pack of pencils for $.99, a notebook for $1.29, and scissors for $1.39. A discount store sells the same pack of pencils for $1.09, the notebook for $1.25, and the scissors for $1.19. Write an inequality comparing the total cost of school supplies at each store. _____

Practice 4-2

Solving Inequalities Using Addition and Subtraction

Solve each inequality. Check the solution.

1. $n - 7 \geq 2$ **2.** $10 + y > 12$ **3.** $3.2 < r + 4.7$ **4.** $7 + b > 13$

5. $n + \frac{3}{4} > \frac{1}{2}$ **6.** $-\frac{5}{7} \geq c + \frac{2}{7}$ **7.** $g + 4.6 < 5.9$ **8.** $0 > d - 2.7$

9. $f + 4 \geq 14$ **10.** $x + 1 \leq -3$ **11.** $d - 13 \leq -8$ **12.** $m - 7 \geq -8$

13. $12 + v < 19$ **14.** $-4 \leq t + 9$ **15.** $6 < y - 3$ **16.** $a + 15 > 19$

17. $8 + d < 9$ **18.** $s + 3 \leq 3$ **19.** $9 + h \leq 5$ **20.** $7.6 \geq t - 2.4$

Write and solve an inequality that models each situation.

21. It will take at least 360 points for Kiko's team to win the math contest. The scores for Kiko's teammates were 94, 82, and 87, but one of Kiko's teammates lost 2 of those points for an incomplete answer. How many points must Kiko earn for her team to win the contest?

22. This season, Nora has 125 at-bats in softball. By the end of the season she wants to have at least 140 at-bats. How many more at-bats does Nora need to reach her goal?

23. The average wind speed increased 19 mi/h from 8 A.M. to noon. The average wind speed decreased 5 mi/h from noon to 4 P.M. At 4 P.M., the average wind speed was at least 32 mi/h. What is the minimum value of the average wind speed at 8 A.M.?

24. Suppose it takes no more than 25 min for you to get to school. If you have traveled for 13.5 min already, how much longer, at most, might you take to get to school?

25. Joan has started a physical fitness program. One of her goals is to be able to run at least 5 mi without stopping. She can now run 3.5 mi without stopping. How many more miles must she run non-stop to achieve her goal?

26. Suppose you can get a higher interest rate on your savings if you maintain a balance of at least $1000 in your savings account. The balance in your savings account is now $1058. You deposit $44.50 into your account. What is the greatest amount that you can withdraw and still get the higher interest rate?

Solve each inequality. Graph and check the solution.

27. $\frac{3}{4} + z \geq -\frac{3}{4}$ **28.** $12 + d + 3 \leq 10$ **29.** $v - \frac{3}{4} > 1\frac{1}{4}$ **30.** $8 + m > 4$

31. $2 + f > -3$ **32.** $-27 \geq w - 24$ **33.** $b + \frac{1}{2} > \frac{3}{4}$ **34.** $12 + t < 4 - 15$

35. $-14 > -16 + u$ **36.** $-7 \leq -11 + z$ **37.** $38 \geq 33 + b$ **38.** $k - 27 < -29$

39. $a + 8 \leq 10$ **40.** $b + 6 > 17$ **41.** $13 < 8 + k - 6$ **42.** $j + 1.3 > 2.8$

4-2 • Guided Problem Solving

GPS Student Page 209, Exercise 62

Gymnastics Suppose your sister wants to qualify for a regional gymnastics competition. At today's competition she must score at least 34.0 points. She scored 8.8 on the vault, 7.9 on the balance beam, and 8.2 on the uneven parallel bars. The event that remains is the floor exercise.

  a. Write and solve an inequality that models the information.

  b. Explain what the solution means in terms of the original situation.

  c. **Open-Ended** Write three scores your sister could make that would allow her to qualify for the regional gymnastics competition.

Read and Understand

1. How many points must your sister score at today's competition? _____

2. How many points did she score on the vault? _____ balance beam? _____ uneven parallel bars? _____

Plan and Solve

3. How many total points has your sister scored at the competition so far? _____

4. Write an inequality that models the information. _____

5. What is the solution to the inequality? _____

6. Explain what the solution means in terms of the original situation. _____

_____

7. Write three scores that your sister could make that would allow her to qualify for the regional gymnastics competition. _____

Look Back and Check

8. Check each of your scores by adding 24.9 to each one. Your answers should all be at least 34.0.

_____

Solve Another Problem

9. Samuel's mother has set a limit of 8 hours per week of Internet use. On Monday Samuel used the Internet for 0.75 hours, on Tuesday for 1.5 hours, and on Wednesday for 0.5 hours. Write and solve an inequality in order to determine the maximum amount of Internet time Samuel has for the remaining days of the week.

_____

Practice 4-3

Solving Inequalities Using Multiplication and Division

Solve each inequality. Graph and check the solution.

1. $\frac{15}{8} \le \frac{5}{2}s$

2. $60 \le 12b$

3. $-\frac{4}{5}r < 8$

4. $\frac{5}{2} < \frac{n}{8}$

5. $-9n \ge -36$

6. $\frac{n}{7} \ge -6$

7. $-7c < 28$

8. $16d > -64$

9. $-\frac{t}{3} < -5$

10. $54 < -6k$

11. $\frac{w}{7} > 0$

12. $2.6v > 6.5$

13. $-4 < -\frac{2}{5}m$

14. $17 < \frac{p}{2}$

15. $0.9 \le -1.8v$

16. $-5 \le -\frac{x}{9}$

17. $-1 \ge \frac{d}{7}$

18. $-3x \ge 21$

19. $\frac{c}{12} < \frac{3}{4}$

20. $\frac{a}{4} \le -1$

Write and solve an inequality that models each situation.

21. Suppose you and a friend are working for a nursery planting trees. Together you can plant 8 trees per hour. What is the greatest number of hours that you and your friend would need to plant at most 40 trees?

22. Suppose the physics club is going on a field trip. Members will be riding in vans that will hold 7 people each including the driver. At least 28 people will be going on the field trip. What is the least number of vans needed to make the trip?

23. You need to buy stamps to mail some letters. The stamps cost $.34 each. What is the maximum number of stamps that you can buy with $3.84?

24. The Garcias are putting a brick border along one edge of their flower garden. The flower garden is no more than 31 ft long. If each brick is 6 in. long, what is the greatest number of bricks needed?

25. Janet needs to travel 275 mi for a conference. She needs to be at the conference in no more than 5.5 h. What is the slowest average speed that she can drive and still arrive at the conference on time?

Solve each inequality. Graph and check the solution.

26. $\frac{1}{4}h < 4.9$

27. $\frac{7}{3}x < 21$

28. $-\frac{1}{9}a > 9$

29. $\frac{b}{6} \le 2.5$

30. $-\frac{3}{5}q > 15$

31. $84 \le 21b$

32. $\frac{c}{12} > -\frac{5}{6}$

33. $80.6 \le -6.5b$

34. $-\frac{1}{9}p > \frac{1}{3}$

35. $-9z > 45$

36. $\frac{1}{7}y \le 6$

37. $-\frac{5}{7} > -\frac{k}{14}$

38. $6.8 > \frac{y}{5}$

39. $75 \le 15b$

40. $39 < -13k$

41. $2d < 8.8$

42. $8.5v > 61.2$

43. $-11n \ge -55$

44. $\frac{1}{4}y < 17$

45. $92 < -23k$

4-3 • Guided Problem Solving

GPS **Student Page 216, Exercise 76**

A friend calls you and asks you to meet at a location 3 miles from your home in 20 minutes. You set off on your bicycle after the telephone call. Write and solve an inequality to find the average rate in miles per minute you could ride to be at your meeting place within 20 minutes.

Read and Understand

1. How far away is the meeting location? _____

2. How much time do you have to get there? _____

3. What unit should be used to represent rate? _____

Plan and Solve

4. Let r represent your rate. Write and solve an inequality to find the average rate you could ride to be at your meeting place *within* 20 minutes.

   _____

5. Express your minimum rate as miles/hour. _____

Look Back and Check

6. Give one rate in mi/min that would allow you to meet your friend within 20 minutes. Check your answer by multiplying your rate by 20. Your answer is the distance you will travel at that rate in 20 minutes. Is your answer more than 3 miles?

   _____

Solve Another Problem

7. The student council is planning the next school dance. The total expenses for the dance will be $2500 and they expect 200 students to attend. Write and solve an inequality to find the minimum ticket price per student that should be charged in order to cover expenses.

   _____

Practice 4-4

Solving Multi-Step Inequalities

Solve each inequality. Check the solution.

1. $2z + 7 < z + 10$

2. $4(k - 1) > 4$

3. $1.5 + 2.1y < 1.1y + 4.5$

4. $h + 2(3h + 4) \geq 1$

5. $r + 4 > 13 - 2r$

6. $6u - 18 - 4u < 22$

7. $2(3 + 3g) \geq 2g + 14$

8. $2h - 13 < -3$

9. $-4p + 28 > 8$

10. $8m - 8 \geq 12 + 4m$

11. $5 + 6a > -1$

12. $\frac{1}{2}(2t + 8) \geq 4 + 6t$

13. $-5x + 12 < -18$

14. $2(3f + 2) > 4f + 12$

15. $13t - 8t > -45$

16. $2(c - 4) \leq 10 - c$

17. $\frac{1}{2}t - \frac{1}{3}t > -1$

18. $3.4 + 1.6v < 5.9 - 0.9v$

Write and solve an inequality that models each situation.

19. Ernest works in the shipping department loading shipping crates with boxes. Each empty crate weighs 150 lb. How many boxes, each weighing 35 lb, can Ernest put in the crate if the total weight is to be no more than 850 lb?

20. Beatriz is in charge of setting up a banquet hall. She has five tables that will seat six people each. If no more than 62 people will attend, how many tables seating four people each will she need?

21. Suppose it costs $5 to enter a carnival. Each ride costs $1.25. You have $15 to spend at the carnival. What is the greatest number of rides that you can go on?

22. The cost to rent a car is $19.50 plus $.25 per mile. If you have $44 to rent a car, what is the greatest number of miles that you can drive?

23. The student council is sponsoring a concert as a fund raiser. Tickets are $3 for students and $5 for adults. The student council wants to raise at least $1000. If 200 students attend, how many adults must attend?

Solve each inequality. Check the solution.

24. $-18 < 2(12 - 3b)$

25. $5n + 3 - 4n < -5 - 3n$

26. $36 > 4(2d + 10)$

27. $2(5t - 25) + 5t < -80$

28. $3j + 2 - 2j < -10$

29. $\frac{2}{5}(5x - 15) \geq 4$

30. $7(2z + 3) > 35$

31. $2(3b - 2) < 4b + 8$

32. $\frac{1}{2}y + \frac{1}{4}y \geq -6$

33. $8(3f - 6) < -24$

34. $\frac{3}{4}k < \frac{3}{4} - \frac{1}{4}k$

35. $3(4g - 6) \geq 6(g + 2)$

36. $\frac{1}{2}(2g + 4) > -7$

37. $4(1.25y + 4.2) < 16.8$

38. $38 + 7t > -3(t + 4)$

39. $4(2d + 1) > 28$

40. $4(n - 3) < 2 - 3n$

41. $\frac{3}{4}d - \frac{1}{2} \leq 2\frac{1}{2}$

Algebra 1 Lesson 4-4

4-4 • Guided Problem Solving

GPS **Student Page 223, Exercise 43**

Expenses The sophomore class is planning a picnic. The cost of a permit to use a city park is $250. To pay for the permit, there is a fee of $.75 for each sophomore and $1.25 for each guest who is not a sophomore. Two hundred sophomores plan to attend. Write and solve an inequality to find out how many guests must attend for the sophomores to pay for the permit.

Read and Understand

1. What is the cost of a permit? _____

2. How many sophomores are expected to attend? _____

3. What is the cost for each guest that attends? _____

Plan and Solve

4. How much money will the class earn from sophomores? _____

5. Write and solve an inequality to find out how many guests must attend for the sophomores to pay for the permit. _____

Look Back and Check

6. Use your original inequality to check if the sophomores would be able to pay for the permit if 90 guests attended. _____

Solve Another Problem

7. Mark and Anthony are going to a movie tonight. They know that each ticket will cost $9. Together they have $30 to spend on tickets and a large popcorn for each of them. Write and solve an inequality to determine how much the popcorn can cost in order for Mark and Anthony to have enough money.

_____

Practice 4-5

Compound Inequalities

Solve each compound inequality and graph the solution.

1. $-5 < s + 5 < 5$

2. $1 < 3x + 4 < 10$

3. $k - 3 > 1$ or $k - 3 < -1$

4. $b - 2 > 18$ or $3b < 54$

5. $-4d > 8$ and $2d > -6$

6. $-4 < t + 2 < 4$

7. $-3 < 3 + s < 7$

8. $3j \geq 6$ or $3j \leq -6$

9. $-1 < \frac{1}{2}x < 1$

10. $g + 2 > -1$ or $g - 6 < -9$

11. $-6 < 9 + 3y < 6$

12. $3f > 15$ or $2f < -4$

13. $d - 3 > 4$ or $d - 3 < -4$

14. $1 > 2h + 3 > -1$

15. $7 + 2a > 9$ or $-4a > 8$

16. $2z > 2.1$ or $3z < -5.85$

17. $c - 1 \geq 2$ or $c - 1 \leq -2$

18. $h + 2.8 < 1.8$ or $h + 2.8 > 4.8$

Write and solve a compound inequality that represents each situation. Graph your solution.

19. The crowd that heard the President speak was estimated to be 10,000 people. The actual crowd could be 750 people more or less than this. What are the possible values for the actual crowd size?

20. Susie has designed an exercise program for herself. One part of the program requires her to walk between 25 and 30 miles each week. She plans to walk the same distance each day five days a week. What is the range of miles that she should walk each day?

21. A box of cereal must weigh more than 629.4 g and less than 630.6 g to pass inspection. The box in which the cereal is packaged weighs 5.5 g. What are the possible weights for the cereal?

22. Carmen works in a sporting goods store. Her goal is to sell between $500 and $600 worth of sporting equipment every week. So far this week, she has sold $395 worth of equipment. During the rest of the week, what dollar amount must Carmen sell in order to reach her goal?

Solve each compound inequality and graph the solution.

23. $2n - 1 \geq 1$ or $2n - 1 \leq -1$

24. $2k - 3 > 3$ or $2k - 3 < -3$

25. $-1 < h - 2 < 1$

26. $2.2 + p > 1$ and $1.5p < -0.3$

27. $9 < x + 2 < 11$

28. $5m + 8 < 23$ or $6m > 48$

29. $-3 \leq \frac{3}{2}x + 6 \leq 3$

30. $7 > 5 - x > 6$

31. $\frac{1}{2}x + 1 > 1$ or $\frac{1}{2}x + 1 < -1$

32. $-2 \leq s - 4 \leq 2$

33. $w - 3 > 4$ or $w - 3 < -4$

34. $6 > 4x - 2 > -6$

35. $t + 5 < 2$ or $3t + 1 > 10$

36. $2g > 12$ and $3g < 24$

37. $6x - 3 \geq 3$ or $6x - 3 \leq -3$

38. $2y - 3 > -1$ or $5 - y > 4$

Algebra 1 Lesson 4-5 **311**

4-5 • Guided Problem Solving

GPS **Student Page 231, Exercise 46**

Meteorology The graph below shows the average monthly high and low temperatures for Detroit, Michigan, and Charlotte, North Carolina. Write a compound inequality for Charlotte's average temperature in June.

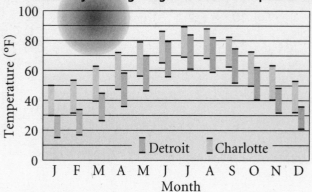

Monthly Average High and Low Temperatures

SOURCE: Statistical Abstract of the United States

Read and Understand

1. What is the high temperature in June for Charlotte? _____

2. What is the low temperature in June for Charlotte? _____

Plan and Solve

3. Will this compound inequality be formed by the word *and* or the word *or*? _____

   Explain. _____

   _____

4. Write a compound inequality for Charlotte's average temperature in June. _____

Look Back and Check

5. Explain why your inequality makes sense. _____

   _____

Solve Another Problem

6. Write a compound inequality for Detroit's average temperature
   in the winter months of December, January, February, and March. _____

Practice 4-6

Absolute Value Equations and Inequalities

· ·

Solve each inequality. Graph the solution.

1. $|d| > 2$ **2.** $|h| > 6$ **3.** $|2k| > 8$ **4.** $|s + 4| > 2$

5. $|3c - 6| \geq 3$ **6.** $|2n + 3| \leq 5$ **7.** $|3.5z| > |7|$ **8.** $\left|\frac{2}{3}x\right| \leq 4$

9. $9 > |6 + 3t|$ **10.** $|j| - 2 \geq 6$ **11.** $5 > |v + 2| + 3$ **12.** $|4y + 11| < 7$

13. $|2n - 1| \geq 1$ **14.** $\left|\frac{1}{2}x + 1\right| > 1$ **15.** $-2|h - 2| > -2$ **16.** $3|2x| \leq 12$

17. $3|s - 4| + 21 \leq 27$ **18.** $-6|w - 3| < -24$ **19.** $-\frac{1}{2}|6x - 3| \leq -\frac{3}{2}$ **20.** $-2|3j| - 8 \leq -20$

Solve each equation. If there is no solution, write *no solution*.

21. $|a| = 9.5$ **22.** $|b| = -2$ **23.** $|d| - 25 = -13$ **24.** $|6z| + 3 = 21$

25. $|3c| - 45 = -18$ **26.** $-2 = -\frac{|z|}{7}$ **27.** $|x| = -0.8$ **28.** $-4|7 + d| = -44$

Write and solve an absolute value equation or inequality that represents each situation.

29. The average number of cucumber seeds in a package is 25. The number of seeds in the package can vary by three. Find the range of acceptable numbers of seeds in each package.

30. The mean distance of the earth from the sun is 93 million miles. The distance varies by 1.6 million miles. Find the range of distances of the earth from the sun.

31. Leona was in a golf tournament last week. All four of her rounds of golf were within 2 strokes of par. If par was 72, find the range of scores that Leona could have shot for each round of the golf tournament.

32. Victor's goal is to earn \$75 per week at his after-school job. Last month he was within \$6.50 of his goal. Find the range of amounts that Victor might have earned last month.

33. Members of the track team can run 400 m in an average time of 58.2 s. The fastest and slowest times vary from the average by 6.4 s. Find the range of times for the track team.

34. The ideal length of a particular metal rod is 25.5 cm. The measured length may vary from the ideal length by at most 0.025 cm. Find the range of acceptable lengths for the rod.

35. When measured on a particular scale, the weight of an object may vary from its actual weight by at most 0.4 lb. If the reading on the scale is 125.2 lb, find the range of actual weights of the object.

36. One poll reported that the approval rating of the job performance of the President of the United States was 63%. The poll was said to be accurate to within 3.8%. What is the range of actual approval ratings?

· ·

4-6 • Guided Problem Solving

GPS **Student Page 238, Exercise 57**

Elections In a poll for the upcoming mayoral election, 42% of likely voters said they planned to vote for Lucy Jones. This poll has a margin of error of ± 3 percentage points. Use the inequality $|v - 42| \le 3$ to find the least and greatest percent of voters v likely to vote for Lucy Jones according to this poll.

Read and Understand

1. What percentage of voters said they planned to vote for Lucy Jones? _____

2. What is the margin of error for this poll? _____

Plan and Solve

3. Write an inequality to determine the greatest percent of voters. _____

4. Solve the inequality in Step 3. _____

5. What is the greatest percent of voters? _____

6. Write an inequality to determine the least percent of voters. _____

7. Solve the inequality in Step 6. _____

8. What is the least percent of voters? _____

Look Back and Check

9. Show that your answers fall within the margin of error for this poll. _____

_____

Solve Another Problem

10. On average a household of 4 people uses 242 gallons of water each day. A 30-gallon change from the previous months could indicate a problem. More than a 30-gallon increase in water use could indicate a leak in a pipe. More than a 30-gallon decrease in water use could indicate a faulty water meter. Solve the inequality $|g - 242| \le 30$ to determine the upper and lower limits of normal water usage.

upper limit: _____

lower limit: _____

4A: Graphic Organizer

For use before Lesson 4-1

Study Skill Before you start your new chapter, read the major headings and summaries. This will give you a good overview of the chapter.

Write your answers.

1. What is the chapter title? _____

2. Find the Table of Contents page for this chapter at the front of the book.
Name four topics you will study in this chapter.

_____   _____

_____   _____

3. Complete the graphic organizer as you work through the chapter.
   1. Write the title of the chapter in the center oval.
   2. When you begin a lesson, write the name of the lesson in a rectangle.
   3. When you complete that lesson, write a skill or key concept from that lesson in the outer oval linked to that rectangle.
   Continue with steps 2 and 3 clockwise around the graphic organizer.

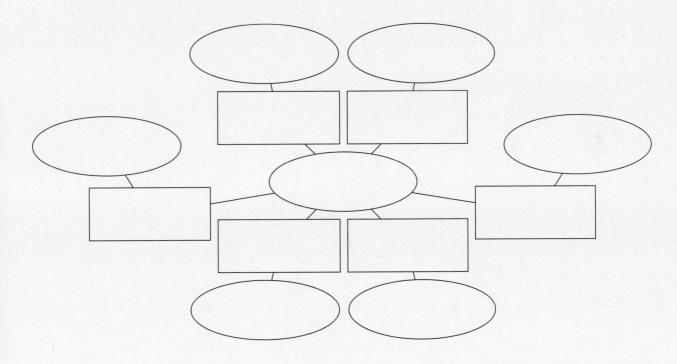

4B: Reading Comprehension

Study Skill When reading a word problem, it is sometimes difficult to determine which inequality sign should be used.

For Exercises 1–8, match each expression in Column A with its corresponding inequality symbol or expression in Column B by drawing a line between them.

	Column A		Column B
1.	is less than	**A.**	$\geq$
2.	is greater than	**B.**	$\leq$
3.	is less than or equal to	**C.**	$>$
4.	is greater than or equal to	**D.**	$<$
5.	Connie (c) is not as tall as Jose (j).	**E.**	$c \geq j$
6.	Cory (c) is older than Janishia (j).	**F.**	$c \leq j$
7.	Chris (c) is at least as tall as Julie (j).	**G.**	$c > j$
8.	Carol (c) is at most the same height as Jane (j).	**H.**	$c < j$

Write True or False for each statement.

_____ **9.** A 13-year-old is at least 10 years old.

_____ **10.** A 13-year-old is at most 10 years old.

_____ **11.** A 13-year-old is no less than 20 years old.

_____ **12.** A 13-year-old is no more than 20 years old.

13. **High-Use Academic Words** What does *corresponding* mean in the direction line?
   a. closely related
   b. writing back and forth

4C: Reading/Writing Math Symbols

For use after Lesson 4-2

Study Skill Keep your homework in a special notebook or section in a loose-leaf binder. This way you will always be able to find it quickly.

Write how to read each symbol.

1. $<$ _____

2. $>$ _____

3. $\leq$ _____

4. $\geq$ _____

5. $=$ _____

Write how to read each expression.

6. $8 > 4$ _____

7. $12 < 25$ _____

8. $3x \leq 15$ _____

9. $4x + 2 \geq 12$ _____

10. $12x = 36$ _____

Write each phrase in symbols.

11. 8 is less than 12 _____

12. 17 is greater than 2 _____

13. $12x$ is more than 36 _____

14. $15x$ minus 8 is less than 32 _____

15. $10x$ plus 4 is greater than or equal to 15 _____

16. $3x$ take away 12 is less than or equal to 21 _____

17. $32x$ equals $4x$ more than 12 _____

4D: Visual Vocabulary Practice

For use after Lesson 4-6

Study Skills When a math exercise is difficult, try to determine what makes it difficult. Is it a word that you don't understand? Are the numbers difficult to use?

Concept List

absolute value	absolute value inequality	Addition Property of Inequality
compound inequality	graph of a compound inequality	graph of an inequality
equivalent inequalities	identity	inequality

Write the concept that best describes each exercise.
Choose from the concept list above.

1. $\lvert -10 \rvert$ _____	2. _____	3. $-2 < x < 10$ _____
4. $2m - 6 \geq 2(m - 3)$ _____	5. $x - 5 > 2$ $x > 7$ _____	**6.** $p \leq -12$ _____
7. If $a < b$, then $a + c < b + c$. _____	8. $-4\ -3\ -2\ -1\quad 0\quad 1$ _____	**9.** $\lvert -6r + 7 \rvert > 12$ _____

4E: Vocabulary Check

Study Skill Strengthen your vocabulary. Use these pages and add cues and summaries by applying the Cornell Notetaking style.

Write the definition for each word at the right. To check your work, fold the paper back along the dotted line to see the correct answers.

_____ Inequality

_____

_____

_____ Solution of an inequality

_____

_____

_____ Variable

_____

_____

_____ Identity

_____

_____

_____ Evaluate an expression

_____

_____

Vocabulary and Study Skills

4E: Vocabulary Check (continued)

Write the vocabulary word for each definition. To check your work, fold the paper forward along the dotted line to see the correct answers.

An mathematical sentence that compares the value of two expression using a less-than or greater-than symbol.

_____

The value or values of a variable in an inequality that makes the inequality true.

_____

A symbol, usually a letter, that represents one or more numbers.

_____

An equation that is true for every value.

_____

Substitute a given number for each variable, and then simplify.

_____

4F: Vocabulary Review Puzzle

For use with Chapter Review

Study Skill You will encounter many new terms as you read a mathematics textbook. Read aloud or recite the new terms as you read them. This will help you remember and recall rules, definitions, and formulas for future use.

Unscramble the UPPERCASE letters to form a math word or phrase that completes each sentence.

1. The multiplicative inverse of a number is always its RLREIPACCO.

2. An XENNPTEO shows repeated multiplication.

3. LOHWE SURBEMN are the nonnegative integers.

4. A EVBALRAI is a symbol, usually a letter, that represents one or more numbers.

5. The numerical factor when a term has a variable is a CINCEFFITOE.

6. A coordinate plane is divided by its axes into four TANQAUSRD.

7. An TEITINYD is an equation that is true for every value.

8. COOPDUNM EUNIISAQELTI are joined by *and* or *or*.

Practice 5-1

The graph shows the speed a student traveled on the way to school.

Trip to School

1. What do the flat parts of the graph represent?

2. Circle the sections of the graph that show the speed decreasing.

The graph shows the relationship between time and distance from home.

Your Bicycle Ride

3. What do the flat parts of the graph represent?

4. What do the sections from 3 P.M. to 4 P.M. and from 5 P.M. to 6 P.M. represent?

5. What does the section from 12 P.M. to 1 P.M. represent?

Sketch a graph to describe the following. Explain the activity in each section of the graph.

6. your elevation above sea level as you hike in the mountains

7. your speed as you travel from home to school

8. the height of an airplane above the ground flying from Dallas, Texas to Atlanta, Georgia

9. the speed of a person driving to the store and having to stop at two stoplights

The graph shows the relationship between time and speed for an airplane.

Speed vs. Time

10. Circle the sections of the graph that show the speed increasing.

11. Circle the section of the graph that shows the plane not moving.

12. Circle the section of the graph that shows the plane moving at a constant speed.

5-1 • Guided Problem Solving

GPS **Student Page 255, Exercise 15**

A student uses a graphing calculator, a data collector, and a motion detector to make the graph at the right, which shows a classmate's distance from the motion detector.

a. Copy the graph and label each section.
b. During which section was the student walking toward the motion detector?
c. During which section(s) was the student walking at constant speed?

Read and Understand

1. What variables do the horizontal and vertical axes on the graph represent? _____

2. What are you asked to do? _____

Plan and Solve

3. Label each of the three segments of the graph in terms of whether the student's distance from the motion detector is increasing, decreasing, or remaining constant over that interval.

4. What is the student doing when the graph is horizontal? _____

5. How should the graph look when the student is walking toward the detector? _____

6. Which section of the graph matches the answer to Step 5? _____

7. Constant speed means distance changing steadily over time. What should the graph look like when this is happening? _____

8. Which sections does the answer to Step 7 describe? _____

Look Back and Check

9. Give a verbal description of the student's behavior from start to finish. Is this description consistent with your earlier answers?

_____

Solve Another Problem

10. Suppose the graph were rotated 180 degrees, putting the flat portion on the left. (You can rotate the page to visualize the result.) Give a verbal description of the student's behavior as described by the resulting graph.

_____

Practice 5-2

Relations and Functions

Find the domain and range of each relation.

1. $\{(-3, -7), (-1, -3), (0, -1), (2, 3), (4, 7)\}$

2. $\{(-5, -4), (-4, 2), (0, 2), (1, 3), (2, 4)\}$

Determine whether each of the following relations is a function.

3. $\left\{(-4, -3), (-2, -2), (0, -1), \left(1, -\frac{1}{2}\right)\right\}$

4. $\{(0, 0), (1, 1), (4, 2), (1, -1)\}$

5.

6.

7.

8.

Evaluate each function rule for $x = 3$.

9. $f(x) = 2x - 15$

10. $f(x) = -x + 3$

11. $g(x) = \frac{2}{3}x - 1$

12. $h(x) = -\frac{1}{2}x - \frac{1}{2}$

13. $h(x) = -0.1x + 2.1$

14. $g(x) = -\frac{x}{6} + \frac{3}{2}$

Evaluate each function rule for $x = -\frac{1}{2}$.

15. $f(x) = 4x - 2$

16. $f(x) = -\frac{1}{2}x + 1$

17. $g(x) = -|x| + 3$

18. $h(x) = x - \frac{1}{2}$

Find the range of each function for the given domain.

19. $f(x) = -3x + 1; \{-2, -1, 0\}$

20. $f(x) = x^2 + x - 2; \{-2, 0, 1\}$

21. $h(x) = -x^2; \{-3, -1, 1\}$

22. $g(x) = -\frac{1}{2}|x| + 1; \{-2, -1, 1\}$

23. For a car traveling at a constant rate of 60 mi/h, the distance traveled is a function of the time traveled.

    a. Express this relation as a function.

    b. Find the range of the function when the domain is $\{1, 5, 10\}$.

    c. What do the domain and range represent?

5-2 • Guided Problem Solving

GPS **Student Page 261, Exercise 42**

Travel Suppose your family is driving home from vacation. The car averages 25 miles per gallon, and you are 180 miles from home. The function $d = 180 - 25g$ relates the number of gallons of gas g the car will use to your distance from home d.

a. Make a table for $d = 180 - 25g$. Use 2, 4, 6, and 8 as domain values.

b. **Estimation** Based on the table, how many gallons of gasoline are needed to get home?

c. The gas tank holds 15 gallons when it is full. Describe a reasonable domain and range for this situation. Explain your answer.

Read and Understand

1. Explain where the equation $d = 180 - 25g$ comes from.

   _____

2. What are you asked to do? _____

Plan and Solve

3. Using $d = 180 - 25g$, fill in the value of d for each value of g.

g	2	4	6	8
d				

4. Home is reached when $d = 0$. Based on the table, approximately what value of g would lead to $d = 0$? _____

5. Since the gas tank can hold up to 15 gallons, what is a reasonable domain for d as a function of g? In other words, what values of g are possible? _____

6. Use the answers to Step 5, together with $d = 180 - 25g$, to find the range for d as a function of g—that is, what values of d are possible. _____

Look Back and Check

7. Check that your answer to Step 4 is reasonable by finding how far the car will travel on this many gallons. Is this distance close to 180 miles? _____

Solve Another Problem

8. A double cheeseburger contains 520 calories. A 150-lb adult, jogging, burns about 115 calories per mile. Write a function that describes how many calories still remain to be burned off after the adult has eaten the burger and then run a certain number of miles.

   _____

Guided Problem Solving

Practice 5-3

Function Rules, Tables, and Graphs

Model each rule with a table of values and a graph.

1. $f(x) = x + 1$

2. $f(x) = 2x$

3. $f(x) = 3x - 2$

4. $f(x) = \frac{3}{2}x - 2$

5. $f(x) = \frac{1}{2}x$

6. $f(x) = -\frac{2}{3}x + 1$

7. $f(x) = x^2 + 1$

8. $f(x) = -x^2 + 2$

9. $f(x) = x - 3$

10. Suppose a van gets 22 mi/gal. The distance traveled $D(g)$ is a function of the gallons of gas used.

a. Use the rule $D(g) = 22g$ to make a table of values and then a graph.

b. How far did the van travel if it used 10.5 gallons of gas?

c. Should the points of the graph be connected by a line? Explain.

11. The admission to a fairgrounds is $3.00 per vehicle plus $.50 per passenger. The total admission is a function of the number of passengers.

a. Use the rule $T(n) = 3 + 0.50n$ to make a table of values and then a graph.

b. What is the admission for a car with six people in it?

c. Should the points of the graph be connected by a line? Explain.

Graph each function.

12. $f(x) = 4x + 2$

13. $f(x) = |-2x|$

14. $f(x) = -3x + 7$

15. $f(x) = -|x| - 1$

16. $f(x) = 8 - \frac{3}{4}x$

17. $f(x) = \frac{2}{3}x - 7$

18. $f(x) = -\frac{2}{3}x + 6$

19. $f(x) = x^2 - 2x + 1$

20. $f(x) = -\frac{1}{2}x + 3$

21. $y = -x^2 + 1$

22. $y = 9 - x^2$

23. $y = 2x^2 + x - 2$

Make a table of values for each graph.

24.

25.

26.

5-3 • Guided Problem Solving

GPS **Student Page 267, Exercise 38**

a. Make a table for the perimeters of the rectangles formed by each set of darkened tiles.

b. The perimeter $P(t)$ is a function of the number of tiles t. Write a rule for the data in your table and graph the function.

Fig. 1   Fig. 2   Fig. 3   Fig. 4

Read and Understand

1. How many darkened tiles are there in each figure? _____

2. What are you asked to find? _____

Plan and Solve

3. Counting each darkened tile as a 1-by-1 square, find the perimeter of each block of tiles. Enter the answers in the table.

Number of tiles (*t*)	1	2	3	4
Perimeter (*P*)				

4. Find two numbers *a* and *b* that allow you to write a rule for the data in the form $P(t) = at + b$. _____

5. Graph the function found in Step 4.

Look Back and Check

6. Draw a block of five tiles in a row, and verify that the function from Step 4 correctly predicts the perimeter. _____

Solve Another Problem

7. Write a function rule based on the following table. _____

x	1	2	3	4
y	4	1	−2	−5

Practice 5-4

Writing a Function Rule

Write a function rule for each table.

1.

x	f(x)
0	3
2	5
4	7
6	9

2.

x	f(x)
0	0
1	3
3	9
5	15

3.

x	f(x)
5	0
10	5
15	10
20	15

4. a. Write a function rule to calculate the cost of buying bananas at $.39 a pound.

   b. How much would it cost to buy 3.5 pounds of bananas?

5. To rent a cabin, a resort charges $50 plus $10 per person.

   a. Write a function rule to calculate the total cost of renting the cabin.

   b. Use your rule to find the total cost for six people to stay in the cabin.

Write a function rule for each table.

6.

x	f(x)
−4	−2
−2	−1
6	3
8	4

7.

x	f(x)
−3	9
0	0
1	1
5	25

8.

x	f(x)
0	20
2	18
4	16
8	12

9. Pens are shipped to the office supply store in boxes of 12 each.

   a. Write a function rule to calculate the total number of pens when you know the number of boxes.

   b. Calculate the total number of pens in 16 boxes.

10. a. Write a function rule to determine the change you would get from a $20 bill when purchasing items that cost $1.25 each.

   b. Calculate the change when five of these items are purchased.

   c. Can you purchase 17 of these items with a $20 bill?

11. You invest $209 to buy shirts and then sell them for $9.50 each.

   a. Write a function rule to determine your profit.

   b. Use your rule to find your profit after selling 24 shirts.

   c. How many shirts do you need to sell to get back your investment?

Algebra 1 Lesson 5-4   **329**

5-4 • Guided Problem Solving

GPS **Student Page 273, Exercise 24**

Water Usage Use the function in the table at the right.

a. Identify the dependent and independent variables.
b. Write a rule to describe the function.
c. How many gallons of water would you use for 7 loads of laundry?
d. **Critical Thinking** In one month, you used 442 gallons of water for laundry. How many loads did you wash?

Water Used for Laundry	
1 load	34 gallons
2 loads	68 gallons
3 loads	102 gallons
4 loads	136 gallons

Read and Understand

1. What are the dependent and independent variables? _____

2. After you have identified the dependent and independent variables, what else are you asked to do? _____

Plan and Solve

3. Subtract 34 from 68, then subtract 68 from 102, and then subtract 102 from 136. The answer should be the same each time. What is it? _____

4. Complete the sentence: "Each load of laundry requires _____."

5. Use the answer to Step 4 to write a function rule. _____

6. Use the function found in Step 5 to find the number of gallons of water required for 7 loads of laundry. _____

7. Set the function found in Step 5 equal to 442 gallons, then solve the resulting equation to find the number of loads. _____

Look Back and Check

8. No loads of laundry should require zero gallons of water. Check that the function you wrote supports this conclusion. _____

Solve Another Problem

9. A motorcycle on the freeway gets 45 miles per gallon. Write a rule that describes miles covered as a function of gallons used. _____

Practice 5-5

Is each equation a direct variation? If it is, find the constant of variation.

1. $y = 5x$

2. $8x + 2y = 0$

3. $y = \frac{3}{4}x - 7$

4. $y = 2x + 5$

5. $3x - y = 0$

6. $y = \frac{3}{5}x$

7. $-3x + 2y = 0$

8. $-5x + 2y = 9$

9. $8x + 4y = 12$

10. $6x - 3y = 0$

11. $x - 3y = 6$

12. $9x + 5y = 0$

The ordered pairs in each exercise are for the same direct variation. Find each missing value.

13. $(3, 2)$ and $(6, y)$

14. $(-2, 8)$ and $(x, 12)$

15. $(4, y)$ and $(16, 12)$

16. $(x, 8)$ and $(6, -16)$

17. $(3, y)$ and $(9, 15)$

18. $(2, y)$ and $(10, 15)$

19. $(-4, 3)$ and $(x, 6)$

20. $(3, y)$ and $(1.5, 6)$

21. $\left(\frac{2}{3}, 2\right)$ and $(x, 6)$

22. $(2.5, 5)$ and $(x, 9)$

23. $(4.8, 5)$ and $(2.4, y)$

24. $(9, 3)$ and $(x, -2)$

For the data in each table, tell whether y varies directly with x. If it does, write an equation for the direct variation.

25.

x	y
4	8
7	14
10	20

26.

x	y
−3	−2
3	2
9	6

27.

x	y
4	3
5	4.5
11	13.5

28.

x	y
−2	−2.8
3	4.2
8	11.2

29. Charles's Law states that at constant pressure, the volume of a fixed amount of gas varies directly with its temperature measured in degrees Kelvin. A gas has a volume of 250 mL at 300 K.

   a. Write an equation for the relationship between volume and temperature.

   b. What is the volume if the temperature increases to 420 K?

30. Your percent grade varies directly with the number of correct answers. You got a grade of 80 when you had 20 correct answers.

   a. Write an equation for the relationship between percent grade and number of correct answers.

   b. What would your percent grade be with 24 correct answers?

31. The amount of simple interest earned in a savings account varies directly with the amount of money in the savings account. You have $1000 in your savings account and earn $50 in simple interest. How much interest would you earn if you had $1500 in your savings account?

5-5 • Guided Problem Solving

GPS **Student Page 281, Exercise 45**

Biology The amount of blood in a person's body varies directly with body weight. A person who weighs 160 lb has about 5 qt of blood.

  a. Find the constant of variation.
  b. Write an equation relating quarts of blood to weight.
  c. **Open-Ended** Estimate the number of quarts of blood in your body.

Read and Understand

1. What is another way of saying "y varies directly with x"? _____

2. What are you being asked to do? _____

Plan and Solve

3. What is the general form of a direct variation? _____

4. When $x = 160$, $y = 5$. Use this information to find k, the constant of variation. _____

5. Use the answer to Step 4 to write an equation relating quarts of blood to weight in pounds. _____

6. Use the equation found in Step 5 to estimate the volume of blood in your own body. _____

Look Back and Check

7. If blood volume varies directly with body weight, and a 160-lb person has 5 quarts of blood, then a person twice as big ought to have twice as much blood. Verify that your equation supports this conclusion. _____

Solve Another Problem

8. "A pint is a pound the whole world round." That's not exactly true, but it's pretty close for a liquid such as water or blood. Since 1 quart = 2 pints, a quart of blood weighs about 2 pounds. Write an equation relating *pounds* of blood to pounds of overall body weight. What fraction of your body weight consists of blood? _____

Practice 5-6

Inverse Variation

Suppose y varies inversely with x. Write an equation for each inverse variation.

1. $x = 9$ when $y = 6$

2. $x = 3.6$ when $y = 5$

3. $x = \frac{3}{4}$ when $y = \frac{2}{9}$

4. $x = 7$ when $y = 13$

5. $x = 8$ when $y = 9$

6. $x = 4.9$ when $y = 0.8$

7. $x = 11$ when $y = 44$

8. $y = 8$ when $x = 9.5$

9. $y = 12$ when $x = \frac{5}{6}$

Each pair of points is on the graph of an inverse variation. Find the missing value.

10. $(5, 8)$ and $(4, m)$

11. $(16, 5)$ and $(10, h)$

12. $(14, 8)$ and $(c, 7)$

13. $(3, 18)$ and $(a, 27)$

14. $(4, 28)$ and $(3, p)$

15. $(100, 25)$ and $(4, a)$

16. $(x, 7)$ and $(2, 14)$

17. $\left(\frac{2}{5}, \frac{3}{2}\right)$ and $\left(k, \frac{5}{2}\right)$

18. $(16, 3)$ and $(g, 24)$

19. $(2.4, 19.8)$ and $(h, 13.2)$

20. $(12.4, 6.6)$ and $(f, 8.8)$

21. $(3.2, k)$ and $(9.2, 0.8)$

22. $(18, 24)$ and $(72, v)$

23. $(17, 0.9)$ and $(5.1, x)$

24. $\left(\frac{3}{4}, y\right)$ and $\left(\frac{2}{3}, 18\right)$

Explain whether each situation represents a direct variation or an inverse variation.

25. The cost of a $50 birthday gift is split among some friends.

26. You purchase some peaches at $1.29/lb.

Tell whether the data in each table is a *direct variation*, or an *inverse variation*. Write an equation to model the data.

27.

x	2	7	10
y	35	10	7

28.

x	3	6	24
y	16	8	2

29.

x	5	6	8
y	55	66	88

30.

x	2	8	16
y	9	36	72

31.

x	2	3	9
y	18	12	4

32.

x	2	6	10
y	4.2	12.6	21

33.

x	2	5	12
y	12.8	32	76.8

34.

x	1.2	1.5	2.4
y	5	4	2.5

35.

x	6	9	36
y	3	2	0.5

36. The volume V of a gas in a closed container varies inversely with the pressure p, in atmospheres, that is applied to that gas.

  a. If $V = 20 \text{ m}^3$ when $p = 1$ atm, find V when $p = 4$ atm.

  b. If $V = 24 \text{ m}^3$ when $p = 3$ atm, find p when $V = 36 \text{ m}^3$.

  c. If $V = 48 \text{ m}^3$ when $p = 2$ atm, find V when $p = 5$ atm.

37. The time t to travel a fixed distance varies inversely with the rate r of travel.

  a. If $t = 3$ h and $r = 25$ mi/h, find t when $r = 50$ mi/h.

  b. If $t = 120$ s and $r = 40$ ft/s, find r when $t = 25$ s.

5-6 • Guided Problem Solving

GPS **Student Page 289, Exercise 45**

a. **Earnings** Suppose you want to earn $80. How long will it take you if you are paid $5/h; $8/h; $10/h; $20/h?

b. What are the two variable quantities in part (a)?

c. Write an equation to represent this situation.

Read and Understand

1. What are you asked to find?

_____

Plan and Solve

2. How are the quantities "pay," "hours worked," and "hourly rate of pay" related?

_____

3. Use division to fill in the table with the number of hours needed to earn $80 for each pay rate.

Rate of Pay	$5/hr	$8/hr	$10/hr	$20/hr
Hours Worked				

4. Of the three quantities in Step 2, which one is given as a fixed quantity in this problem? At what value is it fixed? _____

5. What are the variable quantities in the problem? _____

6. Use your answer to Step 2 to write an equation relating the fixed and variable quantities in this problem. _____

Look Back and Check

7. Use the table to confirm that you have written the correct equation.

Solve Another Problem

8. A shopper has $200 to spend and plans to spend all the money to buy a single type of item. Write an equation relating the price of each item and the number of items being purchased to the total amount being spent, which is $200. _____

Practice 5-7

Find the common difference of each arithmetic sequence.

1. 10, 16, 22, 28, . . .

2. 9, 6, 3, 0, . . .

3. −12, −17, −22, −27, . . .

4. −11, −8, −5, −2, . . .

5. $4, 4\frac{1}{2}, 5, 5\frac{1}{2}, \ldots$

6. $7\frac{1}{2}, 7, 6\frac{1}{2}, 6, \ldots$

7. 9, 10.5, 12, 13.5, . . .

8. 1, −1.5, −4, −6.5, . . .

9. 8, 9.1, 10.2, 11.3, . . .

10. −9, −8.1, −7.2, −6.3, . . .

11. −3, −0.6, 1.8, 4.2, . . .

12. 6.2, 4.5, 2.8, 1.1, . . .

Find the next two terms in each sequence.

13. 1, 7, 13, 19, . . .

14. −8, −5, −2, 1, . . .

15. 1, −4, −9, −14, . . .

16. $\frac{1}{2}, -\frac{1}{2}, -\frac{3}{2}, -\frac{5}{2}, \ldots$

17. 2.7, 4, 5.3, 6.6, . . .

18. 9.8, 0.7, −8.4, −17.5, . . .

19. $6\frac{1}{3}, 4\frac{2}{3}, 3, 1\frac{1}{3}, \ldots$

20. $2\frac{1}{2}, \frac{3}{4}, -1, -2\frac{3}{4}, \ldots$

Find the fifth, tenth, and hundredth terms of each sequence.

21. 4, 14, 24, 34, . . .

22. 14, 6, −2, −10, . . .

23. 3, 10, 17, 24, . . .

24. −19, −22, −25, −28, . . .

25. $\frac{1}{4}, -\frac{1}{4}, -\frac{3}{4}, -\frac{5}{4}, \ldots$

26. −1.3, −0.3, 0.7, 1.7, . . .

27. 0, 101, 202, 303, . . .

28. −1, −100, −199, −298, . . .

29. 5, 3.9, 2.8, 1.7, . . .

30. $-3\frac{1}{2}, -3\frac{3}{4}, -4, -4\frac{1}{4}, \ldots$

Determine whether each sequence is arithmetic. Justify your answer.

31. 0.5, 0.3, 0.1, −0.1, . . .

32. −1, 1, −1, 1, . . .

33. 3, 6, 12, 24, . . .

34. 100, 81, 64, 49, . . .

35. Renting a backhoe costs a flat fee of $65 plus an additional $35 per hour.

   a. Write the first four terms of a sequence that represents the total cost
   of renting the backhoe for 1, 2, 3, and 4 hours.

   b. What is the common difference?

   c. What are the 5th, 24th, 48th, and 72nd terms in the sequence?

5-7 • Guided Problem Solving

GPS **Student Page 295, Exercise 55**

The first five rows of Pascal's Triangle are at the right.

a. Predict the numbers in the sixth row.
b. Find the sum of the numbers in each of the first five rows.
c. Predict the sum of the numbers in the sixth row.

```
              1
           1     1
        1     2     1
     1     3     3     1
  1     4     6     4     1
```

Read and Understand

1. What are you asked to do? _____

Plan and Solve

2. Except for the 1's, every number in a row is based
   on two other nearby numbers. What is the relationship? _____

3. Predict the numbers in the sixth row. _____

4. What is the sum of the numbers in each of the first five rows? _____

5. What is the pattern for the sequence of numbers in your answer to Step 4?

   _____

6. Based on the pattern in Step 5, what should be the sum for row six? _____

Look Back and Check

7. Check your answer to Step 6 by adding up the numbers predicted in Step 3.

   _____

Solve Another Problem

8. The first five rows of another triangle of numbers are at the
   right. Predict the numbers in the sixth row.

```
               1
            1     1
         1     3     1
      1     5     5     1
   1     7    13     7     1
```

5A: Graphic Organizer

For use before Lesson 5-1

Vocabulary and Study Skills

Study Skill Develop a method of note taking, including punctuation and abbreviations. Take your notes in a large notebook. A large notebook will allow you to jot down information without running out of paper or space.

Write your answers.

1. What is the chapter title? _____

2. Find the Table of Contents page for this chapter at the front of the book. Name four topics you will study in this chapter.

   _____   _____

   _____   _____

3. Complete the graphic organizer as you work through the chapter.
   1. Write the title of the chapter in the center oval.
   2. When you begin a lesson, write the name of the lesson in a rectangle.
   3. When you complete that lesson, write a skill or key concept from that lesson in the outer oval linked to that rectangle.
   Continue with steps 2 and 3 clockwise around the graphic organizer.

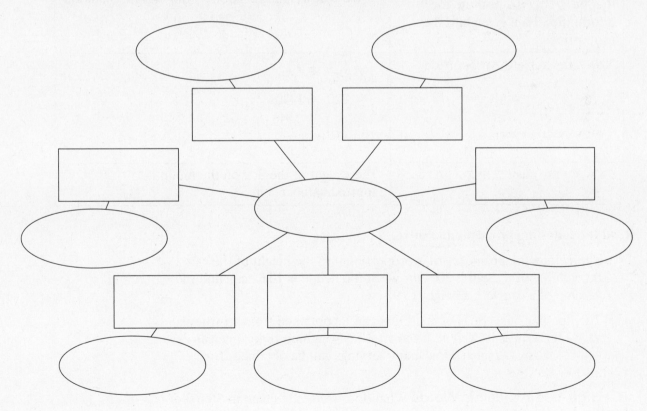

5B: Reading Comprehension

Study Skill After reading a section, try and recall the information. Ask yourself questions. If you cannot remember enough information re-read parts you forgot.

Read the problem and follow along with Carlita as she solves the problem.

> The weight of an object on Earth is directly proportional to the weight of the same object on the moon. A 220-lb astronaut would weigh 36 lb on the moon. How much would a 40-lb dog weigh on the moon?

What Carlita Thinks	What Carlita Writes
I read the problem and write down the important information.	220 lb astronaut = 36 lb on moon 40 lb dog = ?
Where should I start? It says the object is directly proportional, so I set up a proportion.	$\dfrac{\text{astronaut weight on Earth}}{\text{astronaut weight on moon}} = \dfrac{\text{dog weight on Earth}}{\text{dog weight on moon}}$
Since I am looking for the dog weight on the moon, I will let that be x. Now I substitute the information I am given into the proportions.	$\dfrac{\text{astronaut weight on Earth}}{\text{astronaut weight on moon}} = \dfrac{\text{dog weight on Earth}}{\text{dog weight on moon}}$ $\dfrac{220}{36} = \dfrac{40}{x}$
Now I can solve the proportion.	$\dfrac{220}{36} = \dfrac{40}{x}$ $220x = 1440$ $\dfrac{220x}{220} = \dfrac{1440}{220}$ $x \approx 6.5$
I'll write my answer in a sentence.	The weight of the dog on the moon is approximately 6.5 lb.

Read the following problems and solve.

1. The volume of a can of corn is proportional to the height of the can. If the volume of the can is 300 cm^3 when the height is 10.62 cm, find the volume of a can with a height 15.92 cm.

2. The number of servings of meat that can be obtained from a turkey varies directly as its weight. From a turkey weighing 16 kg, one can get 42 servings of meat. How many servings can be obtained from a 10-kg turkey?

3. **High-Use Academic Words** What does *substitute* mean in Step 3 of what Carlita thinks?
   a. replace a description with its numerical value
   b. guess a value for x and see if it makes the proportion true

5C: Reading/Writing Math Symbols

For use after Lesson 5-2

Study Skill When you take notes, it helps if you learn to use abbreviations and symbols that represent words. You should also use math symbols whenever possible.

For Exercises 1–8, match the symbolic expression in Column A with its written expression in Column B by drawing a line between them.

Column A		Column B
1. $k - 14 < 12$	**A.**	15 times x equals 12 more than x
2. $12 + y$	**B.**	twelve times x
3. $|-4|$	**C.**	kilometers per hour
4. $15x = 12 + x$	**D.**	a number take away 14 is less than 12
5. km/h	**E.**	twelve plus y
6. $/gal	**F.**	21 decreased by w
7. $12x$	**G.**	dollars per gallon
8. $21 - w$	**H.**	absolute value of negative four

For Exercises 9–16, match the symbolic expression in Column C with its written expression in Column D by drawing a line between them.

Column C		Column D
9. $12 \geq 12x$	**A.**	miles per gallon
10. 25%	**B.**	dollars per pound
11. $12 < x$	**C.**	12 is greater than or equal to twelve times x
12. $/lb	**D.**	twenty-five percent
13. mi/gal	**E.**	5 times a number x is less than or equal to 25
14. $\frac{1}{4}x$	**F.**	12 is less than a number x
15. $5x \leq 25$	**G.**	4 divided into w parts
16. $4 \div w$	**H.**	one-fourth of x

5D: Visual Vocabulary Practice

For use after Lesson 5-7

Study Skill When you come across something you don't understand, view it as an opportunity to increase your brain power.

Concept List

arithmetic sequence	common difference	conjecture
continuous data	direct variation	discrete data
function notation	inverse variation	relation

Write the concept that best describes each exercise. Choose from the concept list above.

1. an infant's weight over time	**2.** The pattern is "divide the previous term by 5."	**3.** $\{(-2, 1), (3, 0), (5, -9)\}$
4. $y = \dfrac{9}{x}$	**5.** $\underbrace{-4,}_{} \overset{+9}{\longrightarrow} \underbrace{5,}_{+9} \overset{+9}{\longrightarrow} \underbrace{14,}_{+9} \overset{+9}{\longrightarrow} \underbrace{23}_{}$	**6.** the number of children in each family in a neighborhood
7. $-7, -4, -1, 2, 5, 8, \ldots$	**8.** $f(x) = 3x - 11$	**9.** $y = 14x$

5E: Vocabulary Check

Study Skill Strengthen your vocabulary. Use these pages and add cues and summaries by applying the Cornell Notetaking style.

Write the definition for each word at the right. To check your work, fold the paper back along the dotted line to see the correct answers.

_____

_____

_____

Relation

_____

_____

_____

Vertical-line test

_____

_____

_____

Function notation

_____

_____

_____

Continuous data

_____

_____

_____

Direct variation

5E: Vocabulary Check (continued)

Write the vocabulary word for each definition. To check your work, fold the paper forward along the dotted line to see the correct answers.

A set of ordered pairs.

_____

If any vertical line passes through more than one point of the graph, then for some value of x there is more than one value of y.

_____

Using $f(x)$ to indicate the outputs of a function.

_____

Data where numbers between any two data values have meaning.

_____

A function of the form $y = kx$, where $k \neq 0$.

_____

Vocabulary and Study Skills

5F: Vocabulary Review Puzzle

For use with Chapter Review

Study Skill When you read, your eyes make small stops along a line of words. Good readers make fewer stops when they read. The more stops you make when you read, the harder it is for you to comprehend what you've read. Try to concentrate and free yourself of distractions as you read.

Complete the crossword puzzle.

ACROSS	
7. the result of a single trial	**3.** type of reasoning where conclusions are based on patterns you observe
8. a number pattern	**4.** set of second coordinates in an ordered pair
10. an equation involving two or more variables	**5.** a term that has no variable
15. an equation that describes a function	**6.** rational numbers and irrational numbers
	9. each item in a matrix
	11. a comparison of two numbers by division
DOWN	**12.** multiplicative inverse
1. a conclusion you reach by inductive reasoning	**13.** a data value that is much higher or lower than any other data values in the set
2. has two parts, a base and an exponent	**14.** a relation that assigns exactly one value in the range to each value in the domain

Practice 6-1

Rate of Change and Slope

Find the slope of each line.

1.

2.

3.

4.

5.

6.

Find the slope of the line that passes through each pair of points.

7. $(1, 2), (4, 3)$

8. $(7, 2), (3, 5)$

9. $(0, 2), (4, 6)$

10. $(-2, 5), (3, -4)$

11. $(2, 4), (6, 7)$

12. $(-2, -5), (4, 5)$

13. $(-3, -2), (4, -2)$

14. $(4, -2), (4, 9)$

15. $(5, 2), (8, -4)$

Find the rate of change. Explain what the rate of change means for each situation.

16.

17.

18.

Find the slope of the line that passes through each pair of points.

19. $(0, 0), (3, 7)$

20. $(-2, 4), (4, -1)$

21. $(-3, 6), (1, -2)$

22. $(2, 4), (4, -4)$

23. $(2, -10), (5, -6)$

24. $(5, 1), (11, 1)$

25. $(3, 7), (3, 5)$

26. $(7, 9), (2, 9)$

27. $(-5, -2), (-5, 3)$

6-1 • Guided Problem Solving

GPS **Student Page 314, Exercise 42**

Construction An extension ladder has a label that says, "Do not place base of ladder less than 5 ft from the vertical surface." What is the greatest slope possible if the ladder can safely extend to reach a height of 12 ft? Of 18 ft?

Read and Understand

1. How close to the vertical surface can the base of the ladder be placed? _____

2. How high can the ladder safely reach? (Two answers) _____

3. What are you asked to find? _____

Plan and Solve

4. How does the slope of the ladder relate to the height it reaches and to the placement of its base?

_____

5. What placement of the base makes the slope as great as possible? _____

6. When the ladder is set at maximum slope, how high does it reach? (Two answers) _____

7. When the ladder is set at maximum slope, what is the slope? (Two answers) _____

Look Back and Check

8. Which ladder ends up with the greater slope—the one that reaches to 12 ft or the one that reaches to 18 ft? Does the answer make sense?

_____

Solve Another Problem

9. For safety, an extension ladder should not be set at a slope greater than 3. If the ladder is placed against a wall at this slope and reaches a height of 12 ft, how far is the base from the wall?

_____

Practice 6-2

Slope-Intercept Form

Find the slope and *y*-intercept of each equation. Then graph.

1. $y = x + 2$

2. $y + 3 = -\frac{1}{3}x$

3. $y = 2x - 1$

4. $y - \frac{3}{5}x = -1$

5. $y = \frac{1}{2}x - 4$

6. $y - 2x = -3$

7. $y = \frac{2}{5}x + 3$

8. $y + \frac{1}{3}x = -2$

9. $y = -x - 2$

10. $y - 6 = -2x$

11. $y = -5x - 2$

12. $y + x = 0$

13. $y + 4 = 2x$

14. $y = -5x + 5$

15. $y = -4 + x$

16. $y = -4x$

17. $y = \frac{4}{5}x + 2$

18. $y - \frac{3}{4}x = -5$

19. $y = -6$

20. $y - 3 = -\frac{2}{3}x$

21. $y = -\frac{7}{4}x + 6$

22. $y + 3x = 6$

23. $y + \frac{1}{5}x = -2$

24. $y = \frac{3}{7}x$

Write an equation of a line with the given slope and *y*-intercept.

25. $m = 4, b = 8$

26. $m = -2, b = -6$

27. $m = \frac{4}{3}, b = 0$

28. $m = -\frac{9}{5}, b = -7$

29. $m = -6, b = 1$

30. $m = \frac{3}{7}, b = -1$

31. $m = -\frac{1}{5}, b = -3$

32. $m = 9, b = 4$

33. $m = -8, b = 11$

34. $m = \frac{2}{9}, b = 0$

35. $m = -11, b = 13$

36. $m = -\frac{7}{2}, b = -6$

Write the slope-intercept form of the equation for each line.

37.

38.

39.

40.

41.

42.

43. A television production company charges a basic fee of $4000 and then $2000 per hour when filming a commercial.

    a. Write an equation in slope-intercept form relating the basic fee and per-hour charge.

    b. Graph your equation.

    c. Use your graph to find the production costs if 4 hours of filming were needed.

6-2 • Guided Problem Solving

GPS **Student Page 321, Exercise 57**

a. A candle begins burning at time $t = 0$. Its original height is 12 in. After 30 min the height of the candle is 8 in. Draw a graph showing the change in the height of the candle.

b. Write an equation that relates the height of the candle to the time it has been burning.

c. How many minutes after the candle has been lit will it burn out?

Read and Understand

1. What is the candle's starting height at time $t = 0$? _____

2. What is the candle's height at time $t = 30$ min? _____

3. What are you asked to do? _____

Plan and Solve

4. Plot two points to represent the candle heights at different times. Graph the changing candle height by drawing a ray from the first point through the second one.

5. What is the y-intercept of the graph? _____

6. What is the slope of the graph? _____

7. Use the y-intercept and the slope to write the slope-intercept form of the equation relating candle height h to time t. _____

8. Use the equation from Step 7 to find t when the candle height h equals zero. _____

Look Back and Check

9. Check that the time it takes the candle to burn down its full length of 12 in. is three times the time it takes to burn down a third of that distance, namely 4 in. _____

Solve Another Problem

10. A stalk of bamboo is 30 cm tall when measured one day (call this $t = 0$) and is 42 cm tall 24 hours later. Write an equation that relates height in cm to time in hours. Then predict the time when the bamboo reaches a height of 90 cm.

_____

Practice 6-3

Model each situation with a linear function and graph. Is it reasonable to include negative numbers in the range?

1. A gas station that fills portable propane tanks (such as are used for camping and for outdoor barbecues) charges $2.60 per gallon.

2. The weight of a bucket of golfballs is a function of the number of balls, each of which weighs 1.6 oz. The bucket itself weighs 2 lb.

3. It costs a farmer $110 to bring 150 pounds of tomatoes to market, and the tomatoes sell for $2 per pound. The difference between the income from sales and the cost is the farmer's profit.

4. A newly-started high school hopes to enroll 80 students in its first year and to increase enrollment by 40 students per year over the next five years.

5. Temperature on the Fahrenheit scale is a linear function of temperature on the Celsius scale. Ten degrees Celsius equals 50 degrees Fahrenheit, and 25 degrees Celsius equals 77 degrees Fahrenheit.

6. Natalie spends 90 minutes doing her math and English homework. The time she spends on her math homework is a function of the time she spends on her English homework.

Write a linear function for each graph, and state and interpret the slope and the y-intercept in each case.

7. A caterer charges a flat fee to put on an event, plus a per-person cost based on how many guests attend.

8. Total cost of operating a rental car for one day is a function of rental fee plus cost of gasoline.

6-3 • Guided Problem Solving

GPS **Student Page 326, Exercise 7**

Shopping Clothing Connection and Teen World are having sales. The graphs show the discounted price as a function of the original price for merchandise from each shop.

Clothing Connection

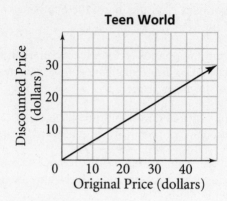

Teen World

a. Which store has a greater discount? Explain.

b. Write a linear function to model the situation in each store.

c. A customer buys merchandise originally priced at $16 from each store. What is the discounted price at each store?

Read and Understand

1. What do each of the two graphs show? _____

2. What are you asked to do? _____

_____

Plan and Solve

3. What is the *y*-intercept of each graph? _____

4. What is the slope of each graph? _____

5. Use the *y*-intercept and the slope to write the discount price
   (*y*) as a function of the original price (*x*) for each store. _____

6. Use the functions from Step 5 to find the discount
   price at each store for an original price of $16. _____

Look Back and Check

7. Do the answers from Step 6 match the graphs
   for Clothing Connection and Teen World? Explain. _____

Solve Another Problem

8. Suppose a third store has a graph similar to the ones for
   Clothing Connection and Teen World, but it passes through
   the point (40, 30). Write a linear function for this store,
   and find the discount price when the original price is $16. _____

Practice 6-4

Graph each equation using *x*- and *y*-intercepts.

1. $x + y = 3$ **2.** $x + 3y = -3$ **3.** $-2x + 3y = 6$ **4.** $5x - 4y = -20$

5. $3x + 4y = 12$ **6.** $7x + 3y = 21$ **7.** $y = -2.5$ **8.** $2x - 3y = 4$

9. $x = 3$ **10.** $3x - 2y = -6$ **11.** $5x + 2y = 5$ **12.** $-7x + 2y = 14$

13. $3x + y = 3$ **14.** $-3x + 5y = 15$ **15.** $2x + y = 3$ **16.** $8x - 3y = 24$

17. $3x - 5y = 15$ **18.** $x + 4y = 4$ **19.** $x = -3.5$ **20.** $y = 6$

Write each equation in standard form using integers.

21. $y = 4x - 11$ **22.** $y = 2x - 6$ **23.** $y = -2x - 3$ **24.** $y = 5x - 32$

25. $y = \frac{2}{3}x - \frac{25}{3}$ **26.** $y = 43 - 4x$ **27.** $y = -\frac{4}{5}x + \frac{6}{5}$ **28.** $y = -\frac{x}{5}$

29. $y = \frac{5}{2}x - 22$ **30.** $y = \frac{7}{3}x + \frac{25}{3}$ **31.** $y = -\frac{x}{3} + \frac{2}{3}$ **32.** $y = -6x - 38$

33. The drama club sells 200 lb of fruit to raise money. The fruit is sold in 5-lb bags and 10-lb bags.

   a. Write an equation to find the number of each type of bag that the club should sell.

   b. Graph your equation.

   c. Use your graph to find two different combinations of types of bags.

34. The student council is sponsoring a carnival to raise money. Tickets cost $5 for adults and $3 for students. The student council wants to raise $450.

   a. Write an equation to find the number of each type of ticket they should sell.

   b. Graph your equation.

   c. Use your graph to find two different combinations of tickets sold.

35. Anna goes to a store to buy $70 worth of flour and sugar for her bakery. A bag of flour costs $5, and a bag of sugar costs $7.

   a. Write an equation to find the number of bags of each type Anna can buy.

   b. Graph your equation.

36. You have $50 to spend on cold cuts for a party. Ham costs $5.99/lb, and turkey costs $4.99/lb. Write an equation in standard form to relate the number of pounds of each kind of meat you could buy.

6-4 • Guided Problem Solving

GPS **Student Page 334, Exercise 48**

You are sent to the store to buy sliced meat for a party. You are told to get roast beef and turkey, and you are given $30. Roast beef is $4.29/lb and turkey is $3.99/lb. Write an equation in standard form to relate the pounds of each kind of meat you could buy at the store with $30.

Read and Understand

1. How much money do you have to spend? _____

2. What is the cost per pound for roast beef? For turkey? _____

3. What are you asked to do? _____

Plan and Solve

4. What will the variables x and y represent in this situation? _____

5. Write an expression for how much money is spent on roast beef, and another expression for how much money is spent on turkey. _____

6. Write an expression for how much money is spent altogether. _____

7. Write an equation which says that the total amount spent equals the amount you have to spend. _____

Look Back and Check

8. Suppose you bought all beef and no turkey. How much beef would you bring back to the party? Does this seem like a reasonable real-world amount? _____

_____

Solve Another Problem

9. A street vendor who sells hot dogs and sodas makes $0.75 of profit on every soda but loses $0.10 on every hot dog. Using x for sodas and y for hot dogs, write an equation in standard form to describe a morning on which the vendor made a profit of exactly $81.

_____

Practice 6-5

Point-Slope Form and Writing Linear Equations

Write an equation in point-slope form for the line through the given points or through the given point with the given slope.

1. $(5, 7), (6, 8)$ **2.** $(-2, 3); m = -1$ **3.** $(1, 2), (3, 8)$ **4.** $(-2, 3); m = 4$

5. $(4, 7); m = \dfrac{3}{2}$ **6.** $(6, -2); m = -\dfrac{4}{3}$ **7.** $(0, 5), (-3, 2)$ **8.** $(8, 11), (6, 16)$

9. $(4, 2), (-4, -2)$ **10.** $(15, 16), (13, 10)$ **11.** $(0, -7); m = -4$ **12.** $(-3, 4), (1, 6)$

13. $(1, 2); m$ undefined   **14.** $(-6, 7); m = -\dfrac{1}{2}$ **15.** $(21, -2), (27, 2)$ **16.** $(7, 5); m = 0$

17. $(8, -2), (14, 1)$ **18.** $(4, 8), (2, 12)$ **19.** $(-5, 13), (-10, 9)$ **20.** $(6, 2); m = \dfrac{3}{4}$

21. $(5, -3); m = -2$ **22.** $(4, 3.5); m = 0.5$ **23.** $(-6, 2); m = \dfrac{5}{3}$ **24.** $(100, 90), (80, 120)$

25. $(-3, 6), (3, -6)$ **26.** $(11, 7), (9, 3)$ **27.** $(2, 7); m = \dfrac{5}{2}$ **28.** $(-9, 8); m = -\dfrac{5}{3}$

Is the relationship shown by the data linear? If it is, model the data with an equation.

29.

x	y
2	3
3	7
4	11
5	15

30.

x	y
-3	4
-1	6
1	7
3	10

31.

x	y
-4	12
-1	8
5	-4
10	-8

32.

x	y
-2	5
3	-5
7	-13
11	-21

33.

x	y
-6	-5
-2	1
0	4
8	16

34.

x	y
-6	11
-3	9
6	3
15	-3

35.

x	y
-7	-3
-5	0
-1	3
3	7

36.

x	y
-4	1
2	4
6	6
14	10

Write an equation of each line in point-slope form.

37.

38.

39.

6-5 • Guided Problem Solving

GPS **Student Page 340, Exercise 55**

Environment Worldwide carbon monoxide emissions are decreasing about 2.6 million metric tons each year. In 1991, carbon monoxide emissions were 79 million metric tons. Use a linear equation to model the relationship between carbon monoxide emissions and time. Let $x = 91$ correspond to 1991.

Read and Understand

1. What is the annual rate of decrease of worldwide carbon monoxide emissions?

   _____

2. What was the total of worldwide carbon monoxide emissions in 1991? _____

3. What are you being asked to do? _____

Plan and Solve

4. Write the information about worldwide emissions
   in 1991 as an ordered pair representing a data point. _____

5. How does the rate of emissions describe the graph of the relation
   between time and emissions? What form of linear equation is
   easiest to write, given the information in the problem?

   _____

6. Write the appropriate linear equation. _____

7. Convert the equation to slope-intercept form. _____

Look Back and Check

8. Substitute 91 for x in the final equation and verify that the corresponding value of y is 79.

Solve Another Problem

9. An accountant at a manufacturing company assumes that
   a particular piece of company-owned machinery declines
   in value by $1800 per year. When the machine is 3 years old,
   it is valued at $21,600. Use a linear equation to model the
   relation between the machine's age and its accounting value. _____

Practice 6-6

Parallel and Perpendicular Lines

Find the slope of a line parallel to the graph of each equation.

1. $y = 4x + 2$

2. $y = \frac{2}{7}x + 1$

3. $y = -9x - 13$

4. $y = -\frac{1}{2}x + 1$

5. $6x + 2y = 4$

6. $y - 3 = 0$

7. $-5x + 5y = 4$

8. $9x - 5y = 4$

9. $-x + 3y = 6$

10. $6x - 7y = 10$

11. $x = -4$

12. $-3x - 5y = 6$

Write an equation for the line that is perpendicular to the given line and that passes through the given point.

13. $(6, 4); y = 3x - 2$

14. $(-5, 5); y = -5x + 9$

15. $(-1, -4); y = \frac{1}{6}x + 1$

16. $(1, 1); y = -\frac{1}{4}x + 7$

17. $(12, -6); y = 4x + 1$

18. $(0, -3); y = -\frac{4}{3}x - 7$

19.

20.

21.

Write an equation for the line that is parallel to the given line and that passes through the given point.

22. $(3, 4); y = 2x - 7$

23. $(1, 3); y = -4x + 5$

24. $(4, -1); y = x - 3$

25. $(4, 0); y = \frac{3}{2}x + 9$

26. $(-8, -4); y = -\frac{3}{4}x + 5$

27. $(9, -7); -7x - 3y = 3$

28.

29.

30.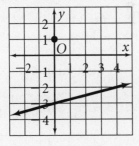

Tell whether the lines for each pair of equations are *parallel*, *perpendicular*, or *neither*.

31. $y = 3x - 8$
$3x - y = -1$

32. $3x + 2y = -5$
$y = \frac{2}{3}x + 6$

33. $y = -\frac{5}{2}x + 11$
$-5x + 2y = 20$

34. $9x + 3y = 6$
$3x + 9y = 6$

35. $y = -4$
$y = 4$

36. $x = 10$
$y = -2$

6-6 • Guided Problem Solving

GPS Student Page 347, Exercises 47–49

Use the map below to answer the questions that follow.

a. What is the slope of New Hampshire Avenue?

b. Show that the parts of Pennsylvania Avenue and Massachusetts Avenue near New Hampshire Avenue are parallel.

c. Show that New Hampshire Avenue is not perpendicular to Pennsylvania Avenue.

Read and Understand

1. Find New Hampshire Avenue, Pennsylvania Avenue, and Massachusetts Avenue on the map. What is the white grid for? _____

Plan and Solve

2. Find the slope of New Hampshire Avenue by examining the segment that runs from Pennsylvania Avenue to a little more than one grid square past Massachusetts Avenue.

_____

3. Staying on the left half of the map, find the slopes of Pennsylvania Avenue and Massachusetts Avenue. If those two streets have the same slope, they are parallel. _____

4. For New Hampshire Avenue and Pennsylvania Avenue to be perpendicular, their slopes must be negative reciprocals of each other. Are they? _____

Look Back and Check

5. On the left half of the map, draw a line with a slope of 2 through Pennsylvania Avenue and Massachusetts Avenue, and verify by inspection that the line is perpendicular to those two streets and not parallel to New Hampshire Avenue.

Solve Another Problem

6. What slope would a street have to have to be perpendicular to New Hampshire Avenue? Draw a line on the map to verify your result. _____

Practice 6-7

Scatter Plots and Equations of Lines

Decide whether the data in each scatter plot follow a linear pattern. If they do, find the equation of a trend line.

1.

2.

3.

Use a graphing calculator to find the equation of the line of best fit for the following data. Find the value of the correlation coefficient *r* and determine if there is a strong correlation between the data.

4.

x	y
1	7
2	5
3	−1
4	3
5	−5

5.

x	y
1	6
2	15
3	−5
4	1
5	−2

6.

x	y
1	5
4	8
8	3
13	10
19	13

7.

x	y
12	28
15	50
18	14
21	28
24	36

Draw a scatter plot. Write the equation of the trend line.

8.

x	y
1	17
2	20
3	22
4	26
5	28
6	31

9.

Year	U.S. Union Membership (millions)
1988	17.00
1989	16.96
1990	16.74
1991	16.57
1992	16.39
1993	16.60
1994	16.75
1995	16.36
1996	16.27
1997	16.11
1998	16.21

Source: *World Almanac 2000*, p. 154.

10.

x	y
1	18
2	20
3	24
4	30
5	28
6	33

11.

Year	U.S. Unemployment Rate (%)
1988	5.5
1989	5.3
1990	5.6
1991	6.8
1992	7.5
1993	6.9
1994	6.1
1995	5.6
1996	5.4
1997	4.9
1998	4.5

Source: *World Almanac 2000*, p. 145.

6-7 • Guided Problem Solving

GPS **Student Page 354, Exercise 12**

Geometry Students measured the diameters and circumferences of the tops of a variety of cylinders. Below is the data they collected.

Cylinder Tops

Diameter (cm)	3	3	5	6	8	8	9.5	10	10	12
Circumference (cm)	9.3	9.5	16	18.8	25	25.6	29.5	31.5	30.9	39.5

a. Graph the data.
b. Find the equation of a trend line.
c. What does the slope of the equation mean?
d. Find the diameter of a cylinder with a circumference of 45 cm.

Read and Understand

1. What are the lower and upper limits on the range of diameter? Of circumferences?

_____

2. In simple, nonquantitative terms, what is the relation between diameter and circumference?

_____

Plan and Solve

3. Select graph ranges and plot each pair of diameter and circumference values as a data point.

_____

4. Using visual inspection, add a trend line to the graph.

5. Using two convenient points on the trend line, write a point-slope equation for the line.

_____

6. Convert the equation from Step 5 to slope-intercept form. _____

7. What does the slope of the equation mean? (*Hint:* Treat the *y*-intercept as approximately 0.)

_____

Look Back and Check

8. Compare your results with what you know about the relation between the ratio of a circle's circumference to its diameter. _____

Solve Another Problem

9. Choose two other data points and repeat Steps 5–8. _____

Practice 6-8

Graphing Absolute Value Equations

Graph each equation by translating $y = |x|$.

1. $y = |x| - 3$

2. $y = |x| + 4$

3. $y = |x| - 1$

4. $y = |x| + \frac{1}{2}$

5. $y = |x| + 2\frac{1}{2}$

6. $y = |x| + 3$

7. $y = |x + 2|$

8. $y = |x - 4|$

9. $y = |3x|$

10. $y = |x + 3| - 2$

11. $y = |x - 2| + 1$

12. $y = |x - 3| + 2$

Graph each equation by translating $y = -|x|$.

13. $y = -|x| + 1$

14. $y = -|x + 2|$

15. $y = -|x| - 5$

16. $y = -|x - 4| + 2$

17. $y = -|x - 5|$

18. $y = -|x| + 4.5$

19. $y = -|x - 3| + 1$

20. $y = -|x + 1| + 3$

21. $y = -|x + 2| - 4$

Write an equation for each translation of $y = |x|$.

22. left 7 units

23. right 5 units

24. up 6 units

25. up 2 units, right 3 units

26. down 3 units, left 1 unit

27. down 1 unit, right 2 units

28. left 2 units, up 4 units

29. right 3 units, up 2 units

30. left 4 units, down 3.5 units

Write an equation for each translation of $y = -|x|$.

31. 3 units up

32. 3.5 units left

33. $\frac{3}{4}$ unit down

34. down 3 units

35. up 2 units, right 1 unit

36. down 5 units, left 1 unit

37. right 3 units, up 2 units

38. down 4 units, left 2 units

39. up 4 units, right 3 units

Write an equation for the given graphs.

40.

41.

42.

43.

6-8 • Guided Problem Solving

GPS **Student Page 362, Exercises 32–35**

Write an equation for each translation of $y = -|x|$.

a. 2 units up   **b.** 2.25 units left

c. $\frac{3}{2}$ units down   **c.** 4 units right

Read and Understand

1. Draw the graph of $y = -|x|$.

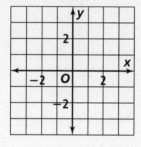

2. What does it mean to write an equation for a translation? _____

_____

Plan and Solve

3. How does one shift the graph of the equation $y = -|x|$ up or down? _____

_____

4. How does one shift the graph of the equation $y = -|x|$ left or right? _____

_____

5. Write the equation that translates the graph of $y = -|x|$ up 2 units. Then write the equation

that translates $y = -|x|$ down $\frac{3}{2}$ units. _____

6. Write the equation that translates the graph of $y = -|x|$ right 4 units. Then write the equation

that translates $y = -|x|$ left 2.25 units. _____

Look Back and Check

7. Pick one of your answers in Steps 5 and 6 and graph the equation. Verify that it is shifted the
way it is supposed to be.

Solve Another Problem

8. Write an equation for the translation of $y = |x| + 5$ down 5 units,

then simplify the right side. Why does the result make sense? _____

6A: Graphic Organizer

For use before Lesson 6-1

Study Skill When taking notes, do not try and write down everything that the teacher is saying. Spend more time listening and write down the main points and examples. If you are writing as fast as you can, you cannot be listening as well.

Write your answers.

1. What is the chapter title? _____

2. Find the Table of Contents page for this chapter at the front of the book. Name four topics you will study in this chapter.

   _____   _____

   _____   _____

3. Complete the graphic organizer as you work through the chapter.
   1. Write the title of the chapter in the center oval.
   2. When you begin a lesson, write the name of the lesson in a rectangle.
   3. When you complete that lesson, write a skill or key concept from that lesson in the outer oval linked to that rectangle.
   Continue with steps 2 and 3 clockwise around the graphic organizer.

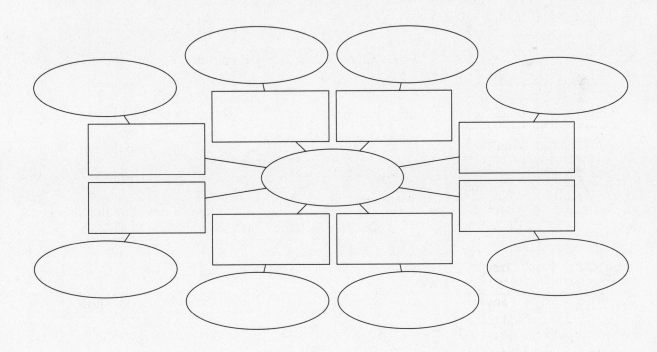

6B: Reading Comprehension

Study Skill Reading and interpreting diagrams, graphs, and charts is an important skill in algebra and in everyday life. When you read diagrams, graphs, and charts, pay close attention to the details they contain.

Interpret each graph. Then match the graph to the sentence that describes the relationship shown.

1.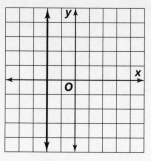

A. As *x* increases, *y* increases.

2.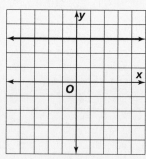

B. As *x* increases, *y* decreases.

3.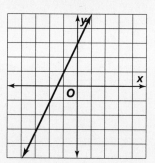

C. As *x* increases, *y* is constant.

4.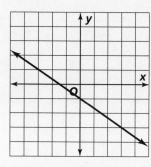

D. As *y* increases, *x* is constant.

5. High-Use Academic Words In the direction line, what does *interpret* mean for you to do?

    a. identify the slope and *y*-intercept   **b.** understand what is being conveyed

6C: Reading/Writing Math Symbols

For use after Lesson 6-6

Study Skill Many times you need to refer to concepts taught in previous lessons. Use the Table of Contents or Index to locate these concepts.

Write what each of the symbols, variables, or equations represents. The first one is done for you.

1. $(x, 0)$ _____ x-intercept _____

2. $|x|$ _____

3. $\geq$ _____

4. $y = mx + b$ _____

5. $<$ _____

6. $Ax + By = C$ _____

7. $=$ _____

8. m, in $y = mx + b$ _____

9. b, in $y = mx + b$ _____

10. $-x$ _____

11. $(0, y)$ _____

12. $\times$ _____

6D: Visual Vocabulary Practice
High-Use Academic Words

For use after Lesson 6-8

• •

Study Skills Use Venn diagrams to understand the relationship between words whose meanings overlap, such as *square*, *rectangle*, and *quadrilateral* or *real number*, *integer*, and *counting number*.

Concept List

analyze	common	equivalent
graph	order	pattern
property	rule	table

Write the concept that best describes each exercise. Choose from the concept list above.

1. To solve an inequality in the form $\lvert A \rvert < b$, where A is a variable expression and $b > 0$, solve $-b < A < b$. _____	**2.** $y = -\frac{3}{2}$ and $4y = -6$ _____	**3.** _____
4. $-8, 16, -32, 64, \ldots$ _____	**5.** A Day's Commute _____	**6.** $-5, -2, 0, \frac{1}{2}, 7$ _____
7. The difference between terms in the sequence $17, 13, 9, 5, \ldots$ _____	**8.** $-4 \cdot 3 = 3 \cdot -4$ _____	**9.** Jorge found the percent of change from \$15 to \$10 to be 50%. What error did he make? _____

6E: Vocabulary Check

Study Skill Strengthen your vocabulary. Use these pages and add cues and summaries by applying the Cornell Notetaking style.

Write the definition for each word at the right. To check your work, fold the paper back along the dotted line to see the correct answers.

_____

_____

_____   Rate of change

_____

_____

_____   Slope

_____

_____

_____   Linear equation

_____

_____

_____   Parent function

_____

_____

_____   Slope-intercept form

_____

_____

6E: Vocabulary Check (continued)

For use after Lesson 6-3

Write the vocabulary word for each definition. To check your work,
fold the paper forward along the dotted line to see the correct answers.

Change in the dependent
variable divided by
change in the independent
variable.

_____

The rate of change
of a line on a graph.

_____

An equation whose
graph is a line.

_____

The simplest equation
of a function.

_____

$y = mx + b$.

_____

6F: Vocabulary Review

Study Skill Always read direction lines before doing any exercises. What you think you are supposed to do may be different from what the directions call for.

Circle the word that best completes the sentence.

1. (*Parallel lines*, *Perpendicular lines*) are lines in the same plane that never intersect.

2. The point where a line crosses the *y*-axis is known as the (*x-intercept*, *y-intercept*).

3. The linear equation $y = mx + b$ is in (*slope-intercept*, *point-slope*) form.

4. The (*slope*, *equation*) of a line is its rate of vertical change over horizontal change.

5. The (*domain*, *range*) of a relation is the set of second coordinates in the ordered pairs.

6. (*Dependent*, *Independent*) events are events that do not influence one another.

7. The (*mean*, *median*) is the middle value in a set of numbers when arranged in numerical order.

8. A(n) (*exponent*, *variable*) is a symbol, usually a letter, that represents one or more numbers.

9. The (*absolute value*, *reciprocal*) of a number is its multiplicative inverse.

10. The equation $3 + 4 = 4 + 3$ illustrates the (*Identity Property of Addition*, *Commutative Property of Addition*).

11. When a value is less than its original amount, the percent of (*increase*, *decrease*) can be found.

12. A V-shaped graph that points upwards or downwards is the graph of a(n) (*linear*, *absolute value*) equation.

Practice 7-1

Solving Systems by Graphing

Solve by graphing. Write *no solution* or *infinitely many solutions* where appropriate.

1. $y = 3x - 1$
$y = -2x + 4$

2. $y = x - 1$
$y = -x + 7$

3. $y = \frac{3}{4}x + 2$
$\frac{3}{4}x - y = 4$

4. $y = 4x + 7$
$y = -3x$

5. $y = x - 3$
$y = \frac{1}{7}x + 3$

6. $y = -3x - 4$
$3x + y = -4$

7. $y = -x - 3$
$y = -2x - 8$

8. $y = -x + 2$
$3x + 3y = 12$

9. $y = x$
$y = 3x + 2$

10. $y = 4x - 3$
$y = -3x - 3$

11. $y = \frac{5}{3}x - 4$
$y = 2x - 6$

12. $y = 3x + 2$
$2x + y = -8$

13. $x = y + 4$
$y = x + 4$

14. $x + y = 2$
$y = -2x - 1$

15. $2x - y = 3$
$y = x + 4$

16. $3x - 6y = 12$
$2x - 4y = 8$

17. $x - y = 1$
$y = \frac{3}{4}x + 1$

18. $y = x$
$x = 2y + 2$

19. $3x - y = 9$
$y = x + 1$

20. $2x + y = 0$
$y = 2x - 4$

21. $y = 2x - 6$
$x + y = 9$

22. $y = -x$
$y = 3x + 12$

23. $4x + y = 6$
$y = -4x - 1$

24. $y = 4x$
$y = -3x$

25. $y = x$
$2x + y = \frac{3}{2}$

26. $3x + y = 6$
$2x - y = \frac{3}{2}$

27. $x + 4y = -\frac{1}{2}$
$-2x - 3y = 1$

28. $x - y = -\frac{3}{2}$
$-2x + 5y = -4.5$

Solve each system by using a graphing calculator. Write *no solution* or *infinitely many solutions* where appropriate.

29. $y = x + 6$
$y = 2x - 7$

30. $y = \frac{7}{2}x - 6$
$y = 3x - 2$

31. $y = 2x - 20$
$y = -x + 34$

32. $y = \frac{2}{3}x + 4$
$2x - 3y = 3$

33. $y = -x - 5$
$y = 3x - 105$

34. $x + y = -10$
$2x + 3y = -30$

35. $3x - 4y = 0$
$2x + y = 110$

36. $y = \frac{1}{7}x + 10$
$x - 2y = 0$

37. $2x + y = 6$
$3y = -6x + 9$

38. $y = \frac{5}{6}x + 12$
$y = \frac{4}{3}x - 6$

39. $2x - y = 8$
$3x - 2y = 0$

40. $x + 2y = 2$
$3x + 4y = 22$

41. $y = 2x + 0.75$
$y = -4x - 8.25$

42. $1.25x + 3.25y = -5.75$
$0.5x - 1.5y = 0.5$

43. $x = -2y - 3.5$
$-5x + 3y = -15$

7-1 • Guided Problem Solving

GPS **Student Page 378, Exercise 25**

Soccer Jim and Tony are on opposing teams in a soccer match. They are running after the same ball. Jim's path is the line $y = 3x$. Tony's path is the line $y = -2x + 100$. Solve by graphing to find the coordinates of the ball.

Read and Understand

1. What is the equation for Jim's path to the ball? _____

2. What is the equation for Tony's path to the ball? _____

3. What are you asked to find? _____

Plan and Solve

4. Find the slope and y-intercept for $y = 3x$. _____

5. Find the slope and y-intercept for $y = -2x + 100$. _____

6. Graph the two equations on the same set of axes.

100 m

0 m   73 m

7. What are the coordinates of the point where the two lines cross? _____

Look Back and Check

8. Does it makes sense that the paths of two opposing players would cross at the ball? Would it make sense for two players on the same team?

    _____

Solve Another Problem

9. Suppose Tony's path were instead given by $y = -x + 40$. Where would you locate the ball?

Practice 7-2

Solving Systems Using Substitution

Solve each system using substitution. Write *no solution* or *infinitely many solutions* where appropriate.

1. $y = x$
$y = -x + 2$

2. $y = x + 4$
$y = 3x$

3. $y = 3x - 10$
$y = 2x - 5$

4. $x = -2y + 1$
$x = y - 5$

5. $y = 5x + 5$
$y = 15x - 1$

6. $y = x - 3$
$y = -3x + 25$

7. $y = x - 7$
$2x + y = 8$

8. $y = 3x - 6$
$-3x + y = -6$

9. $x + 2y = 200$
$x = y + 50$

10. $3x + y = 10$
$y = -3x + 4$

11. $y = 2x + 7$
$y = 5x + 4$

12. $3x - 2y = 0$
$x + y = -5$

13. $4x + 2y = 8$
$y = -2x + 4$

14. $6x - 3y = 6$
$y = 2x + 5$

15. $2x + 4y = -6$
$x - 3y = 7$

16. $5x - 3y = -4$
$x + y = -4$

17. $y = -\frac{2}{3}x + 4$
$2x + 3y = -6$

18. $2x + 3y = 8$
$\frac{3}{2}y = 4 - x$

19. $3x - y = 4$
$2x + y = 16$

20. $x + y = 0$
$x = y + 4$

21. $5x + 2y = 6$
$y = -\frac{5}{2}x + 1$

22. $2x + 5y = -6$
$4x + y = -12$

23. $4x + 3y = -3$
$2x + y = -1$

24. $y = -\frac{2}{3}x + 1$
$4x + 6y = 6$

25. $5x - 6y = 19$
$4x + 3y = 10$

26. $2x + y = 6.6$
$5x - 2y = 0.3$

27. $2x - 4y = 3.8$
$3x - y = 17.7$

28. $3x + 4y = 8$
$4.5x + 6y = 12$

29. $3x - 4y = -5$
$x = y + 2$

30. $y = \frac{1}{3}x + 10$
$x = 3y + 6$

31. $2x + 5y = 62$
$3x - y = 23.3$

32. $-5x + y = 6$
$2x - 3y = 60$

33. $x = \frac{3}{4}y - 6$
$y = \frac{4}{3}x + 8$

34. $5x + 6y = -76$
$x + 2y = -44$

35. $3x - 2y = 10$
$y = \frac{3}{2}x - 1$

36. $-3x + 2y = -6$
$-2x + y = 6$

37. At an ice cream parlor, ice cream cones cost $1.10 and sundaes cost $2.35. One day, the receipts for a total of 172 cones and sundaes were $294.20. How many cones were sold?

38. You purchase 8 gal of paint and 3 brushes for $152.50. The next day, you purchase 6 gal of paint and 2 brushes for $113.00. How much does each gallon of paint and each brush cost?

Name _____ Class _____ Date _____

7-2 • Guided Problem Solving

GPS **Student Page 384, Exercise 24**

Buying a Car Suppose you are thinking about buying one of two cars.
Car A will cost $17,655. You can expect to pay an average of $1230 per year
for fuel, maintenance, and repairs. Car B will cost about $15,900. Fuel,
maintenance, and repairs for it will average about $1425 per year. After how
many years are the total costs for the cars the same?

Read and Understand

1. What are the costs involved in owning car A? _____

2. What are the costs involved in owning car B? _____

3. What are you asked to find? _____

Plan and Solve

4. Write an equation for car A that describes total cost as a function of time. _____

5. Write another equation that does the same for car B. _____

6. Why will solving the two equations as a system give the answer to the problem?

   _____

7. To solve the system of two equations, does
   it make more sense to replace c with an
   expression containing t, or vice versa? Explain. _____

8. Make the appropriate replacement, then solve for the remaining variable. _____

9. Use your answer to Step 8 to give the solution to the problem as stated. _____

Look Back and Check

10. Explain why it makes sense that the total costs
    would be the same after several years of ownership. _____

Solve Another Problem

11. Suppose car C costs $16,815 to buy and $1350 per year to operate.
    At what time are the total costs the same as for car A? At what time
    are they the same as for car B?

    _____

Practice 7-3

Solving Systems Using Elimination

Solve by elimination. Show your work.

1. $x + 2y = 7$
$3x - 2y = -3$

2. $3x + y = 20$
$x + y = 12$

3. $5x + 7y = 77$
$5x + 3y = 53$

4. $2x + 5y = -1$
$x + 2y = 0$

5. $3x + 6y = 6$
$2x - 3y = 4$

6. $2x + y = 3$
$-2x + y = 1$

7. $9x - 3y = 24$
$7x - 3y = 20$

8. $2x + 7y = 5$
$2x + 3y = 9$

9. $x + y = 30$
$x - y = 6$

10. $4x - y = 6$
$3x + 2y = 21$

11. $x + 2y = 9$
$3x + 2y = 7$

12. $3x + 5y = 10$
$x - 5y = -10$

13. $2x - 3y = -11$
$3x + 2y = 29$

14. $8x - 9y = 19$
$4x + y = -7$

15. $2x + 6y = 0$
$-2x - 5y = 0$

16. $-2x + 3y = -9$
$x + 3y = 3$

17. $4x - 3y = 11$
$3x - 5y = -11$

18. $3x + 7y = 48$
$5x - 7y = -32$

19. $-2x + 3y = 25$
$-2x + 6y = 58$

20. $3x + 8y = 81$
$5x - 6y = -39$

21. $8x + 13y = 179$
$2x - 13y = -69$

22. $-x + 8y = -32$
$3x - y = 27$

23. $2x + 7y = -7$
$5x + 7y = 14$

24. $x + 6y = 48$
$-x + y = 8$

25. $6x + 3y = 0$
$-3x + 3y = 9$

26. $7x + 3y = 25$
$-2x - y = -8$

27. $3x - 8y = 32$
$-x + 8y = -16$

28. $4x - 7y = -15$
$-4x - 3y = -15$

29. $5x + 7y = -1$
$4x - 2y = 22$

30. $6x - 3y = 69$
$7x - 3y = 76$

31. $x + 8y = 28$
$-3x + 5y = 3$

32. $8x - 6y = -122$
$-4x + 6y = 94$

33. $2x + 9y = 36$
$2x - y = 16$

34. $-6x + 12y = 120$
$5x - 6y = -48$

35. $-x + 3y = 5$
$-x - 3y = 1$

36. $10x - 4y = 6$
$10x + 3y = 13$

37. $6x + 3y = 27$
$-4x + 7y = 27$

38. $6x - 8y = 40$
$5x + 8y = 48$

39. $3x + y = 27$
$-3x + 4y = -42$

40. $2x + 8y = -42$
$-x + 8y = -63$

41. $5x + 9y = 112$
$3x - 2y = 8$

42. $-3x + 2y = 0$
$-3x + 5y = 9$

43. $8x - 2y = 58$
$6x - 2y = 40$

44. $7x - 9y = -57$
$-7x + 10y = 68$

45. $9x + 3y = 2$
$-9x - y = 0$

46. Shopping at Savers Mart, Lisa buys her children four shirts and three pairs of pants for $85.50. She returns the next day and buys three shirts and five pairs of pants for $115.00. What is the price of each shirt and each pair of pants?

47. Grandma's Bakery sells single-crust apple pies for $6.99 and double-crust cherry pies for $10.99. The total number of pies sold on a busy Friday was 36. If the amount collected for all the pies that day was $331.64, how many of each type were sold?

7-3 • Guided Problem Solving

GPS **Student Page 392, Exercise 30**

a. **Business** A company sells brass and steel machine parts. One shipment contains 3 brass and 10 steel parts and costs $48. A second shipment contains 7 brass and 4 steel parts and costs $54. Find the cost of each machine part.

b. How much would a shipment containing 10 brass and 13 steel machine parts cost?

Read and Understand

1. What kind of information are you given about each of the two shipments?

_____

2. What are you asked to find? _____

Plan and Solve

3. Write an equation relating the known cost of the first shipment to the unknown cost of each type of part. Use *b* for brass and *s* for steel. _____

4. Write another equation that does the same for the second shipment. _____

5. What will be the first step in solving the pair of equations by the elimination method?

_____

6. Eliminate the variable *s* to obtain an equation in *b* only. _____

7. Solve the equation from Step 6 for *b*, then substitute the value for *b* back into one of the original equations and find the value for *s*. Interpret the results.

_____

_____

8. Use the cost of each part to predict the cost of a shipment containing 10 brass and 13 steel parts.

_____

_____

Look Back and Check

9. Does it seem right that one type of part costs significantly more than the other? Explain.

_____

Solve Another Problem

10. You have $10,000 to divide between two investments. One investment will yield a profit of 3%, while the other will yield 5%. How much would you put into each investment for a profit of $445?

_____

Guided Problem Solving

Practice 7-4

Use a system of linear equations to solve each problem.

1. Your teacher is giving you a test worth 100 points containing 40 questions. There are two-point and four-point questions on the test. How many of each type of question are on the test?

2. Suppose you are starting an office-cleaning service. You have spent $315 on equipment. To clean an office, you use $4 worth of supplies. You charge $25 per office. How many offices must you clean to break even?

3. The math club and the science club had fundraisers to buy supplies for a hospice. The math club spent $135 buying six cases of juice and one case of bottled water. The science club spent $110 buying four cases of juice and two cases of bottled water. How much did a case of juice cost? How much did a case of bottled water cost?

4. On a canoe trip, Rita paddled upstream (against the current) at an average speed of 2 mi/h relative to the riverbank. On the return trip downstream (with the current), her average speed was 3 mi/h. Find Rita's paddling speed in still water and the speed of the river's current.

5. Kay spends 250 min/wk exercising. Her ratio of time spent on aerobics to time spent on weight training is 3 to 2. How many minutes per week does she spend on aerobics? How many minutes per week does she spend on weight training?

6. Suppose you invest $1500 in equipment to put pictures on T-shirts. You buy each T-shirt for $3. After you have placed the picture on a shirt, you sell it for $20. How many T-shirts must you sell to break even?

7. A light plane flew from its home base to an airport 255 miles away. With a head wind, the trip took 1.7 hours. The return trip with a tail wind took 1.5 hours. Find the average airspeed of the plane and the average windspeed.

8. Suppose you bought supplies for a party. Three rolls of streamers and 15 party hats cost $30. Later, you bought 2 rolls of streamers and 4 party hats for $11. How much did each roll of streamers cost? How much did each party hat cost?

9. A new parking lot has spaces for 450 cars. The ratio of spaces for full-sized cars to compact cars is 11 to 4. How many spaces are for full-sized cars? How many spaces are for compact cars?

10. While on vacation, Kevin went for a swim in a nearby lake. Swimming against the current, it took him 8 minutes to swim 200 meters. Swimming back to shore with the current took half as long. Find Kevin's average swimming speed and the speed of the lake's current.

7-4 • Guided Problem Solving

GPS **Student Page 401, Exercise 21**

Consumer Decisions Suppose you are trying to decide whether to buy ski equipment. Typically, it costs you $60 a day to rent ski equipment and buy a lift ticket. You can buy ski equipment for about $400. A lift ticket alone costs $35 for one day.

a. Find the break-even point.
b. **Critical Thinking** If you expect to ski 5 days a year, should you buy the ski equipment? Explain.

Read and Understand

1. What are your total costs if you buy the equipment? If you don't? _____

2. What are you asked to find out? _____

Plan and Solve

3. Write an equation relating your total cost to the number of days you ski, assuming you buy the equipment. _____

4. Write another equation relating costs to days, assuming you don't buy the equipment.

_____

5. Which method of solving the system is best? Explain why. _____

6. Solve the system to find the break-even point. Interpret the answer. _____

7. If you expect to ski 5 days a year, does it make sense to buy the ski equipment? Give your reasons.

_____

_____

Look Back and Check

8. Does the break-even point seem realistic? _____

_____

Solve Another Problem

9. Suppose you cannot afford the new equipment but have an opportunity to buy used equipment for $275. If the used equipment can be expected to last two seasons, what should you do?

_____

_____

Guided Problem Solving

Practice 7-5

Linear Inequalities

Graph each linear inequality.

1. $y \geq -4$

2. $x + y < -2$

3. $y < x$

4. $x > 2$

5. $4x + y > -6$

6. $-3x + y \leq -3$

7. $x + 4y \leq 8$

8. $y > 2x + 6$

9. $y > -x + 2$

10. $2x + 3y < -9$

11. $y \leq \frac{3}{7}x + 2$

12. $4x + 2y < -8$

13. $y \leq \frac{3}{4}x + 1$

14. $x - y > 4$

15. $y \geq -\frac{2}{5}x - 2$

16. Suppose your class is raising money for the Red Cross. You make $5 on each basket of fruit and $3 on each box of cheese that you sell. How many items of each type must you sell to raise more than $150?

 a. Write a linear inequality that describes the situation.

 b. Graph the inequality.

 c. Write two possible solutions to the problem.

17. Suppose you intend to spend no more than $60 buying books. Hardback books cost $12 and paperbacks cost $5. How many books of each type can you buy?

 a. Write a linear inequality that describes the situation.

 b. Graph the inequality.

 c. Write two possible solutions to the problem.

18. Suppose that for your exercise program, you either walk 5 mi/d or ride your bicycle 10 mi/d. How many days will it take you to cover a distance of at least 150 mi?

 a. Write a linear inequality that describes the situation.

 b. Graph the inequality.

 c. Write two possible solutions to the problem.

Graph each linear inequality.

19. $6x - 4y > -16$

20. $y \geq -\frac{1}{4}x - 3$

21. $-5x + 4y < -24$

22. $y < -5x + 6$

23. $6x - 4y < -12$

24. $y \geq -\frac{9}{5}x + 7$

25. $y > \frac{5}{7}x - 3$

26. $y < -5x + 9$

27. $-7x + 3y < -18$

28. $y \geq \frac{6}{5}x - 8$

29. $-12x + 8y < 56$

30. $16x + 6y > 36$

7-5 • Guided Problem Solving

GPS **Student Page 408, Exercise 37**

Budget Suppose you work at a local radio station. You are in charge
of a $180 budget for new tapes and CDs. Record companies will give
you 21 promotional (free) CDs. You can buy tapes for $8 and CDs for $12.

Let x = the number of CDs you can buy.
Let y = the number of tapes you can buy.

a. Write an inequality that shows
the number of tapes and CDs
you can buy.

b. Graph the inequality.

c. Is $(8, 9)$ a solution of the inequality? Explain
what the solution means.

d. If you buy only tapes and you buy as many as
possible, how many new recordings will the station get?

Read and Understand

1. How much do tapes cost? _____

2. How much do CDs cost? _____

3. How much do you have to spend? _____

4. How many CDs can you get for free? _____

Plan and Solve

5. Write an inequality which says that the amount spent on tapes and
CDs has to be less than or equal to $180, using x for CDs and y for tapes. _____

6. Graph the inequality.

7. Does the point $(8, 9)$ lie inside the solution region? If yes, what does does that mean?

   _____

   _____

   _____

8. Assuming you buy only tapes (which are cheaper), how many can
you buy? Consult the graph. Then add the free CDs to find the
maximum number of recordings you can obtain on your budget. _____

Look Back and Check

9. How many recordings could you obtain if you bought only CDs? Does it make sense that the
answer is less than for Step 8?

Solve Another Problem

10. How many tapes and CDs should you buy to end up with twice as many CDs as tapes (including
the free CDs), while having as little money left over as possible? _____

Practice 7-6

Solve each system by graphing. Show your work.

1. $y < 6$
$\quad\ y > 3$

2. $x < 7$
$\quad\ y > 2$

3. $x < 2$
$\quad\ x > 5$

4. $\quad x + y > -2$
$\quad -x + y < \ 1$

5. $x + y < 2$
$\quad x + y > 5$

6. $y < -5x + 6$
$\quad\ y > 2x - 1$

7. $y < 2x - 3$
$\quad -2x + y > 5$

8. $-x + 3y < 12$
$\qquad\ y \geq -x + 4$

9. $y \leq -\frac{1}{2}x + 3$
$\quad\ y \geq -\frac{5}{3}x + 2$

10. $y \geq \frac{3}{4}x + 1$
$\qquad y \geq -\frac{2}{3}x - 1$

11. $\quad 6x + 4y > 12$
$\quad -3x + 4y > 12$

12. $\quad 3x + y < 6$
$\quad -2x + y < 6$

13. $-4x + 2y < -2$
$\quad -2x + \ y > \ \ 3$

14. $-5x + y > -2$
$\quad\ 4x + y < \ \ 1$

15. $y < \frac{9}{5}x - 8$
$\quad -9x + 5y > 25$

16. $5x + 4y < 1$
$\quad\ 8y \geq -10x + 24$

17. $\quad 6x + 8y < 32$
$\quad -4x + 6y < 24$

18. $x + 7y < 14$
$\quad x - 6y > -12$

19. In basketball you score 2 points for a field goal and 1 point for a free throw. Suppose that you have scored at least 3 points in every game this season, and have a season high score of 15 points in one game. How many field goals and free throws could you have made in any one game?

   a. Write a system of two inequalities that describes this situation.

   b. Graph the system to show all possible solutions.

   c. Write one possible solution to the problem.

20. Suppose you need to use at least $1.00 worth of stamps to mail a package. You have as many $.03 stamps as you need but only four $.32 stamps. How many of each stamp can you use?

   a. Write a system of two inequalities that describes this situation.

   b. Graph the system to show all possible solutions.

   c. Write one possible solution to the problem.

21. A grandmother wants to spend at least $40 but no more than $60 on school clothes for her grandson. T-shirts sell for $10 and pants sell for $20. How many T-shirts and pants could she buy?

   a. Write a system of two inequalities that describes this situation.

   b. Graph the system to show all possible solutions.

   c. Write two possible solutions to the problem.

7-6 • Guided Problem Solving

GPS **Student Page 416, Exercise 35**

a. Business A clothing store has a going-out-of-business sale. They are selling pants for $10.99 and shirts for $4.99. You can spend as much as $45 and want to buy at least one pair of pants. Write and graph a system of inequalities that describes this situation.

b. Suppose you need to buy at least three pairs of pants. From your graph, find all the ordered pairs that are possible solutions.

Read and Understand

1. What is the cost of a pair of pants, and of two shirts, and how much can you spend?

   _____

2. What other restrictions are there on how many pants and shirts you buy?

   _____

3. What are you asked to do? _____

Plan and Solve

4. Write an inequality which says that the amount spent on pants and shirts has to be less than or equal to $45, using x for pants and y for shirts. Write another inequality stating that you buy at least 1 pair of pants. _____

5. Graph the system of inequalities.

6. List all the ordered pair solutions where x is greater than or equal to 3.

   _____

Look Back and Check

7. Suppose you were to buy just pants, as many as you could. How many would you buy? Is this one of the solutions found in Step 6? _____

Solve Another Problem

8. Suppose that instead of having to buy some minimum number of pants, you had to buy at least 6 shirts. List all the ordered pair solutions. _____

7A: Graphic Organizer

For use before Lesson 7-1

Study Skill When taking notes, write as clearly as possible.
Use abbreviations of your own invention when possible.
The amount of time needed to recopy messy notes would
be better spent rereading and thinking about them.

Write your answers.

1. What is the chapter title? _____

2. Find the Table of Contents page for this chapter at the front of the book.
   Name four topics you will study in this chapter.

   _____   _____

   _____   _____

3. Complete the graphic organizer as you work through the chapter.
   1. Write the title of the chapter in the center oval.
   2. When you begin a lesson, write the name of the lesson in a
      rectangle.
   3. When you complete that lesson, write a skill or key concept from
      that lesson in the outer oval linked to that rectangle.
   Continue with steps 2 and 3 clockwise around the graphic organizer.

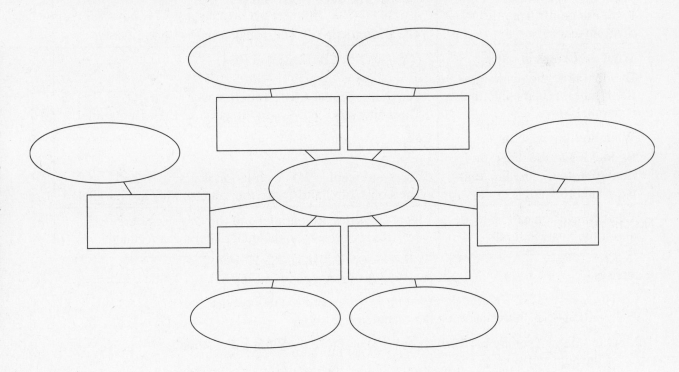

7B: Reading Comprehension

For use after Lesson 7-5

Study Skill Reading a math textbook requires being able to extract information from a graph, figure, diagram, or picture. Take time to look for relationships between lines, points, etc.

Follow the thought process that Matthew thinks and writes.

> In the graph, a quadrilateral is formed by four intersecting lines denoted $\ell_1, \ell_2, \ell_3,$ and ℓ_4. Find the equation of each line. Use this information to draw a conclusion about the quadrilateral.

What Matthew Thinks	What Matthew Writes
I have to find the equations of four lines. What information appears to be true about the lines?	There appear to be two pairs of parallel lines. If that is true, there will only be two slopes. The shape also appears to be a rectangle. If that is true, the two slopes will be negative reciprocals of each other since the lines are perpendicular.
What do I know about ℓ_1? I must look at the diagram to find points that the line passes through.	ℓ_1 passes through $(0, 0)$ and $(2, 2)$. $m = \frac{2 - 0}{2 - 0} = 1$ The y-intercept is 0. The equation of ℓ_1 is $y = x$.
What do I know about ℓ_2? I will use points from the diagram again.	ℓ_2 passes through $(0, 0)$ and $(-1, 1)$. $m = \frac{1 - 0}{-1 - 0} = -1$ The y-intercept is 0. The equation is $y = -x$.
What do I know about ℓ_3? By looking at the diagram, I think that this is the line that is parallel to ℓ_2.	ℓ_3 passes through $(2, 2)$ and $(0, 4)$. $m = \frac{4 - 2}{0 - 2} = \frac{2}{-2} = -1$ The y-intercept is 4. The equation is $y = -x + 4$. The slopes of ℓ_2 and ℓ_3 are the same so they are parallel.
What do I know about ℓ_4? By looking at the diagram, I think that this is the line that is parallel to ℓ_1.	ℓ_4 passes through $(0, 2)$ and $(-2, 0)$. $m = \frac{0 - 2}{-2 - 0} = \frac{-2}{-2} = 1$ The y-intercept is 2. The equation is $y = x + 2$. The slopes of ℓ_1 and ℓ_4 are the same so they are parallel.
What conclusion can be made about the quadrilateral?	Opposite sides are parallel and the two slopes are negative reciprocals, so the quadrilateral is a rectangle.

Exercises

1. Three vertices of a rectangle are at $(1, 1)$, $(5, 1)$ and $(5, 5)$. Find the equation of each line forming the rectangle.

2. One side of a square has vertices at $(2, 3)$ and $(-2, 1)$. What is the slope of the adjacent sides?

3. **High-Use Academic Words** In the direction box at the top of the page, what does *draw a conclusion* mean for you to do?
    a. identify special characteristics
    b. identify general characteristics

7C: Reading/Writing Math Symbols

For use after Lesson 7-2

Study Skill Many graphs look very similar. You must look for details in the graphs and their equations, and decide what those details symbolize.

Look at each inequality, and then choose its correct graph.

1. $y \geq 3$

  A.   **B.**   **C.**

2. $x < 2$

  A.   **B.**   **C.**

3. $y \leq x + 2$

  A.   **B.**   **C.**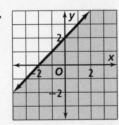

4. $y > 2x + 5$

  A.   **B.**   **C.**

7D: Visual Vocabulary Practice

For use after Lesson 7-6

Study Skill Making sense of mathematical symbols is like reading a foreign language that uses different letters.

Concept List

elimination method	infinitely many solutions	solution of a system of equations
no solution	linear inequality	solution of a system of linear inequalities
solutions of an inequality	substitution method	system of linear inequalities

Write the concept that best describes each exercise.
Choose from the concept list above.

1. $y = 4 - 3x$ $x + 2y = -1$ $x + 2(4 - 3x) = -1$ _____	**2.** 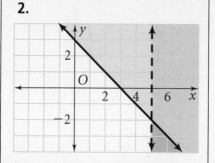 _____	**3.** $y > 9x + 8$ _____
4. _____	**5.** $5x + 9y = 11$ $-5x + 3y = -5$ $12y = 6$ _____	**6.** $4x - y = 10$ $8x - 2y = 20$ _____
7. $y \geq 3x - 1$ $6x + y < 5$ _____	**8.** $3x + 5y = 10$ $3x + 5y = -2$ _____	**9.** _____

Name _____ Class _____ Date _____

7E: Vocabulary Check

For use after Lesson 7-4

Vocabulary and Study Skills

Study Skill Strengthen your vocabulary. Use these pages and add cues and summaries by applying the Cornell Notetaking style.

Write the definition for each word at the right. To check your work, fold the paper back along the dotted line to see the correct answers.

_____

System of linear equations

Solution of a system

No solution

Substitution method

Elimination method

All rights reserved.

© Pearson Education, Inc., publishing as Pearson Prentice Hall.

Vocabulary and Study Skills

Algebra 1 Chapter 7 — 385

7E: Vocabulary Check (continued)

For use after Lesson 7-4

Write the vocabulary word for each definition. To check your work, fold the paper forward along the dotted line to see the correct answers.

Two or more linear equations together.

_____

Any ordered pair in a system that makes *all* the equations true.

_____

A system of equations whose graphs do not intersect.

_____

Solving a system by replacing one variable with an equivalent expression containing the other variable.

_____

Using the Addition and Subtraction Properties of Equality to solve a system.

_____

7F: Vocabulary Review

For use with Chapter Review

Study Skill To be successful in math you need to understand meanings of words. Learn one term at a time, moving on to the next when you are confident of your knowledge of the first.

For Exercises 1–7 match each term in Column A with its definition in Column B by drawing a line between them.

Column A

1. system of linear equations
2. solutions of an inequality
3. constant
4. linear inequality
5. parallel lines
6. variable
7. ratio

Column B

A. a comparison of two numbers by division

B. two or more linear equations using the same variables

C. a term that has no variable

D. lines in the same plane that never intersect

E. a statement representing a region of the coordinate plane

F. a symbol that represents one or more numbers

G. the coordinates of the points that make the inequality true

For Exercises 8–14 match each term in Column C with its definition in Column D by drawing a line between them.

Column C

8. outcome
9. substitution method
10. power
11. solution of the system
12. sequence
13. reciprocal
14. slope

Column D

A. any ordered pair that makes all of the equations in the system true

B. multiplicative inverse

C. a method of solving systems of equations by replacing one variable with an equivalent expression

D. a number pattern

E. has 2 parts, a base and an exponent

F. the rate of vertical change to horizontal change of a line

G. the result of a single trial

Practice 8-1

Zero and Negative Exponents

Simplify each expression.

1. 16^0

2. 4^{-2}

3. 3^{-3}

4. 8^{-4}

5. $\dfrac{1}{2^{-5}}$

6. $\dfrac{4}{4^{-3}}$

7. $\dfrac{3}{6^{-1}}$

8. $\dfrac{2^{-1}}{2^{-5}}$

9. $3 \cdot 8^0$

10. $16 \cdot 2^{-2}$

11. 12^{-1}

12. -7^{-2}

13. $16 \cdot 4^0$

14. 9^0

15. $\dfrac{32^{-1}}{8^{-1}}$

16. $\dfrac{9}{2^{-1}}$

17. $\dfrac{8^{-2}}{4^0}$

18. $\dfrac{9^{-1}}{3^{-2}}$

19. $5(-6)^0$

20. $(3.7)^0$

21. $(-9)^{-2}$

22. $(-4.9)^0$

23. $-6 \cdot 3^{-4}$

24. $\dfrac{7^{-2}}{4^{-1}}$

Evaluate each expression for $a = -2$ and $b = 6$.

25. b^{-2}

26. a^{-3}

27. $(-a)^{-4}$

28. $-b^{-3}$

29. $4a^{-3}$

30. $2b^{-2}$

31. $(3a)^{-2}$

32. $(-b)^{-2}$

33. $2a^{-1}b^{-2}$

34. $-4a^{-2}b^{-3}$

35. $3^{-2}a^{-2}b^{-1}$

36. $(3ab)^{-2}$

Simplify each expression.

37. x^{-8}

38. xy^{-3}

39. $a^{-5}b$

40. m^2n^{-9}

41. $\dfrac{1}{x^{-7}}$

42. $\dfrac{3}{a^{-4}}$

43. $\dfrac{5}{d^{-3}}$

44. $\dfrac{6}{r^{-5}s^{-1}}$

45. $3x^{-6}y^{-5}$

46. $8a^{-3}b^2c^{-2}$

47. $15s^{-9}t^{-1}$

48. $-7p^{-5}q^{-3}r^2$

49. $\dfrac{d^{-4}}{e^{-7}}$

50. $\dfrac{3m^{-4}}{n^{-8}}$

51. $\dfrac{6m^{-8}n}{p^{-1}}$

52. $\dfrac{a^{-2}b^{-1}}{cd^{-3}}$

Write each number as a power of 10 using a negative exponent.

53. $\dfrac{1}{10,000}$

54. $\dfrac{1}{1,000,000}$

55. $\dfrac{1}{10,000,000}$

56. $\dfrac{1}{1,000,000,000}$

Write each expression as a decimal.

57. 10^{-5}

58. 10^{-8}

59. $4 \cdot 10^{-1}$

60. $6 \cdot 10^{-4}$

Evaluate each expression for $m = 4, n = 5,$ and $p = -2$.

61. m^p

62. n^m

63. p^p

64. n^p

65. $m^p n$

66. m^{-n}

67. p^{-n}

68. mn^p

69. p^{-m}

70. $\dfrac{m}{n^p}$

71. $\dfrac{1}{n^{-m}}$

72. $-n^{-m}$

8-1 • Guided Problem Solving

GPS **Student Page 434, Exercise 79**

Probability Suppose your history teacher gives you a multiple-choice quiz. There are four questions, each with five answer choices. The probability p of guessing the answer to a question correctly is $\frac{1}{5}$. The probability q of guessing the answer to each question incorrectly is $\frac{4}{5}$.

a. The table has expressions to find the probability of correctly guessing a certain number of answers on this quiz. Complete the table.

Multiple-Choice Quiz

Number Correct	Expression	Probability
0	p^0q^4	$\left(\frac{1}{5}\right)^0\left(\frac{4}{5}\right)^4 = 0.4096$
1	$4p^1q^3$	
2	$6p^2q^2$	
3	$4p^3q^1$	
4	p^4q^0	

b. Which number of correct answers is most likely?

Read and Understand

1. How many questions are there on the quiz, and how many choices for each question? _____

2. For any one question, what is the chance of getting a right answer? A wrong answer? _____

Plan and Solve

3. Using the answer to Step 2, evaluate $4p^1q^3$. In the table, fill in the probability for 1 correct.

4. Fill in the rest of the Probability column in the same way.

5. Which number(s) of correct answers have the highest probability? _____

Look Back and Check

6. Since the number of correct answers is sure to be either 0, 1, 2, 3 or 4, the sum of all the probabilities should equal 1. Does it? _____

Solve Another Problem

7. Suppose that each quiz question has 4 answer choices instead of 5, so that $p = \frac{1}{4}$ and $q = \frac{3}{4}$. Repeat Steps 3 through 5.

Practice 8-2

Scientific Notation

Write each number in standard notation.

1. 7×10^4 **2.** 3×10^{-2} **3.** 2.6×10^5 **4.** 7.1×10^{-4}

5. 5.71×10^{-5} **6.** 4.155×10^7 **7.** 3.0107×10^2 **8.** 9.407×10^{-5}

9. 31.3×10^6 **10.** 83.7×10^{-4} **11.** 0.018×10^{-1} **12.** 0.016×10^5

13. 8.0023×10^{-3} **14.** 6.902×10^8 **15.** 1005×10^2 **16.** 0.095×10^{-1}

Write each number in scientific notation.

17. 51,000,000   **18.** 975,000,000,000   **19.** 0.00000012   **20.** 0.000005008

21. 1560 billion   **22.** 0.5 million   **23.** 2 thousandths   **24.** 1095 millionths

25. 194×10^3 **26.** 154×10^{-3} **27.** 0.05×10^6 **28.** 0.031×10^{-4}

29. 790 thousand   **30.** 25 hundredths   **31.** 0.000000000159   **32.** 5,000,900,000,000

Order the numbers in each list from least to greatest.

33. $7 \times 10^{-7}, 6 \times 10^{-8}, 5 \times 10^{-6}, 4 \times 10^{-10}$

34. $5.01 \times 10^{-4}, 4.8 \times 10^{-3}, 5.2 \times 10^{-2}, 5.6 \times 10^{-2}$

35. $62,040, 6.2 \times 10^2, 6.207 \times 10^3, 6.34 \times 10^{-1}$

36. $10^{-3}, 5 \times 10^{-3}, 8 \times 10^{-2}, 4 \times 10^{-1}$

Simplify. Write each answer using scientific notation.

37. $4(3 \times 10^5)$ **38.** $5(7 \times 10^{-2})$ **39.** $8(9 \times 10^9)$

40. $7(9 \times 10^6)$ **41.** $3(1.2 \times 10^{-4})$ **42.** $2(6.1 \times 10^{-8})$

43. $3(1.2 \times 10^{-4})$ **44.** $3(4.3 \times 10^{-4})$ **45.** $3(3.2 \times 10^{-2})$

Complete the table.

		Units of Area in Square Feet	
	Unit	**Standard Form**	**Scientific Notation**
46.	1 in.^{2}		6.9444×10^{-3}
47.	1 link^2	0.4356	
48.	1 rod^2	272.25	
49.	1 mi^2		2.78×10^7
50.	1 cm^2	0.001076	
51.	1 hectare		1.08×10^7

8-2 • Guided Problem Solving

GPS Student Page 439, Exercise 43

Computers A computer can perform 4.66×10^8 instructions per second.
How many instructions is that per minute? Per hour? Use scientific
notation.

Read and Understand

1. How many instructions can the computer perform in one second? _____

2. What are you asked to do? _____

Plan and Solve

3. What conversion factor do you multiply by to convert
   instructions per second into instructions per minute? _____

4. Perform the multiplication to find the number of instructions
   per minute. Do not yet worry about proper scientific notation form. _____

5. Now put the answer from Step 4 in proper scientific notation
   form, by moving the decimal point and adjusting the exponent on the 10. _____

6. Repeat Steps 3 through 5 for the conversion from
   instructions per minute to instructions per hour. _____

Look Back and Check

7. You should be able to get the answer to Step 6
   by converting directly from instructions per second
   to instructions per hour. Verify that this works. _____

Solve Another Problem

8. Light travels at a speed of 3×10^8 meters per second. Use the
   number of seconds in a minute, the number of minutes in an hour,
   the number of hours in a day, and the number of days in a year
   to write the speed of light in meters per year. Then convert to
   kilometers per year. Use scientific notation.

_____

Practice 8-3

Multiplication Properties of Exponents

Simplify each expression.

1. $(3d^{-4})(5d^8)$
2. $(-8m^4)(4m^8)$
3. $n^{-6} \cdot n^{-9}$

4. $a^3 \cdot a$
5. $3^8 \cdot 3^5$
6. $(3p^{-15})(6p^{11})$

7. $p^7 \cdot q^5 \cdot p^6$
8. $(-1.5a^5b^2)(6a)$
9. $(-2d^3e^3)(6d^4e^6)$

10. $\dfrac{1}{b^{-7} \cdot b^5}$
11. $p^5 \cdot q^2 \cdot p^4$
12. $\dfrac{1}{n^7 \cdot n^{-5}}$

13. $(8d^4)(4d^7)$
14. $x^{-9} \cdot x^3 \cdot x^2 = +^{\square}$
15. $2^3 \cdot 2^2$

16. $r^7 \cdot s^4 \cdot s \cdot r^3$
17. $b^7 \cdot b^{13}$
18. $(7p^4)(5p^9)$

19. $2^8 \cdot 2^{-9} \cdot 2^3$
20. $(6r^4s^3)(9rs^2)$
21. $4^3 \cdot 4^2$

22. $m^{12} \cdot m^{-14}$
23. $s^7 \cdot t^4 \cdot t^8$
24. $(-3xy^6)(3.2x^5y)$

25. $5^{-7} \cdot 5^9$
26. $\dfrac{1}{h^7 \cdot h^3}$
27. $\dfrac{1}{t^{-5} \cdot t^{-3}}$

28. $f^5 \cdot f^2 \cdot f^0$
29. $r^6 \cdot r^{-13}$
30. $5^{-6} \cdot 5^4$

Simplify each expression. Write each answer in scientific notation.

31. $(7 \times 10^7)(5 \times 10^{-5})$
32. $(3 \times 10^8)(3 \times 10^4)$
33. $(9.5 \times 10^{-4})(2 \times 10^{-5})$

34. $(4 \times 10^9)(4.1 \times 10^8)$
35. $(7.2 \times 10^{-7})(2 \times 10^{-5})$
36. $(5 \times 10^7)(4 \times 10^3)$

37. $(6 \times 10^{-6})(5.2 \times 10^4)$
38. $(4 \times 10^6)(9 \times 10^8)$
39. $(6.1 \times 10^9)(8 \times 10^{14})$

40. $(2.1 \times 10^{-4})(4 \times 10^{-7})$
41. $(1.6 \times 10^5)(3 \times 10^{11})$
42. $(9 \times 10^{12})(0.3 \times 10^{-18})$

43. $(4 \times 10^9)(11 \times 10^3)$
44. $(5 \times 10^{13})(9 \times 10^{-9})$
45. $(7 \times 10^6)(4 \times 10^9)$

46. $(6 \times 10^{-8})(12 \times 10^{-7})$
47. $(6 \times 10^{15})(3.2 \times 10^2)$
48. $(5 \times 10^8)(2.6 \times 10^{-16})$

49. In 1990, the St. Louis metropolitan area had an average of 82×10^{-6} g/m^3 of pollutants in the air. How many grams of pollutants were there in 2×10^3 m^3 of air?

50. Light travels approximately 5.87×10^{12} mi in one year. This distance is called a light-year. Suppose a star is 2×10^4 light-years away. How many miles away is that star?

51. The weight of 1 m^3 of air is approximately 1.3×10^3 g. Suppose that the volume of air inside of a building is 3×10^6 m^3. How much does the air inside the building weigh?

52. Light travels 1.18×10^{10} in. in 1 second. How far will light travel in 1 nanosecond or 1×10^{-9} s?

8-3 • Guided Problem Solving

GPS **Student Page 445, Exercise 56**

Medicine Medical X-rays, with a wavelength of about 10^{-10} meter, can penetrate your skin.

a. Ultraviolet rays, which cause sunburn by penetrating only the top layers of skin, have a wavelength about 1000 times the wavelength of an X-ray. Find the wavelength of ultraviolet rays.

b. **Critical Thinking** The wavelengths of visible light are between 4×10^{-7} meters and 7.5×10^{-7} meters. Are these wavelengths longer or shorter than those of ultraviolet rays? Explain.

Read and Understand

1. What is given as the wavelength of medical X-rays? _____

2. What is the conversion factor relating the wavelengths of medical X-rays and ultraviolet rays?

_____

3. What are you asked to do? _____

_____

Plan and Solve

4. Multiply the wavelength of medical X-rays by the appropriate conversion factor to find the approximate wavelength of ultraviolet rays. _____

5. Compare the wavelengths of ultraviolet rays to the wavelengths for visible light. Which is longer? Explain. _____

Look Back and Check

6. If ultraviolet rays can burn the skin more than visible light rays can, what would you expect for X-rays, given how all the wavelengths compare? Explain. Does your conclusion fit with what you know to be true?

_____

_____

Solve Another Problem

7. Infrared rays have wavelengths in the neighborhood of 10^{-5} meter. Is this longer or shorter than X-rays? Than ultraviolet rays? Than visible light?

_____

_____

Practice 8-4

More Multiplication Properties of Exponents

Simplify each expression.

1. $(4a^5)^3$

2. $(2^{-3})^4$

3. $(m^{-3}n^4)^{-4}$

4. $(x^5)^2$

5. $2^5 \cdot (2^4)^2$

6. $(4x^4)^3(2xy^3)^2$

7. $x^4 \cdot (x^4)^3$

8. $(x^5y^3)^3(xy^5)^2$

9. $(5^2)^2$

10. $(a^4)^{-5} \cdot a^{13}$

11. $(3f^4g^{-3})^3(f^2g^{-2})^{-1}$

12. $x^3 \cdot (x^3)^5$

13. $(d^2)^{-4}$

14. $(a^3b^4)^{-2}(a^{-3}b^{-5})^{-4}$

15. $(x^2y)^4$

16. $(12b^{-2})^2$

17. $(m^{-5})^{-3}$

18. $(x^{-4})^5(x^3y^2)^5$

19. $(y^6)^{-3} \cdot y^{21}$

20. $n^6 \cdot (n^{-2})^5$

21. $(m^5)^{-3}(m^4n^5)^4$

22. $(a^3)^6$

23. $b^{-9} \cdot (b^2)^4$

24. $(4^{-1}s^3)^{-2}$

25. $(5a^3b^5)^4$

26. $(b^{-3})^6$

27. $(y^6)^3$

28. $a^{-4} \cdot (a^4b^3)^2$

29. $(x^4y)^3$

30. $d^3 \cdot (d^2)^5$

Simplify. Write each answer in scientific notation.

31. $10^{-9} \cdot (2 \times 10^2)^2$

32. $(3 \times 10^{-6})^3$

33. $10^4 \cdot (4 \times 10^6)^3$

34. $(9 \times 10^7)^2$

35. $10^{-3} \cdot (2 \times 10^3)^5$

36. $(7 \times 10^5)^3$

37. $(5 \times 10^5)^4$

38. $(2 \times 10^{-3})^3$

39. $(5 \times 10^2)^{-3}$

40. $(3 \times 10^5)^4$

41. $(4 \times 10^8)^{-3}$

42. $(1 \times 10^{-5})^{-5}$

43. $10^5 \cdot (8 \times 10^7)^3$

44. $(10^2)^3(6 \times 10^{-3})^3$

45. $10^7 \cdot (2 \times 10^2)^4$

46. The kinetic energy, in joules, of a moving object is found by using the formula $E = \frac{1}{2}mv^2$, where m is the mass and v is the speed of the object. The mass of a car is 1.59×10^3 kg. The car is traveling at 2.7×10^1 m/s. What is the kinetic energy of the car?

47. The moon is shaped somewhat like a sphere. The surface area of the moon is found by using the formula $S = 12.56r^2$. What is the surface area of the moon if the radius is 1.08×10^3 mi?

48. Because of a record corn harvest, excess corn is stored on the ground in a pile. The pile is shaped like a cone. The height of the pile is 25 ft, and the radius of the pile is 1.2×10^2 ft. Use the formula $V = \frac{1}{3}\pi r^2h$ to find the volume.

49. Suppose the distance in feet that an object travels in t seconds is given by the formula $d = 64t^2$. How far would the object travel after 1.5×10^3 seconds?

8-4 • Guided Problem Solving

GPS **Student Page 450, Exercise 51**

a. **Geometry** Write an expression for the surface area of each cube.
b. How many times greater than the surface area of the small cube is the surface area of the large cube?
c. Write an expression for the volume of each cube.
d. How many times greater than the volume of the small cube is the volume of the large cube?

2x

4x

Read and Understand

1. What are you asked to do? _____

Plan and Solve

2. How many faces (sides) does a cube have? _____

3. For a cube whose edges have length s, what expression represents the area of each face?

_____

4. Write an expression for the surface area of a cube with edges of length s. Then write an expression for the surface area of each cube pictured above. _____

5. Use division to find the ratio of the large cube's surface area to the small cube's surface area.

_____

6. Write an expression for the volume of a cube with edges of length s. _____

7. Write an expression for the volume of each cube pictured above. _____

8. Use division to find the ratio of the large cube's volume to the small cube's volume. _____

Look Back and Check

9. If the side length s of a cube is doubled, by what factor should the quantity s^2 increase? What about the quantity s^3? Check that your answer agrees with your earlier findings. _____

Solve Another Problem

10. Suppose the larger cube had a side length of $6x$ instead of $4x$. Write expressions for its surface area and volume, and compare those to the surface area and volume of the small cube.

_____

Practice 8-5

Division Properties of Exponents

Simplify each expression.

1. $\dfrac{c^{15}}{c^9}$

2. $\left(\dfrac{x^3 y^{-2}}{z^{-5}}\right)^{-4}$

3. $\dfrac{x^7 y^9 z^3}{x^4 y^7 z^8}$

4. $\left(\dfrac{a^2}{b^3}\right)^5$

5. $\dfrac{3^7}{3^4}$

6. $\left(\dfrac{a^3}{b^2}\right)^4$

7. $\left(\dfrac{2}{3}\right)^{-2}$

8. $\left(\dfrac{p^{-3} q^{-2}}{q^{-3} r^5}\right)^4$

9. $\dfrac{a^6 b^{-5}}{a^{-2} b^7}$

10. $\dfrac{7^{-4}}{7^{-7}}$

11. $\dfrac{a^7 b^6}{a^5 b}$

12. $\left(\dfrac{a^2 b^{-4}}{b^2}\right)^5$

13. $\left(-\dfrac{3}{2^3}\right)^{-2}$

14. $\dfrac{z^7}{z^{-3}}$

15. $\left(\dfrac{5a^0 b^4}{c^{-3}}\right)^2$

16. $\dfrac{x^4 y^{-8} z^{-2}}{x^{-1} y^6 z^{-10}}$

17. $\dfrac{m^6}{m^{10}}$

18. $\left(\dfrac{2^3 m^4 n^{-1}}{p^2}\right)^0$

19. $\left(\dfrac{s^{-4}}{t^{-1}}\right)^{-2}$

20. $\left(\dfrac{2a^3 b^{-2}}{c^3}\right)^5$

21. $\left(\dfrac{x^{-3} y}{x z^{-4}}\right)^{-2}$

22. $\dfrac{h^{-13}}{h^{-8}}$

23. $\dfrac{4^6}{4^8}$

24. $\left(\dfrac{1}{3}\right)^3$

25. $\dfrac{x^5 y^3}{x^2 y^9}$

26. $\left(\dfrac{m^{-3} n^4}{n^{-2}}\right)^4$

27. $\dfrac{4^{-1}}{4^2}$

28. $\left(\dfrac{a^8 b^6}{a^{11}}\right)^5$

29. $\dfrac{n^9}{n^{15}}$

30. $\left(\dfrac{r^3 s^{-1}}{r^2 s^6}\right)^{-1}$

31. $\dfrac{n^{-8}}{n^4}$

32. $\dfrac{m^8 n^3}{m^{10} n^5}$

Simplify each quotient. Write each answer in scientific notation.

33. $\dfrac{3.54 \times 10^{-9}}{6.15 \times 10^{-5}}$

34. $\dfrac{9.35 \times 10^{-3}}{3.71 \times 10^{-5}}$

35. $\dfrac{495 \text{ billion}}{23.9 \text{ million}}$

36. $\dfrac{8 \times 10^9}{4 \times 10^5}$

37. $\dfrac{9.5 \times 10^9}{5 \times 10^{12}}$

38. $\dfrac{6.4 \times 10^9}{8 \times 10^7}$

39. $\dfrac{298 \text{ billion}}{49 \text{ million}}$

40. $\dfrac{1.8 \times 10^{-8}}{0.9 \times 10^3}$

41. $\dfrac{3.6 \times 10^6}{9 \times 10^{-3}}$

42. $\dfrac{8.19 \times 10^7}{4.76 \times 10^{-2}}$

43. $\dfrac{65 \text{ million}}{19.5 \text{ billion}}$

44. $\dfrac{4.9 \times 10^{12}}{7 \times 10^3}$

45. $\dfrac{36.2 \text{ trillion}}{98.5 \text{ billion}}$

46. $\dfrac{3.9 \times 10^3}{1.3 \times 10^8}$

47. $\dfrac{5.6 \times 10^{-5}}{8 \times 10^{-7}}$

48. $\dfrac{40 \text{ million}}{985 \text{ million}}$

49. The half-life of uranium-238 is 4.5×10^9 years. The half-life of uranium-234 is 2.5×10^5 years. How many times greater is the half-life of uranium-238 than that of uranium-234.

8-5 • Guided Problem Solving

GPS **Student Page 457, Exercise 50**

Telecommunications In 2000, there were 97.4 million households with telephones. The people in these households made 544 billion local calls and 97 billion long distance calls.

a. Write each number in scientific notation.

b. What was the average number of local calls placed per household? Round to the nearest whole number.

c. What was the average number of long distance calls placed per household? Round to the nearest whole number.

Read and Understand

1. How many households had telephones in the year 2000? _____

2. How many local and long distance calls did these households make? _____

3. What are you being asked to find? _____

Plan and Solve

4. What are 1 million and 1 billion written as powers of 10? _____

5. Write 97.4 million households, 544 billion local calls, and 97 billion long distance calls using the powers of 10 from Step 4, then convert to scientific notation.

_____

6. Use division to find the average number of local calls per household to the nearest whole number.

_____

7. Use division to find the average number of long distance calls per household to the nearest whole number. _____

Look Back and Check

8. The ratio of your answers in Steps 6 and 7 should equal the ratio of total local calls to total long distance calls. What is that ratio? _____

Solve Another Problem

9. In 2000, Los Angeles County, with an area of 4061 square miles, was home to 6.1 million motor vehicles. Write each number in scientific notation and find the average number of vehicles per square mile to the nearest whole number. _____

Guided Problem Solving

Practice 8-6

Geometric Sequences

Find the next three terms of each sequence.

1. $4, 12, 36, 108, \ldots$

2. $2, -8, 32, -128, \ldots$

3. $18, 9, \frac{9}{2}, \frac{9}{4}, \ldots$

4. $1, -\frac{1}{3}, \frac{1}{9}, -\frac{1}{27}, \ldots$

5. $-2, 20, -200, 2000, \ldots$

6. $30, -10, \frac{10}{3}, -\frac{10}{9}, \ldots$

7. $\frac{1}{3}, 1\frac{1}{3}, 5\frac{1}{3}, 21\frac{1}{3}, \ldots$

8. $20, 4, \frac{4}{5}, \frac{4}{25}, \ldots$

9. $-100, -40, -16, -6.4, \ldots$

10. $40, 20, 10, 5, \ldots$

Determine whether each sequence is arithmetic or geometric.

11. $-8, -10, -12.5, -15.625, \ldots$

12. $5, 1, -3, -7, \ldots$

13. $1, \frac{2}{5}, \frac{4}{25}, \frac{8}{125}, \ldots$

14. $-0.2, -0.02, -0.002, -0.0002, \ldots$

15. $-10, -5, 0, 5, \ldots$

16. $6, -3, \frac{3}{2}, -\frac{3}{4}, \ldots$

Write a rule for each sequence.

17. $4, 12, 36, 108, \ldots$

18. $2, -8, 32, -128, \ldots$

19. $18, 9, \frac{9}{2}, \frac{9}{4}, \ldots$

20. $1, -\frac{1}{3}, \frac{1}{9}, -\frac{1}{27}, \ldots$

21. $-2, 20, -200, 2000, \ldots$

22. $30, -10, \frac{10}{3}, -\frac{10}{9}, \ldots$

23. $1, 4, 16, 64, \ldots$

24. $6, 12, 24, 48, \ldots$

25. $125, 25, 5, 1, \ldots$

26. $50, 25, 12.5, 6.25, \ldots$

Find the first, fourth, and eighth terms of each sequence.

27. $A(n) = 2 \cdot 3^{n-1}$

28. $A(n) = 3 \cdot 4^{n-1}$

29. $A(n) = 3 \cdot 2^{n-1}$

30. $A(n) = -1 \cdot 5^{n-1}$

31. $A(n) = 4 \cdot 2^{n-1}$

32. $A(n) = \frac{1}{2} \cdot 2^{n-1}$

33. $A(n) = 0.1 \cdot 4^{n-1}$

34. $A(n) = -2.1 \cdot 3^{n-1}$

35. $A(n) = 10 \cdot 5^{n-1}$

Write a rule and find the given term in each geometric sequence described below.

36. What is the sixth term when the first term is 4 and the common ratio is 3?

37. What is the fifth term when the first term is -2 and the common ratio is $-\frac{1}{2}$?

38. What is the tenth term when the first term is 3 and the common ratio is -1.2?

39. What is the fourth term when the first term is 5 and the common ratio is 6?

40. Suppose a manufacturer invented a computer chip in 1978 that had a computational speed of *s*. The company improves its chips so that every 3 years, the chip doubles in speed. What would the chip's speed have been for the year 2002? Write your solution in terms of *s*.

8-6 • Guided Problem Solving

GPS **Student Page 464, Exercise 41**

Physics On the first swing, a pendulum swings through an arc of length
36 centimeters. On each successive swing, the length of the arc is 90% of
the length of the previous swing.

  a. Write a rule to model this situation.
  b. **Critical Thinking** What value of n would you use to find the length
    of the arc on the sixth swing? Explain.
  c. Find the length of the arc on the sixth swing, to the nearest tenth of
    a centimeter.

Read and Understand

  1. What is the arc length of the first swing of the pendulum? _____

  2. What is the ratio of each successive swing length to the one before it? _____

  3. What are you asked to find? _____

Plan and Solve

  4. Write the arc lengths of the first four swings. _____

  5. Using $A(n) = a \cdot r^{n-1}$, write a formula for the arc length of the nth swing. _____

  6. What does n equal for the first swing? The sixth swing? _____

  7. Use the formula to find the arc length of the sixth swing, to the nearest 0.1 cm. _____

Look Back and Check

  8. Make sure you are using the correct values of n by explaining how the formula for $A(n)$ matches
    up with the problem statement.

    _____

    _____

Solve Another Problem

  9. A mechanism ticks as it winds down. The silence following
    the first tick lasts 0.2 seconds, and each silence is 10% longer
    than the silence before it. Find the length of the silence
    between the fourth and fifth ticks, to three decimal places. _____

Practice 8-7

Complete the table for each exercise.

1. Investment increases by 1.5 times every 5 yr.

Time	Value of Investment
Initial	$800
5 yr	$1200
10 yr	$1800
15 yr	$2700
20 yr	▨
25 yr	▨
▨	▨
▨	▨

2. The number of animals doubles every 3 mo.

Time	Number of Animals
Initial	18
3 mo	36
6 mo	72
9 mo	▨
12 mo	▨
▨	▨
▨	▨
▨	▨

3. The amount of matter halves every year.

Time	Amount of Matter
Initial	3200 g
1 yr	1600 g
2 yr	800 g
3 yr	▨
▨	▨
▨	▨
▨	▨
▨	▨

Evaluate each function for the domain {–2, 0, 1, 2, 4}.

4. $y = 2^x$

5. $y = 3.1^x$

6. $y = 0.8^x$

7. $y = 2 \cdot 4^x$

8. $y = 10 \cdot 3^x$

9. $y = 25 \cdot 5^x$

10. $y = \left(\frac{2}{3}\right)^x$

11. $y = 100 \cdot \left(\frac{1}{10}\right)^x$

12. $y = \frac{1}{4} \cdot 8^x$

Graph each function.

13. $y = 3^x$

14. $y = 6^x$

15. $y = 1.5^x$

16. $y = 7^x$

17. $y = 10 \cdot 5^x$

18. $y = 16 \cdot 0.5^x$

19. $y = \frac{1}{8} \cdot 2^x$

20. $y = \frac{1}{2} \cdot 4^x$

21. $y = 8 \cdot \left(\frac{5}{2}\right)^x$

Evaluate each function rule for the given values.

22. $y = 5.5^x$ for $x = 1, 3,$ and 4

23. $y = 4 \cdot 1.5^x$ for $x = 2, 4,$ and 5

24. $y = 3 \cdot 4^x$ for $x = 1, 3,$ and 5

25. $y = 6^x$ for $x = 2, 3,$ and 4

26. $y = 0.7^x$ for $x = 1, 3,$ and 4

27. $y = 3.1^x$ for $x = 1, 2,$ and 3

28. $y = 180 \cdot 0.5^x$ for $x = 0, -2,$ and $-\frac{1}{2}$

29. $y = 4.3^x$ for $x = -2, -1,$ and 0

30. $y = 100 \cdot 0.1^x$ for $x = -4, -1,$ and 2

31. $y = 5^x$ for $x = -2, -3,$ and 4

Solve each equation.

32. $5^x = 625$

33. $2 \cdot 4^x = 128$

34. $4^x = \frac{1}{64}$

35. $4 \cdot 5^x = \frac{4}{125}$

8-7 • Guided Problem Solving

GPS Student Page 471, Exercise 34

Biology A certain species of bacteria in a laboratory culture begins with 75 cells and doubles in number every 20 min.

a. Extend the table to find when there will be more than 5,000 bacteria cells.

Time (min)	Number of 20-min Time Periods	Pattern	Number of Bacteria Cells
Initial	0	75	75
20	1	$75 \cdot 2$	$75 \cdot 2^{\square} =$
40		$75 \cdot 2 \cdot 2$	$75 \cdot 2^{\square} =$
60			$75 \cdot 2^{\square} =$

b. Write a function rule to model the situation.

Read and Understand

1. How many bacteria cells are in the culture to start with? _____

2. How long does it take for the number of cells to double? _____

3. What are you asked to do? _____

Plan and Solve

4. Complete the table above.

5. Add lines to the table until the number of bacteria cells exceeds 5000. How many 20-minute periods does that take? _____

Look Back and Check

6. Write a function rule, and verify that $A(x) > 5000$ for the x found in Step 5. _____

Solve Another Problem

7. What would the formula be if the initial number of cells were 2? _____

Practice 8-8

Exponential Growth and Decay

Write an exponential function to model each situation. Find each amount after the specified time.

1. Suppose one of your ancestors invested $500 in 1800 in an account paying 4% interest compounded annually. Find the account balance in each of the following years.

   a. 1850   **b.** 1900   **c.** 2000   **d.** 2100

2. Suppose you invest $1500 in an account paying 4.75% annual interest. Find the account balance after 25 yr with the interest compounded the following ways.

   a. annually   **b.** semiannually **c.** quarterly   **d.** monthly

3. The starting salary for a new employee is $25,000. The salary for this employee increases by 8% per year. What is the salary after each of the following?

   a. 1 yr   **b.** 3 yr   **c.** 5 yr   **d.** 15 yr

4. Carbon-14 has a half-life of 5,700 years. Scientists use this fact to determine the age of things made of organic material. Suppose the average page of a book containing approximately 0.5 mg of carbon-14 is put into a time capsule. How much carbon-14 will each page contain after each of the following numbers of years?

   a. 5700   **b.** 11,400   **c.** 22,800   **d.** 34,200

5. The tax revenue that a small city receives increases by 3.5% per year. In 1990, the city received $250,000 in tax revenue. Determine the tax revenue in each of the following years.

   a. 1995   **b.** 1998   **c.** 2000   **d.** 2006

6. Suppose the acreage of forest is decreasing by 2% per year because of development. If there are currently 4,500,000 acres of forest, determine the amount of forest land after each of the following.

   a. 3 yr   **b.** 5 yr   **c.** 10 yr   **d.** 20 yr

7. A $10,500 investment has a 15% loss each year. Determine the value of the investment after each of the following.

   a. 1 yr   **b.** 2 yr   **c.** 4 yr   **d.** 10 yr

8. A city of 2,950,000 people has a 2.5% annual decrease in population. Determine the city's population after each of the following.

   a. 1 yr   **b.** 5 yr   **c.** 15 yr   **d.** 25 yr

9. A $25,000 purchase decreases 12% in value per year. Determine the value of the purchase after each of the following.

   a. 1 yr   **b.** 3 yr   **c.** 5 yr   **d.** 7 yr

8-8 • Guided Problem Solving

GPS Student Page 481, Exercise 47

Population Growth Since 1990, the population of Virginia has grown at an average annual rate of about 1%. In 1990, the population was about 6,284,000.

   a. Write an equation to model the population growth in Virginia since 1990.
   b. Suppose this rate of growth continues. Predict Virginia's population in 2010.

Read and Understand

1. What is the annual growth rate of Virginia's population? _____

2. What was the population in 1990? _____

3. What are you asked to find? _____

Plan and Solve

4. In the equation $y = a \cdot b^x$ modeling the situation, what is a, the starting amount? _____

5. What is b, the growth factor? (*Hint:* It is not 0.01.) _____

6. Write the equation that models the situation. What does x represent? _____

7. What is x in 2010? _____

8. Use the equation to predict the population of Virginia in 2010. _____

Look Back and Check

9. Does the population increase over 20 years seem reasonable? _____

Solve Another Problem

10. Since 1995, the population of Alaska has been growing at an average annual rate of about 1%. In 1995, the population was about 604,000.

   a. Write an equation to model the population growth in Alaska since 1995.

   _____

   b. Suppose this rate of growth continues. Predict Alaska's population in 2010.

   _____

8A: Graphic Organizer

For use before Lesson 8-1

Study Skill When taking notes, write down everything written on the chalkboard or overhead. What you write down may be a clue as to what might be on an exam or test.

Write your answers.

1. What is the chapter title? _____

2. Find the Table of Contents page for this chapter at the front of the book. Name four topics you will study in this chapter.

   _____   _____

   _____   _____

3. Complete the graphic organizer as you work through the chapter.
   1. Write the title of the chapter in the center oval.
   2. When you begin a lesson, write the name of the lesson in a rectangle.
   3. When you complete that lesson, write a skill or key concept from that lesson in the outer oval linked to that rectangle.
   Continue with steps 2 and 3 clockwise around the graphic organizer.

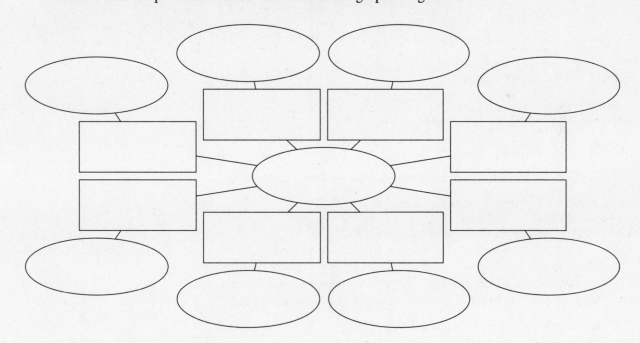

8B: Reading Comprehension

For use after Lesson 8-7

Study Skill You often need to follow written directions. Read carefully and slowly, and do not skip steps.

The following procedure can be used to measure the height of tall objects.

Step 1. Draw a vertical line to represent the tall object.

Step 2. Draw a horizontal line to represent the object's shadow.

Step 3. Draw a vertical line to represent the height of something you can measure, such as your height or the height of a mailbox.

Step 4. Draw a horizontal line to represent the shadow of the measurable object.

Step 5. Connect endpoints of the segments to make two similar triangles.

Step 6. Measure the second object and the two shadows, and label each corresponding part of the drawing. Make sure the measurements are in the same unit. Label the missing height x.

Steps 1–4

Steps 5 and 6

Step 7 Write a proportion.

$$\frac{tall\ object's\ height}{tall\ object's\ shadow} = \frac{measurable\ object's\ height}{measurable\ object's\ shadow} \Rightarrow \frac{x}{12.5} = \frac{3.5}{2.5}$$

Step 8 Solve the proportion.

$2.5x = 43.75$ Write cross products.

$x = 17.5$ The unknown height is 17.5 feet.

Use the steps above to find the missing heights.

1. Mark needs to determine the height of a radio tower. He measured the shadow of the tower and found that it was 40 ft long. His own shadow was 3 ft long. If Mark is 6 ft tall, how tall is the radio tower?

2. Celia needed to find the height of a tree for her botany report. She measured the shadow of the tree and found it was 5 m long. Her own shadow was 0.8 m long. If Celia is 1.6 m tall, how tall is the tree?

3. A girl who is 172 cm tall wants to find the height of a flagpole. If her shadow is 120 cm and the shadow of the flagpole is 4.5 m, how tall is the flagpole? (*Hint:* Make sure all units are the same before calculating.)

4. **High-Use Academic Words** In Step 6, what does *measure* mean for you to do?
   a. use a tool to find the weight of an object
   b. use a tool to find the distance from one point to another

Vocabulary and Study Skills

8C: Reading/Writing Math Symbols

For use after Lesson 8-2

Study Skill After completing your homework, take a break. Then come back and check your homework. You will sometimes discover mistakes that you missed before.

Write how you would read each of the following expressions. The first one has been done for you.

Expression	Read as:
1. $2x^3y^4$	2 times x cubed, y to the fourth power
2. 4^{-3}	_____
3. x^2	_____
4. xy	_____
5. $(x^2)^3$	_____
6. $\dfrac{x}{y}$	_____
7. $5x \cdot y^4$	_____
8. $x^5 + x^7$	_____
9. $\sqrt{x^2y}$	_____
10. $8x^2 - 3y$	_____
11. $\dfrac{x^2}{x^8}$	_____
12. $4x^{11}$	_____

8D: Visual Vocabulary Practice

For use after Lesson 8-6

Study Skill A rational number can be written as a decimal, a fraction, in factored form or in scientific notation. Use the context of the situation to choose the form.

Concept List

algebraic expression	base	common ratio
exponent	geometric sequence	integers
order of operations	scientific notation	power

Write the concept that best describes each exercise. Choose from the concept list above.

1. The number 3 for the sequence $1, 3, 9, 27, \ldots$ because $\frac{3}{1} = \frac{9}{3} = \frac{27}{9} \ldots = 3$	**2.** $3^{7-5} + 4 = 3^2 + 4$ $= 9 + 4$ $= 13$	**3.** The number 4 in the expression 4^5
4. 7.36×10^8	**5.** $2, 4, 8, 16, \ldots$	**6.** $\ldots, -2, -1, 0, 1, 2, \ldots$
7. The number 2 in the expression 7^2	**8.** $3x - 5^x$	**9.** An expression like 5^x

8E: Vocabulary Check

Study Skill Strengthen your vocabulary. Use these pages and add cues and summaries by applying the Cornell Notetaking style.

Write the definition for each word at the right. To check your work, fold the paper back along the dotted line to see the correct answers.

_____

_____

_____   Equivalent equations

_____

_____   Exponent

_____

_____   Base

_____

_____   Power

_____

_____   Scientific notation

_____

Vocabulary and Study Skills

8E: Vocabulary Check (continued)

Write the vocabulary word for each definition. To check your work, fold the paper forward along the dotted line to see the correct answers.

Equations that have the same solution.

_____

A number that shows repeated multiplication.

_____

A number that is multiplied repeatedly.

_____

The base and the exponent of an expression of the form a^x.

_____

A number expressed in the form $a \times 10^n$, where n is an integer and $1 \le a < 10$.

_____

8F: Vocabulary Review

Study Skill Always read direction lines carefully before doing any exercises.

Circle the word that best completes the sentence.

1. A number in (*standard form, scientific notation*) is written as a product of two factors in the form $a \times 10^n$, where *n* is an integer and $1 \leq a < 10$.

2. Each number in a sequence is called a (*term, constant*).

3. In a(n) (*arithmetic, geometric*) sequence you multiply a term in the sequence by a fixed number.

4. The (*Substitution, Elimination*) method is a way of solving systems of equations by replacing one variable with an equivalent expression.

5. A system of linear equations has (*no solution, many solutions*) when the graphs of the equations are parallel lines.

6. In the function $f(x) = 5^x$, as the values of the domain increase, the values of the range (*increase, decrease*).

7. When a bank pays interest on both the principal and interest the account has already earned, the bank is paying (*simple, compound*) interest.

8. A(n) (*interest, growth*) period is the length of time over which interest is calculated.

9. Lines in the same plane that intersect to form a 90° angle are said to be (*perpendicular, parallel*).

10. The result of a single trial is called the (*outcome, probability*).

11. In the exponential function $y = a \cdot b^x$, $a > 0$ and $b > 1$, the base (*b*) is the (*decay, growth*) factor.

12. $-2, 4, \frac{1}{2}, \frac{3}{4}, -8, 6$ are examples of (*real numbers, integers*).

Practice 9-1

Adding and Subtracting Polynomials

Write each polynomial in standard form. Then name each polynomial based
on its degree and number of terms.

1. $4y^3 - 4y^2 + 3 - y$ **2.** $x^2 + x^4 - 6$ **3.** $x + 2$

4. $2m^2 - 7m^3 + 3m$ **5.** $4 - x + 2x^2$ **6.** $7x^3 + 2x^2$

7. $n^2 - 5n$ **8.** $6 + 7x^2$ **9.** $3a^2 + a^3 - 4a + 3$

10. $5 + 3x$ **11.** $7 - 8a^2 + 6a$ **12.** $5x + 4 - x^2$

13. $2 + 4x^2 - x^3$ **14.** $4x^3 - 2x^2$ **15.** $y^2 - 7 - 3y$

16. $x - 6x^2 - 3$ **17.** $v^3 - v + 2v^2$ **18.** $8d + 3d^2$

Simplify. Write each answer in standard form.

19. $(3x^2 - 5x) - (x^2 + 4x + 3)$ **20.** $(2x^3 - 4x^2 + 3) + (x^3 - 3x^2 + 1)$

21. $(3y^3 - 11y + 3) - (5y^3 + y^2 + 2)$ **22.** $(3x^2 + 2x^3) - (3x^2 + 7x - 1)$

23. $(2a^3 + 3a^2 + 7a) + (a^3 + a^2 - 2a)$ **24.** $(8y^3 - y + 7) - (6y^3 + 3y - 3)$

25. $(x^2 - 6) + (5x^2 + x - 3)$ **26.** $(5n^2 - 7) - (2n^2 + n - 3)$

27. $(5n^3 + 2n^2 + 2) - (n^3 + 3n^2 - 2)$ **28.** $(3y^2 - 7y + 3) - (5y + 3 - 4y^2)$

29. $(2x^2 + 9x - 17) + (x^2 - 6x - 3)$ **30.** $(3 - x^3 - 5x^2) + (x + 2x^3 - 3)$

31. $(3x + x^2 - x^3) - (x^3 + 2x^2 + 5x)$ **32.** $(d^2 + 8 - 5d) - (5d^2 + d - 2d^3 + 3)$

33. $(3x^3 + 7x^2) + (x^2 - 2x^3)$ **34.** $(6c^2 + 5c - 3) - (3c^2 + 8c)$

35. $(3y^2 - 5y - 7) + (y^2 - 6y + 7)$ **36.** $(3c^2 - 8c + 4) - (7 + c^2 - 8c)$

37. $(4x^2 + 13x + 9) + (12x^2 + x + 6)$ **38.** $(2x - 13x^2 + 3) - (2x^2 + 8x)$

39. $(7x - 4x^2 + 11) + (7x^2 + 5)$ **40.** $(4x + 7x^3 - 9x^2) + (3 - 2x^2 - 5x)$

41. $(y^3 + y^2 - 2) + (y - 6y^2)$ **42.** $(x^2 - 8x - 3) - (x^3 + 8x^2 - 8)$

43. $(3x^2 - 2x + 9) - (x^2 - x + 7)$ **44.** $(2x^2 - 6x + 3) - (2x + 4x^2 + 2)$

45. $(2x^2 - 2x^3 - 7) + (9x^2 + 2 + x)$ **46.** $(3a^2 + a^3 - 1) + (2a^2 + 3a + 1)$

47. $(2x^2 + 3 - x) - (2 + 2x^2 - 5x)$ **48.** $(n^4 - 2n - 1) + (5n - n^4 + 5)$

49. $(x^3 + 3x) - (x^2 + 6 - 4x)$ **50.** $(7s^2 + 4s + 2) + (3s + 2 - s^2)$

51. $(6x^2 - 3x + 9) - (x^2 + 3x - 5)$ **52.** $(3x^3 - x^2 + 4) + (2x^3 - 3x + 9)$

53. $(y^3 + 3y - 1) - (y^3 + 3y + 5)$ **54.** $(3 + 5x^3 + 2x) - (x + 2x^2 + 4x^3)$

55. $(x^2 + 15x + 13) + (3x^2 - 15x + 7)$ **56.** $(7 - 8x^2) + (x^3 - x + 5)$

57. $(2x + 3) - (x - 4) + (x + 2)$ **58.** $(x^2 + 4) - (x - 4) + (x^2 - 2x)$

Name _____ Class _____ Date _____

9-1 • Guided Problem Solving

GPS **Student Page 497, Exercise 39**

Find an expression for the perimeter of the figure.

Read and Understand

1. Describe how to determine the perimeter of a rectangle. _____

_____

2. What do the single and double marks drawn on the sides of the figure mean? _____

_____

Plan and Solve

3. What additional information do you need to know before
you can determine the perimeter of the rectangle above? _____

4. Label the lengths of the two missing sides of the rectangle above.

5. Write an expression for the perimeter of the rectangle. _____

Look Back and Check

6. Check the reasonableness of your answer by substituting a number for c.
Substitute the number in the expressions for each side of the rectangle.
Add the numbers and determine the perimeter. Substitute the same number
in the expression you wrote for the perimeter and simplify. The answers should
be the same.

Solve Another Problem

7. Find an expression for the perimeter of the rectangle above
if the length is $7x - 2$ and the width is $5x + 1$.

_____

Guided Problem Solving

Practice 9-2

Multiplying and Factoring

Simplify each product.

1. $4(a - 3)$

2. $-5(x - 2)$

3. $-3x^2(x^2 + 3x)$

4. $4x^3(x - 3)$

5. $-5x^2(x^2 + 2x + 1)$

6. $3x(x^2 - 5x - 3)$

7. $-x^2(-2x^2 + 3x - 2)$

8. $4d^2(d^2 - 3d - 7)$

9. $5m^3(m + 6)$

10. $a^2(2a + 4)$

11. $4(x^2 - 3) + x(x + 1)$

12. $4x(5x - 6)$

Find the GCF of the terms of each polynomial.

13. $8x - 4$

14. $15x + 45x^2$

15. $x^2 + 3x$

16. $4c^3 - 8c^2 + 8$

17. $12x - 36$

18. $12n^3 + 4n^2$

19. $14x^3 + 7x^2$

20. $8x^3 - 12x$

21. $9 - 27x^3$

22. $25x^3 - 15x^2$

23. $11x^2 - 33x$

24. $4n^4 + 6n^3 - 8n^2$

25. $8d^3 + 4d^2 + 12d$

26. $6x^2 + 12x - 21$

27. $8g^2 + 16g - 8$

Factor each polynomial.

28. $8x + 10$

29. $12n^3 - 8n$

30. $14d - 2$

31. $6h^2 - 8h$

32. $3z^4 - 15z^3 - 9z^2$

33. $3y^3 - 8y^2 - 9y$

34. $x^3 - 5x^2$

35. $8x^3 - 12x^2 + 4x$

36. $7x^3 + 21x^4$

37. $6a^3 - 12a^2 + 14a$

38. $6x^4 + 12x^2$

39. $3n^4 - 6n^2 + 9n$

40. $2w^3 + 6w^2 - 4w$

41. $12c^3 - 30c^2$

42. $2x^2 + 8x - 14$

43. $4x^3 + 12x^2 + 16x$

44. $16m^3 - 8m^2 + 12m$

45. $4a^3 - 20a^2 - 8a$

46. $18c^4 - 9c^2 + 7c$

47. $6y^4 + 9y^3 - 27y^2$

48. $6c^2 - 3c$

49. A circular pond will be placed on a square piece of land. The length of a side of the square is $2x$. The radius of the pond is x. The part of the square not covered by the pond will be planted with flowers. What is the area of the region that will be planted with flowers? Write your answer in factored form.

50. A square poster of length $3x$ is to have a square painting centered on it. The length of the painting is $2x$. The area of the poster not covered by the painting will be painted black. What is the area of the poster that will be painted black?

51. The formula for the surface area of a sphere is $A = 4\pi r^2$. A square sticker of side x is placed on a ball of radius $3x$. What is the surface area of the sphere not covered by the sticker? Write your answer in factored form.

415

9-2 • Guided Problem Solving

GPS **Student Page 502, Exercise 33**

Building Models Suppose you are building a model of
the square castle shown on the right. The moat of the model castle
is made of blue paper.

a. Find the area of the moat using the diagram with the photo.

b. Write your answer in factored form.

Read and Understand

1. What shape is the moat? _____

2. What is the formula for finding the area of a circle? _____

3. What does the white square in the middle of the blue circle represent? _____

Plan and Solve

4. Suppose the entire circle were shaded blue.
Write an expression for the area of the entire blue circle. _____

5. Write an expression that represents the area of the castle. _____

6. Write an expression that represents the area of the moat only. _____

7. Write your answer in factored form. _____

Look Back and Check

8. Of the three different areas determined above (complete circle,
castle, moat), which should have the largest area? Check the
reasonableness of your answer by determining each area if $x = 5$.

_____

Solve Another Problem

9. Determine the area of the moat if the castle is rectangular, with a
width of $2x$ and a length of $3x$.

_____

Guided Problem Solving

Practice 9-3

Multiplying Binomials

Find each product. Write in standard form.

1. $(x + 3)(2x - 5)$

2. $(x^2 + x - 1)(x + 1)$

3. $(3w + 4)(2w - 1)$

4. $(x + 5)(x + 4)$

5. $(2b - 1)(b^2 - 3b + 4)$

6. $(a - 11)(a + 5)$

7. $(2g - 3)(2g^2 + g - 4)$

8. $(3s - 4)(s - 5)$

9. $(4x + 3)(x - 7)$

10. $(x + 6)(x^2 - 4x + 3)$

11. $(5x - 3)(4x + 2)$

12. $(3y + 7)(4y + 5)$

13. $(3x + 7)(x + 5)$

14. $(5x - 2)(x + 3)$

15. $(3m^2 - 7m + 8)(m - 2)$

16. $(a - 6)(a + 8)$

17. $(x + 2)(2x^2 - 3x + 2)$

18. $(a^2 + a + 1)(a - 1)$

19. $(x - 2)(x^2 + 4x + 4)$

20. $(2r + 1)(3r - 1)$

21. $(k + 4)(3k - 4)$

22. $(2n - 3)(n^2 - 2n + 5)$

23. $(p - 4)(2p + 3)$

24. $(3x + 1)(4x^2 - 2x + 1)$

25. $(2x^2 - 5x + 2)(4x - 3)$

26. $(x + 7)(x + 5)$

27. $(6x - 11)(x + 2)$

28. $(2x + 1)(4x + 3)$

29. $(3x + 4)(3x - 4)$

30. $(6x - 5)(3x + 1)$

31. $(n - 7)(n + 4)$

32. $(3x - 1)(2x + 1)$

33. $(d + 9)(d - 11)$

34. $(2x^2 + 5x - 3)(2x + 1)$

35. $(b + 8)(2b - 5)$

36. $(2x - 5)(x + 4)$

37. $(3x + 5)(5x - 7)$

38. $(x - 5)(2x^2 - 7x - 2)$

39. $(2x^2 - 9x + 11)(2x + 1)$

40. $(2x^2 + 5x - 4)(2x + 7)$

41. $(x^2 + 6x + 11)(3x + 5)$

42. $(5x + 7)(7x + 3)$

43. $(4x - 7)(2x - 5)$

44. $(x - 9)(3x + 5)$

45. $(2x - 1)(x^2 - 7x + 1)$

46. The width of a rectangular painting is 3 in. more than twice the height.
A frame that is 2.5 in. wide goes around the painting.

   a. Write an expression for the combined area of the painting
and frame.

   b. Use the expression to find the combined area when the height of
the painting is 12 in.

   c. Use the expression to find the combined area when the height of
the painting is 15 in.

47. The Robertsons put a rectangular pool with a stone walkway around it
in their backyard. The total length of the pool and walkway is 3 times
the total width. The walkway is 2 ft wide all around.

   a. Write an expression for the area of the pool.

   b. Find the area of the pool when the total width is 10 ft.

   c. Find the area of the pool when the total width is 9 ft.

48. The Cutting Edge frame shop makes a mat by cutting out the
inside of a rectangular board. Use the diagram to find the
length and width of the original board if the area of the mat
is 184 in².

Name _____ Class _____ Date _____

9-3 • Guided Problem Solving

Student Page 508, Exercise 39

Construction You are planning a rectangular garden. Its length is twice its width *x*. You want a walkway 2 ft wide around the garden.

 a. Write an expression for the area of the garden and walk.
 b. Write an expression for the area of the walk only.
 c. You have enough gravel to cover 76 ft² and want to use it all on the walk. How big should you make the garden?

Read and Understand

1. Draw a picture of the garden and its walk. Shade in the walk only.

2. Label the dimensions of the garden.

3. Label the dimensions of the outside of the walkway.

Plan and Solve

4. Write an expression for the area of the garden and walk. _____

5. Write an expression for the area of the walk only. _____

6. You have enough gravel to cover 76 ft² and want to use it all on the walk. How big should you make the garden? _____

Look Back and Check

7. Check if your answer is reasonable by subtracting the area of the garden from the area of the garden and walk and verifying that this amount is less than or equal to 76 ft².

Solve Another Problem

8. How big should you make the garden if you now have 100 ft² of gravel?

_____

Name _____ Class _____ Date _____

Practice 9-4   **Multiplying Special Cases**

Find each product.

1. $(w - 2)^2$ **2.** $(y + 4)^2$

3. $(4w + 2)^2$ **4.** $(w - 9)^2$

5. $(3x + 7)^2$ **6.** $(3x - 7)^2$

7. $(2x - 9)^2$ **8.** $(x - 12)^2$

9. $(6x + 1)^2$ **10.** $(4x - 7)^2$

11. $(x + 8)(x - 8)$ **12.** $(x - 11)(x + 11)$

13. $(x - 12)(x + 12)$ **14.** $(y + w)(y - w)$

15. $(2x + 1)(2x - 1)$ **16.** $(5x - 2)(5x + 2)$

17. $(6x + 1)(6x - 1)$ **18.** $(2x - 4)(2x + 4)$

19. $(x^2 + y^2)^2$ **20.** $(2x^2 + y^2)^2$

21. $(a^2 - b^2)^2$ **22.** $(y^2 - 4w^2)^2$

23. $(3 - 6x^2)^2$ **24.** $(4a - 3y)^2$

25. $(3y + 2a)(3y - 2a)$ **26.** $(x^2 + 2y)(x^2 - 2y)$

27. $(3x^2 + 4w^2)(3x^2 - 4w^2)$ **28.** $(4x + 3w^2)(4x - 3w^2)$

29. $(2a + 7b)(2a - 7b)$ **30.** $(5a^2 - 6x)(5a^2 + 6x)$

31. 18^2 **32.** $(64)^2$

33. $(29)(31)$ **34.** $(97)(103)$

35. $(19)(42)$ **36.** $(95)(205)$

Find the area.

37.   **38.**

2x + 1, 2x + 1

3x − 2, 3x + 2

Find the area of the shaded region.

39.   **40.**

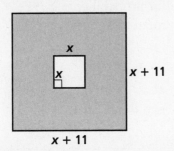

x, x, x + 11, x + 11

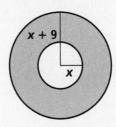

x + 9, x

9-4 • Guided Problem Solving

GPS **Student Page 516, Exercise 40**

Biology The coat color of shorthorn cattle is determined by two genes, Red *R* and White *W*.

RR produces red, *WW* produces white, and *RW* produces a third type of coat color called roan.

a. Model the Punnett square with the square of a binomial.
b. If both parents have *RW*, what is the probability the offspring will also be *RW*?
c. Write an expression to model a situation where one parent is *RW* while the other is *RR*.
d. What is the probability that the offspring of the parents in step (c) will have a white coat?

Read and Understand

1. Describe the information given in the Punnett square. _____
   _____

2. Explain how to determine the probability that an event will occur. _____
   _____

3. What does the notation *RW* mean? _____

Plan and Solve

4. Model the Punnett square with the square of a binomial. _____

5. If both parents have *RW*, what is the probability the offspring will also be *RW*? _____

6. Write an expression to model a situation where one parent is *RW* and the other is *RR*. _____

7. What is the probability that the offspring of the parents in Step 6 will have a white coat? _____

Look Back and Check

8. Check that the probability you found in Step 7 is a possible value for probability.
   That is, check that it is greater than or equal to 0 and less than or equal to 1.

Solve Another Problem

9. Write an expression to model a situation where one parent is *RW* and the other is *WW*.
   _____
   _____

Practice 9-5

Factoring Trinomials of the Type $x^2 + bx + c$

Factor each expression.

1. $x^2 + 8x + 16$ **2.** $d^2 + 8d + 7$ **3.** $y^2 + 6y + 8$

4. $b^2 - 2b - 3$ **5.** $s^2 - 4s - 5$ **6.** $x^2 + 12x + 32$

7. $x^2 - 9x + 20$ **8.** $x^2 - 5x + 6$ **9.** $a^2 + 3a + 2$

10. $p^2 - 8p + 7$ **11.** $d^2 + 6d + 5$ **12.** $n^2 + n - 6$

13. $x^2 + 5x - 14$ **14.** $b^2 + 9b + 14$ **15.** $x^2 + 14x + 45$

16. $a^2 + 7a + 12$ **17.** $x^2 + 13x + 22$ **18.** $x^2 + 3x - 4$

19. $x^2 - 8x + 12$ **20.** $x^2 + 7x - 18$ **21.** $n^2 - 7n + 10$

22. $s^2 - 5s - 14$ **23.** $x^2 - 9x + 8$ **24.** $x^2 - 2x - 24$

25. $x^2 - 6x - 27$ **26.** $x^2 - 16x - 36$ **27.** $x^2 + 7x + 10$

28. $x^2 - 3x - 28$ **29.** $m^2 - 4m - 21$ **30.** $x^2 - 2x - 15$

31. $x^2 - 5x - 24$ **32.** $b^2 - 4b - 60$ **33.** $x^2 - 3x - 18$

34. $m^2 + 7m + 10$ **35.** $n^2 - n - 72$ **36.** $k^2 - 6k + 5$

37. $x^2 + 9x + 20$ **38.** $x^2 - 10x + 9$ **39.** $x^2 - 8x + 16$

40. $d^2 - 4d + 3$ **41.** $b^2 - 26b + 48$ **42.** $n^2 - 15n + 26$

43. $n^2 - n - 6$ **44.** $z^2 - 14z + 49$ **45.** $x^2 + 7x + 12$

46. $x^2 - 18x + 17$ **47.** $x^2 + 16x + 28$ **48.** $t^2 - 6t - 27$

49. $b^2 + 4b - 12$ **50.** $d^2 + 11d + 18$ **51.** $x^2 + x - 20$

52. $x^2 - 13x + 42$ **53.** $x^2 + x - 6$ **54.** $x^2 + 4x - 21$

55. $a^2 + 2a - 35$ **56.** $h^2 + 7h - 18$ **57.** $x^2 + 3x - 10$

58. $p^2 - 12p - 28$ **59.** $y^2 + 6y - 55$ **60.** $b^2 + 3b - 4$

61. $x^2 + 2x - 63$ **62.** $x^2 - 2x - 8$ **63.** $x^2 - 11x - 60$

64. $r^2 + 2r - 35$ **65.** $c^2 - 3c - 10$ **66.** $x^2 + 8x + 15$

67. $x^2 - 8x + 15$ **68.** $n^2 - 23n + 60$ **69.** $c^2 + 3c - 10$

70. $x^2 - 9x + 14$ **71.** $x^2 - 10x + 24$ **72.** $x^2 + 6x - 27$

73. $y^2 - 16y + 64$ **74.** $n^2 + 10n + 25$ **75.** $r^2 - 14r - 51$

76. $x^2 + 3x - 40$ **77.** $x^2 - x - 42$ **78.** $n^2 - 2n - 63$

79. $a^2 + 7a + 6$ **80.** $x^2 - 14x + 48$ **81.** $x^2 - 11x + 28$

82. $n^2 + 16n - 36$ **83.** $n^2 - 4n - 21$ **84.** $y^2 + 16y - 17$

9-5 • Guided Problem Solving

GPS **Student Page 522, Exercise 55**

Write the standard form for the polynomial modeled below. Then factor the expression.

$4x^2$	$10x$
$2x$	5

Read and Understand

1. Explain what the standard form of a polynomial is. _____

    _____

2. Describe how you can write a polynomial from a rectangle model. _____

    _____

Plan and Solve

3. Write the standard form of the polynomial by adding the area of each rectangle. _____

4. Factor the standard form of the polynomial you wrote in Step 3. _____

Look Back and Check

5. Check the reasonableness of your answer in Steps 3 and 4 by substituting a number in each expression. Why should the result be the same for each expression?

Solve Another Problem

6. Write the standard form for the polynomial modeled below. Then factor each expression.

$9x^2$	$3x$
$6x$	2

Guided Problem Solving

Practice 9-6

Factoring Trinomials of the Type $ax^2 + bx + c$

••

Factor each expression.

1. $2x^2 + 3x + 1$

2. $2x^2 + 5x + 3$

3. $2n^2 + n - 6$

4. $3x^2 - x - 4$

5. $2y^2 - 9y - 5$

6. $5x^2 - 2x - 7$

7. $7n^2 + 9n + 2$

8. $3c^2 - 17c - 6$

9. $3x^2 + 8x + 4$

10. $6x^2 - 7x - 10$

11. $3x^2 - 10x + 8$

12. $3y^2 - 16y - 12$

13. $5x^2 + 2x - 3$

14. $3x^2 + 7x + 2$

15. $7x^2 - 10x + 3$

16. $3x^2 + 8x + 5$

17. $2x^2 + 9x + 4$

18. $5x^2 - 7x + 2$

19. $5x^2 - 22x + 8$

20. $4x^2 + 17x - 15$

21. $5x^2 - 33x - 14$

22. $3x^2 - 2x - 8$

23. $3y^2 + 7y - 6$

24. $2x^2 + 13x - 24$

25. $4y^2 - 11y - 3$

26. $2y^2 + 9y + 7$

27. $5y^2 - 3y - 2$

28. $7y^2 + 19y + 10$

29. $7x^2 - 30x + 8$

30. $3x^2 + 17x + 10$

31. $2x^2 + 5x - 3$

32. $2x^2 - 5x + 3$

33. $3x^2 + 10x + 3$

34. $2x^2 - x - 21$

35. $5x^2 - 11x + 2$

36. $4x^2 + 4x - 15$

37. $6x^2 - 19x + 15$

38. $2x^2 - x - 15$

39. $3x^2 - 7x - 6$

40. $2x^2 - 5x - 12$

41. $6x^2 - 7x - 5$

42. $4x^2 + 7x + 3$

43. $12y^2 - 7y + 1$

44. $6y^2 - 5y + 1$

45. $6x^2 - 11x + 4$

46. $12x^2 + 19x + 5$

47. $7y^2 + 47y - 14$

48. $11x^2 - 54x - 5$

49. $15x^2 - 19x + 6$

50. $8x^2 - 30x + 25$

51. $14y^2 + 15y - 9$

52. $22x^2 + 51x - 10$

53. $14x^2 - 41x + 15$

54. $8y^2 + 17y + 9$

55. $8x^2 + 65x + 8$

56. $20x^2 + 37x + 15$

57. $24y^2 + 41y + 12$

58. $18x^2 - 27x + 4$

59. $10x^2 + 3x - 4$

60. $10y^2 - 29y + 10$

9-6 • Guided Problem Solving

GPS **Student Page 526, Exercise 31**

a. Write each area as a product of two binomials.

b. Are the products equal?

c. **Critical Thinking** Explain how the two products you found in part (a) can equal the same trinomial.

Read and Understand

1. What does the word *product* mean? _____

2. What are binomials? _____

Plan and Solve

3. Write each area as a product of two binomials. _____

4. Are the products equal? _____

5. Explain how the two products you found in Step 3 can equal the same trinomial.

_____

_____

Look Back and Check

6. Check the reasonableness of your answer by factoring each product completely to show that they are the same.

Solve Another Problem

7. Show that these two products are equal: $(3x - 1)(2x + 2)$ and $(6x - 2)(x + 1)$.

_____

Practice 9-7

Factoring Special Cases

....

Factor each expression.

1. $x^2 - 9$

2. $4m^2 - 1$

3. $a^2 + 2a + 1$

4. $4x^2 + 12x + 9$

5. $x^2 - 22x + 121$

6. $n^2 - 4$

7. $9x^2 - 4$

8. $16c^2 - 49$

9. $9x^2 - 30x + 25$

10. $4x^2 - 20x + 25$

11. $2a^2 - 18$

12. $x^2 - 24x + 144$

13. $3n^2 - 3$

14. $9h^2 + 60h + 100$

15. $9d^2 - 49$

16. $81a^2 - 400$

17. $r^2 - 36$

18. $3a^2 - 48$

19. $b^2 + 4b + 4$

20. $10x^2 - 90$

21. $25x^2 - 64$

22. $12w^2 - 27$

23. $g^3 - 25g$

24. $x^2 + 6x + 9$

25. $a^2 - 25$

26. $36s^2 - 225$

27. $4b^2 + 44b + 121$

28. $x^2 - 16x + 64$

29. $x^2 - 2x + 1$

30. $d^2 - 49$

31. $x^3 - 36x$

32. $9y^2 - 289$

33. $x^2 - 30x + 225$

34. $100a^2 - 9$

35. $2x^2 + 4x + 2$

36. $5n^3 - 20n$

37. $9n^2 + 12n + 4$

38. $d^2 - 169$

39. $4a^2 - 81$

40. $x^2 - 121$

41. $5x^2 + 40x + 80$

42. $16n^2 + 56n + 49$

43. $3n^2 - 30n + 75$

44. $a^2 + 26a + 169$

45. $25x^2 - 144$

46. $9d^2 - 64$

47. $n^2 - 28n + 196$

48. $49a^2 - 14a + 1$

49. $y^2 + 8y + 16$

50. $y^2 - 400$

51. $x^2 - 10x + 25$

52. $4x^2 - 60x + 225$

53. $3x^2 - 363$

54. $y^2 - 81$

55. $a^2 - 100$

56. $256a^2 - 1$

57. $n^2 + 34n + 289$

58. $2d^3 - 50d$

59. $y^2 + 22y + 121$

60. $144x^2 - 25$

61. $4x^2 - 169$

62. $x^2 - 12x + 36$

63. $64r^2 + 80r + 25$

64. $50m^3 - 32m$

65. $b^2 - 225$

66. $x^2 - 18x + 81$

67. $b^2 - 64$

68. $16x^2 - 72x + 81$

69. $b^2 - 256$

70. $x^2 + 24x + 144$

71. $225x^2 - 16$

72. $2x^3 + 40x^2 + 200x$

73. $4r^2 - 25$

74. $16x^2 + 8x + 1$

75. $b^2 - 14b + 49$

76. $x^2 + 30x + 225$

77. $m^2 - 28m + 196$

78. $9r^2 - 256$

79. $b^2 + 20b + 100$

80. $m^2 - 16$

81. $4x^2 - 32x + 64$

82. $x^2 - 196$

83. $8x^3 - 32x$

84. $25x^2 - 30x + 9$

85. $8m^2 - 16m + 8$

86. $9x^2 - 400$

87. $m^2 - 144$

....

9-7 • Guided Problem Solving

GPS **Student Page 532, Exercise 54**

a. Geometry Write an expression in terms of n and m for the area of the top of the block that was drilled at the right. Use 3.14 for π. Factor your expression.
b. Find the area of the top of the block if $n = 10$ in. and $m = 3$ in.

Read and Understand

1. Describe the information given to you in the picture. _____

_____

2. What is the formula used to find the area of a rectangle? _____

3. What is the formula used to find the area of a circle? _____

Plan and Solve

4. Write an expression for the area of the rectangular block. _____

5. Write an expression for the area of the circular hole drilled into the block. _____

6. Write an expression for the area of the top of the block that was drilled. _____

7. Factor your expression from Step 6. _____

8. Find the area of the top of the block if $n = 10$ and $m = 3$. _____

Look Back and Check

9. In Steps 6 and 7 you wrote two different expressions for the area of the block. Check your answer in Step 8 by substituting the values into the expression that you did not use.

Solve Another Problem

10. What is the area of the top of the block if $n = 15$ and $m = 6$?

_____

Practice 9-8

Factoring by Grouping

Factor each expression.

1. $x(a + 2) - 2(a + 2)$

2. $3(x + y) + a(x + y)$

3. $m(x - 3) + k(x - 3)$

4. $a(y + 1) - b(y + 1)$

5. $x^2 + 3x + 2xy + 6y$

6. $y^2 - 5wy + 4y - 20w$

7. $xy + 4y - 2x - 8$

8. $ab + 7b - 3a - 21$

9. $ax + bx + ay + by$

10. $ax + bx - ay - by$

11. $2x^2 - 6xy + 5x - 15y$

12. $3x^2 - 6xy + 2x - 4y$

13. $2ax + 6xc + ba + 3bc$

14. $x^2y - 3x^2 - 2y + 6$

15. $6 + 2y + 3x^2 + x^2y$

16. $2x^2 - 3x + 1$

17. $2x^2 - 7x + 3$

18. $6x^2 + 7x + 2$

19. $4x^2 + 8x + 3$

20. $6x^2 - 7x + 2$

21. $4x^2 - 9x + 2$

22. $2x^2 - 3x - 2$

23. $12x^2 - x - 1$

24. $6x^2 + 19x + 3$

25. $12y^2 - 5y - 2$

26. $10y^2 + 21y - 10$

27. $5y^2 + 13y + 6$

28. $16y^2 + 10y + 1$

29. $16x^2 - 14x + 3$

30. $16x^2 + 16x + 3$

31. $10x^2 - 3x - 1$

32. $9x^2 + 25x - 6$

33. $14x^2 + 15x - 9$

34. $2x^3 + 8x^2 + x + 4$

35. $8x^4 + 6x - 28x^3 - 21$

36. $5x^3 - x^2 + 15x - 3$

37. $x^3 + 3x^2 + 4x + 12$

38. $6x^3 + 3x^2 + 2x + 1$

39. $3x^3 + 9x^2 + 2x + 6$

40. $9x^3 - 12x^2 + 3x - 4$

41. $10x^3 - 25x^2 + 4x - 10$

42. $4x^3 - 20x^2 + 3x - 15$

Find expressions for the possible dimensions of each rectangular prism.

43. The volume of the prism is given.

44. The volume of the prism is given.

$144x^3 - 258x^2 + 105x$

$28x^3 + 212x^2 + 112x$

9-8 • Guided Problem Solving

GPS **Student Page 538, Exercise 39**

Geometry The polynomial shown at the right represents the volume of the rectangular prism. Factor the polynomial to find possible expressions for the length, width, and height of the prism.

$84w^3 + 82w^2 + 10w$

Read and Understand

1. What is the formula for finding the volume of a rectangular prism? _____

   _____

2. What is the first type of factoring that you should look for? _____

   _____

Plan and Solve

3. What is the common factor for the expression $84w^3 + 82w^2 + 10w$? _____

4. What polynomial is left after factoring out the common factor? _____

5. Factor the polynomial you wrote in Step 5. _____

6. What are the three factors that represent the length, width, and height of the prism?

   _____

Look Back and Check

7. Multiply the three factors you wrote for Step 7. How can you tell if these are the correct factors?

   _____

   _____

Solve Another Problem

8. What are the possible expressions for the length, width, and height of a rectangular prism that has a volume of $18m^3 + 33m^2 + 9m$?

   _____

9A: Graphic Organizer

For use before Lesson 9-1

Study Skill To remember the math concepts, you can study with a friend. Quiz each other on the details of the algebra rules and procedures. Use your notes to help you determine possible test questions. Reviewing right before bedtime will help you retain the material you study.

Write your answers.

1. What is the chapter title? _____

2. Find the Table of Contents page for this chapter at the front of the book. Name four topics you will study in this chapter.

   _____   _____

   _____   _____

3. Complete the graphic organizer as you work through the chapter.
   1. Write the title of the chapter in the center oval.
   2. When you begin a lesson, write the name of the lesson in a rectangle.
   3. When you complete that lesson, write a skill or key concept from that lesson in the outer oval linked to that rectangle.
   Continue with steps 2 and 3 clockwise around the graphic organizer.

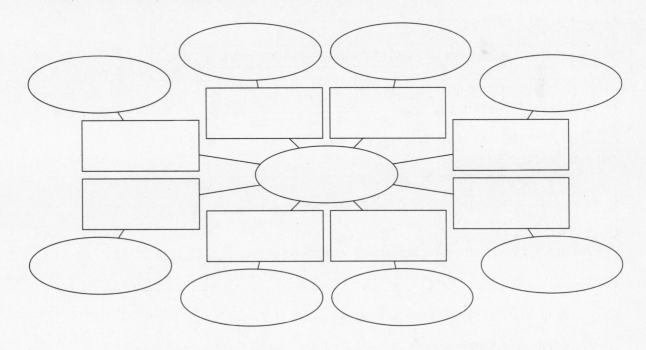

9B: Reading Comprehension

For use after Lesson 9-2

Study Skill Many reading passages contain a great amount of information. It is essential to recognize which information is necessary for a particular question. You can designate corresponding information by circling, underlining, or boxing that information.

Read the passage below and answer the following questions.

Radioactive material is here today and gone tomorrow. Radioisotopes disintegrate into stable isotopes of different elements at a decreasing rate, but never quite reach zero. Radioactive material is measured in curies (Ci) and 1 Ci = 3.7×10^{10} atoms. A mathematical formula known as the radioactive decay law can measure the rate of radioactive decay and the quantity of material present at any given time. From this formula we obtain a quantity known as half-life. Half-life is the amount of time required for a quantity of radioactive material to be reduced to one-half its original quantity.

Each radioisotope has a unique half-life. For example I-131 has a half-life of 8 days, C-11 has a half-life of 20 minutes, and H-6 has a half-life of 0.8 seconds.

Although this can sound quite difficult, it does not have to be. The following chart can help you calculate the amount of radioactive material that has decayed.

Half-life number	1	2	3	4	5	6	7
Radioactivity remaining	50%	25%	12.5%	6.25%	3.12%	1.56%	0.78%

1. What is the half-life of I-131? _____

2. If you have 100 mCi of I-131, how much would remain after 1 half-life?

   _____

3. How much would remain after 2 half-lives? _____

4. If 40 mCi of I-131 was present on January 3rd at noon,
   how much was remaining on January 19th at noon? _____

5. What is the half-life of C-11? _____

6. You have 50 mCi of H-6. How much remains after 4 seconds? _____

7. **High-Use Academic Words** What does *unique* mean in the second paragraph of the passage?

   a. unpredictable   **b.** its own

9C: Reading/Writing Math Symbols

For use after Lesson 9-7

Study Skill Make mental pictures from what you read. This will help you remember it.

In equations and inequalities, *x* and *y* represent coordinates of points, *b* represents the *y*-intercept, and *m* represents the slope. Inequality symbols mean to shade on one side of a boundary line. Match each equation or inequality to the graph that best represents it.

1. $y < b$

2. $x = k$

3. $y = mx + b; m < 0$

4. $y \geq mx + b$

5. $y < mx + b; b \neq 0$

6. $y = mx; m > 0$

A.

B.

C.

D.

E.

F.

9D: Visual Vocabulary Practice
High-Use Academic Words

Study Skill Mathematics is like learning a foreign language. You have to know the vocabulary before you can speak the language correctly.

Concept List

apply	consecutive	formula
interpret	methods	notation
simplify	solve	test

Write the concept that best describes each exercise. Choose from the concept list above.

1. $f(x)$ for y	**2.** The slope of the linear graph is 3, which indicates the class charged $3 per car.	**3.** n and $n + 1$
4. $A(n) = a \cdot r^{n-1}$	**5.** Expenses are $.90 for printing and mailing a newsletter, plus $600 for writing. The price is $1.50 per copy. Find the number of copies that must be sold to break even.	**6.** $2(c + 4) - 5c = -3c + 8$
7. 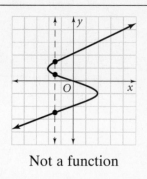 Not a function	**8.** $2(5x - 3) = 14$ $10x - 6 = 14$ $10x = 20$ $x = 2$	**9.** Solving systems by • Graphing • Substitution • Elimination

9E: Vocabulary Check

Study Skill Strengthen your vocabulary. Use these pages and add cues and summaries by applying the Cornell Notetaking style.

Write the definition for each word at the right. To check your work, fold the paper back along the dotted line to see the correct answers.

_____

_____

_____

Degree of a monomial

_____

_____

Polynomial

_____

_____

Standard form of a polynomial

_____

_____

_____

Degree of a polynomial

_____

_____

Greatest common factor

_____

_____

Vocabulary and Study Skills

9E: Vocabulary Check (continued)

Write the vocabulary word for each definition. To check your work, fold the paper forward along the dotted line to see the correct answers.

The sum of the exponents of its variables.

_____

A monomial or the sum or difference of two or more monomials.

_____

The form of a polynomial in which the degree of the terms decreases from left to right.

_____

The degree of the term with the greatest exponent for a polynomial in one variable.

_____

The greatest factor that divides evenly into each term of the expression.

_____

9F: Vocabulary Review Puzzle

For use with Chapter Review

Study Skill When you complete a puzzle such as a word search, remember to read the list of words carefully and completely. As you identify each word in the word search, circle it and then cross off the word from the list. Pay special attention to the spelling of each word.

Complete the word search.

binomial	interest	translation
factor	common ratio	median
monomial	sequence	distributive
standard form	scatter plot	variable
polynomial	outlier	probability
trinomial	reciprocal	degree
systems	elimination	substitution

```
E  Y  R  N  P  O  L  Y  N  O  M  I  A  L  N
L  T  E  E  O  L  A  I  M  O  N  I  R  T  O
I  I  C  J  S  I  S  F  A  C  T  O  R  S  I
M  L  I  L  M  C  T  M  L  Q  H  M  T  E  T
I  I  P  A  R  O  A  U  E  A  P  O  V  Q  A
N  B  R  I  E  M  N  T  T  T  B  B  Y  U  L
A  A  O  M  I  E  D  O  T  I  S  T  H  E  S
T  B  C  O  L  D  A  L  M  E  T  Y  N  N
I  O  A  N  T  I  R  W  Q  I  R  S  S  C  A
O  R  L  I  U  A  D  W  M  U  A  P  B  E  R
N  P  V  B  O  N  F  I  Z  W  W  L  L  U  T
S  Q  C  O  M  M  O  N  R  A  T  I  O  O  S
Q  V  I  N  T  E  R  E  S  T  E  M  S  T  T
E  E  R  G  E  D  M  E  L  B  A  I  R  A  V
E  V  I  T  U  B  I  R  T  S  I  D  G  B  W
```

Practice 10-1

Exploring Quadratic Graphs

Identify the vertex of each graph. Tell whether it is a minimum or a maximum.

1. $y = -3x^2$ **2.** $y = -7x^2$ **3.** $y = 0.5x^2$

4. $y = 5x^2$ **5.** $y = -4x^2$ **6.** $y = \frac{3}{2}x^2$

Order each group of quadratic functions from widest to narrowest graph.

7. $y = x^2, y = 5x^2, y = 3x^2$ **8.** $y = -8x^2, y = \frac{1}{2}x^2, y = -x^2$

9. $y = 5x^2, y = -4x^2, y = 2x^2$ **10.** $y = -\frac{1}{2}x^2, y = \frac{1}{3}x^2, y = -3x^2$

11. $y = 6x^2, y = -7x^2, y = 4x^2$ **12.** $y = \frac{3}{4}x^2, y = 2x^2, y = \frac{1}{5}x^2$

Graph each function.

13. $y = x^2$ **14.** $y = 4x^2$ **15.** $y = -3x^2$

16. $y = -x^2 - 4$ **17.** $y = 2x^2 - 2$ **18.** $y = 2x^2 + 3$

19. $y = \frac{1}{2}x^2 + 2$ **20.** $y = \frac{1}{2}x^2 - 3$ **21.** $y = \frac{1}{3}x^2 + 5$

22. $y = \frac{1}{3}x^2 - 4$ **23.** $y = 2.5x^2 + 3$ **24.** $y = 2.5x^2 + 5$

25. $y = 5x^2 + 8$ **26.** $y = 5x^2 - 8$ **27.** $y = -3.5x^2 - 4$

28. The price of a stock on the NYSE is modeled by the function $y = 0.005x^2 + 10$, where x is the number of months the stock has been available.

  a. Graph the function.

  b. What x-values make sense for the domain? Explain why.

  c. What y-values make sense for the range? Explain why.

29. You are designing a poster. The poster is 24 in. wide by 36 in. high. On the poster, you want to place a square photograph and some printing. If each side of the photograph is x in., the function $y = 864 - x^2$ gives the area of the poster available for printing.

  a. Graph the function.

  b. What x-values make sense for the domain? Explain why.

  c. What y-values make sense for the range? Explain why.

30. You are placing a circular drawing on a square piece of poster board. The poster board is 15 in. wide. The part of the poster board not covered by the drawing will be painted blue. If the radius of the drawing is r, the function $A = 225 - 3.14r^2$ gives the area to be painted blue.

  a. Graph the function.

  b. What x-values make sense for the domain? Explain why.

  c. What y-values make sense for the range? Explain why.

10-1 • Guided Problem Solving

GPS **Student Page 555, Exercise 39**

Suppose that a pizza must fit into a box with a base that is 12 in. long and 12 in. wide. You can use the quadratic function $A = \pi r^2$ to find the area of a pizza in terms of its radius.

- **a.** What values of r make sense for the function?
- **b.** What values of A make sense for the function?
- **c.** Graph the function. Round values of A to the nearest tenth.

Read and Understand

1. What shape is the pizza? _____

2. What shape is the box? _____

3. What information is given to you in the problem? _____

Plan and Solve

4. What values of r make sense for the function? _____

5. What values of A make sense for the function? _____

6. Graph the function. Round values of A to the nearest tenth.

Look Back and Check

7. The equation $A = \pi r^2$ is a quadratic function. What shape is the graph of a quadratic function? Verify the reasonableness of your graph by verifying that it is the shape you would expect.

_____

Solve Another Problem

8. If the size of the box is changed so the base is now 10 in. long and 10 in. wide, what values of r and A would make sense? _____

Practice 10-2

Quadratic Functions

Find the equation of the axis of symmetry and the coordinates of the vertex
of the graph of each function.

1. $y = x^2 - 10x + 2$

2. $y = x^2 + 12x - 9$

3. $y = -x^2 + 2x + 1$

4. $y = 3x^2 + 18x + 9$

5. $y = 3x^2 + 3$

6. $y = 16x - 4x^2$

7. $y = 0.5x^2 + 4x - 2$

8. $y = -4x^2 + 24x + 6$

9. $y = -1.5x^2 + 6x$

Graph each function. Label the axis of symmetry and the vertex.

10. $y = x^2 - 6x + 4$

11. $y = x^2 + 4x - 1$

12. $y = x^2 + 10x + 14$

13. $y = x^2 + 2x + 1$

14. $y = -x^2 - 4x + 4$

15. $y = -4x^2 + 24x + 13$

16. $y = -2x^2 - 8x + 5$

17. $y = 4x^2 - 16x + 10$

18. $y = -x^2 + 6x + 5$

19. $y = 4x^2 + 8x$

20. $y = -3x^2 + 6$

21. $y = 6x^2 + 48x + 98$

Graph each quadratic inequality.

22. $y > x^2 + 1$

23. $y \geq x^2 - 4$

24. $y < -x^2 + 1$

25. $y > x^2 + 6x + 3$

26. $y < x^2 - 4x + 4$

27. $y < -x^2 + 2x - 3$

28. $y \geq -2x^2 - 8x - 5$

29. $y \leq -3x^2 + 6x + 1$

30. $y \geq 2x^2 - 4x - 3$

31. You and a friend are hiking in the mountains. You want to climb to a
ledge that is 20 ft above you. The height of the grappling hook you
throw is given by the function $h = -16t^2 - 32t + 5$. What is the
maximum height of the grappling hook? Can you throw it high enough
to reach the ledge?

32. The total profit made by an engineering firm is given by the function
$p = x^2 - 25x + 5000$. Find the minimum profit made by the company.

33. You are trying to dunk a basketball. You need to jump 2.5 ft in the air
to dunk the ball. The height that your feet are above the ground is given
by the function $h = -16t^2 + 12t$. What is the maximum height your
feet will be above the ground? Will you be able to dunk the basketball?

10-2 • Guided Problem Solving

GPS **Student Page 561, Exercise 36**

Road Construction An archway over a road is cut out of rock. Its shape
is modeled by the quadratic function $y = -0.1x^2 + 12$ for $y \geq 0$.

a. Write an inequality that describes the opening of the archway.
b. Graph the inequality.
c. **Critical Thinking** Can a camper 6 ft wide and 7 ft high fit under the
   arch without crossing the median line? Explain.

Read and Understand

1. Make a rough sketch of what the archway should look like.

2. What information do you know about the archway? _____

Plan and Solve

3. Write an inequality that describes the opening of the archway. _____

4. Graph the inequality.

5. On your graph above, show where the camper would be located.

6. Can a camper 6 ft wide and 7 ft high fit under
   the arch without crossing the median line? Explain. _____

_____

Look Back and Check

7. Check the reasonableness of your inequality graph. Pick a point in the
   shaded region and check to see that it makes the inequality true.

Solve Another Problem

8. The road passing through the archway is being converted to a one-
   way road so a trailer with an extra-wide load can pass through it. If
   the trailer's load is 12 feet wide and 10 feet high, can the trailer fit
   under the arch?

Practice 10-3

Solve each equation by finding square roots. If the equation has no real solution, write *no solution*. If necessary, round to the nearest tenth.

1. $x^2 = 16$ **2.** $x^2 - 144 = 0$ **3.** $3x^2 - 27 = 0$

4. $x^2 + 16 = 0$ **5.** $x^2 = 12$ **6.** $x^2 = 49$

7. $x^2 + 8 = -10$ **8.** $3x^2 = 300$ **9.** $2x^2 - 6 = 26$

10. $x^2 = 80$ **11.** $81x^2 - 10 = 15$ **12.** $2x^2 = 90$

13. $x^2 = 300$ **14.** $4x^2 + 9 = 41$ **15.** $2x^2 + 8 = 4$

16. $x^2 + 8 = 72$ **17.** $4x^2 + 6 = 7$ **18.** $x^2 = 121$

19. $5x^2 + 20 = 30$ **20.** $x^2 + 6 = 17$ **21.** $3x^2 + 1 = 54$

22. $2x^2 - 7 = 74$ **23.** $x^2 + 1 = 0$ **24.** $4x^2 - 8 = -20$

25. $9x^2 = 1$ **26.** $x^2 + 4 = 4$ **27.** $3x^2 = 1875$

28. $x^2 = 9$ **29.** $5x^2 - 980 = 0$ **30.** $x^2 - 10 = 100$

31. $4x^2 - 2 = 1$ **32.** $3x^2 - 75 = 0$ **33.** $x^2 + 25 = 0$

34. $2x^2 - 10 = -4$ **35.** $4x^2 + 3 = 3$ **36.** $4x^2 - 8 = 32$

37. $7x^2 + 8 = 15$ **38.** $x^2 + 1 = 26$ **39.** $6x^2 = -3$

40. $x^2 - 400 = 0$ **41.** $7x^2 - 8 = 20$ **42.** $2x^2 - 1400 = 0$

43. $5x^2 + 25 = 90$ **44.** $x^2 + 4x^2 = 20$ **45.** $5x^2 - 18 = -23$

46. $3x^2 - x^2 = 10$ **47.** $2x^2 + 6 - x^2 = 9$ **48.** $x^2 - 225 = 0$

49. $-3 + 4x^2 = 2$ **50.** $7x^2 - 1008 = 0$ **51.** $6x^2 - 6 = 12$

Solve each problem. If necessary, round to the nearest tenth.

52. You want to build a fence around a square garden that covers 506.25 ft². How many feet of fence will you need to complete the job?

53. The formula $A = 6s^2$ will calculate the surface area of a cube. Suppose you have a cube that has a surface area of 216 in.². What is the length of each side?

54. You drop a pencil out of a window that is 20 ft above the ground. Use the formula $V^2 = 64s$, where V is the speed and s is the distance fallen, to calculate the speed the pencil is traveling when it hits the ground.

55. Suppose you are going to construct a circular fish pond in your garden. You want the pond to cover an area of 300 ft². What is the radius of the pond?

56. During the construction of a skyscraper, a bolt fell from 400 ft. What was the speed of the bolt when it hit the ground? Use $V^2 = 64s$.

10-3 • Guided Problem Solving

Framing Find dimensions for the square picture at the right that would make the area of the picture equal to 75% of the total area enclosed by the square frame. Round to the nearest tenth of an inch.

x 12 in.

Read and Understand

1. What information is given to you in the problem? _____

2. What additional information is given to you in the picture? _____

   _____

Plan and Solve

3. Write an expression for the area of the picture only. _____

4. Write an expression for the total area enclosed by the frame. _____

5. What is 75% of the total area enclosed by the frame? _____

6. Write and solve an equation to find the dimensions of the square picture that would make the area of the picture equal to 75% of the total area enclosed by the square frame. _____

Look Back and Check

7. Use the dimensions you found in Step 6 to check if the area of the picture is 75% of the total area enclosed by the square frame. Explain why it is not exactly 75%.

   _____

Solve Another Problem

8. What would the dimensions of the square picture be that would make the area of the picture equal to 60% of the total area enclosed by the square frame?

   _____

Practice 10-4

Factoring to Solve Quadratic Equations

• •

Use the Zero-Product Property to solve each equation.

1. $(x + 5)(x - 3) = 0$

2. $(x - 2)(x + 9) = 0$

3. $(b - 12)(b + 12) = 0$

4. $(2n + 3)(n - 4) = 0$

5. $(x + 7)(4x - 5) = 0$

6. $(2x + 7)(2x - 7) = 0$

7. $(3x - 7)(2x + 1) = 0$

8. $(8y - 3)(4y + 1) = 0$

9. $(5x + 6)(4x + 5) = 0$

Solve by factoring.

10. $x^2 + 5x + 6 = 0$

11. $b^2 - 7b - 18 = 0$

12. $r^2 - 4 = 0$

13. $x^2 + 8x - 20 = 0$

14. $y^2 + 14y + 13 = 0$

15. $s^2 - 3s - 10 = 0$

16. $x^2 + 7x = 8$

17. $x^2 = 25$

18. $h^2 + 10h = -21$

19. $2t^2 + 8t - 64 = 0$

20. $3a^2 - 36a + 81 = 0$

21. $5x^2 - 45 = 0$

22. $2a^2 - a - 21 = 0$

23. $3n^2 - 11n + 10 = 0$

24. $2x^2 - 7x - 9 = 0$

25. $2n^2 - 5n = 12$

26. $3m^2 - 5m = -2$

27. $5s^2 - 17s = -6$

28. $6m^2 = 13m + 28$

29. $4a^2 - 4a = 15$

30. $4r^2 = r + 3$

31. Suppose you are building a storage box of volume 4368 in.^{3}. The length of the box will be 24 in. The height of the box will be 1 in. more than its width. Find the height and width of the box.

32. A banner is in the shape of a right triangle of area 63 in.^{2}. The height of the banner is 4 in. less than twice the width of the banner. Find the height and width of the banner.

33. A rectangular poster has an area of 190 in.^{2}. The height of the poster is 1 in. less than twice its width. Find the dimensions of the poster.

34. A diver is standing on a platform 24 ft above the pool. He jumps from the platform with an initial upward velocity of 8 ft/s. Use the formula $h = -16t^2 + vt + s$, where h is his height above the water, t is the time, v is his starting upward velocity, and s is his starting height. How long will it take for him to hit the water?

Solve each equation.

35. $(x - 9)(x + 8) = 0$

36. $x^2 - 9x - 10 = 0$

37. $(c - 21)(c + 21) = 0$

38. $(x - 12)(5x - 13) = 0$

39. $2a^2 - 21a - 65 = 0$

40. $x^2 + 6x - 91 = 0$

41. $a^2 + 6a - 72 = 0$

42. $4x^2 + 8x - 21 = 0$

43. $20d^2 - 82d + 80 = 0$

44. $3n^2 + 12n - 288 = 0$

45. $2s^2 - 13s - 24 = 0$

46. $x^2 + 5x = 150$

47. $3c^2 + 8c = 3$

48. $30a^2 + 121a - 21 = 0$

49. $c^2 - 81 = 0$

50. $x^2 + 306 = -35x$

51. $x^2 = 121$

52. $x^2 - 21x + 108 = 0$

• **443**

10-4 • Guided Problem Solving

GPS **Student Page 574, Exercise 33**

Baseball Suppose you throw a baseball into the air with an initial upward velocity of 29 ft/s and an initial height of 6 ft. The formula $h = -16t^2 + 29t + 6$ gives the ball's height h in feet at time t in seconds.

a. The ball's height h is 0 when it is on the ground. Find the number of seconds that pass before the ball lands by solving $0 = -16t^2 + 29t + 6$.

b. **Graphing Calculator** Graph the related function for the equation in part (a). Use your graph to estimate the maximum height of the ball.

Read and Understand

1. What information about the baseball is given to you in the problem? _____

_____

2. Explain what each variable in the formula represents. _____

_____

Plan and Solve

3. What method will you use to solve the quadratic equation $0 = -16t^2 + 29t + 6$? _____

_____

4. Solve the equation $0 = -16t^2 + 29t + 6$ to find the number of seconds that pass before the ball lands. _____

5. What is the related function for the equation $0 = -16t^2 + 29t + 6$? _____

6. On your graphing calculator graph the related function from Step 5 and use your graph to estimate the maximum height of the ball.

Look Back and Check

7. Using your graphing calculator, what is the time when the ball reaches the maximum height? Substitute that value for t in the equation to see if your height estimate is reasonable.

_____

Solve Another Problem

8. The formula $h = -16t^2 + 45t + 9$ also gives the ball's height h in feet at time t in seconds. How many seconds pass before the ball lands on the ground?

_____

Practice 10-5

Completing the Square

Find the value of n such that each expression is a perfect square trinomial.

1. $x^2 - 14x + n$

2. $x^2 - \frac{2}{9}x + n$

3. $x^2 - \frac{4}{9}x + n$

4. $x^2 - \frac{2}{6}x + n$

Solve each equation by completing the square. If necessary, round to the nearest hundredth.

5. $x^2 - 4x = 5$

6. $x^2 - x - 2 = 0$

7. $x^2 - 6x = 10$

8. $x^2 + 4x + 4 = 0$

9. $x^2 - 3x = 18$

10. $x^2 - 8x - 4 = 0$

11. $x^2 - 6x = 0$

12. $x^2 - 6x = 8$

13. $x^2 - 7x = 0$

14. $x^2 + 4x - 12 = 0$

15. $x^2 + 11x + 10 = 0$

16. $x^2 + 2x = 15$

17. $x^2 - 8x = 9$

18. $x^2 + 5x = -6$

19. $x^2 - 2x = 120$

20. $x^2 - 22x = -105$

21. $2x^2 = 3x + 9$

22. $2x^2 + 8x - 10 = 0$

23. $2x^2 - 3x - 2 = 0$

24. $2x^2 + 12x - 32 = 0$

25. $3x^2 + 17x - 6 = 0$

26. $2x^2 - x - 28 = 0$

27. $3x^2 - 4x + 1 = 0$

28. $2x^2 - 5x - 3 = 0$

29. $6x^2 - 2x = 28$

30. $2x^2 - 16x = -30$

31. $4x^2 = -2x + 12$

32. $9x^2 + 6x = 3$

33. $10x^2 + 3x = 4$

34. $12x^2 - 29x + 15 = 0$

Algebra 1 Lesson 10-5

445

10-5 • Guided Problem Solving

GPS **Student Page 582, Exercise 35**

Gardening Suppose you want to enclose a rectangular garden plot against a house using fencing on three sides, as shown. Assume you have 50 ft of fencing material and want to create a garden with an area of 150 ft^2.

a. Let w = the width. Write an expression for the length of the plot.
b. Write and solve an equation for the area of the plot. **Round to the nearest tenth of a foot.**
c. What dimensions should the garden have?
d. **Critical Thinking** Find the area of the garden by using the dimensions you found in part (b). Does the area equal 150 ft^2? Explain.

Read and Understand

1. What information is given to you in the problem? _____

   _____

2. How many sides of the garden must be fenced in? _____

Plan and Solve

3. Write an expression for the length of the plot. _____

4. Write and solve an equation for the area of the plot. **Round to the nearest foot.**

   _____

   _____

5. What dimensions should the garden have? _____

Look Back and Check

6. Find the area of the garden by using the dimensions you found in part (b). Does the area equal 150 ft^2? Explain. _____

   _____

Solve Another Problem

7. Suppose you decide to move your garden away from the house, so you now have to use 50 ft of fencing for four sides. The length of the garden must be twice as long as the width. If the area is now 139 ft^2, what dimensions should the garden have?

   _____

Guided Problem Solving

Practice 10-6

Using the Quadratic Formula

Use the quadratic formula to solve each equation. If the equation has no real solutions, write *no real solutions.* If necessary, round to the nearest hundredth.

1. $x^2 + 8x + 5 = 0$ **2.** $x^2 - 36 = 0$ **3.** $d^2 - 4d - 96 = 0$

4. $a^2 - 3a - 154 = 0$ **5.** $4p^2 - 12p - 91 = 0$ **6.** $5m^2 + 9m = 126$

7. $r^2 - 35r + 70 = 0$ **8.** $y^2 + 6y - 247 = 0$ **9.** $x^2 + 12x - 40 = 0$

10. $4n^2 - 81 = 0$ **11.** $x^2 + 13x + 30 = 0$ **12.** $a^2 - a = 132$

13. $6w^2 - 23w + 7 = 0$ **14.** $4x^2 + 33x = 27$ **15.** $7s^2 - 7 = 0$

16. $x^2 + 5x - 90 = 0$ **17.** $5b^2 - 20 = 0$ **18.** $4x^2 - 3x + 6 = 0$

19. $6h^2 + 77h - 13 = 0$ **20.** $5y^2 = 17y + 12$ **21.** $g^2 - 15g = 54$

22. $27f^2 = 12$ **23.** $4x^2 - 52x + 133 = 0$ **24.** $x^2 + 36x + 60 = 0$

25. $a^2 - 2a - 360 = 0$ **26.** $x^2 + 10x + 40 = 0$ **27.** $t^2 - 10t = 39$

28. $4x^2 + 7x - 9 = 0$ **29.** $2c^2 - 39c + 135 = 0$ **30.** $4x^2 + 33x + 340 = 0$

31. $m^2 - 40m + 100 = 0$ **32.** $8x^2 + 25x + 19 = 0$ **33.** $36w^2 - 289 = 0$

34. $4d^2 + 29d - 60 = 0$ **35.** $4z^2 + 43z + 108 = 0$ **36.** $3x^2 - 19x + 40 = 0$

37. $14x^2 = 56$ **38.** $32x^2 - 18 = 0$ **39.** $r^2 + r - 650 = 0$

40. $2y^2 = 39y - 17$ **41.** $5a^2 - 9a + 5 = 0$ **42.** $x^2 = 9x + 120$

43. $8h^2 - 38h + 9 = 0$ **44.** $20x^2 = 245$ **45.** $9h^2 - 72h = -119$

46. $x^2 + 3x + 8 = 0$ **47.** $6m^2 - 13m = 19$ **48.** $9x^2 - 81 = 0$

49. $4s^2 + 8s = 221$ **50.** $6p^2 + 25p - 119 = 0$ **51.** $2s^2 - 59s + 17 = 0$

52. A rectangular painting has dimensions x and $x + 10$. The painting is in a frame 2 in. wide. The total area of the picture and the frame is 900 in.^{2}. What are the dimensions of the painting?

53. A ball is thrown upward from a height of 15 ft with an inital upward velocity of 5 ft/s. Use the formula $h = -16t^2 + vt + s$ to find how long it will take for the ball to hit the ground.

54. Your community wants to put a square fountain in a park. Around the fountain will be a sidewalk that is 3.5 ft wide. The total area that the fountain and sidewalk can be is 700 ft^2. What are the dimensions of the fountain?

55. The Garys have a triangular pennant of area 420 in.^{2} flying from the flagpole in their yard. The height of the triangle is 10 in. less than 5 times the base of the triangle. What are the dimensions of the pennant?

10-6 • Guided Problem Solving

GPS **Student Page 589, Exercise 36**

Geometry Find the base and height of the triangle below.
If necessary, round to the nearest hundredth.

x 20 ft^2

$x + 2$

Read and Understand

1. What is the formula for finding the area of a triangle? _____

2. What information can be found from the figure? _____

Plan and Solve

3. Write an equation for the area of the triangle. _____

4. If the area is 20 ft^2, write your equation in Step 3 in standard form. _____

5. Solve your equation in Step 4. _____

6. What are the base and height of the triangle? _____

Look Back and Check

7. Use the base and height you found in Step 6 to find the area of the
   triangle. What should it be? Explain.

   _____

   _____

Solve Another Problem

8. Find the length and width of the rectangle below.

   _____

15 ft^2 x

$x + 3$

Practice 10-7

Find the number of real solutions of each equation.

1. $x^2 + 6x + 10 = 0$ **2.** $x^2 - 4x - 1 = 0$ **3.** $x^2 + 6x + 9 = 0$

4. $x^2 - 8x + 15 = 0$ **5.** $x^2 - 5x + 7 = 0$ **6.** $x^2 - 4x + 5 = 0$

7. $3x^2 - 18x + 27 = 0$ **8.** $4x^2 - 8 = 0$ **9.** $-5x^2 - 10x = 0$

10. $-x^2 = 4x + 6$ **11.** $4x^2 = 9x - 3$ **12.** $8x^2 + 2 = 8x$

13. $7x^2 + 16x + 11 = 0$ **14.** $12x^2 - 11x - 2 = 0$ **15.** $-9x^2 - 25x + 20 = 0$

16. $16x^2 + 8x = -1$ **17.** $-16x^2 + 11x = 11$ **18.** $12x^2 - 12x = -3$

19. $0.2x^2 + 4.5x - 2.8 = 0$ **20.** $-2.8x^2 + 3.1x = -0.5$ **21.** $0.5x^2 + 0.6x = 0$

22. $1.5x^2 - 15x + 2.5 = 0$ **23.** $-3x^2 + 27x = -40$ **24.** $2.1x^2 + 4.2 = 0$

25. One of the games at a carnival involves trying to ring a bell with a ball by hitting a lever that propels the ball into the air. The height of the ball is modeled by the equation $h = -16t^2 + 39t$. If the bell is 25 ft above the ground, will it be hit by the ball?

26. You are placing a rectangular picture on a square poster board. You can enlarge the picture to any size. The area of the poster board not covered by the picture is modeled by the equation $A = -x^2 - 10x + 300$. Is it possible for the area not covered by the picture to be 100 in.^{2}?

27. The equation $h = -16t^2 + 58t + 3$ models the height of a baseball t seconds after it has been hit.

    a. Was the height of the baseball ever 40 ft?

    b. Was the height of the baseball ever 60 ft?

28. A firefighter is on the fifth floor of an office building. She needs to throw a rope into the window above her on the seventh floor. The function $h = -16t^2 + 36t$ models how high above her she is able to throw a rope. If she needs to throw the rope 40 ft above her to reach the seventh-floor window, will the rope get to the window?

Find the number of x-intercepts of the related function of each equation.

29. $-16 = x^2 + 10x$ **30.** $-5 = x^2 + 3x$ **31.** $7 = x^2 - 2x$

32. $0 = 3x^2 - 3$ **33.** $0 = 2x^2 + x$ **34.** $-1 = 3x^2 + 2x$

35. $4 = x^2 - 8x$ **36.** $-64 = x^2 - 16x$ **37.** $6 = -2x^2 - 5x$

38. $2 = -4x^2 - 5x$ **39.** $36 = -x^2 + 12x$ **40.** $6 = -5x^2 + 11x$

10-7 • Guided Problem Solving

GPS **Student Page 594, Exercise 25**

Business A software company is producing a new computer application. The equation $S = p(54 - 0.75p)$ relates price p in dollars to total sales S in thousands of dollars.

  a. Write the equation in standard form.
  b. Use the discriminant to determine if it is possible for the company to earn $1,000,000 in sales.
  c. According to the model, what price would generate the greatest sales?
  d. **Critical Thinking** Total sales S decrease as p increases beyond the value in part (c). Why does this make sense in the given situation? Explain.

Read and Understand

1. Explain what the equation describes. _____

_____

2. What do the variables S and p represent? _____

Plan and Solve

3. Write the equation in standard form. _____

4. Use the discriminant to determine if it is possible for the company to earn $1,000,000 in sales. _____

5. According to the model, what price would generate the greatest sales? _____

6. Total sales S decrease as p increases beyond the value in part (c). Why does this make sense in the given situation? Explain. _____

_____

Look Back and Check

7. On your graphing calculator, graph the equation. Use your graph to check the reasonableness of the price that would generate the greatest sales.

Solve Another Problem

8. The height of a firework can be modeled by the equation $h = t(256 - 16t)$, which relates the time t in seconds since the firework was released to height h in feet.

  a. Write the equation in standard form. _____

  b. Use the discriminant to determine if it is possible for the firework to reach 1000 ft._____

  c. According to the model, at what time would the firework be at its highest?_____

                                            Guided Problem Solving

Practice 10-8   Choosing a Linear, Quadratic, or Exponential Model

Which kind of function best models the data? Write an equation to model the data.

1. $(-1, 3), (1, 3), (3, 27), (5, 75), (7, 147)$

2. $(-2, 4), (-1, 2), (0, 0), (1, -2), (2, -4)$

3. $\left(-2, \dfrac{1}{16}\right), \left(-1, \dfrac{1}{4}\right), (0, 1), (1, 4), (2, 16)$

4. $(-6, -1), (-3, 0), (0, 1), (3, 2), (6, 3)$

5. $\left(-2, \dfrac{1}{3}\right), (-1, 1), (0, 3), (1, 9), (2, 27)$

6. $(-4, -32), (-2, -8), (0, 0), (2, -8), (4, -32)$

7.

x	y
-3	$\frac{9}{2}$
-2	2
-1	$\frac{1}{2}$
0	0

8.

x	y
-1	-2
0	-4
1	-6
2	-8

9.

x	y
-4	-4
-2	-1
0	0
2	-1

10.

x	y
0	-2
1	-8
2	-32
3	-128

11.

x	y
-7	-245
-5	-125
-3	-45
-1	-5

12.

x	y
-2	$\frac{3}{2}$
0	$\frac{1}{2}$
2	$-\frac{1}{2}$
4	$-\frac{3}{2}$

13. $\left(-2, \dfrac{1}{3}\right), \left(-1, \dfrac{1}{3}\right), \left(0, \dfrac{1}{3}\right), \left(1, \dfrac{1}{3}\right), \left(2, \dfrac{1}{3}\right)$

14. $\left(-1, -\dfrac{1}{4}\right), \left(0, -\dfrac{1}{2}\right), (1, -1), (2, -2), (3, -4)$

15. The cost of shipping computers from a warehouse is given in the table below.

Number of Computers	50	75	100	125
Cost (dollars)	1700	2500	3300	4100

   a. Determine which kind of function best models the data.

   b. Write an equation to model the data.

   c. On the basis of your equation, what is the cost of shipping 27 computers?

   d. On the basis of your equation, how many computers could be shipped for $5500?

16. During a scientific experiment, the bacteria count was taken at 5-min intervals. The data shows the count at several time periods during the experiment.

Time Interval	0	1	2	3
Count	110	132	159	190

   a. Determine which kind of function best models the data.

   b. Write an equation to model the data.

   c. On the basis of your equation, what is the count 1 hr, 45 min after the start of the experiment?

10-8 • Guided Problem Solving

GPS **Student Page 602, Exercise 17**

Population The table at the right shows the world population in millions from 1980 to 2000. The year $t = 0$ corresponds to 1980.

Year	Population (millions)
0	4457
5	4855
10	5284
15	5691
20	6080

SOURCES: U. S. Census Bureau.
Go to **www.PHSchool.com**
for a data update.

a. What is the difference in years?
b. Find the differences of consecutive terms. Divide by the differences in years to find possible common differences.
c. Find the average of the common differences you found in part (b).
d. Write a linear equation to model the data based on your answer to part (c).
e. Use your equation to predict the world population in 2010.

Read and Understand

1. Describe the information given in the table. _____

_____

2. What are the three types of models that could be used? _____

_____

Plan and Solve

3. What is the difference in years? _____

4. Find the differences of consecutive terms. Divide by
   the differences in years to find possible common differences. _____

5. Find the average of the common differences you found in Step 4. _____

6. Write a linear equation to model the data based on your answer in Step 5. _____

7. Use your equation to predict the world population in 2010. _____

Look Back and Check

8. Test the accuracy of your equation by checking to see if it gives a reasonable population for year 5 and year 15 in your table.

Solve Another Problem

9. Write an exponential equation to model the data in the table. _____

10A: Graphic Organizer

For use before Lesson 10-1

Study Skill To help remember formulas and other important information, use a mnemonic. A mnemonic is a memory device to help us associate new information with something familiar. For example, to remember a formula or equation, change it into something meaningful. To remember the metric terms kilo, hecto, deka, deci, centi, and milli in order, use the first letter of each metric term to represent a word, such as *k*angaroo *h*ops *d*own, *d*rinking *c*hocolate *m*ilk. The key is to create your own; then you won't forget them.

Write your answers.

1. What is the chapter title? _____

2. Find the Table of Contents page for this chapter at the front of the book. Name four topics you will study in this chapter.

   _____   _____

   _____   _____

3. Complete the graphic organizer as you work through the chapter.
   1. Write the title of the chapter in the center oval.
   2. When you begin a lesson, write the name of the lesson in a rectangle.
   3. When you complete that lesson, write a skill or key concept from that lesson in the outer oval linked to that rectangle.
   Continue with steps 2 and 3 clockwise around the graphic organizer.

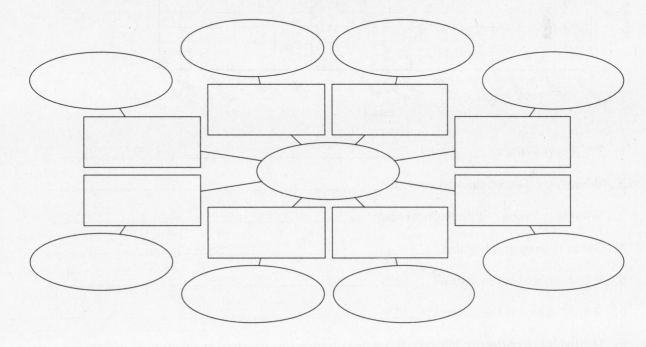

10B: Reading Comprehension

For use after Lesson 10-4

Study Skill Many mathematical applications are related to graphs. Many times you are required to interpret information given in graphs. Being able to identify the specific parts of a graph will help you to answer questions regarding the graph.

In Exercises 1–6, refer to the graph shown below.

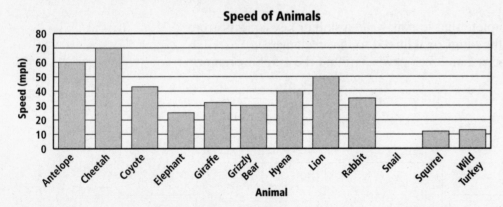

1. What is the title of the graph? _____

2. What is the title of the vertical axis? _____

3. What is the range of the vertical scale? _____

4. What type of graph is this? _____

5. Which animal is the fastest? _____

6. Which animal is the slowest? _____

7. **High-Use Academic Words** What does it mean to *interpret* as mentioned in the study skill?

   a. understand   **b.** verify

10C: Reading/Writing Math Symbols   For use after Lesson 10-6

Study Skill When interpreting mathematical statements, be sure you use the correct words or symbols. Check your written or numerical expressions to make sure you wrote the correct symbols or words.

The graphs below represent the solutions of different linear systems. Some are equations and some are inequalities. The graphs intersect, are parallel, or coincide. Match the graphs with the appropriate system, without actually graphing the systems, by looking for symbols and other indicators (such as slopes and *y*-intercepts).

1. $\begin{cases} x + y = 4 \\ 2x - y = 2 \end{cases}$

A.

2. $\begin{cases} 3x - 2y = -2 \\ 3x - 2y = 6 \end{cases}$

B.

3. $\begin{cases} 2x - 4y \geq 4 \\ x + y < 0 \end{cases}$

C.

4. $\begin{cases} x + y \geq 2 \\ x - y \leq 1 \end{cases}$

D.

10D: Visual Vocabulary Practice

For use after Lesson 10-8

Study Skill Math symbols give us a way to express complex ideas in a small space.

Concept List

completing the square	discriminant	exponential function
factor	linear function	parabola
perfect square trinomial	quadratic formula	Zero-Product Property

Write the concept that best describes each exercise. Choose from the concept list above.

1. $x = \dfrac{-b \pm \sqrt{b^2 - 4ac}}{2a}$ _____	**2.** $y = mx + b$ _____	**3.** $x^2 - 5x - 14$ $(x - 7)(x + 2)$ _____
4. $y = a \cdot b^x$ _____	**5.** _____	**6.** $x^2 - 12x + n$ $x^2 - 12x + 36$ $(x - 6)^2$ _____
7. For every real number a and b, if $ab = 0$ then $a = 0$ or $b = 0$. _____	**8.** $4x^2 - 4x + 1$ _____	**9.** $b^2 - 4ac$ _____

10E: Vocabulary Check

Study Skill Strengthen your vocabulary. Use these pages and add cues and summaries by applying the Cornell Notetaking style.

Write the definition for each word at the right. To check your work, fold the paper back along the dotted line to see the correct answers.

_____

_____

_____

Quadratic function

_____

_____

Axis of Symmetry

_____

_____

Vertex

_____

_____

_____

Standard form of a quadratic equation

_____

_____

Zeros of a quadratic function

_____

_____

10E: Vocabulary Check (continued)

Write the vocabulary word for each definition. To check your work, fold
the paper forward along the dotted line to see the correct answers.

A function that can be
written in the form
$y = ax^2 + bx + c$.

_____

The fold or line that
divides a curve into
two matching halves.

_____

The highest or lowest
point of a parabola.

_____

A quadratic equation
written in the form
$ax^2 + bx + c = 0$.

_____

The solutions of the
quadratic equation.

_____

10F: Vocabulary Review

Study Skill When taking notes, make your original notes as easy to read as possible. The amount of time needed to interpret messy notes would be better spent rereading and thinking about them.

Fill in the blanks with the word(s) that best completes the sentence.

1. The function $y = ax^2 + bx + c$ is a _____ function.

2. The function $Ax + By = C$ is written in _____ form.

3. The _____ of a monomial is the sum of the exponents of its variables.

4. When solving a system of linear equations by graphing, any point where all the lines intersect is the _____.

5. A term that has no variable is known as a _____.

6. The "fold" or line that divides a curve into two matching halves is called the _____.

7. The expression $b^2 - 4ac$ is known as the _____.

8. The _____ of a line is its rate of vertical change over horizontal change.

9. The equation $4(5 - 2 + 3) = 4(5) - 4(2) + 4(3)$ represents the _____ property.

10. A relation that assigns exactly one value in the range to each value in the domain is called a _____.

11. Two or more linear equations together form a _____.

12. When a parabola opens upward, the y-coordinate of the vertex is a _____ value of the function.

13. The point at which a parabola intersects the axis of symmetry is called the _____.

Practice 11-1

Simplifying Radicals

Simplify each radical expression.

1. $\sqrt{32}$ 2. $\sqrt{22} \cdot \sqrt{8}$ 3. $\sqrt{147}$ 4. $\sqrt{\dfrac{17}{144}}$ 5. $\sqrt{a^2 b^5}$

6. $\dfrac{2}{\sqrt{6}}$ 7. $\sqrt{80}$ 8. $\sqrt{27}$ 9. $\dfrac{\sqrt{256}}{\sqrt{32}}$ 10. $\dfrac{8}{\sqrt{7}}$

11. $\sqrt{12x^4}$ 12. $\dfrac{\sqrt{96}}{\sqrt{12}}$ 13. $\sqrt{200}$ 14. $\sqrt{\dfrac{12}{225}}$ 15. $\sqrt{15} \cdot \sqrt{6}$

16. $\sqrt{120}$ 17. $\dfrac{4}{\sqrt{2a}}$ 18. $\left(3\sqrt{2}\right)^3$ 19. $\sqrt{250}$ 20. $\dfrac{\sqrt{65}}{\sqrt{13}}$

21. $\sqrt{84}$ 22. $\sqrt{\dfrac{18}{225}}$ 23. $\sqrt{48s^3}$ 24. $3\sqrt{24}$ 25. $\sqrt{15} \cdot \sqrt{35}$

26. $\sqrt{160}$ 27. $\dfrac{6}{\sqrt{3}}$ 28. $\dfrac{\sqrt{48n^6}}{\sqrt{6n^3}}$ 29. $\sqrt{136}$ 30. $\sqrt{\dfrac{27x^2}{256}}$

31. $\sqrt{m^3 n^2}$ 32. $\dfrac{\sqrt{180}}{\sqrt{9}}$ 33. $\sqrt{18} \cdot \sqrt{8}$ 34. $\left(10\sqrt{3}\right)^2$ 35. $\sqrt{\dfrac{17}{64}}$

36. $\sqrt{50}$ 37. $\sqrt{48}$ 38. $\sqrt{20}$ 39. $\sqrt{8}$ 40. $\sqrt{25x^2}$

41. $\sqrt{\dfrac{7}{9}}$ 42. $\sqrt{\dfrac{13}{81}}$ 43. $\dfrac{\sqrt{48}}{\sqrt{8}}$ 44. $\dfrac{\sqrt{120}}{\sqrt{10}}$ 45. $\dfrac{5}{\sqrt{2}}$

46. $\sqrt{75}$ 47. $\sqrt{300}$ 48. $\sqrt{49a^3}$ 49. $\sqrt{125}$ 50. $\sqrt{28x^4}$

51. $\dfrac{7}{\sqrt{3}}$ 52. $\sqrt{\dfrac{15}{49}}$ 53. $\dfrac{\sqrt{60}}{\sqrt{12}}$ 54. $\dfrac{3}{\sqrt{3}}$ 55. $\dfrac{4}{\sqrt{8}}$

56. $\sqrt{72x^3}$ 57. $\sqrt{50y^3}$ 58. $\sqrt{45x^2 y^3}$ 59. $\sqrt{\dfrac{44x^3}{9x}}$ 60. $\dfrac{\sqrt{4}}{\sqrt{3x}}$

61. $6\sqrt{20}$ 62. $\sqrt{ab^3}$ 63. $\sqrt{a^5 b^6}$ 64. $12\sqrt{60x^2}$ 65. $\left(2\sqrt{3}\right)^2$

66. $\sqrt{12} \cdot \sqrt{27}$ 67. $\left(7\sqrt{5}\right)^2$ 68. $\sqrt{14} \cdot \sqrt{8}$ 69. $\left(5\sqrt{5}\right)^2$ 70. $\sqrt{8x^6 y^7}$

71. $\sqrt{16a^3} \cdot \sqrt{5a^2}$ 72. $\sqrt{8} \cdot \sqrt{7}$ 73. $\sqrt{3x} \cdot \sqrt{5x}$ 74. $2\sqrt{5} \cdot 2\sqrt{5}$

75. $4\sqrt{3} \cdot 2\sqrt{2}$ 76. $6\sqrt{3} \cdot 7\sqrt{8}$ 77. $\dfrac{10}{\sqrt{x}}$ 78. $\dfrac{\sqrt{9}}{\sqrt{2x}}$

79. $\dfrac{4}{\sqrt{20}}$ 80. $\dfrac{\sqrt{12x}}{\sqrt{27x}}$ 81. $\dfrac{3\sqrt{7}}{\sqrt{20x}}$ 82. $\dfrac{4\sqrt{5}}{\sqrt{8y}}$

Name_____ Class_____ Date_____

11-1 • Guided Problem Solving

A square picture on the front page of a newspaper occupies an area of 24 in.^{2}.

  a. Find the length of each side in simplest radical form.
  b. Calculate the length of each side to the nearest hundredth of an inch.

Read and Understand

1. What formula will you use to find the area of a square? _____

2. What is simplest radical form? _____

Plan and Solve

3. Draw a picture to illustrate this situation.

4. Label the picture with the given information and identify the unknown.

5. Write and solve an equation that relates the side length and area.

6. Find the length of each side in simplest radical form. _____

7. Calculate the length of each side to the nearest hundredth of an inch. _____

Look Back and Check

8. Verify the reasonableness of your answers in Steps 6 and 7 by squaring each answer to see if the area is 24 in.^{2}. Explain why the square of your decimal answer in Step 7 is not exactly 24 in.^{2}.

   _____

   _____

Solve Another Problem

9. The area of a square puzzle is 120 cm^2. What is the length of a side? _____

Practice 11-2

Simplify each expression.

1. $3\sqrt{7} + 5\sqrt{7}$

2. $10\sqrt{4} - \sqrt{4}$

3. $4\sqrt{2}(2 + 2\sqrt{3})$

4. $\sqrt{45} + 2\sqrt{5}$

5. $12\sqrt{11} + 7\sqrt{11}$

6. $\sqrt{2}(2\sqrt{3} - 4\sqrt{2})$

7. $\sqrt{28} + \sqrt{63}$

8. $3\sqrt{6} - 8\sqrt{6}$

9. $\sqrt{3}(\sqrt{6} - \sqrt{12})$

10. $\sqrt{18} - \sqrt{50}$

11. $4\sqrt{2} + 2\sqrt{8}$

12. $13\sqrt{15} - 11\sqrt{15}$

13. $3(8\sqrt{3} - 7)$

14. $8(2\sqrt{5} + 5\sqrt{2})$

15. $17\sqrt{21} - 12\sqrt{21}$

16. $\sqrt{6}(7 + 3\sqrt{3})$

17. $8(4 - 3\sqrt{2})$

18. $2\sqrt{12} + 6\sqrt{27}$

19. $19\sqrt{3} + \sqrt{12}$

20. $8\sqrt{26} + 10\sqrt{26}$

21. $\sqrt{10}(3 - 2\sqrt{6})$

22. $9\sqrt{2} - \sqrt{50}$

23. $10\sqrt{13} - 7\sqrt{13}$

24. $12\sqrt{6} - 4\sqrt{24}$

25. $5\sqrt{7} + \sqrt{28}$

26. $8\sqrt{13} - 12\sqrt{13}$

27. $13\sqrt{40} + 6\sqrt{10}$

28. $-3\sqrt{3}(\sqrt{6} + \sqrt{3})$

29. $12\sqrt{29} - 15\sqrt{29}$

30. $10\sqrt{6} - 2\sqrt{6}$

31. $8\sqrt{3} - \sqrt{75}$

32. $3\sqrt{6}(2\sqrt{3} + \sqrt{6})$

33. $17\sqrt{35} + 2\sqrt{35}$

34. $\sqrt{19} + 4\sqrt{19}$

35. $12\sqrt{9} - 4\sqrt{9}$

36. $\sqrt{8}(\sqrt{2} - 7)$

37. $\dfrac{1}{\sqrt{2} - \sqrt{3}}$

38. $\dfrac{5}{\sqrt{7} - \sqrt{3}}$

39. $\dfrac{3}{\sqrt{5} + 5}$

40. $(\sqrt{6} - 3)^2$

41. $(3\sqrt{5} + \sqrt{5})^2$

42. $\dfrac{7}{\sqrt{2} - \sqrt{7}}$

43. $\dfrac{3 - \sqrt{6}}{5 - 2\sqrt{6}}$

44. $\dfrac{-12}{\sqrt{6} - 3}$

45. $\dfrac{2\sqrt{3} - \sqrt{6}}{5\sqrt{3} + 2\sqrt{6}}$

Solve each exercise by using the golden ratio $(1 + \sqrt{5}) : 2$.

46. The ratio of the height : width of a window is equal to the golden ratio. The width of the door is 36 in. Find the height of the door. Express your answer in simplest radical form and in inches.

47. The ratio of the length : width of a flower garden is equal to the golden ratio. The width of the garden is 14 ft. Find the length of the garden. Express your answer is simplest radical form and in feet.

48. The ratio of the width : height of the front side of a building is equal to the golden ratio. The height of the building is 40 ft. Find the width of the building. Express your answer in simplest radical form and in feet.

11-2 • Guided Problem Solving

GPS **Student Page 626, Exercise 54**

You can make a box kite like the one at the right in the shape of a rectangular solid. The opening at each end of the kite is a square.

a. Suppose the sides of the square are 2 ft long. How long are the diagonal struts used for bracing?

b. Suppose each side of the square has length s. Find the length of the diagonal struts in terms of s. Write your answer in simplest form.

Read and Understand

1. What information are you given in the problem? _____

2. What relationship is there between the side lengths and the diagonal? _____

Plan and Solve

3. Write and solve an equation that relates the side lengths of the square and the diagonal.

_____

4. How long are the diagonal struts used for bracing? _____

5. If each side of the square has length s, find the length of the diagonal struts in terms of s^2. _____

6. Write your answer from Step 5 in simplest form. _____

Look Back and Check

7. Substitute the answer you found for the length of the diagonal struts into the equation you used in step 3 to check the reasonableness of your answer.

_____

Solve Another Problem

8. A diagonal board is used to brace a wall that measures 8 ft by 8 ft. How long must the board be?

_____

Practice 11-3

Solve each radical equation. Check your solutions. If there is no solution, write *no solution*.

1. $\sqrt{x} + 3 = 11$ **2.** $\sqrt{x + 2} = \sqrt{3x - 6}$ **3.** $x = \sqrt{24 - 10x}$

4. $\sqrt{4x} - 7 = 1$ **5.** $\sqrt{x} = \sqrt{4x - 12}$ **6.** $x = \sqrt{11x - 28}$

7. $\sqrt{x} = 12$ **8.** $x = \sqrt{12x - 32}$ **9.** $x = \sqrt{13x - 40}$

10. $\sqrt{3x + 5} = \sqrt{x + 1}$ **11.** $\sqrt{x + 3} = 5$ **12.** $\sqrt{6x - 4} = \sqrt{4x + 6}$

13. $2 = \sqrt{x + 6}$ **14.** $x = \sqrt{2 - x}$ **15.** $\sqrt{4x + 2} = \sqrt{x + 14}$

16. $\sqrt{x} + 8 = 9$ **17.** $x = \sqrt{7x + 8}$ **18.** $\sqrt{3x + 8} = \sqrt{2x + 12}$

19. $\sqrt{2x + 3} = 5$ **20.** $\sqrt{3x + 13} = \sqrt{7x - 3}$ **21.** $x = \sqrt{6 + 5x}$

22. $\sqrt{3x} - 5 = 4$ **23.** $\sqrt{3x + 4} = \sqrt{5x}$ **24.** $x = \sqrt{x - 12}$

25. $\sqrt{x - 4} + 3 = 9$ **26.** $x = \sqrt{8x + 20}$ **27.** $12 = \sqrt{6x}$

28. $x = \sqrt{60 - 7x}$ **29.** $\sqrt{x + 14} = \sqrt{6x - 1}$ **30.** $\sqrt{5x - 7} = \sqrt{6x + 11}$

31. $7 + \sqrt{2x} = 3$ **32.** $\sqrt{x + 56} = x$ **33.** $5 + \sqrt{x + 4} = 12$

34. The equation $d = \frac{1}{2}at^2$ gives the distance d in ft that an object travels from rest while accelerating, where a is the acceleration and t is the time.

    a. How far has an object traveled in 4 s when the acceleration is 5 ft/s^2?

    b. How long does it take an object to travel 100 ft when the acceleration is 8 ft/s^2?

35. The equation $v = 20\sqrt{t + 273}$ relates the speed v, in m/s, to the air temperature t in Celsius degrees.

    a. Find the temperature when the speed of sound is 340 m/s.

    b. Find the temperature when the speed of sound is 320 m/s.

36. The equation $V = \sqrt{\frac{Fr}{m}}$ gives the speed V in m/s of an object moving in a horizontal circle, where F is centripetal force, r is radius, and m is mass of the object.

    a. Find r when $F = 6$ N, $m = 2$ kg, and $V = 3$ m/s.

    b. Find F when $r = 1$ m, $m = 3$ kg, and $V = 2$ m/s.

11-3 • Guided Problem Solving

GPS Student Page 633, Exercise 44

The equation $v = 8\sqrt{h - 2r}$ gives the velocity v in feet per second of a car at the top of the loop of a roller coaster.

a. Find the radius of the loop when the hill is 150 ft high and the velocity of the car is 30 ft/sec.

b. Find the approximate speed in mi/h for 30 ft/sec. (*Hint:* 1 mi = 5280 ft)

c. **Critical Thinking** Would you expect the velocity of the car to increase or decrease as the radius of the loop increases? As the height of the hill decreases?

d. Explain your reasoning for your answer in part (c).

Read and Understand

1. What information is given to you in the problem? _____

2. What do the variables v, h, and r represent? _____

Plan and Solve

3. Which variable will you be solving for initially? _____

4. Write the formula with numbers substituted for the two variables. _____

5. Solve your equation for r. _____

6. Find the approximate speed in mi/h for 30 ft/sec. _____

7. Would you expect the velocity of the car to increase or decrease as the radius of the loop increases? _____

8. Would you expect the velocity of the car to increase or decrease as the height of the hill decreases? _____

9. Explain your reasoning in your answer for Step 7 and Step 8. _____

_____

Look Back and Check

10. Does your speed in mi/h in Step 6 seem reasonable? Explain. _____

_____

Solve Another Problem

11. What is the height if the velocity of the car is 40 ft/s and the radius is 90 ft? _____

Guided Problem Solving

Practice 11-4

Graphing Square Root Functions

Find the domain of each function.

1. $f(x) = \sqrt{x - 7}$ **2.** $f(x) = \sqrt{3x - 12}$ **3.** $y = \sqrt{4x + 11}$

4. $y = \sqrt{x - 12}$ **5.** $f(x) = \sqrt{x + 14}$ **6.** $y = \sqrt{x + 8}$

7. $y = \sqrt{5x + 13}$ **8.** $y = \sqrt{2x}$ **9.** $y = \sqrt{6x}$

Make a table of values and graph each function.

10. $y = \sqrt{x} - 12$ **11.** $y = 3\sqrt{x}$ **12.** $y = \sqrt{x + 8}$

13. $y = \sqrt{x + 7} - 6$ **14.** $y = \sqrt{x - 6} - 8$ **15.** $y = \sqrt{x - 10}$

16. $y = 2\sqrt{x - 2}$ **17.** $y = \sqrt{x - 8} + 6$ **18.** $y = \sqrt{x} + 7$

Describe how to translate the graph of $y = \sqrt{x}$ to obtain the graph of each function.

19. $y = \sqrt{x} - 9$ **20.** $y = \sqrt{x} - 8$ **21.** $y = \sqrt{x + 20}$

22. $y = \sqrt{x - 19}$ **23.** $y = \sqrt{x + 18}$ **24.** $y = \sqrt{x - 32}$

25. $y = \sqrt{x} + 11$ **26.** $y = \sqrt{x + 14}$ **27.** $y = \sqrt{x - 4} - 7$

28. The number of people involved in recycling in a community is modeled by the function $n = 90\sqrt{3t} + 400$, where t is the number of months the recycling plant has been open.

     a. Graph the function.

     b. Find the number of people recycling when the plant has been open for 6 mo.

     c. Find the month when about 670 people were recycling.

29. The time t, in seconds, that it takes for an object to drop a distance d, in feet, is modeled by the function $t = \sqrt{\frac{d}{16}}$. Assume no air resistance.

     a. Graph the function.

     b. Find the time it takes for an object to fall 1000 ft.

     c. How far does an object fall in 10 s?

11-4 • Guided Problem Solving

GPS **Student Page 642, Exercise 55**

Business Last year a store had an advertising campaign. The graph shows the sales for single-use cameras. The function $n = 27\sqrt{5t} + 53$ models the sales volume n for the cameras as a function of time t, the number of months after the start of the advertising campaign.

Single-Use Camera Sales

a. Evaluate the function to find how many disposable cameras the store sold in the seventh month.

b. Solve an equation to find the month in which the number of single-use cameras sold was about 175.

Read and Understand

1. Describe the information in the graph. _____

2. Explain what the formula describes. _____

_____

Plan and Solve

3. Write the equation you will use to determine how many disposable cameras the store sold in the seventh month.

_____

4. Simplify your function from Step 3 to determine the number of cameras. _____

5. Write the equation you will solve to determine the month in which the number of single-use cameras sold was about 175.

_____

6. Solve your equation in Step 5. _____

Look Back and Check

7. Check the reasonableness of your answers in Steps 4 and 6 by estimating the answers to both questions by reading the graph.

_____

Solve Another Problem

8. The advertising campaign was so successful it was extended an extra six months. Evaluate the function to see how many cameras were sold after 18 months. _____

Guided Problem Solving

Practice 11-5

Trigonometric Ratios

Use △ABC at the right. Find the value of each expression.

1. sin A   **2.** cos A   **3.** tan A

4. sin B   **5.** cos B   **6.** tan B

Find the value of each expression. Round to the nearest ten-thousandth.

7. tan 59°   **8.** sin 75°   **9.** sin 8°   **10.** cos 13°   **11.** sin 32°

12. tan 67°   **13.** cos 17°   **14.** cos 36°   **15.** tan 19°   **16.** cos 58°

Find the value of x to the nearest tenth.

17.   **18.**

19.   **20.**

21.   **22.**

Use △PQR at the right. Find the value of each expression.

23. sin P   **24.** cos P   **25.** tan P

26. sin R   **27.** cos R   **28.** tan R

29. A 12-ft-long guy wire is attached to a telephone pole 10.5 ft from the top of the pole. If the wire forms a 52° angle with the ground, how high is the telephone pole?

11-5 • Guided Problem Solving

GPS Student Page 649, Exercise 30

Find the value of the variable in the figure below to the nearest tenth.

Read and Understand

1. What information is given to you in the picture? _____

   _____

2. What are the trigonometric ratios that can be used in a right triangle? _____

Plan and Solve

3. Write an equation you will use to solve for p. _____

4. Solve your equation for p. _____

Look Back and Check

5. Explain why the tangent ratio is used for this problem.

   _____

   _____

Solve Another Problem

6. In right triangle ABC, the hypotenuse measures 29 cm, $m\angle A = 15°$.
   How long are the other two sides of the triangle?

   _____

   _____

Practice 11-6

1. A tree casts a shadow that is 20 ft long. The angle of elevation of the sun is 29°. How tall is the tree?

2. Suppose your angle of elevation to the top of a water tower is 78°. If the water tower is 145 ft tall, how far are you standing from the water tower?

3. The angle of elevation from the control tower to an airplane is 49°. The airplane is flying at 5000 ft. How far away from the control tower is the plane?

4. A Boy Scout on top of a 1700-ft-tall mountain spots a campsite. If he measures the angle of depression at 35°, how far is the campsite from the foot of the mountain?

5. A 100-foot kite string makes a 35° angle of elevation to the ground. How high is the kite?

6. A soccer ball is placed 12 ft away from a goal post that measures 8 ft high. You kick the ball and it hits the crossbar at the top of the goal. What was the angle of elevation of your kick?

7. You are standing 10 ft away from a tree. The angle of elevation from your foot to the top of the tree is 65°. How tall is the tree?

11-6 • Guided Problem Solving

GPS Student Page 652, Exercise 8

Hobbies Suppose you are flying a kite. The kite string is 60 m long, and the angle of elevation of the string is 65° from your hand. Your hand is 1 m above the ground. How high above the ground is the kite?

Read and Understand

1. Draw and label a picture that illustrates this situation.

2. In your picture use a variable to label the distance the kite is above the ground.

Plan and Solve

3. What trigonometric function can be used to solve this problem? _____

4. Write and solve an equation to determine the side of your right triangle. _____

5. How high above the ground is the kite? _____

Look Back and Check

6. Explain why the side of your right triangle is not the distance the kite is above the ground.

_____

_____

Solve Another Problem

7. A tree casts a shadow that is 50 ft long. At this time of day, the angle of elevation to the sun is 20°. How tall is the tree?

_____

Guided Problem Solving

11A: Graphic Organizer

For use before Lesson 11-1

Study Skill After reading a section, recall the information. Ask yourself questions about the section. If you cannot recall enough information reread portions you had trouble remembering. The more time you spend studying the more you can recall.

Write your answers.

1. What is the chapter title? _____

2. Find the Table of Contents page for this chapter at the front of the book. Name four topics you will study in this chapter.

   _____   _____

   _____   _____

3. Complete the graphic organizer as you work through the chapter.
   1. Write the title of the chapter in the center oval.
   2. When you begin a lesson, write the name of the lesson in a rectangle.
   3. When you complete that lesson, write a skill or key concept from that lesson in the outer oval linked to that rectangle.
   Continue with steps 2 and 3 clockwise around the graphic organizer.

11B: Reading Comprehension

For use after Lesson 11-3

Study Skill Diagrams of three-dimensional objects have solid lines and dashed lines. The dashed lines are the ones that would be hidden from view if you were to look at the object from the perspective that has been drawn.

Answer the question about each figure to practice extracting and deducing information from diagrams.

1. **a.** What is the shape of the base of the figure?

   _____

   b. If you make a slice through the figure from the top of the figure through the center of the base, what is the shape of the slice?

   _____

   c. What figure is formed by the height of the cone, the radius of the base, and the "slant height" of the cone (the distance *PQ*)?

   _____

   d. How is the slant height of the cone related to the height of the cone and the radius of its base?

   _____

   _____

   _____

2. Assume that the length of the side of the cube is known.

   a. Is it possible to find the length of diagonal *k*? _____

   Explain.

   _____

   b. Is it possible to find the length of diagonal *d*? _____

   Explain. _____

   _____

   _____

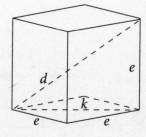

3. **High-Use Academic Words** What does *deducing* mean in the direction line?

   a. observe what is given

   b. figure out by using the given information with other knowledge

11C: Reading/Writing Math Symbols For use after Lesson 11-5

Study Skill When you take notes in any subject, it helps if you learn to use abbreviations and symbols such as @ (at); #, #s (number, numbers); w/ (with); w/o (without); s/b (should be).

Match each written expression or statement in Column A with its symbolic form in Column B by drawing a line between them.

Column A		Column B
1.	eight times x equals 40	**A.** $w \div 6$
2.	the square root of xy	**B.** $8x = 40$
3.	x divided by y	**C.** x^2y^4
4.	the square root of the quantity x plus 4 equals 3	**D.** $5 \le 8$
5.	5 is less than or equal to 8	**E.** $\frac{x}{y}$
6.	x squared y to the fourth power	**F.** $\sqrt{xy}$
7.	w divided into 6 equal parts	**G.** $\sqrt{x+4} = 3$

Match each written expression or statement in Column C with its symbolic form in Column D by drawing a line between them.

Column C		Column D
8.	the quantity x plus four, cubed	**A.** $\frac{1}{3}x$
9.	2 less than 4 times a number	**B.** $8 > 5$
10.	one-third of a number x	**C.** $4x - 2$
11.	three plus x	**D.** $(x + 4)^2$
12.	eight is greater than 5	**E.** $2x^2 - 3y$
13.	two times x squared minus three times y	**F.** $3 + x$
14.	the quantity x plus four, squared	**G.** $(x + 4)^3$

11D: Visual Vocabulary Practice

For use after Lesson 11-6

Study Skill As you master more vocabulary, more concepts are within your reach.

Concept List

angle of elevation	cosine	Division Property of Square Roots
like radicals	radical equation	sine
square root function	tangent	trigonometric ratios

Write the concept that best describes each exercise. Choose from the concept list above.

1. $3\sqrt{2}$ and $5\sqrt{2}$	**2.** $\dfrac{\text{opposite leg}}{\text{hypotenuse}}$	**3.** sine, cosine, tangent
4. $\dfrac{\text{adjacent}}{\text{hypotenuse}}$	**5.** $y = \sqrt{2x + 5}$	**6.** $\sqrt{x + 7} = 5$
7. For every number $a \geq 0$ and $b > 0$, $\sqrt{\dfrac{a}{b}} = \dfrac{\sqrt{a}}{\sqrt{b}}$.	**8.** an angle from the horizontal up to a line of sight	**9.** $\dfrac{\text{opposite leg}}{\text{adjacent leg}}$

11E: Vocabulary Check

Study Skill Strengthen your vocabulary. Use these pages and add cues and summaries by applying the Cornell Notetaking style.

Write the definition for each word at the right. To check your work, fold the paper back along the dotted line to see the correct answers.

_____

_____

Radical expression

_____

_____

Rationalize

_____

_____

Unlike radicals

_____

_____

Conjugates

_____

_____

Extraneous solution

Vocabulary and Study Skills

11E: Vocabulary Check (continued)

Write the vocabulary word for each definition. To check your work, fold the paper forward along the dotted line to see the correct answers.

An expression that contains a radical.

_____

Rewrite as a rational number. It may be necessary to obtain the simplest radical form.

_____

Expressions that do not have the same radicand.

_____

The sum and difference of the same two terms.

_____

A solution that does not satisfy the original equations.

_____

11F: Vocabulary Review Puzzle

For use with Chapter Review

Study Skill When you read, your eyes make small stops along a line of words. Good readers make fewer stops when they read. The more stops you make when you read, the harder it is for you to comprehend what you've read. Try to concentrate and free yourself of distractions as you read.

Complete the crossword puzzle.

Choose a word from the list below for each of the clues.

binomial	converse	cosine	discriminant
extraneous	hypotenuse	leg	midpoint
parabola	polynomial	radical equation	radicand
rationalize	sine	tangent	vertex

ACROSS	DOWN
1. the sum or difference of two or more monomials	**1.** the graph of a quadratic function
4. the expression under the radical sign	**2.** reversing the *if and then* parts of a statement
8. a polynomial with two terms	**3.** multiplying the numerator and denominator by the same radical expression to simplify the denominator
11. a type of equation with a variable in the radicand	**5.** the highest or lowest point of a parabola
13. the expression under the radical sign in the quadratic formula	**6.** divides a segment into two equal segments
14. opposite side over hypotenuse	**7.** a solution that does not satisfy the original equation
15. side opposite the right angle in a right triangle	**9.** each of the sides forming the right angle of a triangle
	10. adjacent side over hypotenuse
	12. opposite side over adjacent side

Practice 12-1

Describe the graph of each function.

1. $f(x) = x^2 - 4$

2. $y = \frac{5}{x} - 1$

3. $y = \frac{3}{x}$

4. $g(x) = \sqrt{x + 2} - 1$

5. $y = -8x + 2$

6. $h(x) = 3x^2 - 4x + 1$

7. $h(x) = |2x + 7|$

8. $y = 0.2^x$

9. $y = \frac{x}{4}$

10. In an electric circuit the resistance R, in ohms, increases when the current I, in amps, in the circuit decreases. The function $R = \frac{1000}{I^2}$ relates the resistance to the current.

    a. What is the resistance when the current is 4 amps?

    b. What is the resistance when the current is 20 amps?

    c. What is the resistance when the current is 10 amps?

11. Light intensity decreases as you move farther away from the source of light. The function $I = \frac{12{,}000}{d^2}$ relates the light intensity I, in lumens, to the distance d, in feet, from the light source.

    a. What is the light intensity 2 ft away from the light source?

    b. What is the light intensity 8 ft away from the light source?

    c. What is the light intensity 25 ft away from the light source?

12. In a cylinder of constant volume, the height increases as the radius decreases. The function $h = \frac{360}{r^2}$ relates the height of the cylinder to the radius of the cylinder.

    a. What is the height of the cylinder when the radius is 5 m?

    b. What is the height of the cylinder when the radius is 12 m?

What value of x makes the denominator of each function equal to zero?

13. $y = \frac{5}{2x - 8}$

14. $y = \frac{12}{x}$

15. $y = \frac{5}{x + 7}$

16. $y = \frac{5x}{4x - 10}$

17. $y = \frac{7x}{x + 3}$

18. $y = \frac{3}{x - 8}$

19. $y = \frac{6}{5x - 6}$

20. $y = \frac{9x}{3x + 5}$

Identify the vertical asymptote of each function. Then graph the function.

21. $y = \frac{2}{x}$

22. $y = \frac{2}{x - 1}$

23. $y = \frac{1}{x + 4}$

24. $y = \frac{2}{x} + 3$

25. $y = \frac{-2}{x + 6}$

26. $y = \frac{2x}{x - 6}$

27. $y = \frac{x + 3}{x - 2}$

28. $y = \frac{3}{x - 1} - 3$

12-1 • Guided Problem Solving

GPS **Student Page 669, Exercise 53**

Light In the formula $I = \dfrac{445}{x^2}$, I is the intensity of light in lumens at a distance x feet from a light bulb with 445 watts. What is the intensity of light 5 ft from the light bulb? 15 ft from the light bulb?

Read and Understand

1. Explain what each variable in the equation represents. _____

2. What information in the problem will not be used? _____

Plan and Solve

3. Write the equation that you will use to find the intensity of light 5 ft away from the light bulb.

   _____

4. Solve your equation in Step 3. _____

5. Write the equation that you will use to find the intensity of light 15 ft away from the light bulb.

   _____

6. Solve your equation in Step 5. _____

Look Back and Check

7. Should the intensity of the light increase or decrease as the distance from the light bulb increases? Check the reasonableness of your answer by seeing if this is true. _____

Solve Another Problem

8. How far away from the light bulb are you if the intensity is 10 lumens? _____

Practice 12-2

Simplify each expression.

1. $\dfrac{6x^4}{18x^2}$

2. $\dfrac{15a^2}{25a^4}$

3. $\dfrac{32h^3}{48h^2}$

4. $\dfrac{12n^4}{21n^6}$

5. $\dfrac{3x-6}{6}$

6. $\dfrac{x^2-2x}{x}$

7. $\dfrac{4t^2-2t}{2t}$

8. $\dfrac{a^3-2a^2}{2a^2-4a}$

9. $\dfrac{21x^2y}{14xy^2}$

10. $\dfrac{32x^3y^2}{24xy^4}$

11. $\dfrac{x^2+3x}{3x+9}$

12. $\dfrac{x^2-5x}{5x-25}$

13. $\dfrac{x^2+13x+12}{x^2-144}$

14. $\dfrac{x^2-9}{x^3-3x^2}$

15. $\dfrac{x^3+x^2}{x+1}$

16. $\dfrac{3x-2y}{2y-3x}$

17. $\dfrac{x^2+x-6}{x^2-x-2}$

18. $\dfrac{x^2+3x+2}{x^3+x^2}$

19. $\dfrac{2x^2-8}{x^2-3x+2}$

20. $\dfrac{2x^2-5x+3}{x^2-1}$

21. $\dfrac{3x+3y}{x^2+xy}$

22. $\dfrac{10+3x-x^2}{x^2-4x-5}$

23. $\dfrac{9-x^2}{x^2+x-12}$

24. $\dfrac{x^2+2x-15}{x^2-7x+12}$

25. $\dfrac{x^2+7x-8}{x^2+6x-7}$

26. $\dfrac{x^2+3x-10}{25-x^2}$

27. Write and simplify the ratio $\dfrac{\text{perimeter of rectangle}}{\text{area of rectangle}}$. The perimeter of the rectangle is $10w$ and the area of the rectangle is $4w^2$.

28. The ratio $\dfrac{3 \cdot \text{volume of cone}}{\text{area of base}}$ determines the height of a cone. Find the height when the volume is $4r^3 + 2r^2$ and the area of the base is $6r^2$.

29. The ratio $\dfrac{2 \cdot \text{area of triangle}}{\text{height of triangle}}$ determines the length of the base of a triangle. Find the length of the base when the area is $3n^2 + 6n$ and the height is $2n + 4$.

30. The ratio $\dfrac{\text{volume of rectangular solid}}{\text{area of rectangular base}}$ determines the height of a rectangular solid. Find the height when the volume is $5s^3 + 10s^2$ and the area is $5s^2$.

12-2 • Guided Problem Solving

GPS Student Page 675, Exercise 35

a. **Construction** To keep heating costs down for a structure, architects want the ratio of surface area to volume as small as possible. Find an expression for the ratio of the surface area to volume for each shape.
   i. square prism   **ii.** cylinder

b. Find the ratio for each figure when $b = 12$ ft, $h = 18$ ft, and $r = 6$ ft.

Read and Understand

1. What is the formula for finding the surface area of a prism?

   _____

2. What is the formula for finding the volume of a prism? _____

3. What is the formula for finding the surface area of a cylinder? _____

4. What is the formula for finding the volume of a cylinder? _____

Plan and Solve

5. Write an expression for the surface area of the square prism. _____

6. Write an expression for the volume of the square prism. _____

7. Write an expression for the ratio of surface area to volume for the square prism. _____

8. Write an expression for the surface area of the cylinder. _____

9. Write an expression for the volume of the cylinder. _____

10. Write an expression for the ratio of the surface area to volume for the cylinder. _____

11. Find the ratio for each figure when $b = 12$ ft, $h = 18$ ft, and $r = 6$ ft.

   square prism: _____   cylinder: _____

Look Back and Check

12. Explain why keeping the ratio of surface area to volume as small as possible will help keep heating costs down.

   _____

Solve Another Problem

13. Write an expression for the ratio of surface area to volume for a square prism that has a length and width of 4 and a height of h. _____

Practice 12-3

Multiplying and Dividing Rational Expressions

Multiply or divide.

1. $\dfrac{5}{9} \cdot \dfrac{6}{15}$

2. $\dfrac{8}{3} \div \dfrac{16}{27}$

3. $\left(-\dfrac{3}{4}\right) \div \dfrac{16}{21}$

4. $\dfrac{2}{9} \div \left(-\dfrac{10}{3}\right)$

5. $\dfrac{18m}{4m^2} \div \dfrac{9m}{8}$

6. $\dfrac{8x}{12} \cdot \dfrac{4x}{6}$

7. $\dfrac{9}{15x} \cdot \dfrac{25x}{27}$

8. $\dfrac{12x^3}{25} \div \dfrac{16x}{5}$

9. $\dfrac{6x^3}{18x} \div \dfrac{9x^2}{10x^4}$

10. $\dfrac{4r^3}{10} \cdot \dfrac{25}{16r^2}$

11. $\dfrac{8n^2}{3} \div \dfrac{20n}{9}$

12. $\dfrac{14x^2}{5} \div 7x^4$

13. $\dfrac{4n^3}{11} \cdot \dfrac{33n}{36n^2}$

14. $\dfrac{24r^3}{35r^2} \div \dfrac{12r}{14r^3}$

15. $\dfrac{a^2 - 4}{3} \cdot \dfrac{9}{a + 2}$

16. $\dfrac{4b - 12}{5b^2} \cdot \dfrac{6b}{b - 3}$

17. $\dfrac{2b}{5} \cdot \dfrac{10}{b^2}$

18. $\dfrac{2b}{b + 3} \div \dfrac{b}{b + 3}$

19. $\dfrac{5y^3}{7} \cdot \dfrac{14y}{30y^2}$

20. $\dfrac{4p + 16}{5p} \div \dfrac{p + 4}{15p^3}$

21. $\dfrac{3(h + 2)}{h + 3} \div \dfrac{h + 2}{h + 3}$

22. $\dfrac{a^3 - a^2}{a^3} \cdot \dfrac{a^2}{a - 1}$

23. $\dfrac{h^2 + 6h}{h + 3} \cdot \dfrac{4h + 12}{h + 6}$

24. $\dfrac{n^2 - 1}{n + 2} \cdot \dfrac{n^2 - 4}{n + 1}$

25. $\dfrac{x^2 - x}{x} \cdot \dfrac{3x - 6}{3x - 3}$

26. $\dfrac{5x - 10}{x + 2} \cdot \dfrac{3}{3x - 6}$

27. $\dfrac{x^2 - 16}{x - 4} \div \dfrac{3x + 12}{x}$

28. $\dfrac{x^2 - 1}{3x - 3} \div \dfrac{x + 1}{3}$

29. $\dfrac{x^2 - 2x - 24}{x^2 - 5x - 6} \cdot \dfrac{x^2 + 5x + 6}{x^2 + 6x + 8}$

30. $\dfrac{x^2 + 2x - 35}{x^2 + 4x - 21} \cdot \dfrac{x^2 + 3x - 18}{x^2 + 9x + 18}$

31. $\dfrac{3x^2 + 14x + 8}{2x^2 + 7x - 4} \cdot \dfrac{2x^2 + 9x - 5}{3x^2 + 16x + 5}$

32. $\dfrac{8 + 2x - x^2}{x^2 + 7x + 10} \div \dfrac{x^2 - 11x + 28}{x^2 - x - 42}$

33. $\dfrac{x^2 - x - 6}{3x - 9} \cdot \dfrac{x^2 - 9}{x^2 + 6x + 9}$

34. $\dfrac{6x^2 + 13x + 6}{4x^2 - 9} \div \dfrac{6x^2 + x - 2}{4x^2 - 1}$

35. $\dfrac{x^2 - 2x - 35}{3x^2 + 27x} \div \dfrac{x^2 + 7x + 10}{6x^2 + 12x}$

36. $\dfrac{x^2 - x - 6}{2x^2 + 9x + 10} \div \dfrac{x^2 - 25}{2x^2 + 15x + 25}$

37. $\dfrac{15 - 14x - 8x^2}{4x^2 + 4x - 15} \div \dfrac{4x^2 + 13x - 12}{3x^2 + 13x + 4}$

38. $\dfrac{x^2 - 4x - 32}{x^2 - 8x - 48} \cdot \dfrac{3x^2 + 17x + 10}{3x^2 - 22x - 16}$

39. $\dfrac{9x^2 - 16}{6x^2 - 11x + 4} \div \dfrac{6x^2 + 11x + 4}{8x^2 + 10x + 3}$

40. Two darts are thrown at random onto the large rectangular region shown. Find the probability that both darts will land in the shaded region.

Practice

Algebra 1 Lesson 12-3   **485**

© Pearson Education, Inc., publishing as Pearson Prentice Hall.

All rights reserved.

Name_____ Class_____ Date_____

12-3 • Guided Problem Solving

Student Page 680, Exercise 41

Geometry Find the volume of the rectangular solid.

Read and Understand

1. What information is given to you in the picture? _____

2. How do you find the volume of a rectangular solid? _____

Plan and Solve

3. Write an expression for the volume of the rectangular solid. _____

4. Explain how you can simplify your expression before multiplying. _____

_____

5. What is the final product? _____

Look Back and Check

6. Check the reasonableness of your answer by evaluating your original expression for $x = 2$ and then evaluating your final product for $x = 2$ also.

Solve Another Problem

7. Find the volume of a cube if each edge measures $\dfrac{3x}{6x^2 + 9x}$. _____

Practice 12-4

Divide.

1. $\dfrac{10x - 25}{5}$

2. $\dfrac{4x^3 - 3x}{x}$

3. $(3x^2 - 6x) \div 3x$

4. $(10x^2 - 6x) \div 2x$

5. $(-8x^5 + 16x^4 - 24x^3 + 32x^2) \div 8x^2$

6. $(15x^2 - 30x) \div 5x$

7. $(x^2 - 14x + 49) \div (x - 7)$

8. $(2x^2 - 13x + 21) \div (x - 3)$

9. $(4x^2 - 16) \div (2x + 4)$

10. $(x^2 + 4x - 12) \div (x - 2)$

11. $(x^2 + 10x + 16) \div (x + 2)$

12. $(12x^2 - 5x - 2) \div (3x - 2)$

13. $(x^2 + 5x + 10) \div (x + 2)$

14. $(x^2 - 8x - 9) \div (x - 3)$

15. $(3x^2 - 2x - 13) \div (x - 2)$

16. $(x^3 + 3x^2 + 5x + 3) \div (x + 1)$

17. $(5 - 23x + 12x^2) \div (4x - 1)$

18. $(24 + 6x^2 + 25x) \div (3x - 1)$

19. $(2x^2 + 11x - 5) \div (x + 6)$

20. $(x^2 + 5x - 10) \div (x + 2)$

21. $(8x + 3 + 4x^2) \div (2x - 1)$

22. $(3x^2 + 11x - 4) \div (3x - 1)$

23. $(x^3 + x - x^2 - 1) \div (x - 1)$

24. $(10 + 21x + 10x^2) \div (2x + 3)$

25. $(6x^2 - 35x + 36) \div (3x - 4)$

26. $(-2x^2 - 33x + x^3 - 7) \div (x - 7)$

27. The volume of a rectangular prism is $15x^3 + 38x^2 - 23x - 6$. The height of the prism is $5x + 1$, and the width of the prism is $x + 3$. Find the length of the prism.

28. The width of a rectangle is $x + 1$, and the area is $x^3 + 2x^2 - 5x - 6$ cm. What is the length of the rectangle?

12-4 • Guided Problem Solving

GPS Student Page 685, Exercise 42

Use the function rule $y = \dfrac{2x + 5}{x + 3}$.

a. Rewrite the function rule as a quotient plus a remainder.
b. Make a table of values and graph the function.
c. What are the vertical and horizontal asymptotes?

Read and Understand

1. What type of function is $y = \dfrac{2x + 5}{x + 3}$? _____

2. Explain how you determine the vertical and horizontal asymptotes.

_____

_____

Plan and Solve

3. Use long division to rewrite the function rule as a quotient plus a remainder. _____

4. Make a table of values and graph the function.

5. What is the vertical asymptote? _____

6. What is the horizontal asymptote? _____

Look Back and Check

7. Check the reasonableness of your graph by choosing another point for your table and verifying that it is on your graph.

Solve Another Problem

8. Rewrite the function $y = \dfrac{3x + 4}{x + 1}$ as a quotient plus a remainder. _____

Guided Problem Solving

Practice 12-5

Adding and Subtracting Rational Expressions

Add or subtract.

1. $\dfrac{3x}{4} - \dfrac{x}{4}$

2. $\dfrac{3}{x} + \dfrac{5}{x}$

3. $\dfrac{5x}{6} - \dfrac{2x}{3}$

4. $\dfrac{x}{3} + \dfrac{x}{5}$

5. $\dfrac{3m}{4} + \dfrac{5m}{12}$

6. $\dfrac{4x}{7} - \dfrac{3x}{14}$

7. $\dfrac{6}{7t} - \dfrac{3}{7t}$

8. $\dfrac{d}{3} + \dfrac{4d}{3}$

9. $\dfrac{7}{2d} - \dfrac{3}{2d}$

10. $\dfrac{3}{2d^2} + \dfrac{4}{3d}$

11. $\dfrac{9}{m+1} - \dfrac{6}{m-1}$

12. $\dfrac{3}{x} - \dfrac{7}{x}$

13. $\dfrac{7a}{6} + \dfrac{a}{6}$

14. $\dfrac{4}{k+3} - \dfrac{8}{k+3}$

15. $\dfrac{3}{4z^2} + \dfrac{7}{4z^2}$

16. $\dfrac{6}{x^2-1} + \dfrac{7}{x-1}$

17. $\dfrac{2x}{x^2-1} - \dfrac{3}{x+1}$

18. $\dfrac{3t}{8} + \dfrac{3t}{8}$

19. $\dfrac{4}{3a^2} - \dfrac{1}{2a^3}$

20. $\dfrac{4}{a+4} + \dfrac{6}{a+4}$

21. $\dfrac{4}{x+3} + \dfrac{6}{x-2}$

22. $\dfrac{6}{7t^3} - \dfrac{8}{3t}$

23. $\dfrac{3}{2x+6} + \dfrac{4}{6x+18}$

24. $\dfrac{5}{8a} - \dfrac{3}{8a}$

25. $\dfrac{5}{r^2-4} + \dfrac{7}{r+2}$

26. $\dfrac{6}{a^2-2} + \dfrac{9}{a^2-2}$

27. $\dfrac{5x}{4} - \dfrac{x}{4}$

28. $\dfrac{4}{3x+6} - \dfrac{3}{2x+4}$

29. $\dfrac{4}{c^2+4c+3} + \dfrac{1}{c+3}$

30. $\dfrac{6}{x^2-3x+2} - \dfrac{4}{x-2}$

31. Brian rode his bike 2 mi to his friend's house. Brian's bike had a flat tire, so he had to walk home. His walking rate is 25% of his biking rate.

   a. Write an expression for the amounts of time Brian spent walking and riding his bike.

   b. If Brian's biking rate is 12 mi/h, how much time did he spend walking and riding his bike?

32. Trudi and Sean are on a river canoeing. Because of the current of the river, their downstream rate is 250% of their upstream rate. They canoe 3 mi upstream and then return to their starting point.

   a. Write an expression for the amount of time Trudi and Sean spend canoeing.

   b. If their upstream rate is 2 mi/h, how much time do Trudi and Sean spend canoeing?

   c. If their upstream rate is 3 mi/h, how much time do Trudi and Sean spend canoeing?

12-5 • Guided Problem Solving

GPS **Student Page 690, Exercise 42**

Rowing A rowing team practices rowing 2 mi upstream and 2 mi downstream. The team can row downstream 25% faster than they can row upstream.

   a. Let r represent their rate upstream. Write and simplify an expression for the amount of time they spend rowing.
   b. Let d represent their rate downstream. Write and simplify an expression for the amount of time they spend rowing.
   c. **Critical Thinking** Do the expressions you wrote in parts (a) and (b) represent the same time? Explain.

Read and Understand

1. Explain why the team rows faster going downstream than upstream. _____

_____

2. What is the relationship between rate, time, and distance that you will need to use? _____

Plan and Solve

3. Let r represent their rate upstream. Write and simplify an expression for the amount of time they spend rowing. _____

4. Let d represent their rate downstream. Write and simplify an expression for the amount of time they spend rowing. _____

5. Do the expressions you wrote in Steps 3 and 4 represent the same time? Explain.

_____

_____

Look Back and Check

6. Check the accuracy of your expressions by verifying that they are equal when $r = 4$ and $d = 5$.

Solve Another Problem

7. Write new expressions for their times upstream and downstream if they can only row downstream 10% faster than they can row upstream. _____

Practice 12-6

Solving Rational Equations

Solve each equation. Check your solution. If there is no solution, write *no solution.*

1. $\dfrac{1}{x} + \dfrac{1}{2x} = \dfrac{1}{6}$

2. $\dfrac{x}{x+2} + \dfrac{4}{x-2} = 1$

3. $\dfrac{1}{3s} = \dfrac{s}{2} - \dfrac{1}{6s}$

4. $\dfrac{x+2}{x+8} = \dfrac{x-2}{x+4}$

5. $1 - \dfrac{3}{x} = \dfrac{4}{x^2}$

6. $\dfrac{7}{3(a-2)} - \dfrac{1}{a-2} = \dfrac{2}{3}$

7. $\dfrac{n}{n-4} = \dfrac{2n}{n+4}$

8. $x + \dfrac{6}{x} = -7$

9. $\dfrac{2}{r^2-r} - 1 = \dfrac{2}{r-1}$

10. $\dfrac{y}{y+3} = \dfrac{6}{y+9}$

11. $\dfrac{d}{3} + \dfrac{1}{2} = \dfrac{1}{3d}$

12. $\dfrac{2m}{m-5} = \dfrac{2m+16}{m+3}$

13. $\dfrac{1}{m-4} + \dfrac{1}{m+4} = \dfrac{8}{m^2-16}$

14. $\dfrac{5}{x-2} = \dfrac{5x+10}{x^2}$

15. $\dfrac{k^2}{k+3} = \dfrac{9}{k+3}$

16. $\dfrac{h-3}{h+6} = \dfrac{2h+3}{h+6}$

17. $\dfrac{h}{6} - \dfrac{3}{2h} = \dfrac{8}{3h}$

18. $4 - \dfrac{3}{y} = \dfrac{5}{y}$

19. $\dfrac{1}{b-3} = \dfrac{b}{4}$

20. $\dfrac{1}{t^2} - \dfrac{2}{t} = \dfrac{3}{t^2}$

21. $\dfrac{2}{3n} + \dfrac{3}{4} = \dfrac{2}{3}$

22. David and Fiona have a house painting business. It takes Fiona 3 days to paint a certain house. David could paint the same house in 4 days. How long would it take them to paint the house if David and Fiona worked together?

23. Suppose the Williams Spring Water Company has two machines that bottle the spring water. Machine X fills the bottles twice as fast as Machine Y. Working together, it takes them 20 min to fill 450 bottles. How long would it take each machine working alone to fill the 450 bottles?

24. Chao, who is an experienced architect, can draw a certain set of plans in 6 h. It takes Carl, who is a new architect, 10 h to draw the same set of plans. How long would it take them working together to draw the set of plans?

25. For exercise, Joseph likes to walk and Vincent likes to ride his bike. Vincent rides his bike 12 km/h faster than Joseph walks. Joseph walks 20 km in the same amount of time that Vincent rides 44 km. Find the rate that each of them travels.

26. The Ryan Publishing Company has two printing presses. It takes the new printing press 45 min to print 10,000 fliers. Together the two presses can print the 10,000 fliers in 30 min. How long does it take the older printing press by itself to print the 10,000 fliers?

12-6 • Guided Problem Solving

GPS **Student Page 696, Exercise 38**

Electricity Lamps can be connected to a battery in a circuit in series or in parallel. You can calculate the total resistance R_T in a circuit if you know the resistance in each lamp. Resistance is measured in ohms (Ω).

$R_1 = 6\ \Omega$ $R_2 = 9\ \Omega$

$R_3 = 5\ \Omega$

Battery

Read and Understand

1. How do you calculate the total resistance in a circuit connected in series with two resistors R_1 and R_2? _____

2. How do you find the total resistance in a circuit with two resistors R_1 and R_2 connected in parallel? _____

Plan and Solve

3. Calculate the total resistance for lamps R_1 and R_2. _____

4. Calculate the total resistance for the lamps connected in parallel. Use your answer in Step 3 as your first resistance. _____

Look Back and Check

5. Verify that you solved the equation in Step 4 correctly by checking that you get a true statement when you substitute the values into the equation.

Solve Another Problem

6. Find R_T.

$R_1 = 4\ \Omega$ $R_2 = 8\ \Omega$

$R_3 = 6\ \Omega$

Battery

Practice 12-7

Simplify each expression.

1. $_7P_2$ **2.** $_{12}P_6$ **3.** $_{11}P_3$ **4.** $_{10}P_3$ **5.** $_9P_8$ **6.** $_{12}P_7$

7. $_{20}P_7$ **8.** $_{15}P_3$ **9.** $_{16}P_4$ **10.** $_{25}P_3$ **11.** $_{17}P_2$ **12.** $_{15}P_2$

13. Suppose a license plate consists of five different letters.

    a. How many five-letter license plates are possible?

    b. In how many ways can a five-letter license plate be made with the letters from APRIL if none of the letters are repeated?

    c. Suppose a license plate is assigned randomly. What is the probability that it will contain the letters from APRIL?

14. In how many ways can nine mopeds be parked in a row?

15. Suppose there are three different ways in which you could go from your house to a friend's house. From your friend's house, there are four different ways in which you could go to the library. In how many different ways can you go from your house to the library after meeting your friend?

16. A sports card collection contains 20 baseball players, 15 basketball players, and 25 football players. In how many ways can you select one of each?

17. Suppose you are electing student council officers. The student council contains 24 students. In how many ways can a president, a vice-president, and a secretary be elected?

18. Suppose the code to a lock consists of three different numbers from the numbers 1 to 20, inclusive.

    a. How many three-number codes are possible?

    b. How many of the codes contain the numbers 6, 13, and 17?

19. A car dealer sells four different models of cars. Each of the cars can come in six different colors. For each of the cars, there are two different option packages available. In how many different ways can you select a car?

20. Teams in a math competition consist of six students. In how many ways can the six students be selected to work a problem on the board?

12-7 • Guided Problem Solving

GPS **Student Page 703, Exercise 27**

License Plate In Indiana, a regular license plate has two numbers that are fixed by county, then one letter, and then four numbers.

a. How many different license plates are possible in each county?

b. There are 92 counties in Indiana. How many license plates are possible in the entire state?

Read and Understand

1. Explain how to use the Fundamental Counting Principle. _____

_____

2. Give an example of one possible license plate. _____

Plan and Solve

3. Which information is not needed in order to determine how many license plates are possible in one county? _____

4. How many different license plates are possible in each county? _____

5. There are 92 counties in Indiana. How many license plates are possible in the entire state?

_____

Look Back and Check

6. Which number should be greater, your answer in Step 4 or your answer in Step 5? Explain.

_____

_____

Solve Another Problem

7. How many license plates are possible in one county if the letter is replaced by another number?

_____

Practice 12-8

Combressive **Combinations**

Simplify each expression.

1. $_9C_4$ **2.** $_{12}C_8$ **3.** $_9C_6$ **4.** $_{15}C_9$ **5.** $_{10}C_8$ **6.** $_{13}C_6$

7. $_{18}C_5$ **8.** $_{16}C_3$ **9.** $_{17}C_7$ **10.** $_9C_5$ **11.** $_{17}C_{13}$ **12.** $_{14}C_7$

13. A group of six tourists arrive at the airport 15 min before flight time. At the gate, they learn that only three seats are left on the airplane. How many different groups of three could get on the airplane?

14. In how many ways can you select 5 greeting cards from a choice of 12 cards at a store?

15. A committee of 4 students is to be formed from members of the student council. The student council contains 13 girls and 12 boys.

   a. How many different committees of four students are possible?

   b. How many committees will contain only boys?

   c. What is the probability that the committee will contain only boys?

16. Suppose your math class consists of 24 students. In how many ways can a group of 5 students be selected to form a math team?

17. A jar of marbles contains 6 yellow and 8 red marbles. Three marbles are selected at random.

   a. How many different groups of three marbles are possible?

   b. How many groups of three marbles will contain only red ones?

   c. What is the probability that the group of marbles will contain only red ones?

18. Suppose two members of your class need to be selected as members of the student council. Your class has 26 students in it. How many groups of two students can be selected?

19. The letters of the alphabet are written on slips of paper and placed in a hat. Three letters are selected at random.

   a. How many different combinations of three letters are possible?

   b. How many combinations consist only of the letters A, C, H, I, K, or Y?

   c. What is the probability that the letters selected consist only of the letters A, C, H, I, K, or Y?

20. Three boys and four girls are running for president and vice-president of the student council. What is the probability that a boy will be elected president and a girl will be elected vice-president?

21. A lottery requires that you match three numbers in order. The three numbers are chosen from the numbers 1–20. What is the probability that you will win this lottery if numbers can be chosen only once?

Algebra 1 Lesson 12-8   **495**

12-8 • Guided Problem Solving

GPS **Student Page 710, Exercise 24**

Locks A lock like the one at the right is called a combination lock. However, mathematically speaking, it should be called a permutation lock! This is because the order of the numbers *is* important. Suppose a three-number sequence opens the lock and no numbers are repeated.

a. How many different sequences are possible?
b. How many sequences use 32 as the first number?
c. What is the probability that the sequence of numbers that opens this lock uses 32 as the first number?
d. Explain why the lock is unlikely to be opened by someone who does not know the correct sequence.

Read and Understand

1. Explain why the combination to a lock like the one described is a permutation. _____
   _____

2. What information do you need from the picture? _____

Plan and Solve

3. How many different sequences are possible? _____

4. How many sequences use 32 as the first number? _____

5. What is the probability that the sequence of
   numbers that opens this lock uses 32 as the first number? _____

6. Explain why the lock is unlikely to be opened by
   someone who does not know the correct sequence. _____

Look Back and Check

7. Check the reasonableness of your answer in Step 4 by multiplying it by 40. Your result should be the total number of different sequences possible.

Solve Another Problem

8. Another type of lock has a set of different rings that must be turned in order to get the correct numbers lined up. If there are 5 rings and each ring has 10 digits, how many combinations are possible? _____

Guided Problem Solving

12A: Graphic Organizer

For use before Lesson 12-1

Study Skill What do the pages before the first page of Chapter 2 tell you? Keep notes as you work through each chapter to help you organize your thinking and to make it easier to review the material when you complete the chapter.

Write your answers.

1. What is the chapter title? _____

2. Find the Table of Contents page for this chapter at the front of the book. Name four topics you will study in this chapter.

   _____   _____

   _____   _____

3. Complete the graphic organizer as you work through the chapter.
   1. Write the title of the chapter in the center oval.
   2. When you begin a lesson, write the name of the lesson in a rectangle.
   3. When you complete that lesson, write a skill or key concept from that lesson in the outer oval linked to that rectangle.
   Continue with steps 2 and 3 clockwise around the graphic organizer.

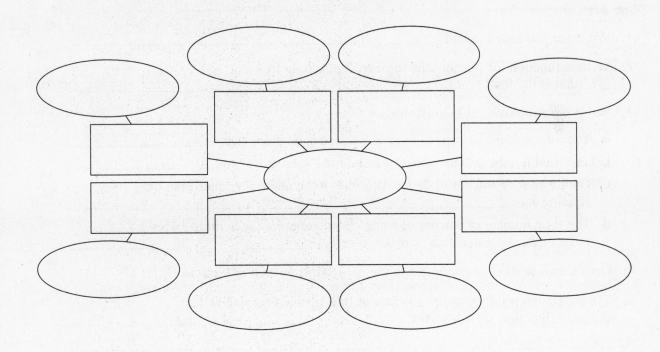

12B: Reading Comprehension

Study Skill Some word problems contain so much information it is difficult to know how to deal with it all. Sometimes it helps to organize information in a table.

Jessica Hernandez bakes and sells gourmet cookies. She bakes two types of cookies: oatmeal and white chocolate macadamia nut. Each batch of oatmeal cookies requires 2 cups of flour and 2 cups of sugar. Each batch of white chocolate macadamia nut cookies requires 3 cups of flour and 1 cup of sugar. Jessica makes a $3 profit on each batch of oatmeal cookies and a $2 profit on each batch of white chocolate macadamia nut cookies. She has 18 cups of flour and 10 cups of sugar on hand. How many batches of each type of cookie should she bake to maximize her profits?

Organize the information you are given into the following table.

	Batches of Cookies	Cups of Flour	Cups of Sugar	Total Profit ($)
Oatmeal	x			
White Chocolate Macadamia Nut	y			
Totals				P

1. What are you asked to find? _____

2. Write a function for the quantity to be maximized. In this case, that is the total profit. _____

3. Write the constraints as inequalities.

   a. The total number of cups of flour to be used is no more than 18. _____

   b. The total number of cups of sugar to be used is no more than 10. _____

   c. The number of batches of oatmeal cookies to be made is greater than or equal to zero. _____

   d. The total number of batches of white chocolate macadamia nut cookies to be made is greater than or equal to zero. _____

4. On a separate sheet of paper, graph the constraints written in Exercise 3.

5. The maximum profit occurs at a vertex of the feasible region. Evaluate the profit function at each vertex. _____

   _____

6. How many batches of each type of cookie need to be made to maximize profit? _____

7. **High-Use Academic Words** What does it mean to *organize* as mentioned in the direction line?

   a. write an equation   **b.** categorize

Algebra 1 Chapter 12

Vocabulary and Study Skills

12C: Reading/Writing Math Symbols   For use after Lesson 12-3

Study Skill It is important to read directions carefully before doing any exercises. Sometimes the directions are asking for more than one answer, or something entirely different than what you think at first glance.

Given the formulas below, write out what the formula means in words, and write a brief description of what the formula is used for or what it represents. The first one is done for you.

1. $a^2 + b^2 = c^2$ leg squared plus leg squared equals

hypotenuse squared; Pythagorean

Theorem—used to find a side of a

right triangle

2. $I = prt$ _____

3. $ax^2 + bx + c = 0$ _____

_____

4. $b^2 - 4ac$ _____

_____

5. $\tan A = \dfrac{\text{opp}}{\text{adj}}$ _____

6. $\cos A = \dfrac{\text{adj}}{\text{hyp}}$ _____

7. $\sin A = \dfrac{\text{opp}}{\text{hyp}}$ _____

8. $\left(\dfrac{x_1 + x_2}{2}, \dfrac{y_1 + y_2}{2} \right)$ _____

_____

9. $x = \dfrac{-b \pm \sqrt{b^2 - 4ac}}{2a}$ _____

_____

10. $d = \sqrt{(x_2 - x_1)^2 + (y_2 - y_1)^2}$ _____

_____

12D: Visual Vocabulary Practice
For use after Lesson 12-6

Study Skill When interpreting a graph, identify the most specific concept represented.

Concept List

absolute value function	asymptotes	exponential function
linear function	quadratic function	rational expression
rational function	rational proportion	square root function

**Write the concept that best describes each exercise.
Choose from the concept list above.**

1.	**2.** The dashed lines in the graph	**3.**
_____	_____	_____
4. 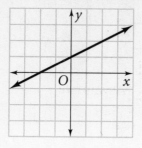	**5.** $\dfrac{x^2 - 3}{x^2 - 6x + 9}$	**6.**
_____	_____	_____
7. 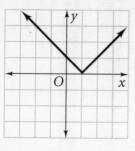	**8.** $\dfrac{5}{x} = \dfrac{1}{x - 2}$	**9.**
_____	_____	_____

Vocabulary and Study Skills

12E: Vocabulary Check

Study Skill Strengthen your vocabulary. Use these pages and add cues and summaries by applying the Cornell Notetaking style.

Write the definition for each word at the right. To check your work, fold the paper back along the dotted line to see the correct answers.

_____

_____

_____

Rational function

_____

_____

Asymptote

_____

_____

_____

Rational expression

_____

_____

_____

Multiplication Counting Principle

_____

_____

_____

Permutation

_____

_____

12E: Vocabulary Check (continued)   For use after Lesson 12-8

**Write the vocabulary word for each definition. To check your work,
fold the paper forward along the dotted line to see the correct answers.**

A function that can be
written in the form
$f(x) = \dfrac{\text{polynomial}}{\text{polynomial}}$.

_____

A line which the graph
of a function gets closer
to x or y gets larger in
absolute value.

_____

An expression which can
be written in the form
$\dfrac{\text{polynomial}}{\text{polynomial}}$.

_____

If there are m ways to
make a first selection and
n ways to make a second
selection, there are $m \times n$
ways to make the two
selections.

_____

An arrangement of some
or all of a set of objects
in a specific order.

_____

12F: Vocabulary Review Puzzle

For use with Chapter Review

Study Skill Read aloud or recite the new terms as you read them. This will help you remember and recall rules, definitions, and formulas for future use.

Unscramble the UPPERCASE letters to form a math word or phrase that completes each sentence.

1. An METPYSTOA is a line that the graph of a function gets closer and closer to, but does not intersect.

2. A OCMINNOIBAT uses the notation $_nC_r$.

3. An SEVNIER ITVIANARO can be written in the form $xy = k$ or $y = \frac{k}{x}$.

4. A RUTTEAPONMI uses the notation $_nP_r$.

5. A TAIRNLOA OFINUTCN can be written in the form $f(x) = \frac{\text{polynomial}}{\text{polynomial}}$.

6. The graph of a quadratic function is a BAAPARLO.

7. The quantity $b^2 - 4ac$ is the RIDNMCITSINA of $ax^2 + bx + c = 0$

8. The highest or lowest point on a parabola is its XTERVE.

9. In a right triangle, the NTNATEG ratio compares the length of the side opposite an acute angle to the length of the side adjacent to the same acute angle.

10. You may TAEZIONILRA the denominator of a radical expression when simplifying the expression.